GRE® Graduate Record Examination

Verbal Workbook

Tenth Edition

For more GRE® prep, Kaplan offers a range of print and digital products, available in stores and online:

Kaplan GRE® Prep Plus with 3 Practice Tests and 500-Question Qbank
Kaplan GRE® Prep with 2 Practice Tests
GRE® Math Workbook
Kaplan GRE® Vocabulary Flashcards

To learn more about Kaplan's comprehensive prep courses for the GRE®, please visit **www.kaptest.com/GRE**.

GRE®

Graduate
Record
Examination

Verbal Workbook

Tenth Edition

GRE® is a registered trademark of the Educational Testing Service, which neither sponsors nor endorses this product.

Published by Kaplan Publishing, a division of Kaplan, Inc.
750 Third Avenue
New York, NY 10017

10 9 8 7 6 5 4 3 2 1

ISBN: 978-1-5062-3529-5

Table of Contents

Acknowledgments

Special thanks to the team that made this book possible:

Arthur Ahn, Matthew Belinkie, Shannon Berning, Lauren T. Bernstein, Kim Bowers, Gerard Cortinez, Elisa Davis, Lola Disparte, Boris Dvorkin, John Evans, Paula Fleming, Darcy Galane, Joanna Graham, Adam Grey, Allison Harm, Jack Hayes, Adam Hinz, Gar Hong, Sunny Hwang, Cinzia Iacono, Avi Lidgi, Kate Lopaze, Keith Lubeley, TJ Mancini, Jennifer Moore, Jason Moss, Walt Niedner, Robert Reiss, S. Ross, Derek Rusnak, Emily Sachar, Stephanie Schrauth, Sheryl Stebbins, Glen Stohr, Sascha Strelka, Gene Suhir, Martha Torres, Liza Weale, Lee A. Weiss, and many others who have contributed materials and advice over the years.

How to Use This Book

Kaplan has prepared students to take standardized tests for more than 75 years. Our team of teachers and researchers knows more about preparation for the GRE than anyone else, and you'll find Kaplan's accumulated knowledge and experience throughout this book. The GRE is a standardized test, so every administration covers the same content in roughly the same way. This is good news for you; it means that the best way to prepare is to focus on the sort of questions you are likely to see on Test Day. The main focus of this book is on strategic reviews, exercises, and practice tests with explanations that will help you brush up on your vocabulary, reading comprehension, and writing skills. If possible, work through this book a little at a time over the course of several weeks. There is a lot of material to absorb, and it's hard to do all at once.

Getting Started

Part 1 of this book, "Getting Started," provides you with background information on the Verbal Reasoning section of the test, what it covers, and how it's organized.

Verbal Reasoning Section

The Verbal Reasoning section of the GRE contains three main question types: Text Completion, Sentence Equivalence, and Reading Comprehension. Part 3 of this book covers these types with strategies and sample questions. Your focus here should be to familiarize yourself with the question types so you won't be trying to figure out how to approach them on Test Day.

Read the explanations to all the questions—even those you got right. Often the explanations will contain strategies that show you how you could have gotten to the answer more quickly and efficiently.

Analytical Writing Section

The analytical writing content review covers grammar, mechanics, and style, as well as strategies for writing effective paragraphs and essays. The final chapters of this workbook cover sample GRE prompts. Using these prompts, you can practice the skills you have learned to write strong essays. In addition to sample prompts, we've also included sample top-scoring essays so you can review the qualities that earn an essay a high score.

Verbal Content Review

Once you have the big picture, focus on the content. Part 2 of this book, "Verbal Content Review," gives you a complete tour of the vocabulary that you will see on Test Day. The material in the verbal content review is divided into particular subjects. Each subject begins with a review, followed by practice questions. This structure makes it easy for you to pinpoint the vocabulary concepts you need to review and quickly get your skills up to speed.

If you find that you would like access to more of Kaplan's practice tests and quizzes, as well as in-depth instruction on the question types and strategies, look into the variety of course options available at **kaptest.com/GRE**.

If you have questions about what you're studying, ask our expert GRE faculty on our Facebook page: **www.facebook.com/KaplanGradPrep**.

Thanks for choosing Kaplan. We wish you the best of luck on your journey to graduate school.

PART ONE

Getting Started

CHAPTER 1

Introduction to GRE Verbal

UNDERSTANDING THE GRE VERBAL REASONING SECTION

The Verbal Reasoning sections of the Graduate Record Exam (GRE) emphasize complex reasoning skills and reward your ability to analyze the relationships among words and sentences as they are used in context. The exam tests vocabulary contextually, and the reading passages are both dense and written with a sophisticated level of diction. The goal of the test's content and emphasis on analytical skills is to provide an accurate indication of your ability to understand what you're reading and to apply reasoning skills to the text's premises and arguments. These are all skills you will need at the graduate level.

To perform well on the Verbal Reasoning section—to answer correctly as many questions as possible—you need to have a good grasp of vocabulary and the ability to apply reasoning skills. Part 2 of this book explains the various question types in detail. Part 3 reviews the foundations of vocabulary. Every chapter offers plenty of opportunities to practice and review your answers.

MST MECHANICS

The GRE is a multi-stage test (MST). While working within a section of the test, you may skip questions and return to them as long as time remains for the section. The test is computer based, presented in an interface with tools such as a Mark button (to indicate a question you want to examine later within the time allowed for that section), a Review button (to see your progress on the entire set of questions in a section), and an optional time display. As you prepare for Test Day, consider how these computer capabilities may help you manage your time for each section.

As best you can, approach the exam as you would a paper-based one. After all, the idea behind the MST is that it will feel more comfortable and familiar than some other computer-based or adaptive tests, on which you cannot move about freely within a section. Use the MST's design to your advantage. If a question looks too daunting, skip it. Use the Mark button to remind you to come back to the question when you have time at the end of that section. By doing so, you can better organize your time by keeping track of which questions you are done with and which ones need a second look.

Finally, having an on-screen timer (which appears in the corner of the display) works to your advantage, helping you keep track of the time remaining in the section. But if you find yourself looking at it so frequently that it becomes a distraction, turn it off for a few minutes and refocus your attention on the test. Use the timer to help you make good decisions about how to spend your time within the section, but don't let it prevent you from concentrating on the questions.

VERBAL REASONING QUESTION TYPES

The GRE MST contains two Verbal Reasoning sections with 20 questions each. Each section lasts 30 minutes and contains a selection of the following question types:

- Text Completion
- Sentence Equivalence
- Reading Comprehension

The Verbal Reasoning portion of the GRE rewards a strong, university-level vocabulary and facility with understanding and analyzing written material. Specifically, it evaluates your ability to do the following:

- accurately paraphrase sentences and paragraphs
- derive a word's meaning based on its context
- detect relationships among words
- understand the logic of sentences and paragraphs
- draw inferences
- recognize major, minor, and irrelevant points
- summarize ideas
- understand passage and paragraph structure
- recognize an author's tone, purpose, and perspective

The GRE assesses those skills with an assortment of Text Completion, Sentence Equivalence, and Reading Comprehension items. The following chart shows how many questions of each type you can expect, as well as the average amount of time you should spend per question.

	Text Completion	Sentence Equivalence	Reading Comprehension
Number of Questions	Approx. 6	Approx. 4	Approx. 10
Time per Question	1–1.5 minutes	1 minute	1–3 minutes, depending on the length, to read the passage and 1 minute to answer each question

TEXT COMPLETION

You will find about six Text Completion questions in each Verbal Reasoning section. These questions consist of single sentences or short paragraphs of two or three sentences. The text has blanks replacing one, two, or three words. Your task is to select one word for each blank from a column of corresponding choices to complete the text logically. This question type tests your ability to read strategically—to recognize the point of a sentence and find the best word(s) to fit its meaning.

Chapter 2 presents the Kaplan Method for answering Text Completion questions and strategies to help you solve them efficiently.

SENTENCE EQUIVALENCE

Each Verbal Reasoning section features approximately four Sentence Equivalence questions. These questions provide a single sentence with one missing word. You must identify two correct words, either of which would complete the sentence. The correct answer choices, when inserted into the blank, will give the same meaning to *both* resulting sentences. These questions test your ability to determine a sentence's meaning and to use vocabulary in context.

You'll find the Kaplan Method for Sentence Equivalence questions and strategies to help solve them efficiently in chapter 3.

READING COMPREHENSION

Reading Comprehension is the only question type that appears on all major standardized tests, and with good reason. No matter what academic discipline you pursue, you'll have to make sense of dense, complex written material. Being able to understand and assess such material is a crucial skill for every graduate student.

To make the test broadly relevant, and to better evaluate your ability to understand comparable material, the testmaker, Educational Testing Service (ETS), adapts Reading Comprehension content from "real-world" graduate-level documents. GRE passages come from four disciplines: social sciences, biological sciences, physical sciences, and the arts and humanities.

The GRE includes roughly ten reading passages between the two Verbal Reasoning sections. Many of these passages are one paragraph in length, although a few are longer. Each passage is accompanied by one to six questions. These questions reward you for ascertaining the author's purpose and meaning, determining what can be validly inferred from the passage, researching details in the text, and understanding the meaning of words and the function of sentences in context.

Chapter 4 contains the Kaplan Method for answering Reading Comprehension questions and strategies to help solve them efficiently.

ANALYTICAL WRITING

The Analytical Writing section assesses not only how well you write, but also the thought processes you employ in formulating and articulating a position. In response to short, descriptive prompts, you produce two essays, one in which you evaluate an argument and one in which you make an argument of your own. Specifically, the Analytical Writing tasks measure your ability to do the following:

- articulate and defend a position
- deconstruct and evaluate a complex argument
- develop a cogent argument
- assess the fundamental soundness of an argument
- recognize major, minor, and irrelevant points
- provide evidence and support for an argument
- detect the flaws in an unsound argument
- write articulately and effectively at a high level

Regardless of your field, you will need these critical thinking skills to perform well in a graduate program.

ANALYTICAL WRITING ESSAY TYPES

The GRE's Analytical Writing section contains two different essay types. You'll be given 30 minutes for each essay. Here are your tasks:

- The Issue Essay Task provides a brief quotation on an issue of general interest and instructions on how to respond to the issue. You can discuss the issue from any perspective, making use of your own educational and personal background, examples from current or historical events, things you've read, or even relevant hypothetical situations. In this task, you develop your own argument in response to the prompt.
- The Argument Essay Task contains a short argument that may or may not be complete and specific instructions on how to evaluate the argument's strength. You will assess the argument's cogency, analyze the author's reasoning, and evaluate the use (or lack) of evidence. In this task, you critique the argument presented in the prompt.

You'll write the essays on the computer, using a simple word processing program with functions allowing you to cut, paste, delete, and insert text but with no spelling or grammar checker. Graders score the Analytical Writing essays based on your ability to plan and compose a logical, well-reasoned essay, one that's responsive to the test's instructions, under timed conditions. Only a score report is sent to the schools to which you apply.

PART TWO

Verbal Reasoning

CHAPTER 2

Text Completion

TEXT COMPLETION: OVERVIEW AND METHOD

You will find about six Text Completion questions per Verbal Reasoning section on the GRE. In each Text Completion question, one, two, or three words from the sentence(s) will be missing. This question type tests your ability to recognize the point of the passage and find the best word(s) to fit its meaning. In addition to testing vocabulary, Text Completion questions require you to read actively and strategically for context. Even an answer choice that "sounds good" when read into the sentence will be incorrect if it does not closely fit the meaning. For Text Completion questions with two or three blanks, all of the blanks must be filled in correctly to earn the point. As elsewhere on the GRE, *no partial credit is given.*

The directions for Text Completion questions will look like this:

> For each blank select one entry from the corresponding column of choices. Fill all blanks in the way that best completes the text.

A Text Completion question with one blank will look like this:

> Although the city's public mass transportation system has been _______ from active service, traces of its presence may be seen in the train stations that have been converted into shopping centers.
>
> (A) dilated
> (B) retired
> (C) metastasized
> (D) frozen
> (E) waxed

THE KAPLAN METHOD FOR TEXT COMPLETION (ONE-BLANK)

STEP 1 **Read the sentence, looking for clues.**

STEP 2 **Predict an answer.**

STEP 3 **Select the answer choice that most closely matches your prediction.**

STEP 4 **Check your answer.**

How the Kaplan Method for Text Completion (One-Blank) Works

Here's how the Kaplan Method for Text Completion (One-Blank) works.

STEP 1

Read the sentence, looking for clues.

There are always clues in the sentence that will point you to the right answer. The missing words in Text Completion questions will usually be similar or opposite to key words in the sentence.

Key words and *key phrases* give context clues that will help you predict the meaning of the missing word(s).

A *road sign* is a structural key word that signals the connection between ideas. Road signs indicate the sentence's direction. Some road signs tell you the sentence is going *straight ahead*—the next idea follows from what has come before. Other road signs, *detour* road signs, indicate that the sentence is changing direction, with the next idea contrasting with what has come before.

Straight-ahead road signs—*and, additionally, moreover, so*—are used when one part of the sentence supports or elaborates on the other part. They continue the sentence in the same direction. The positive or negative connotation of what follows is not changed by these clues.

Detour road signs—*but, however, on the other hand, to the contrary*—change the direction of the sentence. They indicate that one part of the sentence contradicts or qualifies the other part. The positive or negative connotation of an answer is changed by these clues.

On the GRE, a semicolon always connects two closely related independent clauses. If it is not accompanied by a detour road sign, the semicolon functions as a straight-ahead road sign.

Recognizing road signs will help you determine which way a Text Completion sentence is going and predict what word(s) will be used to fill in the blank(s). Here are some examples.

Straight-ahead road signs:	**Detour road signs:**
And	*But*
Since	*Despite*
Also	*Yet*
Thus	*However*
Because	*Unless*
: (colon)	*Rather*
Likewise	*Although*
Moreover	*While*
Similarly	*On the other hand*
In addition	*Unfortunately*
Consequently	*Nonetheless*
Therefore	*Conversely*

STEP 2

Predict an answer.

Once you've found the road sign and the key word(s) relevant to the blank, use them to predict an answer for the blank. Your prediction does not have to be a sophisticated or complex word or phrase, simply a paraphrase that fits logically into the sentence. By predicting, you will know what kind of word you are looking for and be able to efficiently eliminate words that are not a match. This will save you time and help you avoid the trap answers.

STEP 3

Select the answer choice that most closely matches your prediction.

Quickly go through the choices and select the one that most closely matches your prediction of the correct answer. Eliminate choices that do not fit your prediction. If none of the choices matches your prediction, reread the question and revisit Steps 1 and 2.

STEP 4

Check your answer.

Check that your answer choice makes sense in context. Read the sentence to yourself with your choice(s) in the blanks. If the sentence makes sense, confirm your answer(s) and move on. If the sentence does not make sense or just doesn't "sound right," reread the question and revisit Steps 1 through 3.

Apply the Kaplan Method for Text Completion (One-Blank)

Now, apply the Kaplan Method to a Text Completion (One-Blank) question:

Although the city's public mass transportation system has been ______ from active service, traces of its presence may be seen in the train stations that have been converted into shopping centers.

Ⓐ dilated
Ⓑ retired
Ⓒ metastasized
Ⓓ frozen
Ⓔ waxed

STEP 1

Read the sentence, looking for clues.

Begin by paraphrasing the sentence's main idea: The city's transportation system has not disappeared entirely, because traces of it may still be seen. The detour road sign "although" indicates that the verb that will fill the blank will contrast with the second half of the sentence.

STEP 2

Predict an answer.

Based on that paraphrase, you can predict that the correct answer will have a meaning similar to "removed" or "quit."

STEP 3

Select the answer choice that most closely matches your prediction.

Answer choice **(B)** *retired* matches the meaning of your prediction. The system has been "retired" from active service. Choices **(A)** *dilated* and **(E)** *waxed* mean "increased" or "widened"; they are the opposite of your prediction. Similarly, choice **(C)** *metastasized* means something has spread. Choice **(D)** *frozen* makes little sense in this context.

STEP 4

Check your answer.

To make sure your answer is right, simply plug it back into the original sentence:

"Although the city's public mass transportation system has been *retired* from active service, traces of its presence may be seen in the train stations that have been converted into shopping centers."

The sentence is logical, and the answer choice matches your prediction; it's the correct answer.

TEXT COMPLETION (ONE-BLANK) PRACTICE SET

Try the following Text Completion questions using the Kaplan Method:

1. The director is normally lauded for his exciting science-fiction films, but his latest effort is marred by its _______ special effects.

   (A) electrifying
   (B) piquant
   (C) bland
   (D) emotive
   (E) sophisticated

2. Despite her long battle with illness, the dancer displayed astonishing _______ of motion on stage.

   (A) indolence
   (B) hesitancy
   (C) extension
   (D) queasiness
   (E) fluency

3. Having established his competence as a playwright with his first play, the author went on to show greater _______ with his second.

   (A) characterization
   (B) mastery
   (C) understanding
   (D) perception
   (E) insufficiency

4. Such a _______ response to a client is not consistent with the high standards of customer service this company demands.

   (A) politic
   (B) cloying
   (C) meticulous
   (D) boastful
   (E) disrespectful

5. Difficult as it may sometimes be, in all our dealings with both clients and competitors, we must be seen to be above ______.

   (A) profit
   (B) integrity
   (C) ambivalence
   (D) reproach
   (E) scruples

TEXT COMPLETION (ONE-BLANK) PRACTICE SET ANSWER KEY

1. **C**
2. **E**
3. **B**
4. **E**
5. **D**

TEXT COMPLETION (ONE-BLANK) PRACTICE SET ANSWERS AND EXPLANATIONS

1. C

Reading this sentence all the way through reveals that "but" is a detour road sign, indicating that the sentence will change direction. So, while the director is normally "lauded," which means "praised," for his exciting films, his newest one is "marred" by its special effects. Therefore, the word that goes in the blank must be a negatively charged adjective that contrasts with "exciting." You can predict that the correct answer is a word that means "unexciting" or "dull." The answer that fits this prediction is choice **(C)** *bland*. Choices **(A)** *electrifying*, **(B)** *piquant*, and **(D)** *emotive* are related in meaning to "exciting" or "engaging." Choice **(E)** *sophisticated*, meaning "complex" or "refined," also does not logically contrast with "exciting." Sophisticated special effects would tend to make a science fiction film more exciting, not less so. *Bland*, on the other hand, is a direct opposite of "exciting," making **(C)** the correct answer.

2. E

"Despite" is a detour road sign indicating that the correct answer will contrast with the fact that the dancer has endured a long battle with illness. A reasonable prediction is *gracefulness*, which you would not expect from a dancer who has been seriously ill. The best choice is **(E)** *fluency*. "Fluency of motion" has a meaning similar to "gracefulness," so it matches your prediction. Choice **(D)** *queasiness* does not describe movement and also does not follow the detour road sign; there is nothing "astonishing" about nausea in a dancer who has been ill. The same applies for **(B)** *hesitancy*, as you might expect the dancer to be tentative in her movements after an illness. Choice **(A)** *indolence*, which means "laziness," doesn't fit because there would be nothing astonishing about that, either. Choice **(C)** *extension* might have been tempting if you were thinking of ballet or another dance style in which extension of the body is emphasized, but *extension* describes body posture, not movement. Moreover, the sentence is not limited to a particular style of dance, so this choice is too specific for the context.

3. B

The first clause in this sentence describes the playwright as "competent" in his first play, while the second clause asserts that he has progressed beyond mere competence in his second. *Skill* is an excellent prediction. Choice **(B)** *mastery* fits perfectly; the playwright no longer is merely *competent*, but is now *masterful*. You can reject **(E)** *insufficiency* as the opposite of what the sentence needs. Choices **(A)** *characterization*, **(C)** *understanding*, and **(D)** *perception* are all elements of writing that the playwright may have improved upon, but you're looking for a more general word. Nothing in the sentence leads logically to a specific area of improvement.

4. E

The word "not" is a detour road sign indicating that the adjective in the blank (which describes the word "response") must be inconsistent with "high standards of customer service." High customer service standards imply proper etiquette, responsiveness, and professionalism. A simple, accurate prediction of the opposite of those is *rude*. Choice **(E)** *disrespectful* is the answer choice closest to that prediction. Choice **(A)** *politic* has a couple of meanings: "shrewd" and "tactful." Both could describe someone who is good at customer service. Choice **(C)** *meticulous* means "attentive to detail," another good trait in someone who serves customers. Choice **(B)** *cloying* means "too sweet" or "too sentimental." While potentially annoying, this quality does not relate to the context clue of "customer service." Choice **(D)** *boastful* means "full of excessive pride," which does not necessarily make someone rude or inhospitable.

5. D

To unlock this question, recognize that the term in the blank must be a negatively charged word with which a reputable business would not wish to be associated. *Suspicion* works nicely. Choice **(D)** *reproach,* meaning "blame," is the best fit for the context and is the correct answer. You can immediately eliminate **(B)** *integrity* and **(E)** *scruples,* which mean "adherence to ethical principles" and "moral considerations," respectively. These qualities are desirable in a business or company. In context, choice **(A)** *profit* makes little sense; it's not logical to say a company appears to be "above profit," since one of the primary purposes of a business is to make a profit. Similarly, choice **(C)** *ambivalence,* meaning "undecided" or "uncertain," makes little sense in context; indecision is not a quality that would make a company appear disreputable.

THE KAPLAN METHOD FOR TEXT COMPLETION (TWO-BLANK AND THREE-BLANK)

STEP 1 **Read the sentence, looking for clues.**

STEP 2 **Predict the answer for the easier/easiest blank.**

STEP 3 **Select the answer choice that most closely matches your prediction.**

STEP 4 **Predict and select for the remaining blanks.**

STEP 5 **Check your answers.**

A Text Completion question with two blanks will look like this:

Even when faced with continuing (i) _______, the recalcitrant graduate student persisted in her spendthrift ways; she abjured any thought of self-(ii) _______ and spent prodigally.

Blank (i)	Blank (ii)
A lucre	D adumbration
B penury	E aggrandizement
C avarice	F abnegation

A Text Completion question with three blanks will look like this:

Though scientific discoveries are often (i) _______ shortly after they've been accepted as fact, scientists still seem to leap to hasty conclusions, (ii) _______ that the (iii) _______ nature of what can be called "fact" has not eroded their confidence.

Blank (i)	Blank (ii)	Blank (iii)
A validated	D denying	G predictable
B published	E refuting	H incendiary
C disproved	F demonstrating	I illusory

How the Kaplan Method for Text Completion (Two-Blank and Three-Blank) Works

Here's how the Kaplan Method for Text Completion (Two-Blank and Three-Blank) works.

STEP 1

Read the sentence, looking for clues.

Just as with one-blank Text Completion questions, the sentence(s) will contain key words and road signs that point you to the right answer. In particular, the missing words will usually have a meaning either similar or opposite to that of key words or phrases in the sentence(s). Therefore, pay attention to the road signs, which tell you whether there is a straight-ahead relationship or a detour relationship between words. In addition, when there are multiple blanks, a sentence is likely to contain both detour and straight-ahead road signs, indicating different relationships between the different blanks and their context. Pay attention to these relationships as you untangle the sentence(s). You may want to refer to the list of example road signs in the previous section to refresh your memory.

Remember, you must select the correct answer choice for *each* blank for the question to be scored as correct. No partial credit is given.

STEP 2

Predict an answer for the easier/easiest blank.

You do not need to tackle the blanks in order. Instead, identify the easier/easiest blank to work with. This is often one with key words and road signs that help you make a clear prediction. As with one-blank Text Completions, your prediction does not have to be a sophisticated or complex word or phrase. Just come up with a term that logically fits into the sentence at that point. Again, by making a prediction, you can zero in on the choice that matches your prediction, saving time and avoiding trap answers.

When you have correctly filled in one blank, that answer often becomes a key word that provides a clue to another blank(s).

STEP 3

Select the answer choice that most closely matches your prediction.

Quickly go through the choices and see which one matches your prediction.

Simultaneously, eliminate whichever answer choices do not fit your prediction. If none of the choices match your prediction, reread the question and revisit Steps 1 and 2. If one does match, you should proceed to Step 4.

STEP 4

Predict and select for the remaining blanks.

Filling in the easier/easiest blank provides additional context for the remaining blanks.

For two-blank Text Completion questions, use the context to help you choose the answer for the remaining blank. If the answers for the second blank are not working out, you need to go back to Step 2.

For three-blank Text Completion questions, select the easier of the two remaining blanks and predict which choice will most logically complete the sentence. You now have two blanks to provide context for the last, most difficult blank. This approach to two- and three-blank questions is just a logical extension of the Kaplan Method as it applies to one-blank questions.

STEP 5

Check your answers.

Double-check that your answer choices make sense in context by reading the sentence to yourself with your answers plugged in. If the sentence makes sense when you read your choices back into it, confirm your answers and move on. If the sentence doesn't make sense when read with your choices, reread the question and revisit Steps 1 through 4.

APPLY THE KAPLAN METHOD FOR TEXT COMPLETION (TWO-BLANK)

Now, apply the Kaplan Method to a Text Completion (Two-Blank) question:

Even when faced with continuing (i) _______, the recalcitrant graduate student persisted in her spendthrift ways; she abjured any thought of self-(ii) _______ and spent prodigally.

Blank (i)	Blank (ii)
A lucre	D adumbration
B penury	E aggrandizement
C avarice	F abnegation

STEP 1

Read the sentence, looking for clues.

This is a fairly straightforward question, once you wade through all the polysyllabic words. Look at the end of the second clause; you'll notice that the student "spent prodigally," which means "wastefully." Even if you don't know the meaning of the word "prodigally," you can tell from the word "spendthrift" that this is a student who isn't careful with the way she spends her money. If the student is poor at managing money, she likely doesn't have much of it.

STEP 2

Predict the answer for the easier/easiest blank.

Start with the first blank. As noted above, the student is poor at managing money. That means whatever goes in the first blank has a meaning roughly synonymous with "poverty."

STEP 3

Select the answer choice that most closely matches your prediction.

Look at the answer choices for the first blank. Choice **(B)** *penury*, which means "poverty," matches the prediction precisely. You can eliminate **(A)** *lucre* and **(C)** *avarice*, as those mean "wealth" and "greed," respectively.

STEP 4

Predict and select for the remaining blanks.

For the second blank, recall that the student is described as "recalcitrant," which is a term for "stubborn." Also, the student "persisted" in her money-wasting ways. Therefore, she continued to waste money. To "abjure" is to "renounce or repudiate," so she repudiated spending wisely. Thus, "self-________" must carry the meaning of "restraint," since she is renouncing any thought of self-denial or temperance. That points to **(F)** *abnegation*, which means "denial." The root—"negate"—provides a helpful vocabulary clue. Choice **(D)** *adumbration* means a "foreshadowing," or "image of things to come," which makes no sense in this context. Choice **(E)** *aggrandizement* is wrong, as it means "an increase in wealth, power, or rank," and you know she did not shy away from such things if she indulged in overspending.

STEP 5

Check your answers.

Putting both answers back into the sentence, you'll get:

Even when faced with continuing *penury*, the recalcitrant graduate student persisted in her spendthrift ways; she abjured any thought of self-*abnegation* and spent prodigally.

This sentence makes perfect sense.

Apply the Kaplan Method for Text Completion (Three-Blank)

Now, apply the Kaplan Method to a Text Completion (Three-Blank) question:

> Though scientific discoveries are often (i) ______ shortly after they've been accepted as fact, scientists still seem to leap to hasty conclusions, (ii) ______ that the (iii) ______ nature of what can be called "fact" has not eroded their confidence.

Blank (i)	Blank (ii)	Blank (iii)
A validated	D denying	G predictable
B published	E refuting	H incendiary
C disproved	F demonstrating	I illusory

STEP 1

Read the sentence, looking for clues.

Paraphrasing long sentences boils them down to their essentials. Here, you learn that something happens to discoveries shortly after they're accepted as fact; even so, scientists still jump to conclusions.

STEP 2

Predict the answer for the easier/easiest blank.

Because the last part of the sentence refers to "what can be called 'fact,'" you can predict for the first blank that some discoveries are *invalidated* after their acceptance.

STEP 3

Select the answer choice that most closely matches your prediction.

The best match for the prediction is choice **(C)** *disproved*. Choice **(A)** *validated* is the opposite of your prediction, and whether these facts are *published*, choice **(B)**, is irrelevant to their validation.

STEP 4

Predict and select for the remaining blanks.

Now, for the second blank, the only choice that works is **(F)** *demonstrating*. You can see from the sentence structure that the author intends for the scientists' continuing haste to *show* or *demonstrate* a further conclusion. Both choice **(D)** *denying* and choice **(E)** *refuting* are the opposite of what's needed.

Since the sentence posits that some "facts" turn out not to be facts at all, you can predict for the third blank that their nature is *changeable*.

Although it's not an exact match for your prediction, the best choice is **(I)** *illusory*. If the nature of facts was *predictable*, choice **(G)**, they wouldn't get disproved as often. And **(H)** *incendiary* literally refers to setting something on fire but is often used figuratively to describe something that is harmfully provocative or arouses agitation. While the changing nature of fact can no doubt be troubling, the connotation of this word is far too extreme for the context.

STEP 5

Check your answers.

Now, plug your choices into their respective blanks: "Though scientific discoveries are often *disproved* shortly after they've been accepted as fact, scientists still seem to leap to hasty conclusions, *demonstrating* that the *illusory* nature of what can be called 'fact' has not eroded their confidence." These choices fit perfectly, creating a logical, sensible statement.

TEXT COMPLETION (TWO-BLANK AND THREE-BLANK) PRACTICE SET

Try the following Text Completion questions using the Kaplan Method:

1. Despite his insistence to the contrary, the author's (i) _______ hostility was evinced in the tone he used when describing the senator's qualifications; he did not (ii) _______ using words like "craven" and "ill-conceived" liberally when writing about the legislator's voting record.

Blank (i)		Blank (ii)	
A	manifest	D	demur at
B	dubious	E	relish
C	obscure	F	hasten to

2. Given the (i) _______ nature of the evidence, the authorities are unlikely to present a (ii) _______ case against the accused.

Blank (i)		Blank (ii)	
A	abstract	D	weak
B	flimsy	E	convincing
C	rakish	F	tepid

3. Every effort by the bank to determine the origin of the funds met with (i) _______ resulting from the web of (ii) _______ created by the account holder.

Blank (i)	Blank (ii)
A exuberance	D deceit
B apathy	E conviviality
C frustration	F temerity

4. George Gershwin's (i) _______ for the creation of *Rhapsody in Blue* was the kaleidoscope of American life—the melting pot of cultures, the drive of industry, and the bubbling energy of growing cities. Unsurprisingly, the composition was also (ii) _______ by art; two Whistler pieces, *Harmony in Gray and Green* and *Nocturne in Blue and Green*, served as muses for Gershwin while he (iii) _______ the piece during just one week in New York.

Blank (i)	Blank (ii)	Blank (iii)
A conundrum	D inspired	G postponed
B pretense	E biased	H commenced
C context	F captured	I scored

5. (i) _______ competition among buyers in the housing market is a boon for real estate agents, but in a field in which income frequently depends solely on commission, a (ii) _______ agent makes provision for the inevitable weak market. Diversification into property management, rentals, and construction has (iii) _______ many a real estate firm during a turbulent time in the housing market.

Blank (i)	Blank (ii)	Blank (iii)
A Lax	D knowing	G stunted
B Robust	E craven	H terminated
C Dwindling	F brash	I buoyed

TEXT COMPLETION (TWO-BLANK AND THREE-BLANK) PRACTICE SET ANSWER KEY

1. **A, D**
2. **B, E**
3. **C, D**
4. **C, D, I**
5. **B, D, I**

TEXT COMPLETION (TWO-BLANK AND THREE-BLANK) PRACTICE SET ANSWERS AND EXPLANATIONS

1. A, D

Take this question one blank at a time. "Despite" is a standard detour road sign, so you know the sentence will change direction. You know that the author's hostility was evinced (made evident) despite his insisting otherwise. So, whatever goes in the first blank will have a meaning similar to "obvious" or "evident." Choice **(A)** *manifest*, meaning "apparent," works perfectly. Choices **(B)** *dubious* and **(C)** *obscure*, meaning "doubtful" and "unclear," respectively, are the opposite of what you need. For the second blank, remember that if the author were openly hostile, he would be inclined to use negative terms like "craven" and "ill-conceived." Since "not" appears in front of the blank, you're looking for something that means "refrain from." Choice **(D)** *demur at* means to "shy away from." That fits perfectly; if the author were obviously hostile, he would *not* shy away from using strongly negative terms such as "craven" or "ill-conceived." You can rule out **(E)** *relish* and **(F)** *hasten to* straight away. To "relish" is to strongly like something, and to "hasten" is to hurry to do something; these terms produce the wrong meaning in the sentence following the qualifier "not."

2. B, E

This one may be more difficult than it appears at first glance. The word "unlikely" is a detour road sign, indicating that the two correct answers will be opposite in meaning to one another. Since the quality of evidence is directly related to the strength of the case the prosecutors can make against the accused, you can infer that *good* evidence will make them unlikely to present a *bad* case, and *poor* evidence will make them unlikely to present a *good* case. Thus, the correct answers must be oppositely charged. Start with the first blank. You'll notice that **(B)** *flimsy*, meaning "insubstantial," has a negative connotation, while **(A)** *abstract* is neutral and can therefore be ruled out. Choice **(C)** *rakish* means "jaunty" or "dashing"; it makes no sense to describe evidence this way. That leaves **(B)** *flimsy*; the evidence was, therefore, weak. Based on your initial reading of the sentence, you know that the second blank will have to mean "strong." With flimsy evidence, the prosecutors are unlikely to succeed. Choices **(D)** *weak* and **(F)** *tepid* are both negatively charged, while **(E)** *convincing* is positively charged and is a synonym for "strong" when describing a court case. "Given the *flimsy* nature of the evidence, the authorities are unlikely to present a *convincing* case against the accused."

3. C, D

Take this question apart by looking for contextual clues. The phrase "web of ________" is always used in a negative fashion (you're unlikely to ever hear "caught in a web of virtue and delight!"). Start with the second blank, then. The best choice is **(D)** *deceit*, meaning "lies." That makes perfect sense in this context. A web of lies would make it very difficult to determine the origin of the funds. You can immediately rule out **(E)** *conviviality*, as this means "friendliness" or "agreeableness." Choice **(F)** *temerity* means "rashness" or "recklessness." This might, in some cases, be a negative attribute, but the problem in this sentence lies in determining the origin of the funds, which is unlikely to be obscured by the account holder's boldness.

Moving to the first blank, you're looking for a word to characterize the result of an effort that has met with a web of deceit. A good prediction would be *irritation*. Looking at the answer choices, **(C)** *frustration* is a perfect candidate, as it can be a synonym for irritation. Choice **(A)** *exuberance* has a strong positive charge, and it's therefore wrong. Choice **(B)** *apathy,* meaning "indifference," has a neutral charge, so it does not work in this context where you need a negatively charged answer.

4. C, D, I

The straight-ahead road sign "Unsurprisingly" makes the second blank a good place to start. The first sentence discusses "the creation" of a musical work, and the second sentence continues this discussion, saying that two works of art served as "muses" for Gershwin. A muse is a source of inspiration, so *inspired* works as a prediction and, in fact, matches **(D)**. The second sentence in no way indicates that the influence of the artwork *biased* Gershwin's work, or "had a strong and often unfair influence" on it, as the Whistler pieces were but two of many influences on the piece, so **(E)** can be eliminated. **(F)** *captured* in the context of an artistic endeavor means "put into a lasting form," and for this to have occurred, the Whistler paintings would have had to have been produced after *Rhapsody.*

The sentence that contains the third blank ends with "during just one week in New York," giving the time frame in which something was accomplished. Specifically, it refers to when Gershwin *wrote* the musical piece. **(I)** *scored* is a music-specific term for writing, which makes it correct for the blank. Nothing indicates that Gershwin put the piece off until later, which means **(G)** *postponed* can be eliminated. **(H)** *commenced* would mean that Gershwin only "started" the piece of music, but the phrase "during just one week" indicates that the entire piece was completed during that short period.

Finally, the first sentence explains what Gershwin was surrounded by when he wrote *Rhapsody in Blue*: the kaleidoscope of American life during his time in New York, including some specific examples. The first blank describes how this "kaleidoscope" related to Gershwin's composing, so predict that these were the *circumstances* within which he composed. **(C)** *context* means "the situation in which something happens," which is a great match for the prediction. There is no indication that confusion or difficulty led to the creation of the piece, so **(A)** *conundrum*, which means "a confusing or difficult problem," can be eliminated. Finally, a **(B)** *pretense* is "a false reason for something," which is not supported by any information in the text.

5. B, D, I

In the first sentence, the word "is" functions as a straight-ahead road sign, connecting the kind of competition among buyers that is "a boon [a benefit] for real estate agents." Then you learn that real estate agents make money mostly on commission. Therefore, a good market for real estate agents is an active market in which prices are high. Predict *strong* competition and take a look at the answer choices. **(B)** *Robust* means "strong" and works well in the context of this sentence. Both **(A)** *Lax* and **(C)** *Dwindling* would be more apt to describe the "inevitable weak market," since the former means "not strong" and the latter means "decreasing in size."

The second blank describes an agent who plans for a weak market, an idea introduced with the detour road sign "but." Predicting a *wise* agent leads directly to **(D)** *knowing,* which here means "shrewdly or keenly aware." **(E)** *craven,* meaning "cowardly," might work to describe an agent who leaves the real estate field altogether out of fear of the risk involved, but the text is describing people who stay in the business. Although agents who diversify their business are probably confident and perhaps even aggressive, **(F)** *brash* means "confident and aggressive in a rude way"; this negative connotation does not match the neutral tone of the sentence.

The third blank states the positive effect that diversifying has for real estate businesses. The phrase *kept in business* works well as a prediction here. **(I)** *buoyed* means "kept afloat"; this can be in the literal sense of being kept afloat in water, but it can also be used metaphorically to say, *Her mood was buoyed by the good news* or, in this case, *A business is buoyed by diversification.* Both **(G)** *stunted*, which means "slowed in growth," and **(H)** *terminated,* meaning "ended," are negative in tone and are the opposite of what's needed.

KAPLAN'S ADDITIONAL TIPS FOR TEXT COMPLETION QUESTIONS

Look for What's Directly Implied and Not an Ambiguous Interpretation

The questions you'll encounter are written in sophisticated but still logical and straightforward prose. Therefore, the correct answer is the one most directly implied by the meanings of the words in the sentence. These sentences are constructed to allow you to identify the answer using the inferential strategies you just practiced.

Don't Be Too Creative

Read the sentence literally, not imaginatively. Pay attention to the meaning of the words instead of any associations or feelings that might come up for you.

Paraphrase Long or Complex Sentences

You may encounter a sentence that, because of its length or structure, is hard to get a handle on. When faced with a complex sentence, slow down and put it in your own words. Break long, complicated sentences into pieces and tackle one phrase at a time.

Use Word Roots

Use the Resources section of this book to learn the Latin and Greek roots of many common GRE words. If you don't know the meaning of a word, take a look at its root to get close to its meaning or understand what it must refer to. Etymology often provides clues to meaning, especially when you couple a root definition with the word in context.

TEXT COMPLETION PRACTICE SET

Try the following Text Completion questions using the Kaplan Method for Text Completion.

BASIC

1. The strong familial bonds within the elephant herd led to a(n) _______ response in an emergency; as soon as the calf began to trumpet, all of the adult members of the herd rushed to the rescue.

   (A) laggardly
   (B) diminutive
   (C) indignant
   (D) communal
   (E) dilatory

2. Having test-driven this car in a variety of realistic conditions and found its performance lackluster at best, I have to say that its maker's sanguine claims are _______.

   (A) understated
   (B) impeccable
   (C) unfounded
   (D) plausible
   (E) mediocre

3. Even though some of the foremost researchers of cardiovascular disease delivered a harsh critique of the guidelines due to their _______, the nongovernmental organization recommended a "heart-healthy" diet for people in countries with a low per-capita income based on data gathered mainly in affluent nations, thus failing to account for disparities in access to food.

   (A) hindsight
   (B) incompetence
   (C) mendacity
   (D) indiscretion
   (E) inefficacy

4. Although subjected to endless _______, she was unwavering in advocating her theory, claiming to be untroubled by the raillery.

   (A) rebuttal
   (B) approbation
   (C) disavowal
   (D) japery
   (E) consent

5. Practicing psychologists have a variety of resources at their disposal to help individuals characterized as _______ spendthrifts; invariably, ingrained self-destructive habits require accountability and a plan of action.

   (A) inveterate
   (B) intermittent
   (C) indeterminate
   (D) impertinent
   (E) incoherent

6. The idea that the Internet is not a (i) _______ place has become ingrained in popular culture. Because of the increasing number of users, it has become more complicated for authorities to (ii) _______ the breaches of privacy that proliferate on a regular basis. The average user should remain (iii) _______ the exchange of personal data over the Internet.

Blank (i)	Blank (ii)	Blank (iii)
A sensible	D castigate	G indignant about
B secure	E relinquish	H skeptical of
C reliable	F constrain	I prudent in

INTERMEDIATE

7. A (i) _______ platform for accessing government data sets is crucial not only for researchers, statisticians, and political advisers but also for the entire population if citizens are to be informed participants in policy making. As agencies continue to collect an ever-increasing array of information in order to address fiscal and social issues, the technical resources that house that data must be (ii) _______ in kind.

Blank (i)	
A	proprietary
B	static
C	scalable

Blank (ii)	
D	capsulized
E	expanded
F	constringed

8. The global nature of the modern economy means that a financial (i) _______ in one part of the world almost always has detrimental effects on other regions. Moreover, the economies that are least prepared to deal with a crisis are usually the ones that sustain the most (ii) _______ damage.

Blank (i)	
A	boon
B	quagmire
C	variation

Blank (ii)	
D	onerous
E	ephemeral
F	avoidable

9. Studies show that one of the adverse consequences of wage _______ is the need for underemployed individuals to work multiple low-paying jobs in order to raise their household income above the poverty threshold.

   (A) inflation
   (B) stagnation
   (C) sequestration
   (D) remuneration
   (E) consolidation

10. Despite the ever-changing array of convoluted physical regimens that are promoted in the hopes of increasing athletic performance, _______ practices—getting enough sleep, eating a balanced diet, and reducing stress—remain the keys to optimal conditioning.

Ⓐ nebulous
Ⓑ spurious
Ⓒ oblivious
Ⓓ rudimentary
Ⓔ sophisticated

11. In conversation, people usually adjust the register, or (i) _______, of their speech according to the circumstances in which they find themselves. For example, they will be less (ii) _______ in their use of vocabulary and (iii) _______ when relaxing with friends than when they are speaking with clergy or legal officials.

Blank (i)	Blank (ii)	Blank (iii)
A meaning	D thoughtful	G lexicon
B significance	E interested	H grammar
C style	F formal	I verbiage

12. The longstanding pattern in which the majority party is (i) _______ a large number of legislative seats in the election cycle after winning the presidency has more to do with nonpartisan practicality than with (ii) _______ shifts in political ideology. Voters inevitably weary of the problems that afflict society at even the best of times, and they usually find (iii) _______ the party in control.

Blank (i)	Blank (ii)	Blank (iii)
A dispossessed of	D diminutive	G culpable
B recompensed with	E viable	H responsive
C benefitted by	F seismic	I dogmatic

13. Few cities in the world offer such a (i) _______ of culture per square mile as Athens, Greece. The birthplace of Western philosophical ethics, an incubator of the foremost minds in geometric reasoning, and a home to visionary architectural design that is still (ii) _______ in buildings throughout the world, this ancient capital will never (iii) _______ its significance in world history.

Blank (i)	Blank (ii)	Blank (iii)
A plenitude	D disparaged	G usurp
B dearth	E profiled	H rationalize
C plague	F emulated	I cede

14. The English language is unique in that, over the centuries, a (i) _______ of words have been borrowed from other languages. This history has resulted in an interesting (ii) _______ among linguists: the English language holds claim to the largest vocabulary of any language in the world by far, but after the stolen words are (iii) _______ from the total, some scholars argue that this assertion is not accurate.

Blank (i)	Blank (ii)	Blank (iii)
A plenum	D dichotomy	G discounted
B paucity	E paradigm	H tallied
C plethora	F case in point	I queried

15. Many people are familiar with the term "method acting," which is often touted as the (i) _______ technique for achieving realism, but many are surprised to learn of the complexity of the Stanislavsky system of method acting. Nevertheless, among actors it is held as (ii) _______ that adherence to Stanislavsky's tenets requires a (iii) _______ attention to detail and devotion to the craft.

Blank (i)	Blank (ii)	Blank (iii)
A preeminent	D undeniable	G middling
B preternatural	E debatable	H superficial
C accepted	F dubious	I rigorous

Advanced

16. While he uses many traditional training techniques, the fitness instructor's program is (i) _______ and even (ii) _______ approach.

Blank (i)	
A	a prudent
B	an innovative
C	a conventional

Blank (ii)	
D	idiosyncratic
E	spartan
F	cautious

17. The Eastern Woodlands Native Americans who originated lacrosse would likely not recognize how the sport has (i) _______. While early games involved hundreds of players, featured sticks without nets, and required every participant to place a wager, the modern-day sport is played by ten-player teams using sophisticated equipment, mainly at the high school and collegiate level; what does remain are the (ii) _______, such as stick preparation, pep talks, and team chants, which are performed by both sides before every game in hopes of a victory.

Blank (i)	
A	morphed
B	digressed
C	oscillated

Blank (ii)	
D	imprecations
E	rituals
F	antics

18. Although good writing is an art, it is also a (i) _______ skill that most people can master by following the principle that (ii) _______ and economy of language are virtues.

Blank (i)	
A	superfluous
B	fundamental
C	nugatory

Blank (ii)	
D	simplicity
E	preponderance
F	prolixity

19. The danger of (i) ______ assumptions regarding the character of those belonging to certain social classes is a (ii) ______ theme in several of the novels of Jane Austen.

Blank (i)		Blank (ii)	
A	valid	D	sporadic
B	benignant	E	perpetual
C	unfounded	F	recurring

20. Lacking members with a sound sense of (i) ______ knowledge, the explorers were almost certainly (ii) ______ to failure from the start.

Blank (i)		Blank (ii)	
A	geographical	D	doomed
B	general	E	accustomed
C	abstruse	F	immune

TEXT COMPLETION PRACTICE SET ANSWER KEY

1. **D**
2. **C**
3. **E**
4. **D**
5. **A**
6. **B, F, I**
7. **C, E**
8. **B, D**
9. **B**
10. **D**
11. **C, F, H**
12. **A, F, G**
13. **A, F, I**
14. **C, D, G**
15. **A, D, I**
16. **B, D**
17. **A, E**
18. **B, D**
19. **C, F**
20. **A, D**

TEXT COMPLETION PRACTICE SET ANSWERS AND EXPLANATIONS

Basic

1. D

The correct answer will describe the elephant herd's "response." "Led to" is a straight-ahead road sign linking "strong familial bonds" to the nature of the response. Furthermore, the semicolon serves as a straight-ahead road sign in this sentence, and the second part of the sentence states that "all of the adult members" came to the rescue. Thus, *group* response is a good prediction. **(D)** *communal* is correct because it means "to do something as a group," which closely matches the prediction. **(A)** *laggardly* and **(E)** *dilatory* can both be eliminated because they mean to "progress or develop slowly," which is the opposite of what is indicated by "rushed to the rescue." The fact that the response involved the entire herd also rules out **(B)** *diminutive*, which means "very small." **(C)** *indignant* means "angry because of something unjust," and nothing within the sentence indicates that the herd's response was an angry one, only that it was fast. (Be careful not to make assumptions: the sentence doesn't indicate the nature of the emergency. If the baby is trapped in quicksand, for example, the elephants will be very worried but not angry at an injustice.)

2. C

The author characterizes the car's performance as "lackluster," so you know that the word that will go in the blank will say that the maker's "sanguine," or optimistic, claims about the car are groundless. A good, simple prediction is *untrue*. Looking at the answer choices, **(C)** *unfounded* means "baseless," and that's the answer. You can throw out **(A)** *understated,* **(B)** *impeccable,* and **(D)** *plausible. Understated* means "restrained," and that is not a negative characterization. *Impeccable* means "flawless," which is far too positive. *Plausible* means "possible," and the author is expressing doubt, not trust. Choice **(E)** *mediocre* does have a negative charge, but while the car in question is mediocre, the maker's claims need a word that speaks to their truthfulness, not their general quality.

3. E

The sentence begins with the detour road sign "[e]ven though" and mentions some experts' "harsh critique." This criticism is being contrasted with the fact, discussed after the comma, that the organization recommended a diet that is a poor fit for the target population. "The foremost researchers" in the field would believe that such dietary guidelines would be *unhelpful* or *unbeneficial.*

(E) *inefficacy* means "inability to produce a desired result," so this word matches the prediction. **(A)** *hindsight*, "knowledge of an event that is only obtained after it has occurred," is not involved; the researchers criticized the guidelines before the decision to adopt them, and at any rate the blank describes the guidelines, not the researchers or their critique. **(B)** *incompetence*, "lack of ability to do something well," **(C)** *mendacity*, "lack of honesty," and **(D)** *indiscretion*, "lack of good judgment," are all negative qualities that the researchers might accuse the organization of exhibiting, but these are not characteristics of the dietary guidelines.

4. D

The detour road sign "Although" tells you that this person holds to her ideas despite whatever she is subjected to. Therefore, the word in the blank must be negative. A further key to this sentence is the word "raillery," meaning "mockery" or "ridicule." The subject of the sentence is "untroubled by the raillery," so you can determine that what she has been subjected to is a synonym for "raillery." Only **(D)** *japery,* also meaning "mockery," fits this description. Choices **(B)** *approbation* and **(E)** *consent* both mean "approval," so you can eliminate those immediately. Choice **(A)** *rebuttal* is a responding argument, and **(C)** *disavowal* is a rejection; while these terms might be related in idea to the sentence, they are not synonymous with "raillery."

5. A

The word "invariably" and the semicolon are both subtle straight-ahead road signs in this sentence, indicating that the beginning and end of the sentence use similar logic. The second half of the sentence states that the wasteful spending is an "ingrained habit," so a good prediction would be *habitual.* **(A)** *inveterate* is a perfect match for that prediction as it means "well established over a long time." **(B)** *intermittent* can be eliminated because it means "not constant," which is the opposite of the prediction. There is no support in the text for describing the spendthrifts as either **(C)** *indeterminate,* which means "vague," or **(E)** *incoherent,* which means "not easy to understand," so both choices can be eliminated. Finally, **(D)** *impertinent* can be ruled out because no context clues indicate that the spendthrifts are "rude."

6. B, F, I

Since all of the three answer choices fit the first blank, you must read the entire passage first, for context. The phrase "breaches of privacy" suggests that the Internet is a place where unauthorized third parties can obtain data. Choice **(C)** *reliable* doesn't quite fit this context, so you can rule it out. And while it may be true that content posted on the Internet is not always **(A)** *sensible,* there is no context in the sentence to support this idea. Choice **(B)** *secure* is most applicable to the issue at hand, so it is the correct choice.

For the second blank, choice **(F)** *constrain* means "to get under control," **(D)** *castigate* means "to criticize or punish," and **(E)** *relinquish* means "to surrender." *Relinquish* doesn't make sense, and while authorities might try to castigate the people who hack into Internet users' private information, officials do not punish the privacy violations themselves. So **(D)** and **(E)** can be ruled out, and **(F)** is the correct answer.

While one could be **(G)** *indignant about* (angry about) a loss of privacy and **(H)** *skeptical of* (doubtful of) the security of one's data online, the only choice that makes sense relative to "the exchange of personal data" is **(I)** *prudent in.* Given the difficulty in maintaining Internet security, one must indeed be careful about transmitting personal data.

Intermediate

7. C, E

In this question, the key words provide more clues to the second blank than to the first, so start there. The word "[a]s" at the beginning of the second sentence is a straight-ahead road sign, indicating that the first clause in the sentence harmonizes with the second clause. In addition, the phrase "in kind" after the blank means that the technical resources that store the data are doing something similar to what the agencies are doing with the data. The agencies are collecting "an ever-increasing array of information," which means that where the information is stored must *increased in size* as well. **(E)** *expanded* matches the prediction. **(D)** *capsulized* and **(F)** *constringed* mean "made smaller." (What do you do with a time *capsule*? Reduce an entire period of time to a few items that represent the period well. In *constringe*, the prefix *con-* means "with" and the Latin root *stringere* means "to tighten." Other words with that root include *stringent*, *strangle*, and *strict*.)

Now that the second blank is filled in, it can be used to make a prediction for the first blank, which describes the platform used to access data sets. If the technical resources need to be *expanded*, the platform that the information is stored on needs *to be able to grow*. If something is **(C)** *scalable*, it is "capable of being expanded," so this choice is a nice fit with the prediction. **(B)** *static* can be eliminated because "stationary or fixed" is the opposite of the prediction. **(A)** *proprietary* might sound good before "platform," but the government having "an exclusive right to" the platform is contradicted by the sentence, which indicates that many people have access to the data.

8. B, D

The first blank describes a bad economic situation—one that would create "detrimental effects in other regions." The second blank describes the kind of damage experienced by fragile economies—those that are "least prepared to deal with a crisis." "Detrimental effects" is a strong clue, which makes the first blank a good place to start. Predicting a simple negative word like *problem* will allow you to work through the choices. **(B)** *quagmire* means "a bad situation that is difficult to escape," which fits the prediction nicely. **(A)** *boon*, meaning "a benefit or advantage," is the opposite of the prediction, and **(C)** *variation* is too neutral for the the context because "change" can be bad, good, or neither.

"Moreover" serves as a straight-ahead road sign. What kind of "damage" would you expect a bad financial situation to have on a fragile economy? Predict a word like *severe* for the second blank. **(D)** *onerous* is a good match since it means "hard to deal with or burdensome." **(E)** *ephemeral* would mean that the damage is "short-lived," but if anything, the text indicates otherwise. **(F)** *avoidable* is incorrect since the first sentence points out that it is nearly impossible for negative effects in one part of the world not to spread to other parts of the world.

9. B

"Studies show that" serves as a straight-ahead road sign: the noun in the blank is something that is suffering "adverse consequences," one of which is described in the rest of the sentence. Moreover, the word in the blank relates to "wage[s]." If individuals have to work multiple jobs to stay above the poverty line, a good prediction would be *decrease* or *staying the same*. **(B)** *stagnation* means "not increasing," which works with the prediction of *staying the same*. **(A)** *inflation* means an "increase in size or price." This might seem to make sense because *inflation* in general could cause someone to need an extra job, but here *inflation* refers specifically to wages, making it incorrect. **(C)** *sequestration* and **(E)** *consolidation* can both be eliminated because neither word logically describes wages; the former means "the act of keeping groups apart from one another," and the latter means "the act of joining individual units into a whole." Finally, **(D)** *remuneration* simply means "payment," so it can be eliminated as well.

10. D

The detour road sign "[d]espite" indicates that the true keys to optimal conditioning are not the "convoluted physical regimens." The opposite of "convoluted" is *simple*, and the choice that matches that prediction is **(D)** *rudimentary*, which means "related to basic principles" or "lacking complex development." **(A)** *nebulous* would mean that the concepts are "not clear," and if anything, it would be the "convoluted" regimens that are less than clear. Likewise, the sentence does not indicate that the concepts are "based on false ideas," so eliminate **(B)** *spurious*. Be careful not to confuse **(C)** *oblivious* with the word *obvious*; **(C)** *oblivious* means "not aware of something." Finally, **(E)** *sophisticated* is incorrect because it means "highly developed and complex," which is the opposite of the prediction.

11. C, F, H

Use the clues in these sentences to determine which words fit in the blanks. The word for the first blank must be an attribute of speech that is roughly synonymous with "register." Speakers are unlikely to change the **(A)** *meaning* or **(B)** *significance* of their speech to fit the circumstances, but **(C)** *style* fits well as a partner for "register."

The second blank, preceded by "less," suggests a descriptive word in opposition to the phrase "when relaxing with friends." Predict something like *not relaxed*. Neither **(D)** *thoughtful* nor **(E)** *interested* works here, because these qualities of speech do not necessarily change depending on whom one is with. In this case, the remaining word **(F)** *formal* matches the contrast between "friends" and "officials."

Blank (iii) is related to the preceding phrase with the straight-ahead road sign "and," so this will be a noun that is parallel and complementary to "use of vocabulary." Predict that the correct answer will be some other aspect of language use. You may be able to identify that both **(G)** *lexicon* and **(I)** *verbiage* refer to the specific words used, so both of these terms are redundant as a partner to "vocabulary." Instead, **(H)** *grammar* is the correct choice.

12. A, F, G

The strongest clues are provided for the third blank, so start there. The straight-ahead road sign "and" means that this blank describes how voters find the party in control when they get tired of problems. A good prediction is that the voters *blame* the party in power, so predict something like *blameworthy*. This matches the definition of **(G)** *culpable*. **(H)** *responsive* is a positive word. **(I)** *dogmatic* means "very opinionated"; according to the author, the voters are tired of the problems society faces, not tired of anything the party in power might believe.

Now try to fill in the first blank. Voters "find *culpable*" the party that is in control, so a logical prediction is that the party *loses* legislative seats. Predict something like *loss of*. That's a match for **(A)** *dispossessed of*. **(B)** *recompensed with* would mean the party was given more seats, and **(C)** *benefitted by* would also imply that the party gained somehow.

Finally, the second blank is part of the phrase "more to do with *X* than with *Y*," which conveys a contrast. The second sentence indicates that the public is voting against the party in power because it is concerned about problems—this is "nonpartisan practicality." Therefore, predict that the second half of this construction will relate to *partisanship*, specifically *big* shifts in political ideology. Correct choice **(F)** *seismic* means "very great or important." **(D)** *diminutive,* meaning "very small," is the opposite of the prediction, and **(E)** *viable*, which means "capable of succeeding," also does not match the prediction.

13. A, F, I

Subtle road signs provide clues to each blank. The phrases on either side of the first blank constitute a straight-ahead road sign emphasizing that Athens has unusual cultural offerings as compared to other cities. The second sentence lists a number of significant cultural achievements of "this ancient capital," so a good prediction would be *wealth* or *abundance*. **(A)** *plenitude* has the same word root as *plenty* (*plenus*) and means "a large number or amount of something." **(C)** *plague* means "a large amount of something" but specifically "harmful or annoying things," which does not match the strong positive tone of the second sentence. **(B)** *dearth* means "the state of not having enough of something," which is the opposite of the prediction.

Your prediction for the second blank can be guided by the straight-ahead road sign "is still"; this explains how the "visionary architectural design" of ancient Athens relates to modern-day building design. A logical prediction is that Athenian architecture is still *being used* or *copied*. **(F)** *emulated* means "imitated from a motive of admiration," which makes sense given the "visionary" nature of the design. **(D)** *disparaged* is the opposite of the prediction because it means "described as unimportant or bad." Beware of **(E)** *profiled*, which is too neutral in context; it simply means "described briefly."

The final blank describes what "will never" happen to Athens's significance in world history. Since the text focuses on the city's significant cultural milestones, which are more plentiful than those of most other cities, a logical prediction would be that it will never *lose* its place in history. **(I)** *cede* means "relinquish something" and gives the sentence a logical meaning. "To take or keep something in a forceful, violent way," or **(G)** *usurp*, does not fit because there is no sense of struggle or competition here. **(H)** *rationalize* means "to describe something negative in a way that makes it sound more proper or attractive," but the context shows that Athens's significance is legitimate and does not require rationalization.

14. C, D, G

For multi-blank Text Completions, understand how the blanks are related to one another before deciding which one to tackle first. The first blank is a noun denoting how many words have been "borrowed"; the second blank names an "interesting" phenomenon, described after the colon; and the third blank states what is done with words to call into question the claim that English has the largest vocabulary. The third blank has the strongest clues, so start there. The detour road sign "but" means that English has the largest vocabulary until the stolen words are *removed from* or *not included* in the total. **(G)** *discounted* means "left out of consideration" and is correct. **(H)** *tallied*, meaning "counted," is the opposite of what's needed, and **(I)** *queried*, meaning "questioned" does not make sense.

With the third blank filled in, the first blank becomes easier to predict. If not including the words taken from other languages makes English lose its claim to the largest vocabulary, there must be *a lot* of borrowed words. **(C)** *plethora* matches the prediction because it means "an abundance." **(B)** *paucity* means "few," which is the opposite of the prediction, and **(A)** *plenum*, which has several meanings but all relating to "fullness," does not work in context.

Now for blank (ii) before the colon, which functions as a straight-ahead road sign. On the one hand, since the foreign words are now part of the English language, they are counted as part of the language's vocabulary, but on the other hand, some linguists call these words "stolen" and do not count them. This is an interesting *set of contrasting ideas*, which fits **(D)** *dichotomy* well. **(E)** *paradigm* means "example" or "theoretical framework," and **(F)** *case in point* means "example"; neither describes the contrast presented in the rest of the sentence.

15. A, D, I

The word in the first blank describes the "method acting" technique, and the key phrase "often touted" (often promoted) shows that a strong, positive word belongs in the blank. A simple prediction that fits is the *best* technique, which matches the "more important, better than others" meaning of **(A)** *preeminent.* The "natural" in **(B)** *preternatural* might make this choice tempting because the sentence mentions "realism," but *preternatural* actually means "unusual, not realistic." **(C)** *accepted* is too neutral as it does not convey the superiority that comes with "touting" something.

Now, it is easier to make a prediction for the third blank. The detour road sign "[n]evertheless" indicates that even though the complexity of the Stanislavsky system may not be well-known outside the acting community, actors do appreciate its complexity. Predict that actors know they must exercise *great* attention to detail. **(I)** *rigorous,* which means "done carefully, with attention to detail," works well. Neither **(H)** *superficial,* which means "not thorough, incomplete," nor **(G)** *middling,* "average," would describe the attention to detail required by the Stanislavsky system.

The second blank relates to the preceding sentence via the detour road sign "[n]evertheless" and relates to blank (iii) via the straight-ahead road sign "requires." Since the actors know they need to exercise "*rigorous* attention to detail and devotion to craft to use the method," predict that they find this requirement *obvious.* **(D)** *undeniable*, which means "clearly true," matches the prediction. If something is **(E)** *debatable,* it "may or may not be true," and something that is **(F)** *dubious* is "unsure or uncertain"; both of these choices are almost opposites of the prediction.

Advanced

16. B, D

The first part of the sentence tells you that the fitness instructor "uses many traditional training techniques." The detour road sign "[w]hile" signals that the program described by the blanks will be the opposite of traditional. For the first blank, predict "new" or "novel." *Innovative,* **(B)**, which means "using new ideas or methods," matches the prediction. While the program may be *prudent* (meaning "wise" or "sensible") or *conventional,* **(A)** and **(C)** do not contrast with "traditional."

The straight-ahead road sign "even" indicates that the word in the second blank will have the same general meaning as the first but be more emphatic. Since *innovative* is the first word, predict "unique" or "very different." *Idiosyncratic,* **(D)**, describes someone or something "having a peculiar or highly distinctive characteristic." This works in the second blank to describe the fitness program. *Spartan,* **(E)**, means "very disciplined and stern." There is no clue in the sentence to suggest that the program can be described as such. Likewise, there is no clue to conclude that the program is *cautious,* **(F)**.

17. A, E

Two clues can help you make a prediction for the first blank. In the first sentence, it says that the originators of lacrosse "would likely not recognize [it]." Then the next sentence, beginning with the detour road sign "[w]hile," contrasts "early games" with "the modern-day sport." *Changed* works well as a prediction for the first blank and matches **(A)** *morphed*, which means "underwent a transformation." **(B)** *digressed* means "switched to speaking or writing about something other than the main topic." **(C)** *oscillated* means "repeatedly changed from one condition to another." Both **(B)** and **(C)** relate to change, but of a different sort than that undergone by lacrosse.

For the second blank, you can focus on the second half of the second sentence. The blank describes something performed before every game, both in the past ("what does remain") and now, to help ensure victory. The sentence also provides three specific examples: stick preparation, pep talks, and team chants. These could all accurately be described as *routines*, which matches **(E)** *rituals*, "a series of acts performed the same way every time." Neither **(D)** *imprecations*, which means "curses," nor **(F)** *antics*, which means "wildly playful or funny actions," matches the prediction.

18. B, D

"Although" is a detour road sign, so you know that the first blank will detour in meaning from "art," as it is used to describe writing. Something less than "artistic" could be called *basic*. That's a good prediction for the first blank. Choice **(B)** *fundamental* fits perfectly. You can rule out **(A)** *superfluous*, as it means "unnecessary," while you're looking for a term that describes writing at its bare essence. You can also reject choice **(C)** *nugatory*, which means "trifling," since nothing in the sentence indicates that good writing is not important. Moving to the second blank, the straight-ahead road sign "and" tells you that the blank will agree with "economy of language," or short, compact writing without ornamentation. Choice **(D)** *simplicity* is a perfect way to describe basic, fundamental writing. Choice **(E)** *preponderance* and **(F)** *prolixity* both have a meaning related to "excess" and thus are the opposite of what you need.

19. C, F

The second blank, which describes how often the theme of misjudging people occurs, is a good place to start since the sentence says the theme occurs in "several of the novels." Predicting *regular* leads to **(F)** *recurring*, which means "occurring repeatedly." The other two choices are on either end of the "how often" spectrum; **(D)** *sporadic* means "occurring occasionally," and **(E)** *perpetual* means "occurring all the time for an indefinite period." Neither choice conveys the frequency indicated in the sentence.

The first blank describes what kind of assumptions were made. The sentence is discussing the "danger of" these assumptions, so predict a negative word. Specifically, assumptions are potentially dangerous when they are *incorrect*. When something is **(C)** *unfounded*, it "lacks a sound basis," so this word meshes nicely with the prediction. If the assumption is **(A)** *valid*, it is "well-grounded and reasonable," the opposite of the prediction phrase. Finally, **(B)** *benignant* is rarely used but is closely related to the more common *benign*, and it means "favorable or beneficial" (you may have heard the phrase *benign tumor*, which is a tumor that is not harmful). This choice does not match the "danger of" clue.

20. A, D

The phrase "almost certainly" is a straight-ahead road sign, indicating that the second clause in the sentence will continue the direction of the first. Reading the sentence, you can infer that the lack of a certain kind of knowledge affected the explorers' chances of success. A lack of knowledge would not prevent failure, so you can reasonably assume that it "led to" failure. This provides a good prediction for the second blank, so start there. Choice **(D)** *doomed* makes sense. A lack of knowledge *doomed* the explorers. A lack of knowledge would be unlikely to make an expedition **(F)** *immune* to, meaning unaffected by, failure, so **(F)** is wrong. You can also reject choice **(E)** *accustomed*; you have no idea whether the explorers have failed in the past.

For the first blank, you're asked to find the word that characterizes this knowledge. Choice **(A)** *geographical* fits perfectly. It is precisely the type of knowledge an explorer would need and would be doomed without. Choice **(B)** *general* can be rejected; it's not specific enough to indicate why the explorers would be doomed. You can reject choice **(C)** *abstruse*, meaning "obscure" or "hard to understand," since this type of knowledge is not of importance to explorers per se.

CHAPTER 3

Sentence Equivalence

SENTENCE EQUIVALENCE: OVERVIEW AND METHOD

You will find about four Sentence Equivalence questions per Verbal Reasoning section on the GRE. Each consists of a single sentence with one word missing. They differ from Text Completion questions in that there will be six answer choices, two of which are correct. Your job is to identify the two answer choices that, when inserted into the sentence, correctly complete the sentence and produce sentences of similar meaning. These questions are similar to Text Completion questions, as both ask you to deduce the meaning of a missing word in a passage on the basis of incomplete information.

One very important thing to bear in mind when working out a Sentence Equivalence question is that the correct answer choices are often, *but are not necessarily*, synonyms. You must pay close attention to the differing shades of meaning that words have and understand that the key to unlocking the correct answer is to look for choices that create sentences with similar meanings. You must select both correct choices in order to receive credit for the question; no partial credit is given for selecting one of the correct choices.

The directions for Sentence Equivalence questions will look like this:

> Select the two answer choices that, when used to complete the sentence, fit the meaning of the sentence as a whole and produce completed sentences that are alike in meaning.

A Sentence Equivalence question will look like this:

Cora was not known for her reticence; regardless, she only ______ acquiesced to calls to speak at the conference.

- A jejunely
- B exuberantly
- C willfully
- D grudgingly
- E candidly
- F timidly

THE KAPLAN METHOD FOR SENTENCE EQUIVALENCE

STEP 1 **Read the sentence, looking for clues.**

STEP 2 **Predict the answer.**

STEP 3 **Select the two answer choices that most closely match your prediction.**

STEP 4 **Check your answers to see if the sentence retains the same meaning.**

How the Kaplan Method for Sentence Equivalence Works

Here's how the Kaplan Method for Sentence Equivalence works:

STEP 1

Read the sentence, looking for clues.

As you read the sentence, look for specific words in the sentence that will help you understand its meaning. As mentioned in chapter 2, these are key words or phrases, which provide context clues, and road signs, which are structural clues. Use key words and road signs to help you predict the words that go in the blank.

As a reminder, words that show that the second part of a sentence continues or builds on the meaning of the first—"straight-ahead" road signs—include the following:

And	*Because*	*Similarly*
Since	*: (colon)*	*In addition*
Also	*Likewise*	*Consequently*
Thus	*Moreover*	*Therefore*

Words that show that one part of the sentence contradicts or contrasts with the other part—"detour" road signs—include these:

But	*Unless*	*On the other hand*
Despite	*Rather*	*Unfortunately*
Yet	*Although*	*Nonetheless*
However	*While*	*Conversely*

STEP 2

Predict the answer.

Once you have read the sentence and identified clues to words that will complete the sentence, predict an answer. Your prediction should be a simple word that logically completes the sentence. Predict the right answer *before* you look at the answer choices. Characterizing the correct answer before evaluating the choices will help you efficiently eliminate those that don't match your prediction and avoid trap answers.

STEP 3

Select the two answer choices that most closely match your prediction.

Quickly review the six answer choices and choose the two words that, when plugged into the sentence, most closely match its intended meaning and thus your prediction. Eliminate the answer choices that do not fit your prediction. Sometimes you will need to adjust your prediction—often by making it more or less specific—in order to find two answer choices that match it.

STEP 4

Check your answers to see if the sentence retains the same meaning.

Read the sentence with each answer choice to check that you have selected the correct answers. Ensure that both answer choices make sense in the context of the sentence and produce resulting sentences with similar meanings. Pay close attention to the charge of a word's meaning. For example, *dislike* and *despise* both mean the same thing, but *despise* has a much stronger degree of charge to that meaning. If one or both of your answers do not make sense when you reread the sentence, revisit the question and repeat Steps 1, 2, and 3.

Apply the Kaplan Method for Sentence Equivalence

Now let's apply the Kaplan Method to a Sentence Equivalence question:

> Cora was not known for her reticence; regardless, she only ______ acquiesced to calls to speak at the conference.
>
> A jejunely
> B exuberantly
> C willfully
> D grudgingly
> E candidly
> F timidly

STEP 1

Read the sentence, looking for clues.

The first thing you should notice is the structural road sign "regardless," which functions as a detour road sign. Therefore, the clause after the semicolon will depart from the meaning of the first clause. You're told in the first clause that Cora is "not known for her reticence," so the second will indicate hesitance or reluctance.

STEP 2

Predict the answer.

The blank will be an adverb that describes "acquiesced," which means to "give in" or "relent." Since you're looking for a word that shows Cora being uncharacteristically reticent, a good prediction is *reluctantly.*

STEP 3

Select the two choices that most closely match your prediction.

Evaluating the answer choices, you can immediately reject **(A)** *jejunely,* "childishly," which doesn't make sense, and **(B)** *exuberantly,* "gleefully," which implies Cora was anything but reluctant to speak at the conference. You can eliminate **(C)** *willfully,* since it implies that she was headstrong, which does not harmonize with *reluctantly.* Choice **(E)** *candidly,* "openly," doesn't have a meaning close to *reluctantly.* That leaves **(D)** *grudgingly,* meaning "resentfully unwilling," and **(F)** *timidly,* which means "in an easily frightened way." These two are the best matches.

STEP 4

Check your answers to see if the sentence retains the same meaning.

If you check your answers in the context of the original sentence, you'll arrive at two sentences that mean: *Cora was not known for being hesitant, but she only reluctantly agreed to speak at the conference.* Notice that the two answer choices are not precise synonyms. Both connote reluctance, but with different shades of meaning. *Grudgingly* has an undertone of resentfulness, while *timidly* implies that one is fearfully shy. However, both produce sentences with similar meanings, and they're the correct answers.

KAPLAN'S ADDITIONAL TIPS FOR SENTENCE EQUIVALENCE QUESTIONS

Consider All Answer Choices

Make sure to read and check all answer choices in the sentence before making your final choice. An answer may fit well in the sentence and closely match your prediction, but if there is no other answer choice that also completes the sentence with the same meaning, it isn't correct.

Paraphrase the Question

If you rephrase a difficult or longer sentence in your own words, it will be easier to predict the right answer. Paraphrasing will also ensure that you understand the meaning of the sentence.

Look Beyond Synonyms

Simply finding a synonym pair in the answer choices will not always lead you to the correct answer. Answer choices may include a pair of synonyms that do not fit the context of the sentence. Both of those choices are incorrect. The meanings of both resultant sentences must be the same and correct. Be sure to try both words in the sentence, checking that each sentence has the same meaning, before making your final choice.

Use Prefixes, Suffixes, and Roots

If you are struggling to figure out the meaning of a word, think about the meaning of any prefix, suffix, or root that you find in the word. These word parts can provide important clues to the word's definition.

SENTENCE EQUIVALENCE PRACTICE SET

Try the following Sentence Equivalence questions using the Kaplan Method.

Basic

1. Nutritionists are constantly reminding their patients, especially young ones, of the importance of eating mindfully; however, studies show that young people have an increasingly _______ attitude toward healthy eating habits.

   A prescient
   B cognizant
   C frivolous
   D provident
   E cavalier
   F myopic

2. Annual budget cuts and rapid changes in technology over the last decade had made it nearly impossible for the daily newspaper to generate a viable revenue stream for the company; unless management found additional ways to _______ the publication's content, the staff would soon be looking for new jobs.

   A streamline
   B monetize
   C condense
   D integrate
   E depreciate
   F appreciate

3. Following up on a sizable lead in the polls, the gubernatorial candidate established _______ advantage over his incumbent opponent on election night and ultimately gained victory.

   A an inequitable
   B a negligible
   C a decisive
   D a disconcerting
   E a patent
   F an ignominious

4. Although it may seem counterintuitive, students who are forced to choose a profession early in the academic process vary little from students who decide on a career path much later; there is only a _______ difference in the number of students from each group who continue into their chosen field after graduation.

   A negligible
   B minute
   C respectable
   D negative
   E complementary
   F supplementary

5. The residents, who for many years relished the safe, idyllic surroundings of their suburban neighborhood, have in recent months faced _______ of vandalism.

   A a deficiency
   B an epidemic
   C a backlash
   D a scourge
   E an abatement
   F a revelry

6. In her laudatory _______, the food columnist captured the spirit of the hotel dining room.

   A homage
   B paean
   C banter
   D denunciation
   E rebuff
   F examination

7. After losing his entire fortune on Wall Street, the investor abandoned New York City and began a pilgrimage across Europe; in addition, he gave away most of his possessions and _______ materialism.

   A espoused
   B renounced
   C disregarded
   D initiated
   E spurned
   F aggrandized

8. The _______ entourage accompanied Elvis everywhere he went, and they fetched the singer anything he requested—however challenging or ridiculous—at a moment's notice.

   A avaricious
   B obsequious
   C humble
   D belligerent
   E jubilant
   F fawning

9. The CEO felt she should keep the court case under cover so as not to cause alarm, but to do so would contradict her usually _______ management style.

   A transparent
   B pusillanimous
   C aggressive
   D forthright
   E slipshod
   F negligent

10. As a child, he was often lost in thought, a habit that persisted throughout his life, with the result that his contemporaries described him as _______.

   A surly
   B pensive
   C meditative
   D indigenous
   E arcane
   F livid

Intermediate

11. Although the suburban townhouse seemed like a good value, the buyer _______ when the real estate agent asked for a commitment.

    A elaborated
    B ambled
    C vacillated
    D groveled
    E lamented
    F dawdled

12. The newspaper reporter decided to corner the water board commissioner at the town hall meeting; she knew that even though his staff had _______ scheduled interviews for weeks, the politician would be unable to avoid addressing the fraud allegations in that public forum.

    A arranged
    B encumbered
    C censured
    D obstructed
    E authorized
    F sanctioned

13. Within hours the hurricane weakened considerably, serving to _______ the fears of hundreds of residents who had refused to evacuate.

    A assuage
    B emblazon
    C ignite
    D annihilate
    E mediate
    F allay

14. The politician felt that she could no longer empathize with her constituency, so she decided to _______ local establishments in order to discover the concerns of the community.

    A vacate
    B evade
    C patronize
    D skirt
    E aggrandize
    F frequent

15. The movie—adapted from a well-known story—was supposedly intended for all audiences, but many parents felt the content was too _______.

    A ribald
    B arcane
    C superfluous
    D pervasive
    E lascivious
    F esoteric

16. It is an unfortunate but just criticism that some news commentators report certain claims as unimpeachable truths when the claims have undeniably been _______ by researchers.

   A confirmed
   B repudiated
   C disavowed
   D abased
   E resolved
   F validated

17. In his enthusiasm for introducing new scholars to his advanced discipline, Professor Assem endeavors to deliver lectures steeped in economic theory that are _______ to first-year graduate students.

   A accessible
   B enjoyable
   C comprehensible
   D daunting
   E bemusing
   F salient

18. Because the actor has portrayed only comic roles, her opportunities to play characters made _______ by their circumstances will depend on her ability to demonstrate a range of emotions she has not yet shown in her professional work.

   A mirthful
   B doleful
   C capricious
   D bucolic
   E affable
   F morose

19. The singer was renowned for being _______; consequently, anecdotes about her tantrums grew to mythic proportions.

   A captious
   B dissolute
   C irascible
   D profligate
   E smug
   F nettlesome

20. The warriors didn't expect an assault on their olfactory senses; however, they were confronted with such a _______ group of opponents that they decided to beat a hasty retreat.

A cloying
B saccharine
C repulsive
D dejected
E fetid
F malodorous

Advanced

21. In contradistinction to the _______ cat, the dog is the quintessential pack animal.

A transparent
B supercilious
C solitary
D forthright
E maladroit
F aloof

22. The company executive impressed the employees not as incompetent but as _______; despite the executive's public statements, the workers refused to believe that a leader of such vast experience could not understand their obvious frustration.

A guilty
B disingenuous
C complacent
D duplicitous
E sagacious
F erudite

23. The speech was _______, as the speaker did not often resist the temptation to conclude her discussion of every aspect of the topic with some unnecessary side story.

A apposite
B cacophonous
C succinct
D prolix
E loquacious
F compendious

24. The child's inability to _______ with her classmate after he fell off the swing in front of her was worrisome to the teacher; the teacher wondered whether the student's expression of schadenfreude was evidence of a serious mental health issue.

A commiserate
B scuffle
C grimace
D empathize
E weep
F struggle

25. Not only was the author's prose _______, but also his well-known penchant for dissembling colored the way that reviewers read his texts.

A fulsome
B effulgent
C effusive
D unctuous
E cryptic
F vulgar

26. Those scholars who are attracted by the intricacy and esoteric nature of certain topics in geometric topology may be _______ by the formulas describing higher-dimensional relationships, notwithstanding the undeniable appeal of this branch of mathematics to those who have mastered the prerequisite topics.

   A elated
   B inveigled
   C confounded
   D unimpressed
   E nonplussed
   F oppressed

27. The unchecked _______ of state secrets is a source of great concern to intelligence agencies.

   A proliferation
   B retention
   C lassitude
   D acquisition
   E dissemination
   F quality

28. Although the celebrity _______ vociferously on political issues as a guest on several talk shows, her lack of experience in the area led many to ignore her.

   A inveighed
   B declaimed
   C conceded
   D demurred
   E abstained
   F acceded

29. Reginald's _______ aunt was spry for her age but nonetheless required help in ascending the staircase.

   A acrobatic
   B dexterous
   C caustic
   D genial
   E septuagenarian
   F hoary

30. _______, he decided to pass on the project, his professed support notwithstanding.

   A Counterintuitively
   B Unexpectedly
   C Self-indulgently
   D Obscurely
   E Pusillanimously
   F Punctiliously

SENTENCE EQUIVALENCE PRACTICE SET ANSWER KEY

1. **C, E**
2. **B, F**
3. **C, E**
4. **A, B**
5. **B, D**
6. **A, B**
7. **B, E**
8. **B, F**
9. **A, D**
10. **B, C**
11. **C, F**
12. **B, D**
13. **A, F**
14. **C, F**
15. **A, E**
16. **B, C**
17. **A, C**
18. **B, F**
19. **A, C**
20. **E, F**
21. **C, F**
22. **B, D**
23. **D, E**
24. **A, D**
25. **A, D**
26. **C, E**
27. **A, E**
28. **A, B**
29. **E, F**
30. **A, B**

SENTENCE EQUIVALENCE PRACTICE SET ANSWERS AND EXPLANATIONS

Basic

1. C, E

The road sign "however" contrasts how nutritionists want young people to eat with children's attitude toward healthy eating. The nutritionists want children to eat "mindfully," or to pay attention to what they eat. The word in the blank describes young people's attitude, and a good prediction would be *uncaring* or *inattentive*. The two choices that match that prediction are **(C)** *frivolous* and **(E)** *cavalier*, since both can be defined as "not viewing or treating something with seriousness." **(A)** *prescient* and **(D)** *provident* both refer to "planning or knowing about the future" and so run counter to the context clues. **(B)** *cognizant*, "being aware," is the opposite of what's needed; the nutritionists would *like* kids to be *cognizant* of their food choices. **(F)** *myopic* means "lacking in foresight or discernment," which might work in the sentence, but this choice does not have an equivalent among the other choices. For Sentence Equivalence questions, *always* eliminate choices that do not have an equivalent.

2. B, F

The blank in this sentence describes what management needs to do with the newspaper's content. The beginning of the sentence explains that the newspaper is in serious financial trouble, while the detour road sign "unless" shows that management's goal is for the newspaper's content to generate revenue so that the employees do not lose their jobs. A prediction that reflects both the context clues and the road sign would be *make valuable*. **(B)** *monetize* has the same word root as *money* and means "to use as a source of profit." The other correct choice is **(F)** *appreciate*, because one of the definitions of this word is "to increase the value of," which gives the sentence the same general meaning as **(B)** *monetize*. **(E)** *depreciate* means "to decrease the value of" and is the opposite of what the newspaper's management needs to do. **(A)** *streamline* and **(C)** *condense* both have similar meanings, "to make something smaller or simpler," but there is no indication in the sentence that the size of the newspaper is the problem. "To make something part of another larger thing," which is what **(D)** *integrate* means, might be part of a successful strategy to make the content more profitable, but no clues point in that direction and this choice does not have a partner.

3. C, E

The straight-ahead road sign "following up on" indicates that the remainder of the sentence will match the first part. Since the candidate's advantage followed a sizable lead in the polls, it was likely as strong or stronger by election night. You want two words that complement the word "sizable." If something is *decisive*, there can be no doubt about it, so choice **(C)** is one of the correct answer choices. Choice **(E)** *patent* means "clear" or "obvious." An obvious advantage is roughly the same thing as a decisive advantage, so this is the second correct answer. If something is *inequitable*, choice **(A)**, it is not equal, which you may deduce from the word parts *in-* and *equi-*. At first glance, this word may seem to fit. However, it suggests unfairness, and no clues in the sentence imply that the candidate acted unfairly. Choice **(B)** *negligible* means "slight" or "inconsequential in size," so that doesn't agree with the "sizable lead" described earlier. Choice **(D)** *disconcerting* means "upsetting" or "embarrassing," and there is nothing in the sentence to suggest that anyone was upset by the candidate's lead or ultimate victory. The prefix *ig-* in choice **(F)** *ignominious* tells you that, like "ignoble" or "ignorant," this is a negatively charged word. In fact, it means "shameful" and therefore doesn't fit the sentence.

4. A, B

The two detour road signs in the opening phrase of this text, "[a]lthough" and "counterintuitive," effectively cancel each other out. Two groups of students who differ in when they choose a career might be expected to be different in other relevant ways, but in fact they "vary little" from each other. Then the semicolon is a straight-ahead road sign, and the blank describes the "difference" between the two groups of students. Predict that there is a *small* difference between them. **(A)** *negligible* and **(B)** *minute* are the two choices that match the prediction; both words mean "very small or unimportant." Remember that all choices will be the same part of speech, so consider the adjectival use of *minute*, rather than its meaning as a noun of "a unit of time." A **(C)** *respectable* difference would be "a fair amount or quantity" of difference, which is not the same as a small difference. **(E)** *complementary* and **(F)** *supplementary* both have the general meaning "added to something," which does not match the prediction. (In the Quantitative section, you may encounter these words in the context of angles that, when put together, form a right angle or a straight line.) **(D)** *negative* (also a word you'll encounter in the Quant section) means "bad or not positive," which does not match the prediction or any of the other choices, so it can be eliminated.

5. B, D

Read this sentence closely to uncover clues suggesting the direction the sentence is taking (whether the blank will continue or contradict the thoughts that come before). The phrases "for many years" and "in recent months" suggest a change of events. After many years of "safe, idyllic" life, people faced vandalism, which means there probably was not much vandalism before. Look for words that suggest a spike in vandalism. *Epidemic*, choice **(B)**, is a word you have probably heard used to describe outbreaks of disease. It fits the context of a sudden increase in vandalism. The word *scourge*, choice **(D)**, can refer to a cause of widespread suffering. That's the other correct choice. Choice **(A)** *deficiency* does not fit. There is no shortage of vandalism. Choice **(C)** *backlash* may seem like a possible fit, but it is not. A backlash, or sudden reaction, comes after an action or development, and there is nothing in the sentence to indicate that anything happened beforehand to prompt such a response. Eliminate it. *Abatement* is a reduction, the opposite of an increase, so rule out choice **(E)**. Choice **(F)** *revelry* suggests a party atmosphere. That makes no sense, so eliminate it.

6. A, B

"Laudatory," which means "expressing praise," is your key word. You need to find two words that mean "positive review" and rule out any negative trap answers. Choice **(A)** *homage* is an expression of respect and is correct. Choice **(B)** *paean* is a synonym of *homage*. If you didn't know the definition of *paean*, you could still eliminate the remaining choices. Choice **(C)** *banter* is idle chat; this doesn't make sense in context. Choices **(D)** *denunciation* (from *denounce*) and **(E)** *rebuff* both mean "to criticize." That is the opposite of the meaning you want. Choice **(F)** *examination* sounds formal and scientific, and it is netural in tone, not positive; you can rule out this answer.

7. B, E

Paraphrase this sentence to make the contrasting ideas more obvious: "He gave away his possessions and materialism." Someone who gave away _______ possessions would reject material things. Choice **(B)** *renounced* means "gave up," and choice **(E)** *spurned* means "scornfully rejected"; although not exact synonyms, both of these words function similarly in the context of the sentence. Choice **(C)** *disregarded* means "ignored," which is not strong enough for this context, given that the investor is turning his back on his former life. What separates **(B)** and **(E)**, the correct answers, from **(C)** is the intent; the first two suggest using a change in behavior to make a statement, which matches the mood of the sentence. Just as importantly, the words match one another. Choice **(A)** *espoused* means "supported," and choice **(D)** *initiated* means "began"; both are the opposite of the meaning you need, so eliminate them. Choice **(F)** *aggrandized* means "made something look greater or stronger." Aggrandizing materialism is the last thing the investor was trying to do by getting rid of possessions.

8. B, F

You can tell by the straight-ahead road sign "and" that the second half will expand on or clarify the first part. Think about the type of person who would fetch anything another person wanted. In this case, you're looking for words that describe a *toady*. Choice **(B)** *obsequious* describes somebody who will, as a form of flattery, do anything another person says. This is a correct answer choice. See if you can find another word like it. Choice **(C)** *humble* means "modest," which does not explain why the entourage would do absolutely anything for the singer. Choice **(F)** *fawning* means "showing extreme flattery," so it's the other correct answer. You might recall that avarice is greed; you can toss out **(A)** *avaricious*, which describes a greedy person, since the entourage is looking out for Elvis, not themselves. Choice **(D)** *belligerent* contains the root *belli* (meaning "war"), like another more common word, *rebellion*. You can deduce that a *belligerent* person challenges others, which is not the case with those in the entourage. That rules out choice **(D)**. Choice **(E)** *jubilant* is used to describe somebody who is joyfully excited. This might describe Elvis's entourage, but it's not a synonym of *obsequious*, nor does it effectively describe the actions reported in the second half of the sentence.

9. A, D

The detour road sign "but" indicates a turning point in the sentence. You can predict that the words that fill the blank mean the opposite of keeping something under cover. Choice **(A)** *transparent* means "obvious, straightforward" and is correct. Choice **(D)** *forthright* means "straightforward" and is the other correct answer. Choice **(B)** *pusillanimous* means "timid, cowardly in nature," which doesn't fit the sentence. Neither does choice **(C)** *aggressive*. Although one could characterize someone's management style as "aggressive," you need a word meaning "open" or "straightforward" to fit the sentence clues. Choices **(E)** and **(F)**, *slipshod* and *negligent*, mean virtually the same thing, "careless." Neither makes sense in context. The correct pair is choices **(A)** and **(D)**.

10. B, C

The straight-ahead road sign "with the result" signals that the sentence will continue its direction. To understand this sentence, focus on the phrase "lost in thought." What feeling does this bring to mind? Typically, such a person is wistful, curious, or reflective. You want a word that continues this feeling. Choice **(B)** *pensive*, meaning "deep in thought," complements the phrase and is a correct answer. The next word, choice **(C)** *meditative*, is a synonym for *pensive* and is likely the other correct answer. Evaluate the remaining words just to be sure. Choices **(A)** and **(F)** are related words that differ in degree, *surly* being "irritable" and *livid* being "very angry." Neither works because they both carry a negative charge. Choice **(D)** *indigenous* means "native," which doesn't make sense in this sentence. The last choice, **(E)** *arcane*, means "secret" or "mysterious," and it typically is not used to refer to people, nor is there a second choice that would give the sentence the same meaning, so it is incorrect. Choices **(B)** and **(C)** are the correct answers.

Intermediate

11. C, F

The detour road sign "[a]lthough" signifies a contrast. In the first clause, the homebuyer thinks a townhouse is "a good value," so look for the opposite tone after the comma. Find a pair of words that suggest doubt or indecision on the part of the homebuyer. It's important to understand the subtle difference between choices **(B)** *ambled* and **(F)** *dawdled*. To *amble* is "to walk leisurely," while *dawdle* means "to waste time or delay in a decision." Both words suggest taking one's time, but *dawdled* better fits the context and is one of the correct answers. Put *ambled* aside and try to find a better match for *dawdled*. Choice **(C)** *vacillated* also means "wavered." The word *elaborated* **(A)** means "expanded on a subject" and does not make sense in this context. Choice **(D)** *groveled* means "humbled oneself out of fear or service to another." This does not explain the homebuyer's unexpectedly hesitant response to the real estate agent. A person who **(E)** *lamented* mourned or expressed deep regret. Like *groveled*, the word *lamented* is inappropriate in this scenario. The correct answers are choices **(C)** *vacillated* and **(F)** *dawdled*.

12. B, D

The words in the blank will convey the actions of the commissioner's staff. The latter part of the sentence says that "the politician would be unable to avoid addressing the fraud allegations" at the town hall. Thus, the detour road sign "even though" indicates that his staff *had* been able to prevent the reporter from asking her questions. Thus, his staff must have been *preventing* the scheduled interviews. **(D)** *obstructed* means "blocking something," and that fits the prediction. While you may be more familiar with the meaning "burdened" for **(B)** *encumbered*, it also has the meaning "hindered, blocked," and that is a match. **(A)** *arranged*, **(E)** *authorized*, and **(F)** *sanctioned* would all be close in meaning to "approving" the scheduled interviews, so they are the opposite of what's needed in this sentence. Interestingly, *sanctioned* can also mean "imposed a penalty on," and **(C)** *censuring* means "officially criticizing," so these two words are a match for each other. However, if the staff were penalizing or criticizing the interviews, it would mean that the interviews had taken place, but in fact the reporter is hoping to ask her questions at the town hall.

13. A, F

Look at the key phrase "hurricane weakened considerably." This phrase suggests a positive outcome for residents, so the correct answers will reflect this. Choice **(A)** *assuage* means "to lessen or relieve." It makes sense that people's fears were relieved. Choice **(F)** *allay* also means "to lessen or relieve." Only **(A)** and **(F)** give the sentence the same meaning, so they're correct. Even if you didn't know the meaning of either correct answer, you could use the process of elimination to rule out the words you know don't fit. Choice **(D)** *annihilate*, meaning "destroy," is a very negative word, and you need a positive one. Choice **(B)** *emblazon* means "to adorn, decorate, or celebrate." This doesn't work in the sentence. Choice **(C)** *ignite* means "to light a fire" or "to arouse one's passions." This would imply that the residents' fears grew more intense, and you need the opposite meaning. Choice **(E)** *mediate* shares its root with the word *medium*, which means "in the middle." That doesn't make sense in the context of people who've just received news that a threatening storm is abating.

14. C, F

This sentence includes the straight-ahead road sign "so." Thus, her decision to [blank] is a result of her feeling that "could no longer empathize with her constituency." What would a politician do at local establishments to reconnect with her constituents? A good prediction is *spend time*, and that is a match for **(F)** *frequent*, which means "to visit a place often." (You may think of *frequent* as meaning "often," but this is the verb form of this word.) It is also a match for **(C)** *patronize*, which means "to be a frequent customer." These are the correct answers. Both **(B)** *evade* and **(D)** *skirt* mean "to avoid," so they can be eliminated as being opposite the prediction. The politician would also not want to **(A)** *vacate*, meaning "to leave," the local establishments if she wants to connect with her constituency. While some constituents might be pleased if the politician were to **(E)** *aggrandize*, or "to highly praise," local establishments, there is no other choice that would create an equivalent sentence.

15. A, E

Despite the road sign "but," the contrast in this sentence my not be immediately apparent. The use of the words "story" and "parents" are clues that reveal the tone and the element of surprise in the sentence. Think about what kind of movie might concern parents, especially if children are in the audience, and predict the answer may describe the content as *sexy* or *violent*. Choice **(A)** *ribald* is another word for "vulgar." This makes sense in context, so hold on to this choice. **(E)** *lascivious* means "obscene" or "vulgar" and is a match. These are the correct answers. **(B)** and **(F)** are near synonyms; *arcane* means "mysterious, hard to understand," and *esoteric* means "understood to only a few." However, content that was difficult to grasp, while it might not appeal to children, would not cause concern for parents in particular. **(C)** *superfluous* means "more than needed," and **(D)** *pervasive* means "occurring widely or throughout." Neither of these choices fits the context.

16. B, C

The first part of the sentence tells you that "some news commentators" are reporting "claims as unimpeachable truths" ("unimpeachable" means "beyond doubt"). Since the criticism is described as "just," or fair, the commentators' claims must in fact be untrue, or at least questionable. Therefore, predict that the claims have been *rejected* by researchers. *Repudiated*, **(B)**, which means "rejected" or "denied," matches the prediction, so keep this choice. *Disavowed*, **(C)**, also means "rejected," and is therefore correct. *Confirmed*, **(A)**, and *validated*, **(F)**, are the opposite of the prediction. *Abased*, **(D)**, which means "lowered in rank," does not work since it does not make sense to say the researchers "lowered" the claims. *Resolved*, **(E)**, which means "settled" or "determined," may be a tempting choice. However, a matter that has been *resolved*, or settled, may be either accepted as true or rejected as false. Therefore, **(E)** is too neutral to match the prediction.

17. A, C

"In his enthusiasm" functions as a straight-ahead road sign here; Professor Assem's teaching must be informed by his passion for introducing students to his subject matter. If a lecture is "steeped" in theoretical material from an "advanced discipline," you would expect it to be challenging to understand or possibly boring. Therefore, the professor must want to make his lectures *understandable* to students or *entertaining* to students. Either prediction is a possibility, so keep them both in mind. *Accessible*, **(A)**, means "obtainable" or "easy to understand," which matches the prediction. The professor may also hope his lectures are **(B)** *enjoyable*. *Comprehensible*, **(C)**, gives the sentence the same meaning as does *accessible*, so even though **(B)** would fit in the sentence, the correct choices are **(A)** and **(C)**. The material itself may be *daunting*, or "intimidating," and *bemusing*, **(E)**, which means "bewildering" or "confusing," but these words do not describe the lectures Assem hopes to deliver. *Salient*, **(F)**, means "prominent" or "important." While the professor likely wants to deliver *salient* lectures, no other choice has a similar meaning.

18. B, F

The words in the blank will describe the effect of circumstances on certain dramatic characters that might be played by this actor. From the first part of the sentence, you know that the actor has only played "comic roles." "Because" is a straight-ahead road sign indicating that her future opportunities are conditioned by her past work. Toward the end of the sentence, the detour road sign "not yet shown" lets you predict that the characters she might play are different from the ones she has portrayed to date. Thus, predict a word that contrasts with "comic," such as *sad* or *tragic*. *Doleful*, **(B)**, means "melancholy" or "sorrowful." *Morose*, **(F)**, means "gloomy" or "sullen." Both words describe characters that would differ from those the actor has played so far, and the words give the sentence the same meaning. *Mirthful*, **(A)**, means "amusing" or "cheerful" and is the opposite of your prediction. *Capricious*, **(C)**, means "impulsive" or "erratic," and comic characters might behave erratically. *Bucolic*, **(D)**, means "related to country or rural life," and *affable*, **(E)**, means "sociable" or "friendly." Neither of these choices aligns with the context clues.

19. A, C

The hard part about this question is that all of the choices are undesirable traits that could lead to unflattering stories about a performer. However, only two of these answer choices will make sense given the context of the sentence. You're told that the anecdotes (stories) are about the singer's "tantrums," so the correct answers will relate to her irritability. A reasonable prediction for the correct answers is *irritable*. Choice **(A)** *captious,* "easily displeased," is pretty close to your prediction, and it makes sense; if she's difficult to please, she's likely to throw tantrums. Choice **(C)** *irascible*, which means "easily angered," is also worth hanging on to. Someone who's easily angered will throw tantrums. Just as important, the sentence created with *irascible* has a meaning similar to the one created with *captious*. You can immediately reject choices **(B)** *dissolute* and **(D)** *profligate*. Both mean "morally corrupt"; that's negative, but it wouldn't incline someone toward tantrums. Choice **(E)** *smug,* "haughty," is another unpleasant trait, but not one that describes someone who loses her temper. Choice **(F)** *nettlesome,* "annoying," would mean that she is irritating, not that she's easily irritated. The correct answers are **(A)** and **(C)**.

20. E, F

The word "however" is a road sign indicating that the direction of the second clause will take a detour from that of the first. The first clause tells you that the warriors did not expect to encounter an "assault" on their olfactory senses (sense of smell). Since the road sign "however" signals a detour, you can infer that they did indeed encounter something quite smelly. *Smelly* is a simple, serviceable prediction; keep it in mind and scan the answer choices. Choices **(E)** *fetid* and **(F)** *malodorous* both specifically refer to disgusting aromas. They produce sentences with similar meanings and are the correct answers. You can reject **(A)** *cloying* and **(B)** *saccharine*; both mean "excessively sweet," which is the opposite of what you need. Choice **(D)** *dejected* is wrong because *dejected* means "sad" and has nothing to do with smell. Choice **(C)** *repulsive* is more difficult to eliminate (you might say, "That smells repulsive," after all), but the word has too broad a meaning to create a sentence equivalent to either *fetid* or *malodorous*.

Advanced

21. C, F

Your first reaction here should be to notice the rather unusual word "contradistinction," which means "distinction by contrast." You can infer from the root *contra*, which means "in contrast to," that "contradistinction" is acting as a detour road sign. In this sentence, the dog is described as being a "pack animal," which means it is social and communal. Because the cat is in "contradistinction" to the dog, the word in the blank describing the cat must contrast with "pack animal," so predict something like *isolated*. Choice **(C)** *solitary* certainly works well as a contrast to "pack animal." Keep that one. Choice **(F)** *aloof,* meaning "standoffish," fits just as well; those who are standoffish are solitary and dislike company. Choice **(A)** *transparent* doesn't make sense as a way to describe cats. Choice **(B)** *supercilious* may be tempting; it describes a popular view of cats (it means "haughty"), but it does not contrast as strongly with "pack animals." Choice **(D)** *forthright* ("candid") is not necessarily characteristic of someone or something that prefers solitude. The same can be said for choice **(E)** *maladroit*, which means "awkward or clumsy."

22. B, D

From the first part of the sentence, you know how the employees view this executive:

"not as incompetent." In other words, they view the executive as competent, or capable. The second part of the sentence provides the information that the executive also has "vast experience." Based on these two clues, one would expect this manager to understand the situation the workers are dealing with, and in fact the workers do expect this: the employees "refused to believe" that their leader "could not understand their obvious frustration." The detour road sign "despite" indicates that the executive's public statements were at odds with this belief. Therefore, since the employees believe the executive does understand their predicament but is saying he doesn't understand, predict that the workers view the manager as *unbelievable* or *dishonest*. *Disingenuous*, **(B)**, means "being insincere" or "lacking in frankness" and matches the prediction. *Duplicitous*, **(D)**, means "acting in a dishonest or deceitful manner" and gives the sentence the same meaning as does *disingenuous*. These are the correct answers. *Guilty*, **(A)**, may be tempting, since this would indicate that the manager has committed some wrongdoing. However, nothing in the sentence indicates that the executive is *guilty* of causing the problem; the executive is just claiming not to understand it. *Complacent*, **(C)**, means "self-satisfied" or "overly content." There isn't enough evidence to describe the manager as *complacent*. *Sagacious*, **(E)**, and *erudite*, **(F)**, both mean "very smart" or "learned." If you ignore the second part of the sentence, these words would suitably contrast "incompetent," but they do not align with the additional context clues.

23. D, E

The word in the blank will describe the speech. The word "as" is a straight-ahead road sign connecting the blank to the description of how the speaker gave the speech. Specifically, the speaker told a lot of unnecessary side stories. Therefore, predict that the speech was "wordy" or "overly long." *Prolix*, **(D)**, and *loquacious*, **(E)**, both mean "wordy" or "long-winded" and thus match the prediction. These are the correct choices. *Apposite*, **(A)**, means "highly appropriate" or "relevant," which contradicts the prediction; this speaker spent a lot of time talking about irrelevant things. *Cacophonous*, **(B)**, describes a "harsh or discordant sound." There is no indication that the speaker spoke in a harsh manner. *Succinct*, **(C)**, and *compendious*, **(F)**, both mean "concise" or "to the point." These choices directly contradict the prediction.

24. A, D

The semicolon is a straight-ahead road sign here, indicating that the second half of the sentence continues the idea from the first half, in which the teacher is worried because of something the child did. If you are familiar with the word "schadenfreude," this is another useful clue. It comes from the German *Schaden*, which means "harm," and *Freude*, which means joy, and refers to a feeling of enjoyment in the suffering of others. If you're not familiar with this word, the concern about whether the child has "a serious mental health issue" is also a good clue. Having read for the clues, you can ask, "How should a child feel after seeing another child fall off a swing?" A good prediction is *feel sorry for* (keep in mind that the phrase "inability to" means that the prediction is for how the child *should* feel). **(A)** *commiserate* means "to express sadness for someone" and is a match for the prediction. **(D)** *empathize* means "to have the same feelings as another person," and this gives the sentence the same sense. **(B)** *scuffle* and **(F)** *struggle* both mean "to fight," and a teacher would logically not be worried about a student's inability to fight. **(C)** *grimace*, meaning "to distort one's face in pain," and **(E)** *weep*, meaning "to express sorrow by shedding tears," may be how the student who fell off the swing reacted, but the blank is referring to the onlooker.

25. A, D

"Not only" is a straight-ahead road sign. Always paired with "but also," it indicates that the sentence will continue in its original direction. You're told that the author has a penchant for "dissembling," which means "to speak or act hypocritically." Since he dissembles when he writes, his prose can be described as *insincere*. That's a good prediction, so start checking the answer choices. Choice **(A)** *fulsome* means "excessive" or "over-the-top." That's an excellent way to characterize insincere prose, so hang on to it. Choice **(D)** *unctuous* means "excessively smug," which is certainly insincere in its tenor. Choice **(B)** *effulgent,* meaning "radiant" or "shining," doesn't make sense in this context. Choice **(C)** *effusive,* which means "gushing" or "enthusiastic," would describe the emotional tenor of the prose but not the author's sincerity. Choice **(E)** *cryptic,* or "mysterious," is not supported by the context; there is nothing in the sentence to indicate that the author's work was hard to understand. Also, no other answer choice creates a similar sentence. Choice **(F)** *vulgar* can be rejected for the same reason; it also has nothing to do with "dissembling."

26. C, E

The blank in this sentence describes "[t]hose scholars" who like a type of math that is "intrica[te] and esoteric" and is attempted by "those who have mastered the prerequisite topics." From this, you can infer that the formulas of geometric topology are challenging to understand, and you might expect these scholars to be fascinated by its formulas. However, the detour road sign "notwithstanding" contrasts how they respond to the formulas with "the undeniable appeal" of the subject. Thus, despite their enthusiasm for geometric topology, predict that they feel *confused* by the formulas. *Confounded*, **(C)**, means "perplexed," and *nonplussed*, **(E)**, means "unsure what to do." These words both match the prediction and give the sentence the same sense. *Elated*, **(A)**, means "very happy." This is how these scholars feel about difficult math in general but not about the formulas as discussed in this sentence. *Inveigled*, **(B)**, means "lured by flattery." While these mathematicians are attracted by certain math topics, geometric formulas are not capable of deceit. Moreover, this word does not correspond to the detour road sign "notwithstanding." There is no indication that the mathematicians are *unimpressed*, **(D)**, or *oppressed*, **(F)**.

27. A, E

The blank in this sentence takes a verb that describes an action that would concern "intelligence agencies." Since the object of concern is state secrets, it's a good bet the agencies are alarmed by their "spread" or "leaking." Choices **(A)** *proliferation* and **(E)** *dissemination*, both of which are synonymous with "spreading," create similar sentences that make sense: intelligence agencies would be highly concerned about the spread of state secrets. Choices **(B)** *retention* and **(D)** *acquisition* can be ruled out; while intelligence agencies would be keen to both *retain* and *acquire* state secrets, such "unchecked" activity would not "concern" the agencies. Choice **(C)** *lassitude,* "laziness," doesn't make sense in this context (state secrets can't be "lazy"). Choice **(F)** *quality* might be tempting, but no other answer choice produces a similar sentence.

28. A, B

The celebrity in the sentence has done something "vociferously." "Vociferously" means "clamorously" and describes speech, so you know she spoke ardently and loudly. She must also have been trying to convince her audience of something, since her action is contrasted with being ignored. A good prediction is *lectured* or *orated.* When you look at the answer choices, there's nothing that precisely matches your prediction, but **(A)** *inveighed* and **(B)** *declaimed* come close. Both have a connotation of oratory, typically arguing against something. That harmonizes very well with "vociferously." Choices **(C)** *conceded,* "gave in," **(E)** *abstained,* "declined to participate," and **(F)** *acceded,* "agreed," can all be rejected as being too passive and therefore opposite to what you need. Choice **(D)** *demurred,* "raised an objection," is wrong because it isn't strong enough.

29. E, F

This question obliges you to find an adjective to describe Reginald's aunt, who you are told is "spry" (nimble) for her age. The key words "for her age" imply that Reginald's aunt is of an age at which it is unusual to be spry. You can therefore predict answers similar to *elderly.* Choice **(E)** *septuagenarian,* which is a term for someone in her seventies, works well. Choice **(F)** *hoary* means "very old." These are the correct answers. You can reject choices **(A)** *acrobatic* and **(B)** *dexterous,* as these are both synonymous with "agile," in which case she would not need help getting up the stairs. Choices **(C)** *caustic,* "sarcastic or corrosive," and **(D)** *genial,* "pleasant," are also wrong, because they describe her personality, not her fitness.

30. A, B

The fact that the blank is the word that begins the sentence may make this question more challenging than a typical Sentence Equivalence question. The first clause is fairly direct; he passed on the project, and the blank will contain an adverb to describe this decision. The second clause contains the detour road sign "notwithstanding," which means "despite." "Professed," which describes his support, means "stated," so you know he passed on the project despite his vocal support. Therefore, you can predict the first blank to be something like *surprisingly* or *paradoxically.* Choices **(A)** *counterintuitively,* "contrary to intuition," and **(B)** *unexpectedly* both match that prediction quite well. They both create sentences pointing out the subject's seeming inconsistency. Three of the other choices could work on their own in this context: **(C)** *self-indulgently,* "to indulge one's own desires," **(D)** *obscurely,* "vaguely," and **(E)** *pusillanimously,* "cowardly," all characterize the way in which one could decline a project, but none logically contrast with "professed support." Choice **(F)** *punctiliously,* "attentive to detail," does not make sense in this context. Only **(A)** and **(B)** logically complete similar sentences.

CHAPTER 4

Reading Comprehension

READING COMPREHENSION: OVERVIEW AND METHOD

Even though reading is a skill that you've been developing and practicing for most of your life, navigating the often verbose and detailed language of academia can be a challenge. While the GRE tests your ability to assess ideas and information, the greater test of the skills involved will come in the field of higher learning you pursue. Regardless of academic discipline, you will almost certainly be presented with written material at least as difficult to penetrate as the practice set questions to follow.

So that the GRE reflects the real-world nature of postgraduate reading, the passages are drawn from four standard disciplines of higher learning—social sciences, biological sciences, physical sciences, and arts and humanities.

The types of questions the GRE uses fall into three categories, distinguished by the answer choices: standard multiple-choice questions with one correct answer, multiple-choice questions in which one or more of the choices is correct, and questions that ask you to select the sentence from the passage that best answers the question. These different question formats reward a wide range of analytical skills, from determining the best definition of a specific word in context or identifying details that support a main idea to evaluating the author's perspective or drawing inferences from the evidence presented.

A Reading Comprehension passage and question will look like this:

Question 1 is based on the following passage.

A pioneering figure in modern sociology, French social theorist Emile Durkheim examined the effect of societal cohesion on emotional well-being. Believing that scientific methods should be applied to the study of society, Durkheim studied the levels of integration in various social formations and the impact that such cohesion had on individuals within the group. He postulated that social groups with high levels of integration serve to buffer their members from frustrations and tragedies that could otherwise lead to desperation and self-destruction. Integration, in Durkheim's view, generally arises through shared activities and values. Durkheim distinguished between mechanical solidarity and organic solidarity in classifying integrated groups. Mechanical solidarity dominates in groups in which individual differences are minimized and group devotion to a common goal is high. Durkheim identified mechanical solidarity among groups with little division of labor and high degrees of cultural similarity, such as among more traditional and geographically isolated groups. Organic solidarity, in contrast, prevails in groups with high levels of individual differences, such as those with a highly specialized division of labor. In such groups, individual differences are a powerful source of connection rather than of division. Because people engage in highly differentiated ways of life, they are by necessity interdependent. In these societies, there is greater freedom from some external controls, but such freedom occurs in concert with the interdependence of individuals, not in conflict with it. Durkheim realized that societies may take many forms and, consequently, that group allegiance can manifest itself in a variety of ways. In both types of societies outlined previously, however, Durkheim stressed that adherence to a common set of assumptions about the world was a necessary prerequisite for maintaining group integrity and avoiding social decay.

1. Which of the following is NOT a feature of an organic societal formation, according to Emile Durkheim?

   (A) Members are buffered from individual frustration that would lead the individual to cease being a productive member of society.

   (B) Citizens operate independently in their daily lives, but toward a common overall goal.

   (C) Each person must come to accept a series of assumptions that form a collective worldview shared by the formation.

   (D) Workers have an even division of labor and share the work of common tasks.

   (E) Individual differences are celebrated, and have a strengthening effect on the society.

The GRE features three types of Reading Comprehension questions: Select One, Select One or More, and Select-in-Passage. You will review all three types in this chapter.

THE KAPLAN METHOD FOR READING COMPREHENSION

STEP 1 Read the passage strategically.

STEP 2 Analyze the question stem.

STEP 3 Research the relevant text in the passage.

STEP 4 Make a prediction.

STEP 5 Evaluate the answer choices.

HOW THE KAPLAN METHOD FOR READING COMPREHENSION WORKS

Here's how the Kaplan Method for Reading Comprehension works.

STEP 1

Read the passage strategically.

Reading strategically means identifying the topic, scope, and purpose of a passage, as well as noting the passage's structure and main points. The *topic* is the general subject matter, and the *scope* is the specific aspect of the topic that the author focuses on. In order to identify the topic, scope, and purpose, you should target the passage's main ideas, primary arguments, secondary arguments, supporting statements or evidence, and conclusions. Take notes on scratch paper about the points discussed above to create a "passage map" that will be useful to you in answering the questions. For each paragraph, jot down a one- to two-line summary highlighting the main points. For any given passage, you should be able to both summarize the text and identify the main points in your own words before proceeding. It's also important to use the key words and phrases connected to the sentences to identify the important ideas and statements.

With each passage, you need to look for the purpose of the text: why did the author write it? While there will be numerous facts provided in any given piece, not all passages are purely informative. There will be persuasive elements in each passage, even if designed only to convince you of the subject's importance. Identify early on whether the piece is primarily informative or argumentative, and to what degree. You do this by recognizing the author's tone, which reflects the author's attitude towards her subject. Tone is indispensable in identifying an author's purpose, especially if her purpose is not entirely explicit. If the author makes use of comparisons (*better, more effective*) or recommendations (*should, must, need to*), the author is trying to persuade. If the author writes in a more straightforward style with no persuasive or judgmental terminology, the piece is more purely informative. Pieces written in that tone are more likely to have the purpose of explanation or description. Purpose is important for Inference questions, which reward you for identifying the author's opinion on the subject matter.

In general, a social sciences piece is likely to argue a position because the complex nature of human behavior and interaction is open to wide interpretation. Likewise, a discussion of a piece of art or literature will likely contain arguments because the author asserts an interpretation of these art forms. Scientific articles, on the other hand, will be mainly informative, seeking primarily to explain a scientific concept or discovery. Still, there may be arguments or conclusions drawn about the importance of these discoveries or principles in daily application. Pay close attention to the author's tone; it is inseparable from her argument.

STEP 2

Analyze the question stem.

Most GRE Reading Comprehension passages are accompanied by one to three questions. Above the passage on the computer screen, you'll see a note that indicates the number of questions: "Question 11. . ." or "Questions 4–6. . ." Not surprisingly, passages with only one question tend to be shorter (usually one paragraph), while those with several questions may be longer.

When a passage has only one question, it makes sense to read the question stem before reading the passage. You can target the text that answers the specific question. When multiple questions accompany a passage, however, you're better off reading the passage strategically before concerning yourself with the question stems.

When a passage has multiple questions, one stem may be concerned with the author's tone, another focused on a vocabulary term, and still another designed to reward your analytical reasoning skills. Reading with multiple questions in mind makes it difficult to discern the main ideas of the passage. It's usually more valuable to use the question stem to guide research for details in the passage than to try to read for several alternative details at the outset. Your passage map or notes will allow you to find the correct answer(s) quickly while still reading for the big points and main idea. You'll have the answers to general questions—"Which of the following best states the main idea/primary purpose of the passage?"—and the notes to research more specific questions. Likewise, by knowing the author's attitude and purpose, you'll be prepared for questions that ask what an author is most likely or least likely to agree with.

STEP 3

Research the relevant text in the passage.

Notice that this step tells you to *research* the passage, not *reread* it. Once you have analyzed and understood the question stem, you should already have an idea of where in the passage you'll find the answer. Use your passage map or notes, the product of Step 1's strategic reading, to target this research step. Don't consider more text from the passage than is necessary to answer the question. If the question rewards your understanding of vocabulary in context, for example, you need not look further than the sentence in which it appears, and possibly the preceding sentence, to derive the answer.

STEP 4

Make a prediction.

GRE questions will, by design, test your comprehension of what you have read and not just your ability to go into a passage and mine for details. As such, you will often need the ability to formulate a prediction as to the answers of many questions that deal with the main idea, conclusions, arguments, author's meaning, tone, and implications of the information provided. Before moving on to the answer choices, try to either form a response to the stem in your own mind or target the section of the passage that will contain the answer.

At times, you will have to infer an answer based on clues provided in the text, but the test will not ask you for outside information. In these Inference questions, research the relevant sections of the passage, those that provide evidence or details to support (or refute) the opinion or conclusion in question. When you find it difficult to make a specific, word-for-word prediction for the correct answer, remember that the correct answer will be supported by the passage. Use your research to evaluate the answer choices.

STEP 5

Evaluate the answer choices.

You'll take this step a little differently depending on the Reading Comprehension question type you're answering. For a multiple-choice question with one correct answer, look to match your prediction and eliminate violators. When you find the unequivocally correct choice, select it. Time permitting, check the remaining choices and confirm that each is demonstrably incorrect. Eliminating incorrect answers not only helps narrow down options for questions that are hard to answer, it also validates the selection you are considering.

For a multiple-choice question in which multiple answer choices may be correct (a Select One or More question, indicated by "select all that apply"), you must check all of the choices. You receive credit only if you choose all of (and only) the applicable choices. For a Select-in-Passage question, place your cursor over the correct sentence and click. Only one sentence from the passage will be credited as the correct answer.

When you're uncertain about the correct answer, begin by eliminating answers that are demonstrably wrong. Use the same steps as you would for finding the right answer: Weigh the choices against the passage text and eliminate choices that contradict, distort, or fall outside the scope of the passage. Determine the criteria for the correct answer and eliminate choices that violate them. Don't compare answer choices to one another; compare them to the standard of what the correct choice must contain.

Apply the Kaplan Method for Reading Comprehension

Now, apply the Kaplan Method to a Reading Comprehension (Select One) question:

Question 1 is based on the following passage.

A pioneering figure in modern sociology, French social theorist Emile Durkheim examined the effect of societal cohesion on emotional well-being. Believing that scientific methods should be applied to the study of society, Durkheim studied the levels of integration in various social formations and the impact that such cohesion had on individuals within the group. He postulated that social groups with high levels of integration serve to buffer their members from frustrations and tragedies that could otherwise lead to desperation and self-destruction. Integration, in Durkheim's view, generally arises through shared activities and values. Durkheim distinguished between mechanical solidarity and organic solidarity in classifying integrated groups. Mechanical solidarity dominates in groups in which individual differences are minimized and group devotion to a common goal is high. Durkheim identified mechanical solidarity among groups with little division of labor and high degrees of cultural similarity, such as among more traditional and geographically isolated groups. Organic solidarity, in contrast, prevails in groups with high levels of individual differences, such as those with a highly specialized division of labor. In such groups, individual differences are a powerful source of connection rather than of division. Because people engage in highly differentiated ways of life, they are by necessity interdependent. In these societies, there is greater freedom from some external controls, but such freedom occurs in concert with the interdependence of individuals, not in conflict with it. Durkheim realized that societies may take many forms and, consequently, that group allegiance can manifest itself in a variety of ways. In both types of societies outlined previously, however, Durkheim stressed that adherence to a common set of assumptions about the world was a necessary prerequisite for maintaining group integrity and avoiding social decay.

1. Which of the following is NOT a feature of an organic societal formation, according to Emile Durkheim?

   (A) Members are buffered from individual frustration that would lead the individual to cease being a productive member of society.
   (B) Citizens operate independently in their daily lives, but toward a common overall goal.
   (C) Each person must come to accept a series of assumptions that form a collective worldview shared by the formation.
   (D) Workers have an even division of labor and share the work of common tasks.
   (E) Individual differences are celebrated, and have a strengthening effect on the society.

The most common standardized test question—multiple-choice—has a strong presence on the GRE. Most often, the multiple-choice question asks you to select the best answer from a set of five choices. Only one choice is credited as the right answer; the other four options will either be incorrect or less complete than the correct selection.

STEP 1

Read the passage strategically.

As the author sets forth the criteria for Emile Durkheim's theory of social cohesion, he defines two models of social solidarity by introducing qualities that are common to both constructs before addressing the differences between the two. The passage concludes with a prerequisite for social cohesion common to both models. The two models have similarities, but note that the author is contrasting them with one another.

STEP 2

Analyze the question stem.

This question asks which choice is NOT a feature of the organic solidarity model. Normally, you would approach this question type by researching what the passage says *are* features of the organic solidarity model and eliminating answers that mention them. In this case, since the passage contrasts two models of societal formation, the correct answer will likely be a feature of the opposed mechanical solidarity model.

STEP 3

Research the relevant text in the passage.

The relevant text is the part of the passage that discusses the features of the two types of societal formation. Since the question asks you to find what is *not* common to the organic solidarity model, research the portion that defines the mechanical solidarity model as well. The author emphasizes one distinction between the models: the lack of a specialized labor force in the mechanical solidarity model versus the presence of a specialized division of labor in the organic solidarity model.

STEP 4

Make a prediction.

Apply your research to the "call" of the question stem. The correct answer here is a feature not found in organic solidarity groups. Since the author highlights the organic solidarity model's highly specialized division of labor, predict that the correct answer will describe a case in which labor is not differentiated. Now, check the answers to find the choice that matches this prediction.

STEP 5

Evaluate the answer choices.

Choice **(D)** matches your prediction quite well. Societies that distribute labor evenly and parcel out common tasks among everyone are not using a specialized labor force. They fit the mechanical solidarity model, not the organic solidarity one. Choice **(A)** and choice **(C)** are found among the descriptions for both forms of Durkheim's societal formations, the first early in the paragraph and the other toward the end, so they are wrong. Within the section discussing organic solidarity societies, you can find, as part of the definition, differently worded forms of both choice **(B)** and choice **(E)**.

Apply the Kaplan Method for Reading Comprehension

Now, apply the Kaplan Method to a Reading Comprehension (Select One or More) question:

Question 2 is based on the following passage.

A pioneering figure in modern sociology, French social theorist Emile Durkheim examined the effect of societal cohesion on emotional well-being. Believing that scientific methods should be applied to the study of society, Durkheim studied the levels of integration in various social formations and the impact that such cohesion had on individuals within the group. He postulated that social groups with high levels of integration serve to buffer their members from frustrations and tragedies that could otherwise lead to desperation and self-destruction. Integration, in Durkheim's view, generally arises through shared activities and values. Durkheim distinguished between mechanical solidarity and organic solidarity in classifying integrated groups. Mechanical solidarity dominates in groups in which individual differences are minimized and group devotion to a common goal is high. Durkheim identified mechanical solidarity among groups with little division of labor and high degrees of cultural similarity, such as among more traditional and geographically isolated groups. Organic solidarity, in contrast, prevails in groups with high levels of individual differences, such as those with a highly specialized division of labor. In such groups, individual differences are a powerful source of connection rather than of division. Because people engage in highly differentiated ways of life, they are by necessity interdependent. In these societies, there is greater freedom from some external controls, but such freedom occurs in concert with the interdependence of individuals, not in conflict with it. Durkheim realized that societies may take many forms and, consequently, that group allegiance can manifest itself in a variety of ways. In both types of societies outlined previously, however, Durkheim stressed that adherence to a common set of assumptions about the world was a necessary prerequisite for maintaining group integrity and avoiding social decay.

Consider each of the following choices separately and select all that apply.

2. Which of the following might be examples of a mechanical solidarity societal formation as explained by the passage?

   [A] A religious order living in a monastery with an evenly distributed division of labor

   [B] A company that employs architects, carpenters, plumbers, and construction workers who can design and complete all facets of a building project from start to finish

   [C] A xenophobic tribe living in an isolated fishing village amid an uncolonized set of islands

The second form of multiple-choice question offers three choices, but any combination of them could be the correct answer, from a single choice to all three being correct. In order to get the question correct on the test, you must identify all of (and only) the correct choices.

STEP 1

Read the passage strategically.

You've already read the passage strategically, of course. It will come as no surprise that the questions continue to reward you for noting the contrast between Durkheim's two models.

STEP 2

Analyze the question stem.

This question asks you to identify which of three examples meet the criteria supplied by the text to qualify as a society displaying "mechanical solidarity." Notice that the author divides societal formation into "mechanical" and "organic," and the question is only concerned with the former. In a Select One question, once you're confident that you have the correct choice, you can move on. You need not give the remaining choices equal consideration. In Select One or More questions, on the other hand, don't stop once you spot a correct answer. Evaluate all of the choices. More than one may be correct.

STEP 3

Research the relevant text in the passage.

This question rewards you for identifying which of the three examples meet the criteria supplied by the text to qualify as a mechanical solidarity social formation. The author cites "more traditional and geographically isolated groups" as examples of this sort of group. You also know that the author distinguishes mechanical from organic solidarity on the basis of labor specialization.

STEP 4

Make a prediction.

Now, apply your research. You noted the author's illustration of mechanical solidarity groups: "such as more traditional and geographically isolated groups." Make this your prediction.

STEP 5

Evaluate the answer choices.

Your prediction makes choice **(C)** easy to select; it uses much of the same terminology. Knowing that *xenophobic* means "fearful of outsiders" helps, but is not necessary for answering that portion of the question. Keep choice **(C)** as an answer, but check the others as well. Choice **(A)** also meets the criteria. A monastic religious order (such as monks) in which the members do all the same tasks without specialization meets the non-specialized distribution of labor portion of the author's definition as well. Only choice **(B)** fails to meet the definition; even though the workers listed may share a singular goal (of creating a house or building), each worker has very specific specialties and abilities—a feature associated with organic solidarity groups.

Apply the Kaplan Method for Reading Comprehension

Now, apply the Kaplan Method to a Reading Comprehension (Select-in-Passage) question:

Question 3 is based on the following passage.

A pioneering figure in modern sociology, French social theorist Emile Durkheim examined the effect of societal cohesion on emotional well-being. Believing that scientific methods should be applied to the study of society, Durkheim studied the levels of integration in various social formations and the impact that such cohesion had on individuals within the group. He postulated that social groups with high levels of integration serve to buffer their members from frustrations and tragedies that could otherwise lead to desperation and self-destruction. Integration, in Durkheim's view, generally arises through shared activities and values. Durkheim distinguished between mechanical solidarity and organic solidarity in classifying integrated groups. Mechanical solidarity dominates in groups in which individual differences are minimized and group devotion to a common goal is high. Durkheim identified mechanical solidarity among groups with little division of labor and high degrees of cultural similarity, such as among more traditional and geographically isolated groups. Organic solidarity, in contrast, prevails in groups with high levels of individual differences, such as those with a highly specialized division of labor. In such groups, individual differences are a powerful source of connection rather than of division. Because people engage in highly differentiated ways of life, they are by necessity interdependent. In these societies, there is greater freedom from some external controls, but such freedom occurs in concert with the interdependence of individuals, not in conflict with it. Durkheim realized that societies may take many forms and, consequently, that group allegiance can manifest itself in a variety of ways. In both types of societies outlined previously, however, Durkheim stressed that adherence to a common set of assumptions about the world was a necessary prerequisite for maintaining group integrity and avoiding social decay.

3. Select the sentence in the passage that explains why a society displaying organic solidarity tends more toward social codependence than does a mechanical societal formation.

This question type asks you to click on the sentence that meets the criteria or provides the information solicited by the question stem.

STEP 1

Read the passage strategically.

You know from having analyzed the text already that the correct answer will be found somewhere after the introduction of the two forms of societal formations. Keep that in mind.

STEP 2

Analyze the question stem.

This question rewards you for distinguishing the ways in which societies displaying the two forms of solidarity manifest codependence.

STEP 3

Research the relevant text in the passage.

Since the question centers on the organic solidarity model, the best place to start looking is in the part of the passage where the author defines and illustrates organic solidarity. There, you find this cause-and-effect statement: "Because people engage in highly differentiated ways of life, they are by necessity interdependent."

STEP 4

Make a prediction.

Make that sentence your prediction.

STEP 5

Evaluate the answer choices.

The sentence is the right answer; it explains that because the members of an organic society do not have the same skill sets, they are forced to rely on others for those things they are unable to do or do not have the skill for. Click it and confirm your answer.

KAPLAN'S ADDITIONAL TIPS FOR READING COMPREHENSION QUESTIONS

Express the Main Idea in Your Own Words

Summarizing the main idea of the passage not only forms the foundation of your comprehension of the passage, it's also the starting point for your evaluation of the questions. While not every passage has a specific main idea, each passage does have a topic and scope, both of which you should discern by the end of the first paragraph. If you are halfway through a passage and still have not identified these elements, you may be reading too fast and not outlining or identifying key words and phrases in the text.

Focus on Retaining Ideas, Not Facts

Unlike university coursework, you do not have to memorize or retain any of the dates, details, or minutiae of a GRE passage. If you are asked a question about a specific term or detail within the text, such as a date or place, the question will likely ask *why* or *how* the author used the detail rather than what's true about it. You have the text there to refer back to. In that sense, the GRE is an open-book test. Concern yourself with the ideas, arguments, and conclusions the author presents in order to assess the questions accurately and examine them within the context of the passage.

Concentrate on Using Only What the Passage Gives You

As a smart test taker, you can benefit from a passage about a topic completely foreign to you. Whatever the passage is about, it is still presented using familiar patterns of expository and persuasive writing.

A danger occurs when you encounter topics about which you have pre-existing knowledge. Such knowledge can confuse or muddle your ability to answer a question by clouding or expanding the scope of the piece beyond what's written. To best handle the questions, you must be concerned only with the text itself and not be influenced by outside knowledge that may be at odds with the answer as defined by the passage and the question stem. When it comes to answering GRE Reading Comprehension questions, the passage is your "universe."

While you've no doubt honed an ability to question and critique text, on the GRE you should accept the information given in informative passages as true. The questions reward you for determining correct answers "based on the passage" or "according to the passage," not for answers true in the world at large. Even with persuasive passages, and regardless of your own opinions on the author's subject or point of view, correct answers follow from the evidence and arguments given as the groundwork for the passage.

Do Not Approach Highlighted Statement Questions Differently

From time to time, the GRE will highlight words, phrases, clauses, or sentences in the passage in order to ask you about the logic, function, or meaning of the highlighted portion. In the most complex of these—which Kaplan designates as Highlighted Statement questions—the test highlights two portions of text (clauses or sentences) in the passage. It then asks you to determine the functions of both statements or their relationship to one another. Some of the functions a sentence might serve are these:

- development of an argument
- conclusion of an argument
- evidence supporting a conclusion
- evidence supporting part of a conclusion
- evidence supporting an objection to the conclusion
- a secondary argument or support for a secondary argument
- illustration or example of a point
- a principle underlying an argument

While it's natural to focus primarily or exclusively on the highlighted sentences, you may need the entire passage in order to determine the roles played by the highlighted portions. As you read the passage, read strategically to determine the position taken by the author. Identify the argument and its conclusion and note how the author supports them or refutes opposing views. While the highlighted lines are central to the correct answer, the surrounding material provides key context.

Predict the correct answer. Then, move on to evaluating the choices and eliminating obviously incorrect answers. In Highlighted Statement questions, each answer has two parts, one for each highlighted sentence; both must be correct in order for the answer to be correct. If you are unable to predict an answer, or if your prediction is not among the answer choices, eliminate wrong answer choices by looking carefully at the two parts. Get rid of choices in which you find a mischaracterization of the role of a sentence, a reversal of the sentences' roles, a reference to a sentence not highlighted, or a description of something that does not appear in the passage. Once you've eliminated the obviously incorrect answers, you'll more easily be able to identify the answer that best describes the roles of the sentences.

Do Not Get Misled by Variations on Standard Question Stems

While most questions concern themselves with what is stated in or follows from the passage, some questions will ask you to find an answer that is *not* supported by the passage. Don't confuse "true" with correct. Characterize the choices before you evaluate them. Consider a question stem like this one, for example:

According to the passage, each of the following is commonly associated with inflation EXCEPT:

This question has four answers that are "true" according to the passage, but wrong (because of the call of the question stem). The one correct choice is the "false" answer, the one that does not follow from the text. While you should assume passages to be true, veracity is irrelevant to evaluating the answers. Choices are correct because they follow from the passage and answer the question. They're incorrect when they do not. From time to time, the testmakers will ask, "Which of the following, if TRUE, most strengthens the argument?" In such cases, treat the five answer choices as facts, but distinguish the correct answer from the incorrect ones based on the effect they have on the reasoning.

Now try the following section of practice passages and questions to drill and strengthen your Reading Comprehension skills. The following passages are representative in terms of length and number of questions associated with passages on the GRE. Complete the thirty questions and use the explanations that follow to gauge your thinking and refine your test-taking skills.

READING COMPREHENSION PRACTICE SET

Basic

Questions 1–3 are based on the following passage.

Some astrophysicists have postulated that the rings of Saturn are a relatively young feature of the solar system, and data received from the *Cassini* spacecraft have corroborated this theory. Launched by the United States in 1997, *Cassini* provided 13 years of close observation of the planet and its rings. *Cassini*'s data not only reinforced the recent-creation view but also engendered a new theory about how the rings came into being: a cataclysmic collision that created Saturn's rings as well as several of the planet's current inner moons. One of these moons, Enceladus, is widely considered the most promising site in the solar system for the search for extraterrestrial life, and *Cassini* discovered an ocean containing organic molecules and hydrothermal sites beneath the moon's icy crust. It is these components that scientists believe were responsible for the emergence of life on Earth. If Enceladus is determined to both be young and possess life, it would lend support to the argument that life on Earth also appeared quickly after the planet's formation.

Luminosity is one of the ways in which objects in the solar system can be dated. Because the solar system is full of the dark residual dust from comets, the longer objects have been in existence, the more dust they have absorbed, and the darker they appear. The effect is similar to the accumulation of soot on a statue in a city with polluted air; after a number of years, the pollution will settle on the statue and darken its surface. Younger objects, on the other hand, appear brighter. Jeff Cuzzi, a scientist working on the *Cassini* project, and his colleagues compared the density of comet dust on Saturn's rings with the density closer to Saturn's surface, and their preliminary analysis determined the age of Saturn's rings to be somewhere between 200 million and 70 million years. This would put the formation of the rings sometime when dinosaurs walked on Earth, a relatively recent period in Earth's 4-billion-year existence.

The other, and perhaps more remarkable, evidence of the recent creation of Saturn's rings comes from the work of Matija Ćuk and his team, who used the known rate at which the orbits of Saturn's moons are lengthening to extrapolate backward and project the orbits in the past. The results indicate that, about 100 million years ago, two of Saturn's moons would have interacted in such a way as to tilt their orbits, but their orbits are not tilted. Therefore, Ćuk believes this interaction could not have happened. To explain this phenomenon, Ćuk and his colleagues propose that Saturn originally had two moons and that evection, the effect of the sun's attraction on the orbit of the outer moon, destabilized that moon's orbit. The outer moon eventually crashed into the other moon, creating a huge debris field. Some of this debris clumped together due to gravity and formed the set of moons seen today. However, within the Roche limit, the orbital distance within which Saturn's gravity would pull a moon apart, the debris would have been pulled into a disk—the disk that formed Saturn's rings.

If the hypotheses of Cuzzi and Ćuk are confirmed, then further research on Enceladus may offer an intriguing glimpse into the start of life, a glimpse that may add to our knowledge of how life began on Earth.

1. The primary purpose of the passage is to

   (A) compare two theories about how the rings of the planet Saturn were formed.
   (B) discuss reasons Enceladus should be examined for evidence of extraterrestrial life.
   (C) examine new evidence that may contribute to the discussion of how life began on Earth.
   (D) question the proposition that Saturn was one of the older planets in the solar system.
   (E) show how the data from *Cassini* have proven the recent-creation view of the rings of Saturn.

2. Select the sentence in the second or third paragraph that explains a process by which Enceladus may have been created relatively recently.

Consider each of the following choices separately and select all that apply.

3. It can be inferred from the passage that the dark residual dust from comets

   [A] is evenly distributed throughout the solar system
   [B] provides evidence supporting the recent creation of Saturn's rings
   [C] can change the appearance of celestial bodies

Question 4 is based on the following passage.

Richard Wagner's *The Ring of the Nibelung* is perhaps the epitome of a *magnum opus.* If the entire work were to be performed beginning at seven o'clock in the morning, it might not conclude until close to midnight! Despite its immensity, Wagner's epic cycle of four music dramas, filled with familiar melodies such as "Ride of the Valkyries," is still performed and celebrated today. This daunting work is usually divided into a cycle of its four component pieces, which are often performed on successive nights because of the long and arduous level of singing over the course of a full cycle. The performance requirements of *The Ring of the Nibelung* also occasioned a specially constructed opera house in which the orchestra was placed in a covered pit under the stage. This ensured that the size and volume of the orchestra did not drown out the voices of the chorus. This innovation is still in use today. That opera companies are still willing to perform and enthusiasts are still willing to pay for what amounts to multiple consecutive shows is a testament to what some have called the greatest piece of operatic theater ever written.

Consider each of the following choices separately and select all that apply.

4. With which of the following statements would the author be likely to agree?

   [A] Wagner's *The Ring of the Nibelung* cycle is too demanding and logistically difficult to be performed.

   [B] An enduring effect of Wagner's *The Ring of the Nibelung* cycle is the innovation made to the opera house to accommodate the large orchestra.

   [C] Mammoth works such as *The Ring of the Nibelung* are better performed on one day to preserve their full effect.

Questions 5 and 6 are based on the following passage.

Discovered in 2001, the mimic octopus is a creature whose survival abilities are as unique as they are versatile. This talented cephalopod is capable of imitating several different species of creatures found in its environment, and it does so for different purposes. It imitates a crab to get close enough to catch and eat one, it imitates toxic fish to avoid being eaten itself, and it can imitate a predatory sea snake to scare off trespassers. The shape-shifting creature's conscious selection from among multiple forms is an exceptionally rare trait among animals, and one that adds a wrinkle to the more commonly expressed forms of singularly limited camouflage seen in nature. Many species exist that survive in part by resembling sticks, leaves, or other animals. Scientists have suggested that, within these species, members showing adaptive coloring or designs were overlooked by predators while the differently marked members were consumed. The survivors were then left to mate and to pass on their beneficial forms as a natural defense. The mimic octopus's intelligent use of selective disguise suggests a creative and adaptive survival mechanism, more versatile and intriguing than that arising from appearance alone.

5. Select the sentence in the passage that distinguishes how the mimic octopus's camouflage exceeds that of most forms found in nature.

6. The author would most likely agree with which of the following sentences?

   (A) The mimic octopus was probably discovered only recently because of its incredible ability to camouflage itself.
   (B) The mimic octopus's method of conscious and situational disguise discredits current evolutionary theory.
   (C) Mimic octopuses can only imitate the forms of creatures they can see.
   (D) Octopuses must be nearly as intelligent as humans.
   (E) Animal mimicry throughout nature is primarily a defensive mechanism as opposed to a means of attracting food.

Questions 7 and 8 are based on the following passage.

Raj Chetty's research has raised an intriguing question: how can "lost Einsteins," brilliant children in poor or minority families, be identified and nurtured to reach their full potential? Through researching patent filings in the United States, Chetty and his team discovered that children from families whose incomes are in the top 1 percent of all U.S. household incomes are ten times more likely to become inventors than those from families earning incomes in the lower 50 percent. Chetty's results also show similarly large differences correlated with race and gender. Furthermore, Philippe Aghion and his colleagues conducted similar research in Finland, with much the same results. Not only is this imbalance inequitable, but it also indicates a potential reservoir of talent that could be harnessed to solve some of the pressing problems the world faces.

One answer to this question, standardized intelligence testing, has been sharply criticized over the years as minimizing the importance of creativity, practical intelligence, and character, but it is now emerging as an important component in the identification of these high-ability students. The key to the effective use of intelligence testing, however, is that the tests must be administered universally to all students, not selectively to only those students nominated by their parents. Following the universal administration protocol, a school district in Florida found that the number of low-income students qualifying for its high-ability education program increased by 180 percent, the number of qualifying Hispanic students increased by 130 percent, and the number of qualifying African American students increased by 80 percent. While the criticisms of standardized intelligence testing should be addressed and other measures of ability should be considered, such a ready, potent tool for identifying brilliant young minds is ignored at our peril.

Consider each of the following choices separately and select all that apply.

7. Which of the following can be inferred from the passage regarding standardized intelligence testing?

    [A] Since standardized intelligence testing only measures limited aspects of cognition, it must be replaced as means of identifying high-ability students.

    [B] When standardized intelligence testing is administered only to selected groups of students, promising students may be overlooked for high-ability programs.

    [C] The deficiencies of standardized intelligence testing are less important than the immediate benefits this testing may offer.

8. Select the sentence in the passage that provides empirical evidence supporting the author's main point.

Questions 9 and 10 are based on the following passage.

In some key ways, a zoologist's orderly method for identifying and classifying a subject species is at odds with the multi-millennial chaos of adaptive development that led to the species as it is embodied today. If the laws of nature were as rigid as we want our classification system to be, famous taxonomic rebels such as the platypus would be forced, as mammals, to gestate and give birth to live young even if the risk to both parent and child were increased to the point of bringing about the end of the species. We are thus fortunate that the rigid biological nomenclature of science makes concessions for such an unusual marvel, one that not only scorns the basic tenets of its class, but brings new and mystifying qualities to the whole branch of its kingdom. It is hard enough to believe in the existence of a furry, duck-billed, egg-laying, venomous mammal that senses its prey through disturbances in a surrounding electromagnetic field without an unassailable checklist stating that the creature cannot by definition exist.

9. Select the sentence that explicitly states one of the traditional zoological characteristics of a species of mammal.

Consider each of the following choices separately and select all that apply.

10. Which of the following accurately describes the author's intent in writing the passage?

   [A] To indicate the shortcomings of using a highly structured classification system to define radically adaptive animals
   [B] To express admiration for the unusual abilities of the platypus
   [C] To make an argument in favor of changing how scientists classify animals with atypical traits

INTERMEDIATE

Question 11 is based on the following passage.

A healthy national economy is normally in oscillation between a period of freely flowing dollars driving the economy to expansion and a more tightly controlled release of money stabilizing it. All of these actions are initiated by the Federal Reserve (the Fed). When the Fed unleashes money into the system with low interest rates, consumer confidence rises, spending increases, business expands, and the economy itself grows. As wealth accumulates, the pricing of goods and services rises rapidly, creating inflation. The Fed neutralizes inflation by clamping down on the flow of money by setting higher interest rates. With less money available, spending and demand diminishes, usually curtailing or lowering prices. Unfortunately, this balance of control can only operate perfectly in a closed system. In the world economy, external, universal demands for food and oil fuel create an internal inflationary resonance. Increased flow of money is offset by unchecked inflation, and the economy remains flat. When that happens, the Fed is faced with the no-win condition of *stagflation*: it must attempt to increase the flow of dollars into the economy and see inflation skyrocket disproportionately against economic growth, or restrain spending to control inflation, forcing Americans to see their cumulative wealth dissipate.

11. What roles do the highlighted sentences play in the passage?

   (A) The first sentence establishes the author's primary argument, and the second sentence is a detail supporting the argument.
   (B) The first sentence identifies the two subjects of the passage, and the second sentence describes a point of comparison.
   (C) The first sentence states a premise, and the second sentence supplies a criticism of that premise.
   (D) The first sentence defines the primary idea of the passage, and the second sentence states the secondary idea.
   (E) The first sentence provides a definition for the subject of the passage, and the second sentence is an example of the subject.

Questions 12 and 13 are based on the following passage.

After a successful digital grassroots movement resulted in a hosting appearance by accomplished actress Betty White on the sketch comedy show *Saturday Night Live* (or *SNL*), a second movement appeared to get the revered stateswoman of comedy Carol Burnett to host an episode as well. If successful, it would mark an ironic full circle for the show that imagined itself in the 1970s as a counteragent to the supposedly hackneyed antics of Burnett's own successful sketch comedy show. As *SNL* embarked on a path toward the irreverent humor that continues today, the accessible and sentimental *Carol Burnett Show*, which ended every evening with Burnett giving a gentle tug on her ear in symbolic reverence to her grandmother, had already cultivated an audience with an intimate familiarity and genuine appreciation for the unassuming comedienne. Should such a convergence of these shows finally come to pass, will the current show's stars, whose fan bases combined are probably eclipsed by Burnett's own, encourage the show business legend to engage completely in their particular populist stylings? Or will the show that once denounced Burnett's style be willing at last to give a wink, nod, and ear tug to Burnett's highly regarded comedic sensibilities?

12. Select the sentence that most strongly suggests that *The Carol Burnett Show* had been on television prior to *Saturday Night Live*.

13. Which of the following would be the most appropriate title for the passage?

Ⓐ "The Demise and Return of Classic Comedy"
Ⓑ "Saturday Night Success"
Ⓒ "Burnett and *SNL*—Together at Last?"
Ⓓ "The Internet Brings Back a Laughing Legend"
Ⓔ "Carol Burnett: The Mother of Sketch Comedy"

Question 14 is based on the following passage.

In Tildernia, the number of reported paid family leave days taken by employed fathers after the birth of a child has declined 5 percent in the last three years. However, perhaps part of the decline is due to fathers using paid personal leave or vacation days to take time off following the birth of a child. After all, studies show that men who take paid family leave days are more frequently overlooked for promotion than those who do not use this benefit.

14. Which of the following, if true in Tildernia, most strongly supports the proposed explanation?

Ⓐ In the last three years, there has been no increase in the total number of paid personal leave or vacation days used by employed men.
Ⓑ When employees take family leave days after the birth of a child, they also receive a small increase in pay to assist in caring for that child.
Ⓒ A continuing shift in social attitudes has led to an increase in the number of men who assume more responsibilities in the household.
Ⓓ Employers who encourage fathers to take paid family leave after the birth of a child do not in general have lower benefit costs than employers who do not encourage fathers to do so.
Ⓔ In the last three years, the average number of births per household has gradually increased.

Question 15 is based on the following passage.

With the rise of community file-sharing programs that facilitated the easy distribution of data, which initially were used almost exclusively to disseminate music, artists and recording companies faced the possibility of a massive decrease in album sales. While record labels were unified in calling for swift legal crackdowns against file sharing, artists themselves were divided. No one was excited about the prospect of losing royalties, yet a few musicians imagined that the circumstances might lead to a return of the "bardic tradition," in which a musician's living was made through live performances. With large increases in the number of people with access to an artist's music, it was hoped that a potentially larger fan base would translate into better attended shows and concerts. Talented musicians or acts with entertaining showmanship would thrive while contrived or manufactured music groups would disappear, improving the overall quality of music. To date, that imagined future has failed to appear, in part due to rising ticket costs.

Consider each of the following choices separately and select all that apply.

15. Which of the following statements is suggested by the passage?

    [A] Regardless of the ultimate impact of file sharing on the music industry, two certainties will be a decrease in album sales for musicians and an increase in concert tours.

    [B] A subset of musicians would prefer to make their living as touring performers.

    [C] A musician's profits from concert tours are usually greater than those from record sales.

Question 16 is based on the following passage.

Between 1997 and 2002, the incidence of peanut allergies in young children doubled, according to studies by medical allergists. The sharp rise in peanut and other food allergies in adolescents led scientists and doctors to look for possible causes and contributing factors. One idea gaining support is the "hygiene hypothesis," which suggests that the human immune system requires contact with a wide range of environmental pathogens in order to strengthen itself. In a home environment that is kept largely sterile, particularly through the use of antibacterial soaps and sprays, the body does not learn to recognize and later combat some harmful viruses and bacteria. The absence of germs to fight, some theorize, leads the immune system to begin focusing on other, more innocuous substances such as peanuts, milk, and eggs. As a result of the overly clean environment, the developing autoimmune reaction becomes too sensitive to other organisms. Unfortunately, even if there is sufficient evidence to support the hygiene hypothesis, the benefits of that knowledge are mixed. Few people would want to resort to introducing germs, avoiding vaccines, or purposely living less sanitary lives in hopes of preventing a mere possibility of food allergies.

16. In the passage, what purpose do the highlighted sentences serve?

(A) The first sentence states the main idea of the paragraph, and the second sentence states the secondary idea.

(B) The first sentence states a counterargument to the author's argument, and the second sentence provides a supporting detail.

(C) The first sentence identifies a problem, and the second sentence argues a solution.

(D) The first sentence introduces the main idea of the paragraph, and the second sentence is a supporting statement for the conclusion.

(E) The first sentence is the primary argument, and the second sentence is a secondary argument.

Questions 17 and 18 are based on the following passage.

The angiosperms, commonly referred to as the flowering plants, are the dominant plants in most terrestrial ecosystems, but how they came to be so successful is considered one of the most profound mysteries in evolutionary biology. Hundreds of millions of years ago, ferns and conifers were the dominant plant species on Earth; then, about 150 million years ago, angiosperms suddenly appeared, rapidly spread, and diversified to such an extent that they now comprise 90 percent of all living plant species. Charles Darwin called their proliferation an "abominable mystery," fearful that this apparent sudden leap might challenge his theory of evolution. While the cause of their high diversity has been attributed largely to coevolution with pollinators and herbivores, their ability to outcompete the previously dominant ferns and conifers has been the subject of many hypotheses. Common among these is that the angiosperms alone developed leaves with smaller, more numerous stomata and more highly branching venation networks that enable higher rates of transpiration, photosynthesis, and growth. How angiosperms pack their leaves with smaller, more abundant stomata and more veins is unknown, but Kevin Simonin and Adam Roddy have shown that this ability is linked to simple biophysical constraints on cell size. Simonin and Roddy's research provides strong evidence that the success and rapid spread of flowering plants around the world was the result of genome downsizing. Since the genome is located in the nucleus of the cell, a smaller genome allows a plant to build smaller cells. This in turn allows greater carbon dioxide uptake and carbon gain from photosynthesis, the process by which plants use light energy to turn carbon dioxide and water into glucose and oxygen, and maximizes the productivity of the plant's photosynthetic process. The researchers say that genome downsizing happened only in the angiosperms and was "a necessary prerequisite for rapid growth rates among land plants."

17. The author of the passage cites Darwin's sentiment toward the rapid emergence and proliferation of the angiosperms most likely in order to

    (A) emphasize the importance of the enigma of the plants' success.
    (B) explain the basis for Darwin's fear that his theory would be undermined.
    (C) illustrate an example that contradicts Darwin's theory.
    (D) show that the evolution of flowering plants is inconsistent with Darwin's theory.
    (E) suggest that Darwin's fear that his theory would be challenged was unwarranted.

18. The primary purpose of the passage is to

    (A) argue that Darwin's theory of evolution cannot explain the rapid emergence and proliferation of flowering plants.
    (B) compare the prevalence of angiosperms to that of ferns and conifers.
    (C) discuss the reasons a wide variety of species evolved within the angiosperm group.
    (D) explain how flowering plants evolved smaller genomes.
    (E) present evidence suggesting an explanation for the remarkable efficiency and productivity of flowering plants.

Question 19 is based on the following passage.

Thousands who suffer heart attacks each year die before reaching a hospital or clinic where they can benefit from the drugs that dissolve clots found in coronary arteries. The Food and Drug Administration recently approved a new blood clot dissolving agent, which a spokesman claimed could save the lives of many people who would otherwise join this group of heart attack victims.

19. Which of the following statements, if true, would most weaken the argument above?

   (A) The new agent must be administered by a team of doctors in a hospital or clinic setting.
   (B) Many heart attack victims die unnecessarily even though they reach a hospital or clinic in time.
   (C) The new agent can be effectively administered prior to the victim's arrival at a hospital or clinic.
   (D) The Food and Drug Administration has already approved agents that are at least as effective as the new drug in dissolving blood clots.
   (E) The new blood clot dissolving agent causes kidney damage and irregular heart rates in some patients.

ADVANCED

Questions 20 and 21 are based on the following passage.

With computer access for work, education, and personal use reaching near universal saturation, and with many people logging time on more than one networked machine, a vast array of online computers are operated by largely untrained users. These operators' lack of network security awareness presents a large opportunity for hackers and cybercriminals to gain access to sensitive business and personal data. Ironically, it is not these users' computing inexperience that represents the vulnerability. A very small percentage of malicious computer attacks are caused by a "traditional" external attack. Instead of kicking in the door, so to speak, the perpetrators usually convince computer users to open it for them. Through targeted links and ads from dubious websites or fake emails to anonymous contacts made through instant messaging services or social networking sites, cybercriminals rely on people's trusting nature to provide them with the means to infect or gain access to the victims' computers. In some cases, creative criminals will even initiate their attack in the real world, placing advertisements or fake parking tickets on cars that ask the owners to visit a website for more information. The website usually contains invasive software that users then download to their computers.

Consider each of the following choices separately and select all that apply.

20. According to the passage, which of the following are means that the passage suggests cybercriminals can use to illegitimately access another's computer?

[A] Engage in an external attack over a network
[B] Get users to click on a link contained in a deceitful email
[C] Use a seemingly innocuous object to get a person to voluntarily visit a specifically created attack site

21. With which of the following sentences would the author most likely agree?

(A) Since nearly everyone uses computers, the sheer number of computers in use makes the odds of any one computer being hacked too low to merit concern about security.
(B) One way to combat cybercrime is to become more suspicious of anonymous requests or messages sent over social networks.
(C) In order to prevent illegal access to data, only trained personnel should be allowed to use computers.
(D) If a cybercriminal is unable to trick users into giving access to their machines, the criminal will likely attack the users' machines directly.
(E) In order to protect their computers, people should refrain from using instant messaging services and social networks.

Questions 22 and 23 are based on the following passage.

One of the strategic principles for success in the stock market is to refrain from having knee-jerk reactions to possibly deceptive fluctuations in the market's or a particular stock's performance. Before reinvesting in a rapidly falling stock, analysts and investors will often wait for the passing of one or more small upward bumps, referred to as "dead cat bounces." The term reflects the somewhat crude idea that even a dead cat will bounce if it falls from a great height. Upticks in a plummeting stock can be caused by short selling, triggered sell-offs, or overly optimistic reactions to changes made by the company, such as replacing an unpopular CEO. Such a small, unimpressive rise is usually followed by another drop-off that surpasses the previous low. While almost exclusively related to the stock market, the term has found occasional use in describing other areas of misleading improvement. Poll numbers for a candidate losing ground near an election sometimes make a brief, illusory surge. In sports, losing teams that make midseason coaching changes sometimes experience a mild surge of energy that translates to one or more wins before the team reverts to form.

22. According to the passage, each of the following is TRUE of a "dead cat bounce" EXCEPT:

    Ⓐ It occurs when a stock shows a small improvement followed by a much greater decline in performance.
    Ⓑ It only occurs in instances where performance is already showing a rapid decline.
    Ⓒ It provides a good opportunity to sell stock at the peak of the "dead cat bounce" before the stock plummets even further.
    Ⓓ It is a term that primarily exists to explain a regularly occurring feature of the stock market.
    Ⓔ It is capable of occurring multiple times within the same stock's downward collapse before the stock's improvement becomes sustainable.

23. Select the sentence in the passage that demonstrates the traditional investment strategy in regard to a stock experiencing or expected to experience a "dead cat bounce."

Questions 24–26 are based on the following passage.

While most individuals are aware that their bodies are filled with bacteria, both beneficial and pathological, few realize the full spectrum of fungi, viruses, microbes, and archaea that exist within the human microbiome. Some researchers have even posited that the human body is made up of more foreign than human genetic material. One of the major benefits of understanding the complexity of what lives inside the body is that some researchers have changed the way they seek treatments for illness, with a number of innovative techniques being adopted as a result. With a better grasp of how millions of microbial genes interact with the tens of thousands of genes that make up the human genome, researchers are able to divine ways to augment these interactions in order to curb and—in some instances—reverse the progress of disease.

Another important outcome from a better understanding of the human microbiome is a rethinking of the side effects of antibiotics commonly used to treat a wide spectrum of illnesses. One professor has theorized that the proliferation of antibiotics, while doing much to stave off the spread of infectious disease, has also contributed to a new set of diseases far more resistant to currently available remedies. Various antibiotics have detrimental effects on bacteria in the body, and an individual's microbiome not only determines susceptibility to certain autoimmune diseases and allergies, but it may also reduce or increase the likelihood of contracting specific illnesses.

One disease that researchers have applied this new approach to is obesity. The digestive tract is the region of the body with the highest concentration of microbes. Along with lifestyle choices and family history, the microscopic ecosystem of the gut makes a significant contribution to the severity of obesity. Studies of laboratory mice have shown that the same unhealthy diet paired with gut bacteria from different microbiomes can lead to either weight gain or weight loss. Whether the results of these and similar studies will directly translate to humans remains to be seen, but the potential for developing an entirely new branch of pharmaceuticals, microbial medicine, has both intriguing and broad implications.

24. Based on the preceding passage, with which of the following statements about the potential of microbial medicine would the author most likely agree?

   (A) The study of microbes in the digestive tract is unlikely to further the progress of microbial medicine.
   (B) Microbial medicine will be unable to reach its full potential as long as researchers have a limited understanding of the human genome.
   (C) The results of studies of obesity in lab mice may indicate the potential of microbial medicine for humans.
   (D) Despite its potential, microbial medicine is unlikely to have the same impact that antibiotics have had on disease.
   (E) Microbial medicine's main potential benefit is in slowing the progress of specific diseases.

25. Select the sentence that provides a scientific explanation for why antibiotics may not be the best treatment for a condition.

Consider each of the following choices separately and select all that apply.

26. According to the passage, which of the following are possible consequences of a greater understanding of the microbiome within the human body?

 A Researchers have conducted experiments to test hypotheses about the interaction of diet and bacteria in the gut.

 B Researchers use innovative methods to exploit the interaction of human and nonhuman genes.

 C The indiscriminate use of antibiotics to treat illness has been called into question.

Question 27 is based on the following passage.

William Shakespeare is perhaps the most well-known playwright in the world. There is, however, a small but vocal group, known as "anti-Stratfordians," who claim that Shakespeare could not possibly have written the plays and poems attributed to him. They point out that these works show an extraordinary level of sophistication, and there is no evidence that Shakespeare, born to humble beginnings in Stratford-upon-Avon in 1564, received any kind of formal education.

Consider each of the following choices separately and select all that apply.

27. Which of the following, if true, would tend to refute the claim made by the anti-Stratfordians?

 A Other well-known playwrights of the era also came from families of lower socioeconomic status.

 B There is no general consensus among anti-Stratfordians as to who actually wrote Shakespeare's plays.

 C The grammar school in Stratford-upon-Avon has no surviving records for any students from that era.

Question 28 is based on the following passage.

As research into artificial intelligence progresses, some futurists are concerned that computers and robots will take more and more jobs away from humans. However reasonable this fear may seem, humans need not worry about being completely replaced in the job market. Currently, robots have replaced humans only in rote, repetitive jobs, such as automobile assembly lines.

28. Which of the following, if true, would most weaken the argument above?

(A) The average purchase price of an assembly-line robot is equivalent to ten times the annual salaries of the workers it replaces.
(B) Much of the research into artificial intelligence is being conducted by private enterprises rather than public universities.
(C) In a controlled study, a panel of art experts was unable to distinguish paintings created by a machine using artificial intelligence from those created by human artists.
(D) A survey of workers who had been replaced by robots showed that a majority were able to find a job in a new field within a year.
(E) The daily productivity of an assembly-line robot is much higher than that of the human workers it replaces.

Questions 29 and 30 are based on the following passage.

Literature from the Midwestern United States is often relegated to the periphery of the American canon. Jon A. Lauck, in his book *From Warm Center to Ragged Edge*, attributes this marginalization to a statement of literary critic Carl Van Doren published in *The Nation* in 1921, during a period when the hierarchies of aesthetic and social values to be embodied by the canon were first delineated. Van Doren described the most interesting literature from the middle of the United States as that which could be characterized as a "revolt from the village." He celebrated authors who portrayed local life as stifling rather than satisfying and considered them artistic innovators and political visionaries. Lauck argues that Van Doren and other Eastern critics not only completely ignored Midwestern writers whose work deviated from this pattern but also substantially misunderstood the work of the writers who had been assigned to the "revolt" school, resulting in the exclusion of most Midwestern works from the "rootless, urban, elite version of American literature that persists to this day." Although she finds Lauck's omission of a definition of "the Midwest" troubling, Stephanie Foote considers his book "a triumph of research . . . and a compelling narrative" that provokes the reader to "take seriously the debates about which cultures are valued and which are not."

29. Select the sentence that provides Lauck's opinion of Van Doren's assessment of Midwestern literature.

Consider each of the following choices separately and select all that apply.

30. Which of the following statements about the works of Midwestern literature assigned to the "revolt from the village" school can be inferred from the passage?

    [A] Jon Lauck believes that some of the works of Midwestern literature assigned to the "revolt from the village" school were misread by Eastern critics.

    [B] When the American canon of literature was first discussed, some critics considered the works of Midwestern literature assigned to the "revolt from the village" school the most important literature from that region.

    [C] Stephanie Foote finds Lauck's omission of a definition of "the Midwest" sufficient to dismiss his assessment of the works of Midwestern literature assigned to the "revolt from the village" school.

READING COMPREHENSION PRACTICE SET ANSWER KEY

1. **C**
2. *"Some of this debris clumped together due to gravity and formed the set of moons seen today."*
3. **B, C**
4. **B**
5. *"The shape-shifting creature's conscious selection from among multiple forms is an exceptionally rare trait among animals, and one that adds a wrinkle to the more commonly expressed forms of singularly limited camouflage seen in nature."*
6. **E**
7. **B, C**
8. *"Following the universal administration protocol, a school district in Florida found that the number of low-income students qualifying for its high-ability education program increased by 180 percent, the number of qualifying Hispanic students increased by 130 percent, and the number of qualifying African American students increased by 80 percent."*
9. *"If the laws of nature were as rigid as we want our classification system to be, famous taxonomic rebels such as the platypus would be forced, as mammals, to gestate and give birth to live young even if the risk to both parent and child were increased to the point of bringing about the end of the species."*
10. **A, B**
11. **D**
12. *"As* SNL *embarked on a path toward the irreverent humor that continues today, the accessible and sentimental* Carol Burnett Show, *which ended every evening with Burnett giving a gentle tug on her ear in symbolic reverence to her grandmother, had already cultivated an audience with an intimate familiarity and genuine appreciation for the unassuming comedienne."*
13. **C**
14. **E**
15. **B**
16. **D**
17. **A**
18. **E**
19. **A**
20. **A, B, C**
21. **B**
22. **C**

23. *"Before reinvesting in a rapidly falling stock, analysts and investors will often wait for the passing of one or more small upward bumps, referred to as 'dead cat bounces.'"*
24. **C**
25. *"Various antibiotics have detrimental effects on bacteria in the body, and an individual's microbiome not only determines susceptibility to certain autoimmune diseases and allergies, but it may also reduce or increase the likelihood of contracting specific illnesses."*
26. **A, B, C**
27. **C**
28. **C**
29. *"Lauck argues that Van Doren and other Eastern critics not only completely ignored Midwestern writers whose work who deviated from this pattern but also substantially misunderstood the work of the writers who had been assigned to the 'revolt' school, resulting in the exclusion of most Midwestern works from the "rootless, urban, elite version of American literature that persists to this day.'"*
30. **A, B**

READING COMPREHENSION PRACTICE SET ANSWERS AND EXPLANATIONS

Basic

1. C

The purpose of the passage is to present an analysis of data from *Cassini* and an analysis of the orbits of Saturn's moons that support different hypotheses about the timing of the emergence of life on Earth relative to the planet's formation. **(C)** is correct. Eliminate **(A)** because while two pieces of evidence are presented, two theories on the formation of Saturn's rings are not. **(B)** is a subtle distortion of a detail mentioned in the fourth sentence. The author says, "Enceladus is widely considered the most promising site in the solar system for the search for extraterrestrial life" but never *recommends* that the moon be examined for life. The author is not challenging a theory but rather seems excited about the "intriguing glimpse" the researchers' work offers, so eliminate **(D)**. In addition, the text focuses on Saturn's rings, not the planet itself. **(E)** is extreme. Although intrigued by *Cassini*'s evidence, the author never states the theory is "proven."

2. *"Some of this debris clumped together due to gravity and formed the set of moons seen today."*

Enceladus is described as one of the moons of Saturn in the first paragraph, but the question directs you to the second or third paragraph. The third paragraph discusses the formation of "the moons seen today." Since the *Cassini* spacecraft examined Enceladus, it must be one of "the moons seen today."

3. B, C

"The dark residual dust from comets" mentioned in the question is discussed in the second paragraph. Match the choices to the information in the passage. **(A)** is a 180, or opposite, choice and is incorrect. Older objects in the solar system have accumulated more dust than younger objects. **(B)** is the main idea of the second paragraph and is correct. **(C)** describes the effect the dust has on older objects in the solar system and is correct.

4. B

The correct answer to this question can be discerned from one key detail in the text, in which the passage explains that the performance requirements for *The Ring of the Nibelung* necessitated the construction of a newly designed opera house, and that this innovation is still in use today. With that knowledge, you know that **(B)** applies, because that is the only effect mentioned that is still in use today. You can reject **(A)** because the author explains the technical innovations that have allowed such a work to be performed on a regular basis. Choice **(C)** is incorrect because the author nowhere implies that he disapproves of the multi-night performances, and notes the logistical difficulties of a single-day performance.

5. *"The shape-shifting creature's conscious selection from among multiple forms is an exceptionally rare trait among animals, and one that adds a wrinkle to the more commonly expressed forms of singularly limited camouflage seen in nature."*

This sentence best meets the criterion of describing how the camouflage of the mimic octopus exceeds that of other creatures. The sentence asserts that the creature's ability is rare and elaborates that the mimic octopus's ability to take multiple forms is a step above that of most other camouflaging creatures, which possess only a single form of disguise.

6. E

With five-choice questions that are not specific enough for you to make a prediction, it is better to eliminate than attempt to recognize the correct answer initially. Walking down the list of choices, **(A)** doesn't stand up because no details are given concerning the nature of the mimic octopus's discovery, only its year. The most that the passage asserts regarding the mimic octopus's abilities within the scheme of evolutionary theory is that it "adds a wrinkle." The wording of choice **(B)** is too extreme to follow from the passage. As with **(A)**, choice **(C)** makes an inference without any supporting details in the passage. The passage lists three creatures that the octopus mimics and explains how it uses each of those disguises. Nothing suggests that these are the only creatures it imitates or that sight is required for the mimicking process. Choice **(D)**, which acknowledges the mimic octopus's intelligence, falls outside the scope of the passage, which gives no grounds for comparing it to that of humans. Choice **(E)** is the correct answer, not just because it is left standing after the process of elimination, but also because the passage gives us ample discussion of animal camouflage, describing it primarily as defensive. Only the mimic octopus is described as using camouflage to catch prey.

7. B, C

The main idea of the passage is that universal standardized intelligence testing may be useful in identifying high-ability students regardless of their economic status or race. **(A)** is a 180, or opposite, choice, and is incorrect. **(B)** is correct. The second sentence of paragraph 2 says, "The *key* to the effective use of intelligence testing, *however* . . ." is that it be administered universally, that is, to all students. The author supports this idea with the results of universal testing at the Florida school, where dramatic changes were seen in the representation of low-income and minority students in a high-ability educational program. **(C)** is correct. This choice is supported by the last sentence of the passage, where the author acknowledges possible criticisms of standardized intelligence testing but calls it a "ready, potent tool."

8. *"Following the universal administration protocol, a school district in Florida found that the number of low-income students qualifying for its high-ability education program increased by 180 percent, the number of qualifying Hispanic students increased by 130 percent, and the number of qualifying African American students increased by 80 percent."*

The author's main idea is that universal standardized intelligence testing may be useful in identifying low-income and minority students who could benefit from high-ability classes. The data from the Florida school are empirical evidence that supports the author's view.

9. *"If the laws of nature were as rigid as we want our classification system to be, famous taxonomic rebels such as the platypus would be forced, as mammals, to gestate and give birth to live young even if the risk to both parent and child were increased to the point of bringing about the end of the species."*

With a four-sentence passage, your odds of getting this question right are one in four, just on a blind guess. Those odds are better than on a "one right, four wrong" multiple-choice question, but you can do better. Only two sentences—the second and the fourth—discuss mammals. The fourth describes the traits that make the platypus unlike most mammals. You can infer the standard mammalian traits from that, but the question asks for a sentence in which qualities are "explicitly" listed. The second sentence, however, states that, to fit properly within the definition of a "mammal," a creature must produce live young.

10. A, B

Reading strategically, you likely discerned the author's dual purposes. They're indicated by key words indicating her opinion and emphases. The passage centers on the limitations of the standard method of zoological classification, which the author chides for being too rigid to accommodate species that don't fall precisely within certain families. That fits choice **(A)**; the author, indeed, "indicate(s) the shortcomings" of the biological taxonomy. Choice **(C)**, on the other hand, goes too far; the author does not suggest an alternative classification system. The author illustrates her point through a discussion of the platypus. In addition to describing its category-defying traits, the author considers it a "marvel," one we're "fortunate" to experience because it's difficult to define. Attending to the author's tone enables you to discern her admiration for the platypus. That tells you to include choice **(B)** as part of the correct answer.

Intermediate

11. D

In Highlighted Statement questions, in which the sentences to be analyzed are pointed out,. you are best served by forming a prediction for the correct answer before you consider the choices. You should look for the main idea or argument and then determine how the highlighted sentences apply. By predicting the correct answer, you're less likely to let the choices influence you into thinking a sentence does something it does not. Here, for instance, the passage is informative, not persuasive. This means that choices **(A)** and **(C)**—which use the words "argument" and "criticism" to imply that the author expresses a strong opinion on the issue—are incorrect. Even without reading the second highlighted sentence, you can dismiss choice **(B)** because the description of the first sentence, which introduces a single subject, is inaccurate. You might be able to make an argument for the first part of **(E)**, if you see the explanation of the state of a healthy U.S. economy as a definition. But the second part of choice **(E)** is derailed by the word "unfortunately" at the onset of the second highlighted sentence, which suggests not a supporting example but a separate and contrasting idea. Indeed, the second highlighted sentence contains a secondary idea that further refines the main idea. That matches the correct answer, choice **(D)**.

12. *"As* SNL *embarked on a path toward the irreverent humor that continues today, the accessible and sentimental* Carol Burnett Show, *which ended every evening with Burnett giving a gentle tug on her ear in symbolic reverence to her grandmother, had already cultivated an audience with an intimate familiarity and genuine appreciation for the unassuming comedienne."*

It's easy to presume that the second sentence in the passage, which outlines how *SNL* planned to position itself against *The Carol Burnett Show*, would suffice for this question, but it does not assure that the two shows did not arise simultaneously or even that Burnett's show wasn't following in the footsteps but competing for an audience. Only in the third sentence (the correct answer to this question) do the combined statements of "As *SNL* embarked" and "had already cultivated an audience" guarantee us that Burnett had preceded *SNL* into the sketch comedy arena.

13. C

Titles can be difficult to judge. We've all experienced articles and stories with titles at odds with their content. For the purposes of defining a passage such as this, there are qualifiers you should keep in mind. First, the possible title cannot introduce or fixate on some element of discussion that does not appear in the text. Choice **(E)** fails on that standard; nowhere does the passage posit that Burnett invented sketch comedy. Choice **(A)** stumbles on this point as well; you're never told of a "demise" or death of any form of comedy or of any show. You can tell that Burnett's show no longer runs today, but you get no explanation of the conditions under which that occurred. A title must also be an accurate summary of the main subject or idea. Choice **(B)** is not only too bland, but too general, missing the comparison central to the passage. Choice **(D)** misses the boat by targeting an introductory detail rather than the main idea. Choice **(C)**, which most correctly identifies both the longevity and disparate comedy careers of Burnett and *Saturday Night Live* elaborated on in the passage, is the clear choice.

14. E

The question asks you to support the proposed explanation. The author explains men's lower usage of paid family leave by speculating that, because of decreased promotion opportunities, men are now using vacation or personal leave days to take time off from work after the birth of a child. To strengthen this idea, find the choice that provides some evidence for this reasoning, either by providing direct support for the idea that men are using alternative forms of time off or by eliminating a potential alternative explanation.

(A) has no effect on the argument and is incorrect. The number of personal leave or vacation days taken is not related to how those days were used. Perhaps men used to take all their personal and vacation time for other reasons and are now using it to spend time with their newborns, in which case the argument would be strengthened. But perhaps men are using this time off in the way they always have, which would weaken the argument. There is not enough information to make this determination. **(B)** actually *weakens* the argument. If men would receive a salary increase connected to taking family leave, they would be more likely to take this form of time off rather than some other kind. **(C)** has no effect on the argument. The shift in social attitudes may mean men are spending more time with their children, but it doesn't affect how the men classify their hours. **(D)** also has no effect on the argument. The cost of benefits is not mentioned in the argument and would have no effect on men's concerns about receiving promotions. **(E)** is correct. If the number of children born in the last three years had gone down, that would be an alternative explanation for the decrease in the number of family days taken for the birth of a child. **(E)** strengthens the explanation in the argument by removing the possibility of that alternative.

15. B

As always, each statement needs to be considered on its own merits, using only evidence stated in the passage. Remember that you only have to discredit one aspect of a choice to show that it's invalid. Option **(A)** has multiple parts, and none is supported by the text. Whether or not you agree that the end result of music file sharing can't be determined, the passage does not establish that either the decrease in album sales (which the music industry fears) or an increase in the number of concerts (which some musicians anticipate) has or will come to pass. Option **(B)** has merit, and is a correct answer. Indeed, the passage's main idea is that, with the onset of music file sharing, some musicians were optimistic that they could engage in and support themselves through live performance. Option **(C)**, similarly to **(A)**, has multiple undemonstrated aspects. The passage does not compare the profitability of albums and concerts, either before or after the influence of file sharing. There is no basis in the text for this claim.

16. D

The topic of this passage, introduced in the first two sentences, is food allergies and the search for a possible cause. The next sentence presents the main idea: it defines the "hygiene hypothesis" and asserts that it might explain the rise in adolescent food allergies. Once you have recognized that, you can pass over all choices that do not acknowledge that role for the first highlighted sentence, meaning **(B)**, **(C)**, and **(E)** are out. Your understanding of the passage's structure is important, because the conclusion, "Unfortunately, even if there is sufficient evidence to support the hygiene hypothesis, the benefits of that knowledge are mixed," is not one of the highlighted sentences. The final, highlighted sentence supports that conclusion. This puts choice **(A)** by the wayside and indicates **(D)** as the correct choice.

17. A

When asked for the author's reason for including a detail in the passage, consider the main idea of the passage and then decide how the detail contributes to the author's overall purpose. Here, the main idea is that new research is providing strong evidence that may resolve an important, long-standing question. Darwin's sentiment, that this question was an "abominable mystery," and his concern that the answer might undermine his theory show how important he thought it was. This prediction matches **(A)**, the correct answer. **(B)** is incorrect because Darwin's statement expresses his fear but does not explain the reasons behind it; the author does not explain how the rapid emergence of angiosperms might be construed as evidence against evolution. **(C)** is extreme; Darwin was worried that the angiosperms' rapid dominance was evidence against his theory, but the passage does not go on to confirm that fear. **(D)** is a 180, or opposite, choice. The passage goes on to explain how the evolution of one feature of flowering plants explains their rise in a manner consistent with Darwin's theory.

(E) is not addressed in the passage; if anything, the author's careful explanation indicates that the question is an important one and Darwin's fears *were* warranted.

18. E

Predict an answer to a primary purpose question based on your understanding of the author's main thrust in writing. The purpose of this passage is to explain how recent research strongly suggests that the smaller genomes contributed to the rapid proliferation of flowering plants. Keep the author's factual, neutral tone in mind. **(E)** matches the prediction and is correct. The efficiency and productivity of flowering plants is mentioned in the next-to-last sentence as a result of the smaller cells that are needed to house a smaller genome. **(A)** can be eliminated because the passage goes on to give evidence for how the ability of flowering plants to outcompete other plants arose from their evolution in a manner consistent with Darwin's theory. **(B)** is a distortion of information in the passage. The current dominance of flowering plants over ferns and conifers is mentioned, but the text does not compare the different types of plants; the purpose of the passage is to explain how angiosperms became the dominant species. **(C)** is mentioned in the passage, but this is not the main idea. The reasons the flowering plants are so diverse are discussed in the fourth sentence, but it's the rapid emergence and proliferation of angiosperms that are important to the author, not their diversity. **(D)** is a distortion of information in the passage, which explains how a smaller genome promoted the angiosperms' success but not how the smaller genome came about.

19. A

This question asks you to weaken the argument in the stimulus. In the last sentence of the stimulus, a spokesperson says that this dissolving agent will save the lives of many people who would otherwise join "this group of heart attack victims." Which group of heart attack victims? Those who die before reaching a hospital or clinic, who are mentioned earlier in the stimulus.

To weaken the spokesperson's conclusion, you need to find an answer choice that goes against this specific argument. In other words, you want a choice that says people who would die before reaching a hospital *will not be saved* by this drug. Answer choice **(A)** does this, and it is correct; if the new agent can't be administered outside a hospital or clinic setting, it's not going to make a shred of difference for those who die before they get there.

Choice **(B)** is outside the scope of this argument, as this argument only cares about those who die before they hit the hospital. Choice **(C)** actually *strengthens* the argument, attesting to the agent's ability to save pre-hospital patients. And choices **(D)** and **(E)** both begin suggesting reasons why this new drug might not make a difference, but there is too much uncertainty in each of them: for **(D)**, perhaps the more-effective drugs are not yet in wide usage or have some other caveat; for **(E)**, maybe the lives saved would outweigh those endangered by the side effects.

Advanced

20. A, B, C

This is a tough Select One or More question. For the untrained test taker, the difficulty is compounded by the fact that, here, all three choices are correct. Remember not to assume that one of the answers must be wrong. The testmakers may write one, two, or all three of the choices to be applicable to the question stem. In this question, select any answer that lists a way in which the passage tells you a cybercriminal might attack a personal computer. The passage states that direct attack over the network, choice **(A)**, is unlikely, but still a possibility. Likewise, the passage explicitly cites "dubious websites or fake emails," choice **(B)**. The use of "advertisements or fake parking tickets" cited near the end of the passage matches choice **(C)**'s "seemingly innocuous object" reference.

21. B

This question asks for a choice with which the author would agree. Rule out the choices that are not supported in the text. Choice **(A)** contradicts the author; he states that near-universal computer use increases the security risk. You can infer that the author would agree with choice **(B)**; he cites fraudulent requests and messages from unknown sources on social networks and instant messaging systems as a significant source of cyber-vulnerability. This makes **(B)** the correct answer. In this predominantly informative paragraph, the author makes no claims that come close to either of the controversial suggestions in choices **(C)** and **(E)**. Choice **(D)** receives no support from the passage. The author says indirect attack is more common than direct attack, but doesn't state or suggest that criminals turn to direct attack when their indirect schemes fail.

22. C

This is a question that asks for the answer choice that is *not* supported by the passage. That means that the four wrong answers will contain statements you can infer from the text. A solid reading of the text gives you all you need to know about the definition and characteristics of a "dead cat bounce" in order to eliminate choices **(A)** "usually followed by another drop-off that surpasses the previous low," **(B)** "before reinvesting in a rapidly falling stock," **(D)** "occasional use in describing other areas," and **(E)** "one or more small upward bumps." Choice **(C)**, on the other hand, is out of scope and is therefore the correct answer. Nowhere in the passage does the author discuss the strategies that sellers should use to take advantage of a "dead cat bounce."

23. *"Before reinvesting in a rapidly falling stock, analysts and investors will often wait for the passing of one or more small upward bumps, referred to as 'dead cat bounces.'"*

Here, the sentence that provides the definition for a "dead cat bounce" also gives you the conventional wisdom investors use in response: wait out the deceptive event before finding a more opportune time to reinvest.

24. C

This Inference question asks for the author's opinion of "microbial medicine," a term that shows up in the last paragraph. Here, the author discusses the possibility of a "new branch of pharmaceuticals" and states that it has "intriguing and broad implications." This positive language indicates the author's opinion. Microbial medicine is thought to hold promise because of the results of experiments on mice, discussed in the preceding sentence. **(C)** paraphrases the ideas in the last two sentences of the passage and is correct. Note the tentative phrasing "may indicate," which matches the author's caveat that experimental results with mice may not translate to humans.

(A) is incorrect. The second sentence of the third paragraph points out that the digestive tract has "the highest concentration of microbes," so it is actually an ideal part of the body to study in order to further the potential of microbial medicine.

The human genome mentioned in **(B)** is discussed in the first paragraph. Researchers are already using their "better grasp" of how microbial genes interact with human genes to make progress, so while it is possible that a complete understanding of the human genome is necessary for microbial medicine to reach its full potential, the passage does not provide evidence for this idea.

(D) may have been tempting because the author mentions some of the potential harmful effects of antibiotics in the second paragraph. However, the author never compares the relative benefits of microbial medicine and antibiotics, making this choice incorrect.

(E) is incorrect. The first paragraph ends saying that researchers may be able to "curb and—in some instances—*reverse* the progress of disease." Moreover, from the third paragraph, you can infer that since weight loss can be achieved in mice, an application of microbial medicine might be able to reverse obesity and potentially other health conditions, not just slow their progress.

25. *"Various antibiotics have detrimental effects on bacteria in the body, and an individual's microbiome not only determines susceptibility to certain autoimmune diseases and allergies, but it may also reduce or increase the likelihood of contracting specific illnesses."*

Antibiotics are discussed in the second paragraph, and negative information appears in the second sentence, where you're told one professor believes they have "contributed to a new set of diseases." The scientific explanation for why this would occur is given in the next sentence, which describes their effect on the microbiome.

26. A, B, C

This question stem begins with the phrase "[a]ccording to the passage," so this is a Detail question. The passage begins by saying researchers know more about the human microbiome than they used to and goes on to outline a number of potential consequences of this knowledge. Research each choice in this all-that-apply question in the passage. **(A)** reflects information in the last paragraph about experiments on mice to test how different microbiomes affect weight, so this choice is correct. **(B)** paraphrases information from the first paragraph, where the author says that "innovative techniques" are being used because researchers have "a better grasp of how millions of microbial genes interact with the tens of thousands of genes that make up the human genome." **(C)** appears in the second paragraph, where the author cites a professor who believes antibiotics "have also contributed to a new set of diseases" that resist treatment.

27. C

This is an all-that-apply Weaken question. You'll need to determine which of the answer choices make the anti-Stratfordians's claim less likely to be true. First, summarize that claim: Shakespeare could not have written the plays attributed to him. Their evidence is that the plays are sophisticated and there's no proof that Shakespeare had formal schooling. To weaken this claim, a correct answer choice may show how he could have written these plays without having gotten a formal education or how he could have received schooling even though there is no evidence of his enrollment.

(C) is the only correct answer. If the school in Shakespeare's hometown has no records of any kind from that time, then the fact that there are no records of Shakespeare specifically has no special importance. This choice opens up the possibility that Shakespeare did have an education after all, so it weakens the anti-Stratfordian claim. **(A)** shows that other successful playwrights of the era came from similar backgrounds as Shakespeare, but neither piece of this statement addresses the argument made by the anti-Stratfordians, whose argument rests on Shakespeare's lack of education (not his means) and the sophistication (not the success) of the plays. **(B)** shows a weakness in the anti-Stratfordians' thinking about the plays. However, the claim being refuted here is that the author was not Shakespeare; even if they can't agree on who wrote them, they may be right that the author was not Shakespeare, so **(B)** does not weaken this argument.

28. C

The author of this passage makes the claim that most humans shouldn't worry about losing their jobs to robots or computers in the future because, so far, robots have replaced them only in repetitive jobs. Note that the claim is about the future, while the evidence is about the present; as is common when an argument makes a prediction, the author assumes that the future will be similar to the present. Look for a choice indicating that the capability of computers and robots will change, allowing them to do more kinds of jobs. That's what **(C)** does. It shows that an artificial intelligence may be able to succeed in artistic endeavors, an ability that would potentially allow technology to compete with humans for more jobs. This is the correct answer.

(A), if anything, strengthens the argument; if robots are more expensive than people, it may be somewhat less likely that companies will use them. **(B)** is incorrect because who conducts the research is irrelevant; whether created by a business or a university, a robot or computer may be able to take over a human job. **(D)** can be eliminated because it deals only with the past; so far, people have been able to get new jobs, but there's no guarantee that this will hold true in the future. Finally, **(E)** may be tempting because it seems to show an advantage of robots over humans: they're more productive than humans in an assembly line. The author, however, already concedes that robots do this job well; her argument is that they won't be able to expand into other fields.

29. *"Lauck argues that Van Doren and other Eastern critics not only completely ignored Midwestern writers whose work who deviated from this pattern but also substantially misunderstood the work of the writers who had been assigned to the 'revolt' school, resulting in the exclusion of most Midwestern works from the "rootless, urban, elite version of American literature that persists to this day.'"*

The key word "argues" identifies Lauck's opinion. If you chose either of the two previous sentences, you may have misread the question. Those sentences provide Van Doren's opinion. The following sentence provides Stephanie Foote's opinion of Lauck's work.

30. A, B

(A) is supported by Lauck's opinion expressed in the fifth sentence and is correct. If the works were "misunderstood," then they were "misread." **(B)** is also correct. This choice is supported by the third sentence, where it's said that Van Doren, one of the critics responsible for the discussions that led to the formation of the American canon of literature, called these works "the *most* interesting literature from the middle of the United States." Since a canon of literature is a list of the most important or influential books, and since Van Doren's comment is cited in reference to the creation of the American canon, it is inferred that "Van Doren and other Eastern critics" thought the works of the "revolt" school were the most important literature from the Midwestern United States. **(C)** is not supported by the text. While Foote does criticize Lauck's omission of a crucial definition, she also considers Lauck's book "a triumph of research" and so likely supports his assessment of these works. Her criticism is directed toward an issue that is peripheral to the literature assigned to the "revolt from the village" school.

CHAPTER 5

Verbal Reasoning Practice

VERBAL REASONING PRACTICE SET 1

Directions: For each sentence, choose one word for each set of blanks. Select the word or words that best fit(s) the meaning of the sentence as a whole.

1. As a society grows and evolves, so too do its cultural norms. A piece of art or a musical performance that once was viewed as inordinately (i) _______ may now be seen as utterly (ii) _______.

Blank (i)	Blank (ii)
A salacious	D pensive
B adequate	E opulent
C trite	F pedestrian

2. Traditional recipes for beef brisket vary widely between cultures, but one (i) _______ the various preparations is a "low and slow" cooking technique: a long cooking time at a low temperature. This is not a matter of taste but a (ii) _______; the brisket is a working muscle and would otherwise be too tough to eat.

Blank (i)	Blank (ii)
A affinity between	D prerequisite
B variance among	E predilection
C substitution across	F propinquity

3. The story of Milton Humason's long career at Mount Wilson Observatory is a _______ one; from his humble beginnings as a janitor without a high school diploma, let alone a PhD, he went on to make several important cosmological discoveries alongside legendary astronomer Edwin Hubble.

   (A) trivial
   (B) succinct
   (C) singular
   (D) quotidian
   (E) ludicrous

4. Cooper believes that his latest novel presents a very charming story. Notwithstanding this appraisal, he feels this novel is a less _______ work than his more profound earlier novels.

   (A) innovative
   (B) superficial
   (C) delightful
   (D) fanciful
   (E) insightful

5. The conclusion of a tour that had taken the singer to five continents over the course of a year invoked feelings of both (i) _______ and (ii) _______. Despite her disappointment that she would not be performing for her fans for a long time, she was (iii) _______ about the prospect of spending more time with her young children.

Blank (i)	Blank (ii)	Blank (iii)
A dolor	D listlessness	G jubilant
B complaisance	E quiescence	H rueful
C lethargy	F felicity	I apathetic

6. Despite the team owner's (i) _______ comments following the team's final game, many fans became (ii) _______, exacerbating a situation that was already (iii) _______ for the coaching staff.

Blank (i)	Blank (ii)	Blank (iii)
A unrepentant	D highly incensed	G parlous
B conciliatory	E less critical	H inconsequential
C impudent	F more accepting	I amenable

Questions 7 and 8 are based on the following passage.

The psychoactive herb salvia has garnered a great deal of attention for its use among adolescents. Thousands of online videos have sprung up of teenagers filming their hallucinogenic experiences. Most of this footage is uninspired: it shows the subjects losing focus for approximately seven to ten minutes, followed by enthusiastic claims regarding the transformative experience they underwent. These videos serve to compound parents' fear of neurological damage with the more real horrors of compromised personal privacy, documentation of potentially illegal activities, and a seemingly open invitation to online predators.

7. The author would most likely agree with which of the following sentences?

    Ⓐ Salvia is a highly dangerous and addictive substance that causes neurological damage.
    Ⓑ An important protection for our young people is to regulate herbal substances such as salvia.
    Ⓒ Online video sites should require people posting videos of themselves using salvia to prove they are 18 or older.
    Ⓓ People who post salvia videos should be more explicit about the hallucinations they experienced when they come out of the high.
    Ⓔ The videos of teenagers using salvia exemplify multiple concerns faced by today's parents.

Consider each of the following choices separately and select all that apply.

8. Which of the following statements is suggested by the passage?

    [A] The effects of smoking salvia are short-lived, but intense.
    [B] Posting a public video of oneself engaging in the use of mind-altering substances is a cry for help.
    [C] Young people who expose their private drug use could open themselves to being targeted by pushers of more dangerous drugs.

Questions 9 is based on the following passage.

According to recent research, during the final days of planet formation but before planets had fully formed, planetesimals, which were itinerant objects as large as Pluto, may have collided with Earth, Mars, and the moon. It is hypothesized that they deposited siderophiles (elements such as gold, platinum, and palladium) into Earth's crust. Siderophiles are typically drawn to iron, which forms much of the inner core of Earth. Logically, during planet formation, most of these elements would have been drawn into the center of Earth; however, their abundance in Earth's crust has long perplexed scientists. These collisions may also have caused Earth's axis to tilt by 10 degrees and deposited water on the moon.

9. Based on the information in the passage, which of the following best describes planetesimals?

   (A) Free-roaming proto-planets
   (B) Planets that collided with Earth and bounced out of the galaxy
   (C) Objects embedded in Earth's crust
   (D) Highly magnetic bodies that helped form planets
   (E) Large rocks composed of siderophiles

Question 10 is based on the following passage.

Attempts to blame the mayor's policies for the growing inequality of wages are misguided. The sharp growth in the gap in earnings between college and high school graduates in this city during the past decade resulted from overall technological trends that favored the skills of more educated workers. The mayor's response to this problem cannot be criticized, as it would hardly be reasonable to expect her to attempt to slow the forces of technology.

10. Which of the following, if true, casts the most serious doubt on the conclusion drawn in the last sentence in the passage?

   (A) The mayor could have initiated policies that would have made it easier for less-educated workers to receive the education necessary for better-paying jobs.
   (B) Rather than cutting the education budget, the mayor could have increased the amount of staff and funding devoted to locating employment for graduating high school seniors.
   (C) The mayor could have attempted to generate more demand for products from industries that paid high blue-collar wages.
   (D) Instead of reducing the tax rate on the wealthiest earners, the mayor could have ensured that they shouldered a greater share of the total tax burden.
   (E) The mayor could have attempted to protect the earnings of city workers by instituting policies designed to reduce competition from foreign industries.

Directions: Select the two answer choices that, when inserted into the sentence, fit the meaning of the sentence as a whole and yield complete sentences that are similar in meaning.

11. The scientist has a reputation for writing on topics that are far beyond the understanding of most people, including other scientists, but her latest book is surprisingly not ________.

    [A] recondite
    [B] cogent
    [C] abstruse
    [D] clear
    [E] erratic
    [F] lucid

12. As an analyst, Nizar had a reputation for working harmoniously with the rest of the staff. However, when he was promoted to management, he quickly developed a ________ relationship with his employees.

    [A] contentious
    [B] belligerent
    [C] audacious
    [D] courteous
    [E] deferential
    [F] decorous

13. If medical researchers can determine precisely which symptoms are typical in people suffering from this disease, they may be able to identify those pharmaceutical interventions and alternative treatment modalities that are likely to ________ the effects of this condition.

    [A] proscribe
    [B] mitigate
    [C] sully
    [D] supplant
    [E] augment
    [F] palliate

14. In popular culture, the field of archaeology is often depicted as a hunt for lost treasure, full of excitement and adventure. This is _______ by the reality of the profession; an archaeologist is more likely to spend hours painstakingly excavating artifacts at a dig site than to run through the jungle dodging arrows.

  A belied
  B belayed
  C conveyed
  D corroborated
  E refuted
  F buttressed

Question 15 is based on the following passage.

Jean Sibelius's Symphony No. 8 has been the source of controversy and rumor for decades. A towering figure in his native Finland, the world-renowned composer worked on the piece for about a decade following the mid-1920s, but he destroyed the primary score around the end of the Second World War. Although Sibelius claimed periodically that he was continuing to work on the symphony, he refused to release it to the public in any form, and nothing but short fragments, probably sketches he drafted as he initially conceived the work, have ever been identified among his archived manuscripts. The symphony has long been considered completely lost, although some experts have suggested that someday it may be possible to reconstruct the entire work through interpolation, allowing it to be performed. Indeed, excerpts have already been recorded. Others say that, given the nature of the surviving fragments and Sibelius's own actions, this course is undesirable, since the composer suppressed the release of a work he clearly would have viewed as inferior.

15. Based on the passage, which of the following does the author believe to be true about Symphony No. 8 by Jean Sibelius?

  (A) Its publication in its entirety would ensure the international reputation of its composer.
  (B) Sibelius claimed he was working on the symphony even when he was not.
  (C) The work was never published in Sibelius's lifetime because the composer felt it lacked merit.
  (D) The symphony will someday be performed once experts have been able to reconstruct it.
  (E) If a complete copy of the symphony were discovered, it would be found to be an inferior work.

Question 16 is based on the following passage.

The word *atom* is derived from the Greek *atomos*, meaning "uncuttable," and was popularized by Democritus as a fundamental, indivisible building block of natural matter around the turn of the 4th century BCE. Although other philosophers across the world developed similar theories, it was not until the turn of the 19th century that the existence of atoms was definitively proved by science. However, at the turn of the 20th century, J.J. Thompson demonstrated the existence of subatomic particles, and these were in turn found to be reducible into elementary (or fundamental) particles. These discoveries, dividing what was previously considered indivisible, have revolutionized physics and spawned a number of subfields. In 2010, the Large Hadron Collider (a hadron being a type of subatomic particle) gained international attention for creating the highest-energy man-made particle collisions. It is the hope of particle physicists that experiments using the collider will be able to shed light on a number of fundamental questions about the laws of nature.

16. Which of the following statements is NOT supported by the passage?

- (A) The theory of atoms was proposed long before it was proved.
- (B) The hadron is not the smallest type of particle.
- (C) Students of particle physics hope to answer questions about the laws of nature.
- (D) The atom was first discovered by Democritus.
- (E) The theory of atoms was proposed by multiple philosophers.

Questions 17–20 are based on the following passage.

Cinematic renditions of historic pieces of literature provide an informative glimpse into the cultural and social context in which the films were made. Shakespeare's *Henry V* is a prime example, as it has been in circulation within the English-speaking world for over 400 years and has been reinterpreted in a number of different milieus. Since the source material has not changed, the way in which different artists and directors treat the play indicates not only the predispositions of the interpreter, but also the prevailing social and political views of the audience. This is acutely noticeable in a play like *Henry V*, which is highly charged with nationalistic concerns.

The play was written during the reign of Elizabeth I, when English national identity (and the modern English language) had begun to crystallize and the language and culture we know today approached their present form. It is a historical biography of King Henry V of England, who waged a bloody campaign during The Hundred Years War with the aim of conquering France. The introduction of the play features an adviser to the King explaining, in a confusing and nearly incomprehensible fashion, the justification for Henry's claim to the French throne. The text of the play itself has been interpreted as being ambiguous in its treatment of Henry's character. Henry has a number of rousing, heroic speeches, but he is also shown to be coldly unmerciful, as in the case of his refusal to pardon petty thieves.

Shakespeare's play has been adapted in two famous film versions. The first, directed by Laurence Olivier, was made during the Second World War, immediately before the invasion of Normandy was launched in 1944. Critics of the film have emphasized the pageantry, bravado, and nationalistic undertones of this version. The battle scenes in the film are understated and tame, with little of the carnage that would be expected of a medieval melee. They are shot in beautiful weather, and the actors are clad in radiant colors. The scene with Henry's harsh justice is omitted. The film was funded, in part, by the British government and is widely understood to have been intended as a propaganda film, made in anticipation of D-day. The second version, directed by Kenneth Branagh, was made in 1989, only a few years after the Falklands War, and was much harsher in tone. The battle scenes are gory and are shot in gray, dismal weather. The actors wear muddy, blood-smeared costumes reflective of the period. The scene with Henry's harsh justice is included.

17. The primary purpose of this passage is to

   (A) describe Shakespeare's *Henry V.*
   (B) denounce the intrusion of government involvement with the arts.
   (C) describe cinematic interpretation of literature.
   (D) teach the reader about cinematic versions of theater.
   (E) explain the effect of contemporary situations upon interpretation of literature.

Consider each of the following choices separately and select all that apply.

18. The author would most likely agree with which of the following?

    [A] Original works of art are more reflective of their societal contexts than are cinematic adaptations of such works.
    [B] Contemporary events influence the adaptation of historical source material.
    [C] War is likely to produce good cinema.

19. Which of the following most accurately describes the relationship between the highlighted sentences?

    (A) The first is an example of an argument; the second is a counterexample.
    (B) The first is a synthesis of disparate ideas; the second is one of the components of that synthesis.
    (C) The first is the topic of the passage; the second is an argument in support of it.
    (D) The first presents an assertion; the second provides an example to support that assertion.
    (E) The first is a thesis; the second is the antithesis.

20. It can be inferred that the author

    (A) regards texts as being open to interpretation.
    (B) prefers the Olivier version.
    (C) dislikes Henry.
    (D) prefers Branagh's version.
    (E) believes directors should remain as faithful to the original as possible.

VERBAL REASONING PRACTICE SET 1 ANSWER KEY

1. **A, F**
2. **A, D**
3. **C**
4. **E**
5. **A, F, G**
6. **B, D, G**
7. **E**
8. **A**
9. **A**
10. **A**
11. **A, C**
12. **A, B**
13. **B, F**
14. **A, E**
15. **B**
16. **D**
17. **E**
18. **B**
19. **D**
20. **A**

VERBAL REASONING PRACTICE SET 1 ANSWERS AND EXPLANATIONS

1. A, F

There are no obvious road signs here, so read the sentence carefully for clues to the blanks. The first sentence explains that cultural norms, or what a society views as acceptable, evolve over time. The two blanks describe two different views of the same piece of art, and each blank describes a different extreme, as indicated by "inordinately" ("exceeding limits") and "utterly" ("to the highest degree"). Note that there's no way to tell which way the views evolved; they may have gone from acceptable to unacceptable, or vice versa. You'll have to consider both blanks to find words with the appropriate relationship. The only words that fit are **(A)** *salacious*, which means "morally offensive" or "indecent," and **(F)** *pedestrian*, which in this context means "commonplace" or "mundane." Taken together, they describe how a work of art can at one point be seen as shocking but later be seen as ordinary.

(B) *adequate* doesn't fit with "inordinately." It's not possible to be extremely adequate—something either is or is not adequate. **(C)** *trite* means "boring" or "unoriginal." This could potentially fit as one part of the comparison, but there's no appropriately contrasting word for the second blank. **(D)** *pensive* means "thoughtful," and **(E)** *opulent* means "lavish" or "luxurious"; neither of these fits into the context of art and cultural norms, and neither contrasts with a choice for the first blank.

2. A, D

Each blank here is supported by several clues, so start with whichever one you feel more comfortable with. The first blank says something about recipes for beef brisket. The opening clause of the sentence indicates that these recipes "vary widely," and the detour road sign "but" means the blank will be the opposite of that—a word to indicate what they have in common. *Similarity* would be a good prediction. **(A)** *affinity*, or "close resemblance," is a perfect match, so it's the right answer for the first blank. **(B)** *variance* means "difference," so it's the opposite of what you're looking for. **(C)** *substitution* might be tempting because it's a word often used in cooking; if you're out of one ingredient, you'd substitute another. However, it doesn't fit the context here, since the sentence is describing a technique different preparations share, not one that replaces another.

The second blank describes why the "low and slow" technique is used. The first clause says that it's "not a matter of taste but . . . ," a detour construction, so the missing word must contrast with the idea that the cooking method is simply a personal preference. After a semicolon, which functions as a straight-ahead road sign here, the sentence indicates that without this method, the meat would be "too tough" to eat. Since cooking food in a way that makes it inedible defeats the purpose, predict something like *necessity*. **(D)** *prerequisite*, or "something that is necessary," matches this prediction, so it's the correct answer. **(E)** *predilection* means "a liking for," which would fit if the cooking method were just a matter of taste. **(F)** *propinquity*, which means "a closeness or similarity to," does not fit the context.

3. C

The blank in this sentence describes the Humason's career, which is described after the semicolon. He started as a janitor without a formal education and ended up working alongside a "legendary" scientist, so a good prediction would be something like *remarkable*. **(C)** *singular* means exactly that—in this context, "unusual" or "exceptional"—so it's correct. **(A)** *trivial* means "unimportant." This is incorrect as there's no basis for saying the story of Humason's life is not important; if anything, the opposite is true. **(B)** *succinct* means "brief" or "concise." There's no indication that the story is short; indeed, it would be hard to tell the story of such a long and varied career in a concise manner. **(D)** *quotidian*, meaning "commonplace," is the opposite of what's needed. **(E)** *ludicrous* means "ridiculous" or "absurd," which is much too negative to fit the sentence.

4. E

The first sentence presents a positive opinion Cooper has about his new novel: it is "charming." But "[n]otwithstanding" is a detour road sign that indicates Cooper feels his new novel compares poorly to his earlier novels. Specifically, those books were "more profound" than the latest work, in Cooper's estimation. Note the detour road sign "less" before the blank and predict a positive word with a somewhat similar meaning as *profound*. *Insightful*, **(E)**, matches the prediction and is correct. Nothing in the text points to the new work being less *innovative*, **(A)**, than the others, as a story that is not particularly "profound" might still be "inventive." If anything, the new book is more *superficial* than the earlier, "more profound" ones, so eliminate **(B)**. Since the latest novel is described as having a "charming story," it would not make sense to say it is less *delightful*, **(C)**. There is no information in the text about how *fanciful*, **(D)**, or "imaginary or whimsical," the new work is, so eliminate this choice as well.

5. A, F, G

Based on the first sentence alone, it is not possible to predict accurately for the first two blanks. The tour's end could lead to a variety of emotions. The second sentence, however, begins with a detour road sign, "[d]espite," and contrasts the singer's "disappointment" with what she felt about spending more time with her children. Predict that she was *relieved* or *happy* to see more of her family. *Jubilant*, **(G)**, means "very happy" and is correct. *Rueful*, **(H)**, means "regretful" and is the opposite of what you need. *Apathetic*, **(I)**, means "lacking in care or interest." This also runs counter to the prediction.

Now you know that she felt both "disappointment" and happiness. For the first two blanks, predict that one emotion is positive and the other is negative and find a pair of words that match this dual prediction. For the first blank, *dolor*, **(A)**, means "sadness." For the second blank, *felicity*, **(F)**, means "happiness." These two words work together to complete the sentence logically and are the correct answers. *Complaisance*, **(B)**, means "eagerness to please others," and *lethargy*, **(C)**, means "sluggishness" or "drowsiness." *Listlessness*, **(D)**, is similar in meaning to *lethargy*, signifying "lacking energy or spirit." *Quiescence*, **(E)**, means "being at rest" or "in a state of inactivity."

6. B, D, G

Sometimes it is easier to start with the second or third blank. In the last part of the sentence, you have the key word "exacerbating," which means "making worse." The situation that the coaching staff is in, therefore, is bad and becoming worse. For the third blank, predict *bad* or *risky*. *Parlous*, **(G)**, which means "dangerous," provides the right meaning and is correct. *Inconsequential*, **(H)**, means "insignificant," and *amenable*, **(I)**, means "agreeable." Neither choice matches the prediction.

Working your way backward, consider the second blank, which describes the fans who are putting the coaches at risk. *Angry* is a good prediction, and *highly incensed*, **(D)**, means "very upset." *Less critical*, **(E)**, and *more accepting*, **(F)**, are both contrary to the prediction and would not explain why the situation was being exacerbated.

The detour road sign "[d]espite" sets up a contrast between the team owner's comments and the fans' angry reaction. Predict that the coach made positive or diplomatic comments. *Conciliatory*, **(B)**, means "appeasing" or "attempting to reconcile." One who is *conciliatory* would try to make the fans less angry, making **(B)** correct. If the owner made *unrepentant* comments, as in **(A)**, she would fail to express regret or take responsibility for the situation the fans are angry about, and such comments would be expected to make them more angry. *Impudent*, **(C)**, meaning "rude" or "insulting," is also the opposite of the prediction.

7. E

In this Inference question, you are asked to identify the statement that follows from the author's point of view as it's expressed in the passage. The author offers two opinionated statements. He finds the video footage "uninspired" and states that it "serve(s) to compound" parental fears. One of those two statements will be paraphrased in the correct answer. The claim in **(A)** is not actually made in the passage. The author suggests that parents may fear possible neurological damage from salvia but suggests that the other "horrors" are "more real," undermining this statement. Choices **(B)** and **(C)** both go beyond the scope of the passage; the author stops short of recommending solutions for the salvia problem. You can also dismiss choice **(D)** because, although the author does intimate that the videos are rather dull, there is no evidence that the author wants more detail about the experience. Choice **(E)** matches your prediction. It is strongly suggested in the passage's final sentence and therefore is the correct answer.

8. A

Here is another Inference question, this time with the potential for multiple correct answers. You can infer choice **(A)** because the text states that the "spaced out" part only lasts a few minutes but that the experience is intense enough that young people describe it in great detail. There is no evidence for choice **(B)**; the author doesn't opine on the psychological state of salvia users. Choice **(C)** is not suggested by the passage; "online predators," not "drug pushers," are cited as the threat, and salvia is not compared to other drugs.

9. A

Though it is not explicitly stated in the passage, you can, from a few clues, determine that a planetesimal was (1) an object that moved—a sort of wandering body—since they are described as "itinerant," and (2) an object that existed during "planet formation." Choice **(A)** follows from those two inferences and is correct. There is no support for choice **(B)**; the passage makes no mention of objects leaving or bouncing out of the galaxy. You can eliminate choice **(C)** because the passage tells you that components of the planetesimals (the siderophiles) remained in Earth's crust after impact but doesn't say that whole planetesimals did so. Choice **(D)** is beyond the scope of the passage, which doesn't contain information about planetesimals' magnetic characteristics. You can also cross off **(E)** because the passage doesn't describe planetesimals as "rocks," nor does it claim that they are always made up of (or necessarily even contain) siderophiles.

10. A

When asked to cast doubt on a conclusion, as you are here, first locate the author's conclusion. Then, find an answer choice that contradicts it in some way. This question stem explicitly directs you to the last sentence of the passage, where the author is defending the mayor from criticism, asserting that the growing inequality of wages is beyond her control. Since the passage is saying, "This isn't the mayor's fault," predict a correct answer that says, "No, this *is* the mayor's fault."

Choice **(A)** should stand out immediately as going against the passage. If the mayor *could* have initiated policies that would have educated those who are now earning less, then her policies—to be precise, her policy of inaction—*is* at least partially to blame for the problem of wage inequality. This is exactly the sort of additional evidence you want, and choice **(A)** is correct.

The wrong choices largely focus on misleading shifts in terminology from the passage. Choice **(B)** sidesteps the wage issue, as more employment of high school graduates would not necessarily raise their wages. Choice **(C)**'s logic requires that we assume "blue-collar" equals "less-educated," which is too large a shift in terminology. Choice **(D)** only discusses taxes and avoids wages altogether. Choice **(E)** only mentions protection of "city workers," again avoiding the education issue from the passage.

11. A, C

The scientist is known for writing on topics that most people can't understand. The clause with the blank has three detour road signs, so untangle it carefully. "But" and "surprisingly" indicate a contrast between the scientist's previous writings and her latest book, which must therefore be easier to understand. Be careful with the word "not" just before the blank: predict that the scientist's latest book is *not* as hard to understand. Thus, you need two words that mean "hard to understand." *Recondite*, **(A)**, means "hard to understand," as does *abstruse*, **(C)**. *Cogent*, **(B)**, means "convincing and well reasoned," but a book that is *cogent* may or may not be difficult to understand. **(D)** *clear* is the opposite of the prediction, as is **(F)** *lucid*, which also means "clear." *Erratic*, **(E)**, doesn't match the prediction either; nothing in the context indicates that the scientist's work is "unpredictable."

12. A, B

The first sentence tells you that Nizar had a good working relationship with the staff when he was an analyst. "However" is a detour road sign, indicating that when Nizar was promoted, his relationship with the staff became the opposite of "harmonious." *Contentious*, **(A)**, means "quarrelsome" or "argumentative" and matches the prediction, as does *belligerent*, **(B)**, which means "hostile" or "antagonistic." *Audacious*, **(C)**, means "bold" or "daring," which does not work in the blank. *Courteous*, **(D)**, and *deferential*, **(E)**, both mean "respectful," and *decorous*, **(F)**, means "behaving with propriety" or "polite." All three would align with a harmonious relationship rather than the one Nizar had after his promotion.

13. B, F

The word "[i]f" sets up a straight-ahead relationship between the first clause and the second. Since researchers are trying to figure out what symptoms are associated with this disease, they are likely seeking to help people with the condition. They could do this either by finding out which treatments work and should be used or which treatments do not work and should be avoided. The neutral word "identify" doesn't tell you which meaning the author is conveying, so look for a pair of words that either both mean "lessen" or "ease" the bad results of the condition or mean "increase" or "make worse." As it happens, **(B)** and **(F)** are a match with one of the predictions and with each other. **(B)** is correct because *mitigate* means to "make less severe," and *palliate*, **(F)**, means "to provide relief from." *Proscribe*, **(A)**, means to "banish" or "denounce." While health care providers and their patients would undoubtedly like to "banish" symptoms of the disease, that is a legal remedy, not a medical one. *Sully*, **(C)**, means to "make dirty or stain," and *supplant*, **(D)**, means to "take the place of." Neither choice matches the predictions. *Augment*, **(E)**, means "make greater" and does not have a match among the other choices.

14. A, E

The first sentence describes the fictional portrayal of archaeology; the second describes "the reality." The word in the blank will convey the relationship between the two. Fictional archaeology is said to be full of "excitement and adventure" and "dodging arrows," while the real thing is full of "painstaking" ("meticulous or thorough") work. Thus, a good prediction would be that reality *contradicts* the fictional view. **(A)** *belied* and **(E)** *refuted* both mean "disproved" or "showed to be false," so they're the correct answers. **(B)** *belayed* may sound similar to *belied*, but it has a different meaning; it can mean either "secured a rope" or "canceled an order." **(C)** *conveyed* ("imparted" or "communicated") is too neutral to fit. **(D)** *corroborated* and **(F)** *buttressed* are both the opposite of what's needed, as each means "supported with evidence."

15. B

The author states that "[a]lthough Sibelius claimed" to be working on the symphony, neither contemporaries nor later music experts examining his papers have ever seen it. The author's contrast of Sibelius's claim with evidence to the contrary allows you to infer that the author believes the composer was not in fact working on the piece. The correct answer is **(B)**. The author states that Sibelius already has an international reputation, so Symphony No. 8 is not needed to establish one, and **(A)** is incorrect. **(C)** and **(E)** are the opinion of the "[o]thers" mentioned in the last sentence, not the author. Likewise, while "experts" believe the symphony may be performed someday, the author expresses no opinion on this, so **(D)** is incorrect.

16. D

The correct answer to this question is *not* supported in the passage, meaning it either contradicts the passage or falls outside the scope. The four wrong answers *are* supported. The first two sentences of the passage describe the origin of the theory of atoms prior to their scientific discovery, which allows you to eliminate choice **(A)**; furthermore, the author mentions that "philosophers across the world developed similar theories," which supports—and thus eliminates—choice **(E)**. However, the author describes Democritus as having "popularized" the theory of atoms, which is not the same as first discovering the atom; based on this, choice **(D)** is correct. Choices **(B)** and **(C)** both relate to the discussion of subatomic particles, but because elementary particles are smaller than subatomic particles (an example of the latter being the hadron), you may eliminate **(B)**. The conclusion of the passage rules out choice **(C)** in the description of the importance of experiments using the Large Hadron Collider.

17. E

The correct answer to a primary purpose question summarizes what the author is trying to do in the passage. Here, the author uses cinematic depictions of *Henry V* to illustrate how contemporary culture influences the interpretation of art. Choice **(A)** misses the point; the author uses Shakespeare's *Henry V* as an illustration, not for the purpose of describing the play itself. **(B)** distorts the author's purpose, which is to illustrate the cultural influence, not to judge which influences are positive or negative. **(C)** is too broad; the passage isn't about cinematic interpretations of literature writ large. **(D)** is too general in the same way as choice **(C)**. So, choice **(E)** is the correct answer. It cites the effect of contemporary situations on the interpretation of literature, striking at the heart of what the author explores in the passage.

18. B

Questions of this type have three options, but any or all of them could be correct. You can't stop when you come across one correct answer. Evaluate the choices in light of this author's scope and purpose. Choice **(A)** makes an irrelevant comparison. The author discusses the influence of historical and societal context on both Shakespeare's play and the later film adaptations of it but never implies that one is more reflective of its societal context than the other. Choice **(B)** is correct; this paraphrases the author's primary purpose, so he's certain to agree with it. Choice **(C)** is incorrect. The author makes no effort to argue about what makes *good* cinema, only what influences it when it's involved in interpreting classic literary works.

19. D

Questions of this type reward you for understanding the logic of a passage. In this case, the first highlighted sentence is an assertion that lays out the topic and scope of the passage. The second highlighted sentence is a specific example that the author offers to illustrate his main point. Choice **(D)**, the correct answer, hits this prediction squarely. Choice **(A)** is incorrect because the second sentence does not contradict the first. You can reject **(B)** as it mischaracterizes the first sentence; there is nothing disparate about its components. You can reject **(C)** because it gets the second sentence wrong; the second sentence is an example, not an argument (which would need a conclusion supported by evidence). Choice **(E)** distorts the relationship between the two sentences; the second doesn't contradict the first.

20. A

This is another question that asks you to put yourself in the author's shoes and try to reason from his perspective. The tone of the passage is neutral; even when describing Henry's darker moments, the author passes no judgment. You can therefore reject choice **(C)**, as the author is not doing a character study. Though choices **(B)** and **(D)** are mutually exclusive, they are both incorrect. The author states no preference for either of the film versions he describes. Choice **(E)** is incorrect because the author states no preference for cinematic versions that maintain greater fidelity to the source material. Choice **(A)** is correct; it matches the author's purpose for the passage. In order for cultural events to influence the interpretation of classic literature, such literature must be interpretable.

DIAGNOSE YOUR RESULTS

Diagnostic Tool

Tally up your score and write your results in the space provided.

Total

Total Correct: ________ out of 20 correct

Percentage Correct: # you got right × 100 ÷ 20: ________

By Question Type

Text Completion ________ out of 6 correct

Sentence Equivalence ________ out of 4 correct

Reading Comprehension ________ out of 10 correct

Look back at the questions you got wrong and think about your experience answering them.

VERBAL REASONING PRACTICE SET 2

Directions: For each sentence, choose one word for each set of blanks. Select the word or words that best fit(s) the meaning of the sentence as a whole.

1. Many felt the rules for the scholarship competition had been unfairly administered to the applicant pool and that, furthermore, the judges were ________.

   Ⓐ biased
   Ⓑ adequate
   Ⓒ inept
   Ⓓ impartial
   Ⓔ objective

2. We will face the idea of old age with ________ as long as we believe that it invariably brings poverty, isolation, and illness.

   Ⓐ regret
   Ⓑ apprehension
   Ⓒ enlightenment
   Ⓓ veneration
   Ⓔ reverence

3. Usually an articulate speaker, as he had given many public addresses over the years, the doctor (i) ________ the keynote speech at the oncology convention. It was clear from their expressions that the audience members were overcome with (ii) ________ by the end.

Blank (i)	Blank (ii)
A flubbed	D rapture
B perfected	E repulsion
C rescinded	F bewilderment

4. The author's agent approached the contract signing with (i) ________, as she knew full well the reputation of the publisher. The author, finally recognized after years of rejection, was more (ii) ________ by the event.

Blank (i)	
A	incertitude
B	hubris
C	cordiality

Blank (ii)	
D	enraptured
E	humiliated
F	mortified

5. The hikers were eager to summit Mount Everest and (i) ________ warnings about the dangerous storm approaching the camp. It was only when disaster struck that the (ii) ________ of the situation took hold. By this time, however, the descent was (iii) ________, and the survivors fought for their lives.

Blank (i)	
A	recollected
B	scrutinized
C	flouted

Blank (ii)	
D	gravity
E	hypocrisy
F	prestige

Blank (iii)	
G	galvanizing
H	fortuitous
I	baleful

6. The fact that Mark Twain gave orders for his memoir to remain unpublished for 100 years reflects the author's (i) ________ about its contents. Indeed, releasing his more (ii) ________ observations about the world during his own time would have spurred a public response, one that Twain must have foreseen as (iii) ________.

Blank (i)	
A	trepidation
B	buoyancy
C	insouciance

Blank (ii)	
D	quixotic
E	utopian
F	vitriolic

Blank (iii)	
G	enigmatic
H	detrimental
I	salubrious

Questions 7 and 8 are based on the following passage.

Pancreatic beta cells are responsible within a body for monitoring homeostatic cues from a wide variety of hormonal inputs and in turn regulate the insulin needed to maintain balance in the blood sugar. Researchers studying this signaling system have located three key proteins that relay signals. Understanding how these proteins function within the context of the signaling system can help scientists gain more insight into how diabetes compromises the healthy functioning of the system and how to counteract the impact of diabetes once it is identified.

7. The passage implies which of the following about diabetes research?

   (A) When scientists fully understand how these key proteins work, rates of Type II diabetes will be greatly reduced.
   (B) Researchers hope to understand the signaling system of pancreatic beta cells in order to replicate an artificial system.
   (C) Without a complete understanding of these key proteins, diabetes research is at a standstill.
   (D) Future medications for diabetes may include or simulate some of the hormonal cues that pancreatic beta cells monitor.
   (E) One way researchers hope to fight diabetes is by stopping the relay signal system in the pancreas by cutting off the proteins.

8. According to the passage, each of the following is true EXCEPT:

   (A) The pancreas helps a body to maintain homeostasis.
   (B) Diabetes controls the functioning of pancreatic beta cells.
   (C) When the pancreas is stimulated, it releases varying amounts of insulin that help to balance blood sugar.
   (D) Pancreatic beta cells must interpret a wide array of hormonal information.
   (E) Blood sugar can be controlled by insulin.

Question 9 is based on the following passage.

Named after the notorious confidence trickster Charles Ponzi (though not originated by him), the term "Ponzi scheme" describes a particular type of fraud in which individual investors are promised extremely high returns, which are then paid either out of their own money or the money of other investors, creating the appearance of an extremely profitable investment. The entire scheme relies on encouraging investors to donate large amounts of money long-term by offering them the enticement of impossibly high short-term returns. As time progresses, investors who have been paid returns contribute even more money, and new investors are drawn into the scheme. New payments are used to pay off new investors. Excess money is then kept as profit for the creator of the fraud, rather than to create any tangible profits for the investment itself.

9. According to the passage, which is necessary for a Ponzi scheme to be successful?

 (A) Investors should be tempted into long-term investment by large initial returns.
 (B) The investment plan should demonstrate sustainability over the long term.
 (C) The percentage of the investment's profits going to the creator of the scam should be concealed.
 (D) There should be no paper trails of the fraud.
 (E) The culpability for the fraud should be shared among the confidence trickster and investors.

Question 10 is based on the following passage.

Hay-on-Wye is a small town in Wales, just over the border from England. While once a relatively unknown town, the town rose to fame in the second half of the 20th century as a literary hot spot. Influenced by Richard Booth's opening of a secondhand bookshop in a converted fire station, a number of other entrepreneurs followed suit, until the tiny town held over 30 used bookshops; by the 1970s, it became known around the world as the "Town of Books." Aided by Booth's publicity efforts, Hay-on-Wye was turned from a sleepy market town with fewer than 2,000 inhabitants to a thriving tourist destination. The town now boasts half a million tourists per year and hosts a popular annual literary festival. Booth himself was inducted into the Order of the British Empire for his efforts to encourage tourism.

10. Which of the following is the primary purpose of the passage?

 (A) To argue for the importance of secondhand bookshops
 (B) To describe the life of Richard Booth
 (C) To explain the development of Hay-on-Wye as a literary center
 (D) To highlight Richard Booth's publicity efforts to encourage tourism
 (E) To depict the town of Hay-on-Wye

Directions: Select the two answer choices that, when inserted into the sentence, fit the meaning of the sentence as a whole and yield complete sentences that are similar in meaning.

11. Despite its ______ during its initial theatrical run, *Our American Cousin* would likely be forgotten today were it not for one eventful performance at Ford's Theatre on April 14, 1865, during which Abraham Lincoln was shot by John Wilkes Booth.

    A disfavor
    B obscurity
    C renown
    D impeccability
    E repute
    F superiority

12. After an arduous trip across the arid interior of the continent, the surveyors were visibly ______ and were in need of hydration and rest.

    A flagging
    B skittish
    C buoyant
    D sanguine
    E enervated
    F lugubrious

13. After five years of ______ attempts to get a role on a major television show, the young actor decided he would go to college and pursue a career in which success was more likely.

    A futile
    B artless
    C vain
    D bromidic
    E fortuitous
    F apathetic

14. Although his contributions to the metropolitan area are largely forgotten, Eugenius Harvey Outerbridge is commemorated in the name of the Outerbridge Crossing in New York City. He is nonetheless in danger of being forgotten, as the name is often assumed to be derived from the bridge's location in the outermost reaches of the city rather than from its _______ figure.

    A secluded
    B disparate
    C titular
    D manifold
    E eponymous
    F cloistered

Questions 15–17 are based on the following passage.

Characterized as half zebra and half horse, the quagga sounds like a mythical creature, but at one time, it was a very real animal. Only 150 years ago, a great number of quaggas were found in South Africa. Unlike the common zebra, which has black and white stripes that cover its entire body, the quagga has yellow-brown stripes only on its head, neck, and forebody, which gave it its half-horse facade. Its unique appearance caused early explorers to think the quagga was a separate species from the common zebra when it was discovered around 1760, but DNA analysis later revealed that the animal is a subspecies of the zebra. In the 100 years following its discovery, the quagga population diminished. It was frequently hunted for its meat and hide, and settlers who considered the animal a competitor for the grazing of their livestock also callously killed the quagga in great numbers. By 1870, the quagga was no longer found in the wild. The last captive quagga died in 1880 in an Amsterdam zoo. Today, the quagga is categorized as an extinct animal, but researchers in Africa hope to resurrect the native subspecies through genetic modification and selective breeding.

15. What does the author designate as the primary reason for the quagga going extinct?

    (A) DNA analysis revealed that the quagga was susceptible to diseases brought by domesticated animals.
    (B) The quagga did not have enough grazing land.
    (C) The quagga was unable to survive in captivity.
    (D) Settlers eliminated the species through hunting and extermination.
    (E) The quagga did not breed as successfully as the common zebra.

16. With which of the following statements would the author of the passage most likely agree?

    (A) The zebra is a type of quagga.
    (B) Researchers hope to restore the quagga using scientific technology.
    (C) Settlers humanely killed quaggas in an effort to protect their livestock.
    (D) Shortly after the quagga was discovered, its population grew.
    (E) Settlers saw the quagga as a competitor for the prey of their livestock.

Consider each of the following choices separately and select all that apply.

17. Based on the information in the passage, which conclusion can be drawn?

    [A] If it were not for the human influence, the quagga would be a surviving species.
    [B] DNA analysis can help humans better understand the origins of certain species.
    [C] The extinction of species should not be a concern as scientists are able to bring back extinct species through genetic modification.

Questions 18–20 are based on the following passage.

According to a recent survey from the National Institute for Drug Abuse, more U.S. adolescents smoke marijuana than smoke cigarettes. The organization's annual survey revealed an increase in marijuana use among all teen groups and a slight decrease in tobacco use among high-school seniors compared to past years. Federal officials speculate that teens are starting to listen to the warnings about the risks of tobacco use but are receiving mixed messages about the safety of marijuana use. While antidrug organizations such as Drug-Free America maintain their message that marijuana impairs judgment and hampers brain development, clinical studies support the medicinal benefits of marijuana, particularly for those suffering from certain cancers and Crohn's disease. These studies have sparked a national debate about the legalization of marijuana. More than a dozen states and the District of Columbia have legalized the use of medical marijuana, and there is a push for the nationwide legalization of the drug. The White House Office of National Drug Control Policy asserts that the message that marijuana use is okay for some is dangerous. The office insists that both policy makers and the general public should be aware of the effect the debate over the legalization of marijuana has on teens' perception of the drug's risk.

18. The passage implies which of the following about teen drug use?

    Ⓐ The Office of National Drug Control is concerned about teen tobacco use.
    Ⓑ Marijuana has many health benefits for teens.
    Ⓒ Teens are aware of health risks associated with smoking.
    Ⓓ Drug-Free America suspects that teen marijuana use will continue to rise.
    Ⓔ Teens support legislation to legalize marijuana.

19. The passage predicts which of the following would follow the legalization of marijuana?

    Ⓐ It may increase the use of illegal street drugs.
    Ⓑ It may decrease the frequency of teen tobacco use.
    Ⓒ It may cause teens to believe that marijuana use is harmless.
    Ⓓ It may change antidrug organizations' stance on the drug's use.
    Ⓔ It may increase the safety of the drug's use.

20. According to the passage, what is the "mixed message" that teens are receiving about marijuana?

    Ⓐ Its use is acceptable for individuals older than age 18, but not for individuals younger than age 18.
    Ⓑ It has legitimate health benefits for the ill, but it has serious health risks.
    Ⓒ Its use is acceptable in some states, but not acceptable in other states.
    Ⓓ It is safer to use than tobacco, but it is still an unsafe drug.
    Ⓔ Its use is approved by the government, but not by teens' parents.

VERBAL REASONING PRACTICE SET 2 ANSWER KEY

1. **A**
2. **B**
3. **A, F**
4. **A, D**
5. **C, D, I**
6. **A, F, H**
7. **D**
8. **B**
9. **A**
10. **C**
11. **C, E**
12. **A, E**
13. **A, C**
14. **C, E**
15. **D**
16. **B**
17. **B**
18. **C**
19. **C**
20. **B**

VERBAL REASONING PRACTICE SET 2 ANSWERS AND EXPLANATIONS

1. A

Here, "furthermore" indicates that the charge of the word in the blank will be consistent with "unfair." Choice **(A)** *biased* is a good synonym for "unfair," and is the correct answer. Choices **(B)**, **(D)**, and **(E)** all list traits one would want in judges. Choice **(C)** *inept* provides a negative trait, but one that challenges the judges' competence, not their fairness.

2. B

First, read the sentence through, noting any structural road signs and/or key words. Here, "as long as" is a structural clue: we view old age in the same way we do poverty, isolation, and illness. Predict that the correct answer matches a word like *fear* or *despair*. Choice **(B)** *apprehension* is a good match. Check the other answers, to confirm that each is incorrect. Choice **(A)** *regret* may be tempting because of its negative connotation, but it applies to something that has already happened, not what someone will face in the future. Choice **(C)** *enlightenment* doesn't match the sentence's list of negative conditions. Choices **(D)** *veneration* and **(E)** *reverence* both mean "great respect"; that's a positive way to face old age, but not one that matches the way one would face something likely to bring "poverty, isolation, and illness." That confirms that **(B)** is the right answer. Now, plug the answer into the sentence: "We will face the idea of old age with *apprehension* as long as we believe that it invariably brings poverty, isolation, and illness." This certainly makes sense.

3. A, F

Consider the logic of the sentences before approaching the first blank. It might be tempting to choose a positive word, but the structure and tone suggest a contrast from the "usual." It might help to put the word *while* in front of "Usually." The only word that suggests the opposite of "articulate speaker" is choice **(A)** *flubbed*, which means "to make a mess of." Choice **(B)** *perfected* means "made no errors" and choice **(C)** *rescind* means "took back." These words don't fit the context of the clause. How might an audience subjected to a flubbed speech feel? You can rule out choice **(D)** *rapture* since it means "extreme joy." That leaves choice **(E)** *repulsion*, or "disgust," and choice **(F)** *bewilderment*, or "deep confusion." Consider the shades of meaning here: the audience is not likely to respond with an emotion as strong as disgust, especially if the doctor is normally a great speaker. *Bewilderment* is correct.

4. A, D

You can infer that the author must be "happy" to be published after years of rejection, so start with the second blank. The correct answer is choice **(D)** *enraptured*, which means "full of delight." It wouldn't make sense for the author to feel **(E)** *humiliated* or **(F)** *mortified*; she's finally received some recognition, after all. Now for the first blank. The word "more" functions as a subtle detour road sign in this sentence. The author is "more" happy than the agent, so predict something like "skepticism" on the part of the agent. Only **(A)** *incertitude*, which means "uncertainty," fits this context. **(B)** *hubris* is "excessive pride in oneself" that often leads to someone's downfall;

while the agent may have been proud of the author and of herself for getting this contract, nothing in the sentence indicates this pride was excessive. At any rate, this sentence is about the contrast between the author's happiness and the agent's more skeptical perspective, not about any sense of accomplishment the agent may feel. **(C)** *cordiality*, meaning "friendliness," is too positive to work here.

5. C, D, I

The words "and," "only," and "however" are road signs that help you determine the direction of each sentence and choose the appropriate missing words. Overly eager hikers are unlikely to heed warnings, and choice **(C)** *flouted,* which means "defied" or "ignored," captures this relationship best. Neither choice **(A)** *recollected* nor **(B)** *scrutinized,* both of which suggest examining an issue, fits the context. The second blank will contain a word consistent with one's attitude after a disaster. Choice **(E)** *hypocrisy* refers to insincerity; that might describe the hikers (who'd just flouted the warnings), but not the situation they now find themselves in. Choice **(F)** *prestige*, meaning "status" or "consideration," is inappropriate to the context as well. Only choice **(D)** *gravity*, or "seriousness," makes sense here. While the descent may have been **(G)** *galvanizing*, or "exciting," on some level, it was in the context of a dire situation, so keep looking for a better choice. Choice **(H)** *fortuitous* means "lucky." (If you didn't know its definition, notice that it shares the root of "fortune.") You can infer that it doesn't fit logically in the paragraph. Something **(I)** *baleful* appears threatening, or even deadly; this is the correct answer.

6. A, F, H

To complete this sentence, look for key words or phrases that give hints about the context. For instance, "gave orders" in the first sentence indicates a strong feeling, perhaps a concern, so try to find a term that plays off this sentiment. Only choice **(A)** *trepidation*, which means "unease," supports the first sentence. Choice **(B)** *buoyancy* means "quick to recover" (think of the buoy floating in the ocean), and **(C)** *insouciance* means "lightheartedness." Both words suggest unconcern, the opposite of how Twain must have felt when ordering his memoirs to remain sealed for a century. The word in the second blank must describe writing that the author wants to keep private for a long time after his death. Choices **(D)** *quixotic* and **(E)** *utopian* have a similar meaning—"idealistic"—and neither fits the context. Choice **(F)** *vitriolic*, meaning "acidic" or "corrosive," is the best fit. For the third blank, you need a negative word. Choice **(G)** *enigmatic*, or "mysterious," doesn't make sense. Choice **(H)** *detrimental* means "damaging." That is the right answer. Finally, choice **(I)** *salubrious* means "health-promoting," which is too positive and does not fit the context.

7. D

The correct answer follows from the passage, though it may not be stated explicitly. Choice **(A)** is not implied. Although researchers probably hope to stem the occurrence of diabetes, the passage speaks only of combating the disease's impact. There is also no suggestion in the passage of the hope, expressed in choice **(B)**, of creating an artificial system. Choice **(C)** is too extreme. The passage doesn't imply a "standstill" absent "complete" understanding of the proteins. The wording in choice **(D)** is dense, but it's also broad enough to follow from the passage. Researchers may well use their understanding of the hormonal cues monitored by the proteins to develop the treatments mentioned in the final sentence of the passage. Indeed, **(D)** is the correct response. Finally, **(E)** runs counter to the passage. The researchers hope to understand how to help the relay system work, not how to cut it off. You can eliminate **(E)** confidently.

8. B

The four wrong answers to this Detail question are found in the passage. The correct answer will either contradict or distort the passage, or fall outside its scope altogether. Choice **(A)** is true; it is stated in the first sentence of the passage. Choice **(B)** seems like it might be true, but reading carefully, it overstates the role of diabetes as described in the passage: diabetes compromises or impairs the ability of the pancreatic beta cells to function, but you're not told that it *controls* those functions. Choice **(C)** is true and is also stated in the passage's first sentence. Choice **(D)** paraphrases the first main claim of the passage. Choice **(E)** comes from the end of the first sentence.

9. A

The correct answer to this Detail question must paraphrase something stated explicitly in the passage. Choice **(A)** restates the author's definition of Ponzi schemes: the use of short-term payoffs to attract long-term investments. That's the correct answer. Choice **(D)** is incorrect because the passage mentions nothing about paper trails; likewise, it does not address who should share the culpability, ruling out choice **(E)**. Choice **(C)** is initially tempting, but be careful; the final sentence of the passage explicitly states that the investment does not create any real profits, so **(C)**'s recommendations for how to divvy them up must be incorrect. Choice **(B)** is tempting because the schemes attempt to sucker investors into long-term commitments, but the schemes needn't be sustainable in any case.

10. C

By the time you begin to look at questions accompanying a passage, you should have already determined the scope and purpose of the passage. In this case, the author is purely expository; she just wants to relate or explain how Hay-on-Wye became known for books and literature. Choices **(A)**, **(B)**, and **(D)** are related to the passage's subject matter but don't describe the overall purpose of the passage. Choices **(C)** and **(E)** look relatively similar, and the fact that the passage is about Hay-on-Wye makes **(E)** tempting. But the passage focuses on a specific aspect of the town, rather than the town as a whole. This aspect is its rise to fame as the "Town of Books," and thus choice **(C)** is your answer.

11. C, E

"Despite" is a detour road sign; the blank therefore describes a quality of the play that makes it surprising that it would have been forgotten. Predict that the two correct answers will be words meaning something like "popularity." **(C)** *renown*, or "fame," matches this prediction. **(E)** *repute* is the other correct answer; as a noun, it refers to something that is "well-known" or "esteemed." **(A)** *disfavor* is the opposite of what's needed; it means "disapproval." **(B)** *obscurity* ("being unknown") is also contradicted by the sentence; if the play were obscure, it would not be unusual for it to be forgotten. **(D)** *impeccability* and **(F)** *superiority* both go too far, speaking to the quality of the play rather than how well-known it was, and there's no indication that the play is impeccable, or "flawless," or better than other plays.

12. A, E

The blank in this sentence describes the travelers after an "arduous" trip and when they needed water and rest. Predict that the surveyors were visibly *exhausted* or *weakened*. *Flagging*, **(A)**, means "weakening" or "losing energy," which works to describe the surveyors. *Enervated*, **(E)**, means "weakened" or "tired," giving the sentence the same meaning as does *flagging*. These are the correct answers. *Skittish*, **(B)**, means "shy" or "nervous." While the surveyors may have been nervous about their survival during the trip, there is no reason to think they were nervous having finished it. *Buoyant*, **(C)**, and *sanguine*, **(D)**, both mean "cheerfully optimistic." *Lugubrious*, **(F)**, means "very sad" or "mournful." None of these choices describing the surveyors' mood is supported by the context clues.

13. A, C

Since the actor decided to pursue a career in which "success was more likely," he must have failed to be cast on a major television show. Therefore, predict that the attempts were *frustrating* or *unsuccessful*. *Futile*, **(A)**, means "useless" or "ineffective." *Vain*, **(C)**, can mean "overly proud of oneself," but can also mean "useless," and that is its meaning in this context. These choices match the prediction and each other. *Artless*, **(B)**, does not mean "lacking in artistic talent"; instead, it means "free of deceit" or "genuine," which does not fit this context. *Bromidic*, **(D)**, is an uncommonly used word meaning "lacking originality"; the word *bromide* is somewhat more often used and means a "trite or tired expression." At any rate, there is no indication that this actor lacks originality. *Fortuitous*, **(E)**, means "lucky," and *apathetic*, **(F)**, means "lacking emotion." If the actor were lucky, he would have gotten the role he wanted, and if he felt nothing about acting, he would not have pursued it for five years.

14. C, E

The first sentence describes Eugenius Outerbridge, who is only remembered in the name of a bridge, and the second sentence says that he may yet be forgotten. The word in the blank describes Outerbridge in relation to the bridge; since it was named after him, a good prediction would be *namesake*. **(C)** *titular* means "something from which a title was taken." For example, the titular character of a book is one who appears in the book's title (as in *Tess of the d'Urbervilles* or *Harry Potter and the Philosopher's Stone*), so this is a good match for the prediction. **(E)** *eponymous* refers to "something from which a name is derived," so it's another match for the prediction.

(A) *secluded* and **(F)** *cloistered* both mean "hidden" or "isolated." These words might describe the bridge, but the blank relates to Outerbridge. **(B)** *disparate* means "distinct" or "different." There's nothing in this sentence to support this idea, so eliminate it. **(D)** *manifold* means "diverse" or "many," which also doesn't fit here.

15. D

This question asks you to identify a major point in the passage, the "primary reason" for the quagga's extinction. Research leads you to the sentence between those asserting the quagga's decline and its extinction. The quagga was hunted and "callously" exterminated by ranchers who considered it a competitor for their livestock. Choice **(A)** distorts the passage. Settlers considered the quagga a competitor with their herds, but there's nothing to suggest that the domestic species infected the wild animals.

Choice **(C)** distorts the passage, which states that the last quagga died in captivity but not that the species' extinction was a result of captivity. Similarly, choice **(E)** distorts that portion of the passage stating that researchers want to revive the quagga using selective breeding of existing, related species. It does not link the quagga's extinction to its breeding habits. Choices **(B)** and **(D)** are both, in a way, related to grazing. Choice **(B)** is incorrect because it ascribes the problem to the quagga's loss of grazing habitat. You never learn that the quagga was left with an insufficient range. The quagga competed with livestock for grazing, which caused settlers to hunt the species to extinction. Choice **(D)** best reflects what the passage states as the primary reason for the quagga's extinction.

16. B

The correct answer may not be stated explicitly in the passage, but it must follow directly from something that is stated there. The passage states that the quagga is a subspecies of the zebra, not the other way around. That makes choice **(A)** incorrect. The passage also contradicts choice **(D)**; its population "diminished" after discovery. Choice **(C)**, which states that settlers "humanely" killed quaggas, contradicts the passage more subtly but just as fatally. In fact, according to the passage, settlers "callously" killed quaggas. Choice **(E)** distorts the passage. The quagga was a competitor for the pasture of settlers' livestock, not their prey. Indeed, grazing animals have no prey. Choice **(B)** is the correct answer, as the last sentence of the passage states that scientists are hoping to spark the species' return.

17. B

This question asks you to evaluate the statement and identify what conclusions you can draw using the information from the passage. Choice **(A)** overstates the passage. Humans were historically responsible for the quagga's extinction. There's no way to deduce what would have happened absent human contact. Choice **(B)** follows from the portion of the passage in which you learn that DNA analysis helped determine that the quagga is a subspecies of the zebra and not a unique species. That's enough to make the broadly worded choice **(B)** a viable conclusion. Choice **(C)** does not provide a viable answer; it assumes too much information. The passage states that researchers are trying to bring back the extinct quagga, but it doesn't say how likely these efforts are to be successful, nor does it opine on how much concern extinctions should provoke.

18. C

Examine the answer choices one at a time and choose the one that follows from the passage. Choice **(A)** states that the Office of National Drug Control is concerned about teen tobacco use. While you may assume this to be a true statement, the passage doesn't state this directly, commenting only on the office's concern about teen marijuana use. Similarly, it is reasonable to think that choice **(D)** is true, but the passage only addresses Drug-Free America's stance on the risks of marijuana, not the organization's predictions of future use. The passage mentions claimed health benefits of marijuana, but it does not imply choice **(B)**, that marijuana has health benefits for teens. Choice **(C)** is the correct answer. The passage states that officials believe teens to be acting, in part, in response to anti-tobacco warnings. Choice **(E)** may seem reasonable because the passage makes implications about teen perception of the risks of marijuana, but it contains no statements about teens' feelings on the issue of legalization.

19. C

This question asks you to evaluate the possible connections and compare them to the information in the passage. Choice **(A)** seems possible, but the passage contains no information about drug use beyond marijuana and tobacco. Choice **(B)** makes a reference to information about tobacco use, but it distorts the passage, which states that teen tobacco use is down because teens seem to understand the risk of smoking, not because marijuana has been legalized in some states. Choice **(C)** is the most viable choice. The passage states that research on the medical uses of marijuana and the decision to legalize medical marijuana in some states contribute to the message that marijuana is not harmful. Choice **(D)** addresses antidrug organizations' message on marijuana use. This is not a viable choice because the passage states that antidrug organizations maintain their message that marijuana is harmful and gives you no reason to think they would change their views upon legalization. Choice **(E)** is out of scope; the passage does not give any information on how legalizing marijuana will affect the risks of the drug's use.

20. B

This question asks you to identify a detail in the passage. The "mixed message" referred to in the stem is found in the passage's fourth sentence, introduced with the contrast key word "While." That sentence outlines the contrast between antidrug messages (marijuana impairs judgment and hampers brain development) and research about possible health benefits. That matches choice **(B)** to a T. Choice **(E)** misses the scope of the passage by including a statement about the opinions of teens' parents, who aren't mentioned. Choice **(A)** brings in information about the age-appropriateness of marijuana use, another topic that isn't considered in this passage. Choice **(D)** states that marijuana use is safer than tobacco use, but the passage never makes that comparison. Choice **(C)** accurately states the inconsistent legal status of marijuana, but it doesn't answer the question. The mixed message teens receive is about the health effects—not the legality—of marijuana use.

DIAGNOSE YOUR RESULTS

Diagnostic Tool

Tally up your score and write your results in the space provided.

Total

Total Correct: ________ out of 20 correct

Percentage Correct: # you got right × 100 ÷ 20: ________

By Question Type

Text Completion ________ out of 6 correct

Sentence Equivalence ________ out of 4 correct

Reading Comprehension ________ out of 10 correct

Look back at the questions you got wrong and think about your experience answering them.

VERBAL REASONING PRACTICE SET 3

Directions: For each sentence, choose one word for each set of blanks. Select the word or words that best fit(s) the meaning of the sentence as a whole.

1. While most of the crowd was elated at the _______ promises that the politicians made, more cynical observers remained skeptical.

   (A) stolid
   (B) verbose
   (C) whimsical
   (D) extravagant
   (E) diffident

2. In mythology, rarely is a hero completely (i) _______ to any harm; even the greatest heroes have some (ii) _______ part of their body, such as Samson's hair or Achilles's heel.

Blank (i)		Blank (ii)	
A	obdurate	D	gullible
B	impervious	E	impotent
C	oblivious	F	susceptible

3. (i) _______, the demographic group that was most (ii) _______ in their support for the candidate in social media forums and most likely to vote for the candidate in pre-election online surveys was also the group that was least likely to vote on election day. This phenomenon underscores the potentially (iii) _______ nature of online political polls: despite the seemingly objective nature of the data they provide, sometimes they are not accurate.

Blank (i)		Blank (ii)		Blank (iii)	
A	Paradoxically	D	tacit	G	specious
B	Predictably	E	equivocal	H	acerbic
C	Impetuously	F	vociferous	I	mutable

4. Research studies that track the (i) _______ of salmon and their feeding habits are an important factor in making decisions about river release points in attempts to create a more (ii) _______ population. Salmon varieties that travel greater distances to feed have greater growth rates, tend to be healthier, and, on average, (iii) _______ larger populations than species with more localized feeding habits, and researchers plan to introduce more of the hardy salmon species to help revitalize the ecosystem.

Blank (i)	Blank (ii)	Blank (iii)
A immigration	D homogeneous	G yield
B migration	E kindred	H supplant
C evolution	F heterogeneous	I undermine

5. The (i) _______ relationship between patients and their doctors is evidenced by patients' (ii) _______ reactions to the attempts by insurance companies to force patients to see new doctors in different health care networks.

Blank (i)	Blank (ii)
A laconic	D tacit
B stolid	E onerous
C sacrosanct	F antagonistic

6. While the university's adoption of a new policy against plagiarism was intended to (i) _______ the school's faculty, some instructors criticized the policy as a (ii) _______ attempt to address a serious problem.

Blank (i)	Blank (ii)
A obviate	D tepid
B mollify	E pugnacious
C censure	F polarizing

Question 7 is based on the following passage.

Parents of high-school students argue that poor attendance is the result of poor motivation. If students' attitudes improve, regular attendance will result. The administration, they believe, should concentrate less on making stricter attendance policies and more on increasing students' learning.

7. Which of the following, if true, would most effectively weaken the parents' argument?

   Ⓐ Motivation to learn can be improved at home, during time spent with parents.
   Ⓑ The degree of interest in learning that a student develops is a direct result of the amount of time he or she spends in the classroom.
   Ⓒ Making attendance policies stricter will merely increase students' motivation to attend classes, not their interest in learning.
   Ⓓ Showing a student how to be motivated is insufficient; the student must also accept responsibility for his or her decisions.
   Ⓔ Unmotivated students do not perform as well in school as other students.

Questions 8–10 are based on the following passage.

In 2010, the National Aeronautics and Space Administration (NASA) discovered a new species of bacteria, called the *GFAJ-1* strain, that for a while promised to change our understanding of how living things survive. Deep in the waters of Mono Lake in California, NASA scientists discovered a form of bacteria that seemed to use arsenic, plentiful in its habitat, to make DNA and proteins. Most life forms are made from six main building blocks: carbon, hydrogen, nitrogen, oxygen, sulfur, and phosphorus. Arsenic is toxic to most known organisms, but the *GFAJ-1* strain can tolerate high concentrations of arsenic, and initial studies suggested that it could even incorporate the chemical into its cells. Some scientists claimed that this discovery had opened new possibilities for life elsewhere in the universe, as the existence of such a microbe would show that organisms can exist in chemical environments that scientists may not have considered.

8. Which of the following statements best summarizes the passage?

   (A) The presence of arsenic-based bacteria would prove that there is life on other planets.
   (B) Scientists have discovered that arsenic is not toxic to most known organisms.
   (C) Claims made about the *GFAJ-1* strain challenged scientists' perception of how living organisms survive.
   (D) If *GFAJ-1* were established as using arsenic to build its DNA, scientists would need to consider adding this element to the six main building blocks of life.
   (E) The ecosystem of Mono Lake is a scientific phenomenon that scientists will be studying for years.

9. According to the information in the passage, upon discovery of the *GFAJ-1* strain, some scientists believed it was

   (A) a water-based bacteria that had a high tolerance for toxins
   (B) one of the six building blocks of life
   (C) a form of arsenic that was toxic to most living organisms
   (D) a strain of bacteria that incorporated arsenic into its cells
   (E) a form of DNA that did not need phosphorus to grow

Consider each of the following choices separately and select all that apply.

10. Based on the information in the passage, what reasonable conclusions can be drawn?

   [A] If a species of bacteria can use arsenic in cell development, it is possible that planets that have high levels of arsenic might be able to support living organisms.
   [B] If the *GFAJ-1* strain's chemical processes do not follow the same patterns as those of other organisms, the strain must have originated on another planet.
   [C] If scientists have discovered a living organism that uses arsenic in place of one of the six building blocks of life, it is possible that there may be other chemicals in addition to arsenic that can support life.

Directions: Select the <u>two</u> answer choices that, when inserted into the sentence, fit the meaning of the sentence as a whole <u>and</u> yield complete sentences that are similar in meaning.

11. Mr. Phillips' characterization of the political faction as ultra-neoconservative is too ______ to be confirmed without further consideration.

    [A] judicious
    [B] perfunctory
    [C] hasty
    [D] orthodox
    [E] partisan
    [F] senatorial

12. The college newspaper once portrayed the school's scholarship program as anything but unfair; now the paper depicts the program as highly ______.

    [A] reasonable
    [B] unbiased
    [C] lucrative
    [D] inequitable
    [E] fallacious
    [F] discriminatory

13. The success of a fledgling restaurant is highly dependent on the demeanor of every staff member, since any instance of ______ can lead to opprobrious reviews.

    [A] obstinance
    [B] unseemliness
    [C] kindness
    [D] courtesy
    [E] indecorum
    [F] larceny

14. The author's novel, in which the main character copes with all manner of setbacks with equanimity, was known to be a thinly veiled autobiography. Upon meeting the author for the first time, her editor commented on the incongruity of the writer's ______ nature with that of her fictional persona.

    [A] xenophobic
    [B] mercurial
    [C] timorous
    [D] impassive
    [E] dissembling
    [F] volatile

Questions 15 and 16 are based on the following passage.

All artists are reputed to suffer to some degree for their art, but some may physically suffer more than others. As part of *The 3rd I* project, a performance artist agreed to have a camera surgically implanted into the back of his head and the footage gathered from the experiment to be uploaded hourly into a website. The surgery involves slicing and lifting folds of skin and implanting the camera into the back of the skull and is excruciating for the artist. Some critics claim that the visceral reaction of hearing about the camera or its insertion may be orchestrated to shock viewers into learning more about the art or the project. Although the camera can be fitted with a lens cap to protect the privacy of those who request it, every single detail of the artist's life is recorded and open for all to view. One might conclude that this project is an extreme example of the Modernists' tendency to take the creation of art as its subject.

15. This passage implies which of the following about performance art?

    (A) At least some performance art is Modernist in origin.
    (B) Modern technology affords performance artists a wider audience for conveying political messages.
    (C) Critics prefer static visual art to performance art because it typically relies less on shock value.
    (D) By becoming part of the art, a performance artist can convey a powerful message within the art.
    (E) Performance artists suffer more greatly than other types of artists.

Consider each of the following choices separately and select all that apply.

16. The passage implies that the strength of the reaction the artwork evokes would be substantially weakened if which of the following were to happen?

    [A] The content of the video is difficult to make out on-screen.

    [B] Most people who see the video on the website don't know how it was made.

    [C] Certain shots of the video "go viral" and become something that people across the world discuss in real time.

Questions 17 and 18 are based on the following passage.

Upton Sinclair's 1906 novel *The Jungle*, set in the meatpacking plants of early 20th-century Chicago, was intended to provoke a strong public reaction. The book, based on Sinclair's own experience working incognito at a meatpacking plant, tells of the horrific working conditions in the meat industry. The stories of contaminated or diseased meat were intended to incite outrage at the system of worker exploitation that led to these issues; however, the response of both the public and the government focused on food safety. Less than a year after publication of *The Jungle*, Congress passed the Pure Food and Drug Act, which eventually led to the creation of the modern Food and Drug Administration. Sinclair himself was not pleased with what he saw as a misinterpretation of his work; he famously said, "I aimed at the public's heart, and by accident I hit it in the stomach."

The reaction to *The Jungle* is hardly the first time that concerns over food safety and purity have won out over more compassionate objectives. In 1516, Bavaria (then part of the Holy Roman Empire) passed the *Reinheitsgebot*, a law mandating, among other things, that the only ingredients that could be used in the production of beer were barley, hops, and water. Although *Reinheitsgebot* literally translates to "purity order," the main impetus behind the law was not to protect the purity of beer but rather to prevent competition between bakers and brewers for the purchase of grains. By ensuring that wheat and rye would be available only for bakers, the Bavarian government hoped to keep bread affordable for everyone. Many modern breweries, however, tout that their beers conform to the *Reinheitsgebot* in an attempt to convince consumers of the quality and purity of their beer, completely ignoring the original empathetic intent of the law. Perhaps the public's stomach is, in fact, more sensitive than its heart.

17. With which of the following statements about the Pure Food and Drug Act would the author of the passage likely agree?

    Ⓐ It did not do enough to ensure the safety of America's food supplies, given the state of the meatpacking industry.
    Ⓑ It was a misguided response to the transgressions of the meatpacking industry exposed in *The Jungle.*
    Ⓒ Congress enacted the law to limit competition for resources, although its effect was to improve food quality.
    Ⓓ The act was likely to increase the price of food by imposing regulations on the meatpacking industry.
    Ⓔ It was intended to fix problems that were not highlighted in *The Jungle.*

18. Which of the following is true of the effects of the *Reinheitsgebot*, according to the passage?

    Ⓐ It led to the production of higher-quality beer.
    Ⓑ It influenced how beer was made throughout the Holy Roman Empire.
    Ⓒ It resulted in lower bread prices.
    Ⓓ Laws that use it as precedent are still in effect today.
    Ⓔ Some advertisements for beer refer to its requirements.

Questions 19 and 20 are based on the following passage.

Willa Cather (1873–1947) lived in Nebraska and set her novels *O Pioneers!* and *My Ántonia* in the state, describing the land as intricately as she would a main character. However, Nebraska might not have featured so heavily in Cather's work if she had not grown up in the Shenandoah Valley of Virginia. Until she was nine, she lived in the quaint charm of Willow Shade, her grandfather's 300-acre farm. Amid the lush, wooded vegetation, a rustic bridge covered a creek. Box hedges surrounded the house. Willow trees grew large. In 1883, following the lure of fertile farmland in the West, Cather's family left Willow Shade and crossed six states to reach a new farm in Webster County, Nebraska. The new landscape shocked Cather to the core. She felt erased by flat prairies stretching to the horizon, swallowed by the enormous sky. The stark contrast to the mountains of Virginia etched its influence onto her soul. She grew to love the new land, but never forgot the old. Perhaps that is why she identified with immigrants homesick for Czechoslovakia, Norway, and Sweden, the people she wrote about in *O Pioneers!* and *My Ántonia.* She knew how transplanted they felt.

19. Based on the information in the passage, which assumption MOST likely underlies the passage?

   (A) Cather's novels would have been much different if her family had not moved to Nebraska.
   (B) Cather would not have become an author if her family had not moved to Nebraska.
   (C) Cather did not truly remember or value Virginia because she did not use the state as the setting of her most famous novels.
   (D) It was Cather's compassion for immigrant people, rather than her passion for landscape, that inspired her novels.
   (E) The shock Cather felt in Nebraska and her grief for Virginia deepened her soul and made her an artist.

20. Which best states the author's use of rhetorical structure in the passage?

   (A) The passage is a comparison between the different landscapes of Virginia and Nebraska.
   (B) The passage compares Willa Cather's response to the different landscapes of Virginia and Nebraska.
   (C) The author compares the different landscapes of Virginia and Nebraska as a way to emphasize Willa Cather's experience when she first set eyes on Nebraska.
   (D) The author describes how Willa Cather compared the different landscapes of Virginia and Nebraska when she first set eyes on Nebraska.
   (E) The author compares Willa Cather's use of landscapes in her two most famous novels.

VERBAL REASONING PRACTICE SET 3 ANSWER KEY

1. **D**
2. **B, F**
3. **A, F, G**
4. **B, F, G**
5. **C, F**
6. **B, D**
7. **B**
8. **C**
9. **D**
10. **A, C**
11. **B, C**
12. **D, F**
13. **B, E**
14. **B, F**
15. **A**
16. **B**
17. **B**
18. **E**
19. **A**
20. **C**

VERBAL REASONING PRACTICE SET 3 ANSWERS AND EXPLANATIONS

1. D

The key to this question is the contrast between the "elated," or excited, crowd, and the "skeptical," or doubting, cynics. We are looking for a word that would cause the crowd to be excited, but would cast doubt among skeptics. We can immediately eliminate choice **(A)** *stolid,* "unemotional," choice **(B)** *verbose,* "talkative," and choice **(E)** *diffident,* "lacking self-confidence," as these are all negative adjectives for a political speech and would not invoke the excitement of the crowd. Choice **(C)** *whimsical,* "fanciful," seems plausible: the crowd might like a fanciful, idealistic promise, while cynics would remain doubtful of its veracity. However, choice **(D)** *extravagant* is a better choice, as it implies an attractive promise that might not be realistic.

2. B, F

Based on the context, you can assume that the blank will describe a hero's ability to be harmed, so you can predict *resistant*, or *unable*, to describe the hero's relationship to harm. Choice **(A)** *obdurate* has a meaning related to your prediction, but its connotations are more emotional than physical—it means "resistant to persuasion" or "unmoved by pity" and is therefore not appropriate in this context. Choice **(C)** *oblivious* may be tempting, but the second part of the sentence is clearly discussing actual bodily harm, not awareness of harm. Choice **(B)** *impervious* means "unable to be pierced" and is the best choice.

For the second blank, you could use the examples of Achilles's heel and Samson's hair to help you along. But whether or not you are familiar with these stories, you can use the straight-ahead road sign of the semicolon: the second part of the sentence carries the same ideas as the first. Since the first part of the sentence suggests that heroes all have some sort of flaw or problem, predict a word that means "open to harm." Choice **(D)** *gullible* refers to someone who is easily tricked. This adjective does not make sense to describe a part of the body and is therefore incorrect. Choice **(E)** *impotent* describes what might become of a hero who has been harmed, but it does not work as the predicted meaning itself. Only choice **(F)** *susceptible* carries the correct meaning, "open to harm," and is your answer.

3. A, F, G

The key to this question is the contradiction between the group's voting behavior before the election and in the election itself. The single word before the comma in blank (i) is a road sign word setting up this contradiction, so predict something like *Oddly* or *Strangely*. **(A)** *paradoxically* is correct. *Predictably,* **(B)**, is the opposite of the prediction. *Impetuously,* **(C)**, describes quick and thoughtless behavior, and while the people in this group demonstrate inconstancy in their support for the candidate, there are no clues to indicate they are making rash judgments.

The second blank is connected to "most likely to vote for the candidate" by the straight-ahead road sign "and," so predict that this demographic group was *active* or *strong* in its support in online forums. **(F)** matches this prediction since *vociferous* means "very loud" or "insistent." *Tacit,* **(D)**, means "unspoken," which would be the opposite of the prediction. *Equivocal,* **(E)**, means "misleading and vague," which may describe the pre-election survey data, but the word in blank (ii) must describe the people and these individuals expressed a positive view of the candidate.

The word in the final blank will describe the "nature" of online polls, and this is described after the colon. Even though they generate "seemingly objective" data, they can be inaccurate—and *inaccurate* is a good prediction. **(G)** is correct because something that is *specious* is "misleading." *Acerbic*, **(H)**, means "harsh" or "severe," and *mutable*, **(I)**, means "changeable." Although people may behave differently on election day than indicated in pre-election polls and perhaps be considered "changeable," the word in the third blank describes the polls, not the people surveyed.

4. B, F, G

The first blank describes something that researchers would track in order to make decisions about "river release points" that will lead to changes in the salmon population. The GRE does not expect you to be an expert on wildlife biology, so if you're not sure what "river release points" are, don't worry about it. Just focus on the context clues you do understand. In the second sentence, the distance that salmon travel determines how healthy they are and, by extension, how healthy the ecosystem is. Thus, predict that the research studies under discussion look at the fish's *movement*. Two of the choices for the first blank are related to movement, but only one is not specific to humans. **(B)** *migration* means "to move from one place to another" and is correct. **(A)** *immigration* can be eliminated because it means "moving to another country to live there," and fish don't think about which country they're in. The **(C)** *evolution* of the salmon is something that could be under study, but the context clues do not suggest that this research is about that.

The third blank relates salmon varieties that "have greater growth rates" and "tend to be healthier" to "larger populations." The ideas can be connected with the prediction *result in*, which works well with **(G)** *yield*, meaning "to produce something." There is no supporting evidence in the sentence that the hardy salmon species are going to either **(H)** *supplant*, meaning "take the place of," or **(I)** *undermine*, meaning "make something weaker," any other species.

Finally, you can use the clues at the end of the second sentence to make a prediction for the second blank, which describes what kind of population the researchers want to achieve. The goal for researchers is "to introduce more of the hardy salmon species." Based on this information, predict that the researchers want to create a more *diverse* population. A population that is **(F)** *heterogeneous* is one that is "made up of diverse parts," which matches the prediction. Both **(D)** *homogeneous* and **(E)** *kindred* mean "similar" and can be eliminated.

5. C, F

The first blank describes the "relationship" of patients with their doctors, and the second blank describes these patients' "reactions" to being "force[d]" to see different doctors. The key phrase "evidenced by" indicates a straight-ahead relationship between the first blank and the second one. How are patients going to react to insurance companies that try to "force" them to see new doctors? For the second blank, predict that their reactions will be hostile or critical. **(F)** is correct because *antagonistic* means "combative." **(D)** *tacit* means "unspoken," and **(E)** *onerous* means "burdensome."

After you've filled in the second blank, the first blank is easier to predict. You want a positive word that describes the patient–doctor relationship as important. **(C)** is correct because *sacrosanct* means "sacred." **(A)** *laconic* means "using few words," and **(B)** *stolid* means "unemotional."

6. B, D

"While" is a detour road sign, indicating the contrast between what the university intended with the adoption of a new policy and the criticism that the policy received. For the first blank, predict that the policy was intended to *satisfy* or *win the approval of* the faculty. **(B)** is correct because *mollify* means to "appease" or "to make something better"; thus, *mollifying* the faculty would *satisfy* the faculty. **(A)**, *obviate*, means to "prevent" or "eliminate," which does not match the prediction. *Censure*, **(C)**, means "to show disapproval" or "to officially reprimand."

For the second blank, you want a word that indicates how the faculty characterized the university's attempt to address a "serious problem." Since the faculty was critical, predict that they thought the university's policy was a *poor* or *feeble* attempt. **(D)** is correct because *tepid* means "lacking in force" or "unenthusiastic." *Pugnacious*, **(E)**, means "combative" or "inclined to fight." *Polarizing*, **(F)**, means "to divide into sharply opposing groups."

7. B

You are asked here to weaken the parents' argument, which is outlined in the first sentence of the stimulus: parents believe that poor attendance results from poor motivation. This sets up a cause-and-effect relationship between "poor attendance" and "poor motivation," with poor motivation as the cause and poor attendance as the effect. The parents go on to elaborate on their theory and suggest a plan of action, but this cause-and-effect argument is the central issue.

Since you need to *weaken* this argument, you need to find an answer choice that contradicts or otherwise introduces doubt into this assertion. Choice **(B)** does just this by stating that "the degree of interest in learning that a student develops" (i.e., a student's motivation) is a result of "the amount of time he or she spends in the classroom" (his or her attendance). Choice **(B)** establishes a new cause-and-effect relationship with *attendance* as the cause and *motivation* as the effect. Since this reverses the causality from the initial argument, it weakens the stimulus and is the correct answer.

Wrong choices **(A)**, **(D)**, and **(E)** fail to mention both attendance and motivation and therefore sidestep the issue. Choice **(C)** does mention both concepts, but its stance of decrying strict attendance policies is right in line with the last sentence of the stimulus and would thus *strengthen* rather than weaken the argument.

8. C

This question asks you to identify the most accurate summary of the passage. Use your summary of the topic, scope, and purpose of the passage as a prediction of the correct answer. This author is writing to inform the reader about a discovery that was initially exciting: scientists discovered a new bacterium that seemed to have the remarkable ability to use arsenic, and this discovery challenged assumptions about the building blocks of life. That matches the correct answer, **(C)**. Choice **(A)** is extreme; the passage states that the new discovery introduced new possibilities for life in other parts of our universe, but it does not state that this discovery would *prove* that there is life in other parts of our universe. **(B)** contradicts the passage; in fact, "[a]rsenic is toxic to most known organisms." **(D)** does not reflect the passage's main point, which is broader than how many elements can be considered "building blocks of life." **(E)** misses the boat by focusing on a detail in the passage and making a prediction that is not supported.

9. D

The correct answer to this Detail question is directly stated in the passage. *GFAJ-1* can tolerate arsenic and "initial studies suggested that it could even incorporate the chemical into its cells." Choices **(A)** and **(D)** both state that the *GFAJ-1* strain is a form of bacteria. However, **(A)** states that it is a water-based bacteria, which is not supported by information in the passage. **(D)** states that the *GFAJ-1* strain was believed to be a type of bacteria that incorporates arsenic into its cells, which (as noted above) is directly stated in the passage. This is the correct answer. Eliminate **(B)** because it states that the *GFAJ-1* strain is a building block of life, not a bacteria strain that is made up of building blocks of life. Eliminate **(C)** because it states that the *GFAJ-1* strain is a form of arsenic, not a bacteria strain that was thought to be arsenic based. Similarly, eliminate **(E)** because it states that the *GFAJ-1* strain is a form of DNA, whereas the passage says that it seemed to develop DNA from arsenic.

10. A, C

This question asks you to evaluate the statement and identify the conclusions you can validly draw using the information from the passage. Choice **(A)** is a reasonable conclusion because it is based on the claim cited in the passage that arsenic-based bacteria would have "opened new possibilities for life elsewhere in the universe." **(B)** is not based on any information stated in the passage. The passage suggests that the discovery of this new bacteria had implications for the likelihood of finding life on other planets, but it does not suggest that the bacteria came from another planet. **(C)** is a reasonable conclusion because the passage states that initial studies of *GFAJ-1* suggested that "organisms can exist in chemical environments that scientists may not have considered."

11. B, C

Ask yourself what kind of characterization it must be if the characterization hasn't been confirmed. Predict that it must be one that was made too quickly or carelessly. Therefore, you can eliminate *judicious*, **(A)**, which means "using good judgment." *Perfunctory*, **(B)**, means "done without much care" or "done superficially." Making a characterization that hasn't been confirmed would be an instance of acting quickly or without much care, so keep this choice. *Hasty*, **(C)**, means "done quickly" or "done without much thought," giving the sentence the same meaning as does *perfunctory*. Therefore, keep **(C)**. *Orthodox*, **(D)**, which means "adhering to tradition or what is customary," does not make sense in this context. Since Mr. Phillips is characterizing a political faction as ultra-neoconservative, he may indeed be *partisan*, **(E)**, which means being "devoted to a particular group, idea, cause, etc." However, there is not another choice that provides a similar meaning. *Senatorial*, **(F)**, means "relating to a senate or senator," which does not make sense in this context. **(B)** and **(C)** are correct.

12. D, F

Notice the words "once" and "now." These contrasting words indicate that how the newspaper describes the scholarship program has changed; together, they constitute a detour road sign. Be careful taking apart the phrase "anything but unfair"; this means the newspaper used to assess the program as *fair*. "[N]ow," however, the paper must describe the program as *unfair*. This is a good prediction. *Inequitable*, **(D)**, means "unjust" or "unfair," so keep this choice. *Discriminatory*, **(F)**, means "biased" or "prejudicial." This choice gives the sentence the same meaning as does *inequitable* and is the other correct answer. Eliminate *reasonable*, **(A)**, and *unbiased*, **(B)**, as contradicting the prediction. There is no clue that suggests the program is *lucrative*, **(C)**, which means "profitable." *Fallacious*, **(E)**, which means "logically unsound" or "deceptive," may be a tempting choice. However, an unfair program may or may not be *fallacious*. Further, there is no other choice that gives the sentence the same meaning.

13. B, E

Since the restaurant is a "fledgling," or new, business, it needs to avoid bad reviews to be successful. In the second part of the sentence, the term "opprobrious" means "publicly disgraceful" or "shameful." If you did not know the meaning of "opprobrious," given the context of the sentence, you may still have been able to infer that "opprobrious" has a negative charge. Therefore, predict that any instance of *poor or inappropriate behavior* by staff could lead to such bad reviews. *Obstinance*, **(A)**, means "stubbornness." The *obstinance* of a staff member, especially in response to a customer's request, could indeed merit a bad review. *Unseemliness*, **(B)**, means "inappropriate," and staff who behave inappropriately could also earn the restaurant a bad review. Though both **(A)** and **(B)** fit in the sentence, they do not give the text the same meaning. Keep looking for a match. *Indecorum*, **(E)**, means "improper behavior" and gives the sentence the same meaning as does *unseemliness*, so **(B)** and **(E)** are correct. *Kindness*, **(C)**, and *courtesy*, **(D)**, are opposites of your prediction. While *larceny*, **(F)**, or theft, could lead to a bad review if a staff member committed it against a customer, there is not enough context to support this choice, nor is there another choice with the same meaning.

14. B, F

The word "incongruity," which means "a thing that is contrary or lacking consistency," is a detour road sign indicating a contrast between the writer's nature and coping with setbacks "with equanimity." Someone with an equanimous disposition is "even-tempered" or "calm." (Note that the root word *equ* means "even" or "equal.") Predict that the author's nature is *not calm*. Thus, **(B)** *mercurial*, meaning "having unpredictable moods," is a match, as is **(F)** *volatile*. These are the correct choices. *Xenophobic*, **(A)**, means "having a fear or hatred of foreigners." *Timorous*, **(C)**, means "shy" or "fearful." *Impassive*, **(D)**, means "not having or not showing feeling or emotion," and *dissembling*, **(E)**, means "misleading."

15. A

The correct answer to this question will be true based on the passage. With this in mind, **(A)** is the correct answer. If this performance art project is an "example of" Modernist art, it must be the case that at least some performance art is Modernist in origin. Although **(B)** may be true in the real world, it is not an implication of the passage. The author says nothing about the political dimensions of the performance. Consider **(C)** carefully: critics do comment on this aspect of this project's shock value, but nowhere is it suggested that critics prefer visual art to performance art. This passage doesn't make any assessment of how "powerful" the message of the piece is, only suggesting that finding out how the artwork is made is a powerful experience, so **(D)** is incorrect. Choice **(E)** is too vague; the artist described here may suffer more *physically*, but that doesn't translate to a generalized statement that performance artists suffer more than artists of other genres.

16. B

This Inference question asks you to identify statements about people's reaction to the artwork that follow from the passage. According to the critics mentioned in the passage, knowing how the art was created is potentially related to the audience's interest in it. The reaction is mainly reliant on the concept, not the product, of the art. Thus, **(B)** is correct; if the audience doesn't appreciate how the art was made, they may be less interested in it. Choice **(A)** doesn't follow from the passage. Nothing suggests that the beauty or clarity of the images produced affects the success of the project. If **(C)** were true, it would likely increase the popularity of the performance and get people thinking about it. This has the opposite effect called for by the question stem.

17. B

The question asks what the author of the passage would think about the Pure Food and Drug Act; this law is discussed in the first paragraph, so start your research there. The only opinion there is that of Upton Sinclair, who was not happy that the act focused on food safety rather than the worker exploitation he sought to highlight in *The Jungle*. Look further to find the opinion of the passage's author. In the first sentence of the second paragraph, the author indicates an opinion through a comparison, saying that "concerns over food safety and purity . . . won out over more compassionate objectives." Thus, the author feels that Congress with the Pure Food and Drug Act addressed a less important problem than it should have. Then again, in the last sentence of the passage, the author expresses agreement with Sinclair, saying that "the public's stomach is, in fact, more sensitive than its heart." Look for an answer choice that lines up with the opinion. **(B)** does so nicely; the author would think, just as Sinclair did, that this law was a misguided response to *The Jungle*, so this is the correct answer.

(A) is incorrect because the author does not express any opinion on the effectiveness of the law; she thinks a law protecting workers would have been a more appropriate response, but that doesn't mean she thinks the law that was passed didn't work. **(C)** confuses the U.S. law this question asks about with the Bavarian law discussed in the second paragraph. **(D)** is wrong because the only discussion of food prices comes in the second paragraph in connection to the *Reinheitsgebot*, not the Pure Food and Drug Act. **(E)** may be tempting because the author does think the act addressed a problem that should have been a lower priority. However, it's clear that *The Jungle* did highlight a problem with food quality, given its "stories of contaminated or diseased meat," and the law addressed that issue.

18. E

This Detail question asks for a fact about the effects of the *Reinheitsgebot*, which is discussed in the second paragraph. A quick paraphrase of the paragraph's main point will serve as guidance: the law was enacted with the hope of keeping bread affordable, but many today associate it with beer purity.

Keep this in mind as you evaluate the answer choices. **(E)** paraphrases the next-to-last sentence and is correct: "[modern] beers conform to the *Reinheitsgebot*." Even if the claims modern breweries make on this basis are misplaced, beer is being made with only the ingredients stipulated by this 16th-century law. **(A)** is incorrect; the author points out that the law was not intended to raise the quality of beer, and even if that happened as an unintended side effect, it isn't mentioned in the passage. **(B)** can be eliminated; the law was passed in Bavaria, which is said to be part of the Holy Roman Empire, but there's no indication the law was in effect throughout the empire. **(C)** may be tempting, because the author states that the intent of the law was to keep bread affordable. However, the passage never says whether it was successful in meeting this goal. Even though there are breweries that claim to follow the law today, there's no indication that they're legally obligated to; they may be invoking an old law in their advertising to cloak their beer in a mantle of purity. Thus, **(D)** is incorrect.

19. A

This question asks you to make inferences based on the information in the passage. You will need to evaluate each response one by one and weigh its merits. Choices **(A)** and **(B)** are similar in that they refer to Cather's motives in becoming an author. The passage does not prove, however, that she wouldn't have become an author at all if she had stayed in Virginia. Choice **(B)** is not the correct answer. You can also rule out **(C)**; the author tells you explicitly that Cather remembered Virginia. The fact that she was influenced by Nebraska doesn't mean that she devalued her former home. To support the claim in **(D)**, the passage would have to offer summaries of each novel and more information about Cather's relationship to communities of people. You can't draw this inference from the passage. In a literary analysis, an author could possibly support a claim such as the one stated in choice **(E)**. However, based on this passage, **(E)** is emotional hyperbole. Choice **(A)** is the most feasible assumption. According to the passage, Cather certainly would not have written the specific novels she did write if she hadn't moved to Nebraska as a child.

20. C

The correct answer to this Global question summarizes the passage's structure. The passage certainly compares two landscapes, but to correctly answer this question, you must determine *why* the comparison is made. Choice **(C)** includes the main point of the passage—Cather's shock upon first seeing Nebraska and its influence on her writing—and this is correct. You can eliminate choice **(A)** because it does not provide a reason for the comparison. Rule out **(B)** because prior to seeing Nebraska, Cather had nothing to compare to Virginia; we do not know how she "responded" to her home state. Choice **(D)** is similar to the correct answer, but the focus of the passage is not on Cather's thought process as she compared the two landscapes; rather, it's on her reaction to a new landscape and the effect of this experience on her writing. You can also cross off choice **(E)** as there is little to no information about the novels in the passage. Therefore, **(C)** is the correct answer.

DIAGNOSE YOUR RESULTS

Diagnostic Tool

Tally up your score and write your results in the space provided.

Total

Total Correct: ________ out of 20 correct

Percentage Correct: # you got right $\times$ 100 $\div$ 20: ________

By Question Type

Text Completion ________ out of 6 correct

Sentence Equivalence ________ out of 4 correct

Reading Comprehension ________ out of 10 correct

Look back at the questions you got wrong and think about your experience answering them.

VERBAL REASONING PRACTICE SET 4

Directions: For each sentence, choose one word for each set of blanks. Select the word or words that best fit(s) the meaning of the sentence as a whole.

1. It was apparent that the recordings were _______ remastered, as the vocals were barely audible through the wave of noise.

   Ⓐ maladroitly
   Ⓑ copiously
   Ⓒ ingeniously
   Ⓓ shrewdly
   Ⓔ maliciously

2. She cited financial difficulty as her primary motive in the lucrative robbery; nonetheless, even her own family _______ her.

   Ⓐ deluded
   Ⓑ chastised
   Ⓒ absolved
   Ⓓ venerated
   Ⓔ engulfed

3. While the guitar has (i) _______ over the course of its centuries-long history, perhaps most notably with the invention of the electric guitar in the 1930s, the modern guitar exhibits (ii) _______ the *vihuela* of 15th-century Spain. A skilled guitarist would likely be able to pick up this (iii) _______ instrument, also an ancestor of the viol, and competently play a tune.

Blank (i)	Blank (ii)	Blank (iii)
A stagnated	D an incongruity with	G inferior
B evolved	E an affinity to	H archaic
C regressed	F a divergence from	I avant-garde

4. The punctilious wine aficionado was a consummate purist when it came to his tastes. He immediately rejected the (i) _______ of two wines. As an alternative, and as a general rule, he preferred a simple, (ii) _______ wine.

Blank (i)		Blank (ii)	
A	amalgamation	D	pragmatic
B	dissonance	E	unadulterated
C	enigma	F	opaque

5. The belligerent student did everything in her power to (i) _______ the other students with her behavior and classroom conduct. However, the teacher's calm yet stern discipline, acquired through years of dealing with similar situations, quickly (ii) _______ their reactions.

Blank (i)		Blank (ii)	
A	satiate	D	exacerbated
B	antagonize	E	vacillated
C	repudiate	F	assuaged

6. The _______ alumni donors for the university's English department is well documented and acknowledged. It creates _______ in the allocation of university funds when the time comes to decide the annual budget. As things stand now, the available money goes to other university departments, which are not always the most underfunded or _______.

Blank (i)		Blank (ii)		Blank (iii)	
A	paucity of	D	an irritation	G	widespread
B	preponderance of	E	a paradox	H	needy
C	utility of	F	a disparity	I	newsworthy

Questions 7 and 8 are based on the following passage.

Since the Industrial Revolution in the 19th century, societies have wrestled with the question of how to balance the benefits of new technologies with the loss of employment these changes may engender. In our own time, not only have jobs in manufacturing disappeared with the expanding implementation of robotics but also professional careers are now threatened by social media. While many people believe that those enjoying lofty levels of compensation resist redistribution of wealth, a recent book by social media multimillionaire Chris Hughes argues for a guaranteed minimum income, funded primarily by a marginal tax rate of 50 percent on individual annual incomes over $250,000, to offset reduced employment due to technological advances.

Reflecting on his own fortuitous life story, Hughes recounts how his chance selection of Mark Zuckerberg as his roommate in college was the primary determinant of Hughes's own success. Zuckerberg recruited Hughes and a few other friends to help with his side project, Facebook, and within a few years, Hughes's ownership share was worth an inconceivable amount of money. Hughes recognizes that his meteoric rise from the middle class was a product not only of his education and effort but also of luck. In addition, Hughes believes that opportunities for upward economic mobility are becoming less accessible as developments in technology supplant employment opportunities. Social media, Hughes's own vehicle for success, for example, may reduce the number of salespeople or human resource recruiters employed because social media algorithms can connect people to products or to other people more efficiently than can a human intermediary.

While Hughes may be commended for his ethos of generosity and his recognition of an impending social dilemma, his solution suffers the same failings as those offered by other technology moguls. There is no consideration of the formidable political obstacles to his plan or how these obstacles could be overcome.

7. Which of the following best describes the function of the second sentence in the second paragraph ("Zuckerberg recruited . . . money") in the context of the passage as a whole?

   (A) To illustrate that Hughes is wealthy
   (B) To contradict the hypothesis that introduced the passage
   (C) To explain Hughes's motivation for writing his book
   (D) To argue against a view stated previously in the passage
   (E) To support a proposition stated previously in the passage

8. It can be inferred from the passage that the author would likely agree with which of the following proposals for change to the economic system?

   (A) Because the redistribution of wealth would be rejected by most of the individuals whose income would be taxed at higher rates, voluntary charitable contributions should be encouraged to support the unemployed.
   (B) Recent innovations in technology, such as the widespread adoption of social media to conduct business and personal interactions, should be curtailed to prevent widespread loss of employment.
   (C) The role of luck as a factor that enables rapid accumulation of wealth should be mitigated by providing more opportunities for education, especially in technological fields.
   (D) Chris Hughes's plan for the redistribution of wealth is an important development and should be implemented with little modification.
   (E) A system to remedy the impact on personal income when technological advancement reduces the supply of jobs should be considered.

Question 9 is based on the following passage.

Many governments have passed laws requiring that bicyclists must wear helmets while riding. Most of these laws in the United States only apply to children; however, there are some jurisdictions, such as Australia, that have laws mandating helmet usage for adults as well. While these laws are intended to reduce the incidence of injuries, some bicycle safety advocates argue that they should be repealed because they can, in some circumstances, have the contrary effect.

9. Which of the following, if true, most helps to explain the position of the bicycle safety advocates?

   (A) Classes that teach safe bicycling behaviors have been shown to be a more effective method of reducing injuries than are laws requiring helmets.
   (B) A driver overtaking a cyclist who is not wearing a helmet is more likely to pass at a safe distance than if the cyclist were wearing a helmet.
   (C) Bicycle helmet laws have been shown to discourage people from bicycling.
   (D) Children are more vulnerable to head injuries while bicycling than are adults.
   (E) In some severe bicycle crashes, a helmet may not prevent traumatic brain injury.

Question 10 is based on the following passage.

A property management company that operates a large townhouse complex has recently implemented a strict new policy that prohibits tenants from having certain breeds of dogs that it deems overly aggressive. The policy will apply only to new tenants and tenants who renew their leases. There has been a steep increase in the number of dog attacks associated with these breeds over the last two years, and the property manager has concluded that the new policy is the only way to reduce the number of attacks. The tenants' association disagrees, claiming that the new policy will not significantly remedy the situation in the long run.

10. Which of the following, if true, would most effectively undermine the claim made by the tenants' association?

Ⓐ Similar apartment complexes in the area have been able to effectively reduce the number of dog attacks.
Ⓑ There have been some dog attacks from breeds not added to the restricted list.
Ⓒ The apartment owner's insurance policy does not cover any costs associated with dog attacks.
Ⓓ More than 90 percent of the current tenants have leases that expire over the next two years.
Ⓔ A majority of attacks occurred when tenants did not have proper control over their dogs.

Directions: Select the <u>two</u> answer choices that, when inserted into the sentence, fit the meaning of the sentence as a whole <u>and</u> yield complete sentences that are similar in meaning.

11. Caligula, one of the great ______ of history, is best remembered for his lavish, bacchanalian feasts, in which participants indulged in every form of excess.

[A] gadflies
[B] sybarites
[C] philanthropists
[D] puritans
[E] wantons
[F] ascetics

12. Arthur looked positively ______; as he hadn't seen his wife, Deirdre, in weeks, the mere sight of her filled him with elation.

    A ebullient
    B esurient
    C peevish
    D pensive
    E ecstatic
    F execrable

13. For all his ______ in chatting with his friends and coworkers, when Cedric actually had a good reason to speak up in a serious conversation, he became taciturn.

    A oratories
    B declamations
    C palaver
    D blather
    E epigrams
    F opining

14. Despite the falling temperature and the inclement weather that lasted for most of the expedition, the hunting party was in a ______ mood.

    A disconcerted
    B jocund
    C garrulous
    D genial
    E histrionic
    F sententious

Questions 15–17 are based on the following passage.

Contrary to their appearance, polar bears are not white. These arctic dwellers actually have black skin, and the peculiar composition of their guard hairs is responsible for their white appearance. The hair of mammals, including polar bears, is composed of keratin and has a three-layer structure. The outermost layer, the cuticle, is composed of translucent overlapping scales. Below the cuticle is the cortex, which contains bundles of keratin, air spaces, and the pigments that provide the color of the hair. The innermost layer, the medulla, is a structured open space filled with air. This final layer, which is found only in some mammals, is particularly well developed in polar bears. Since the cuticle is translucent, the cortex is devoid of pigment, and the medulla is a wide air space, polar bear hair is translucent. Light enters the hair and is trapped in the medulla, striking tiny light-scattering particles within it, rather than being absorbed by the bear's skin. This scattering of the light waves causes luminescence—an emission of light across the visible spectrum—and makes the polar bear appear white.

15. In the passage, the author is primarily concerned with

   (A) analyzing a pattern of reasoning
   (B) arguing against a traditional belief
   (C) providing an explanation for a phenomenon
   (D) persuading the reader to adopt a point of view
   (E) showing how new information has revised a previous view

Consider each of the following choices separately and select all that apply.

16. Which of the following can be inferred from the passage regarding the composition and characteristics of polar bear hair?

   [A] At least one characteristic of polar bear hair is not widely shared with other mammals.
   [B] The white pigmentation of polar bear hair is located in keratin bundles that reside in the cortex.
   [C] The interaction of the structure of hair and light makes the nearly clear hair of the polar bear appear white.

17. According to the passage, each of the following is true EXCEPT:

   (A) The cortex of polar bear hair is composed of overlapping scales of keratin.
   (B) The cuticle of polar bear hair is located above the cortex and the medulla.
   (C) The guard hairs of the polar bear are composed of three layers.
   (D) The major component of polar bear hair is keratin.
   (E) The structure of the medulla is responsible for the polar bear's white appearance.

Question 18 is based on the following passage.

Online retail sales have been increasing annually for a number of years. When packages fulfilling these sales are delivered to homes, the dogs in those homes bark both when the delivery truck approaches the home and when the doorbell is rung. Because the dogs perceive the delivery activities as a threat to their territory, they bark more loudly and for a longer time then they do when they bark for other reasons. Consequently, there is bound to be an increase in the number of barking-dog nuisance complaints called in to local police departments.

18. Which of the following, if true, most seriously weakens the argument?

   (A) There are indications that in recent years, the daily number of residences visited by each delivery truck has markedly increased.
   (B) The increase in the number of packages delivered per day to residences on weekends has not increased at the same rate as those delivered on weekdays.
   (C) Some people are concerned about crime and want to be aware when their neighborhoods are entered by nonresidents.
   (D) Complaints about barking dogs almost always arise after a longstanding feud between neighbors results in overreactions to common disturbances.
   (E) Due to the intense competition for customers, more online retailers are offering free or discounted shipping fees or requiring smaller minimum orders for free shipping.

Questions 19 and 20 are based on the following passage.

An idea that has gained renewed currency in recent years is that the proliferation of information technology has a deleterious effect on interpersonal relationships. Neil Postman, in his book *Amusing Ourselves to Death*, asserted that television, as a medium, was incapable of fostering intelligent, meaningful discourse around a given subject. Postman wrote his book in the 1980s, when cable television was first becoming widely available. In it, he discusses the way that putatively "serious" news programs are inherently trite. Terse reports on serious, weighty issues such as the war in Iraq are juxtaposed with trivial information, such as celebrity gossip. Often the two are linked, one after another, by the phrase "and now. . ." This leaves the viewer unable to emotionally respond to something traumatic, as he is bombarded with disparate pieces of information in rapid succession. Instant access to a glut of information impoverishes genuine experiences, as it deprives the information of a meaningful context for interpretation.

19. Select the sentence in the passage in which the author cites a concrete example of how mass media has a desensitizing effect.

Consider each of the following choices separately and select all that apply.

20. Based on his views as they're expressed in the passage, Postman would likely agree with which of the following statements?

    - [A] Information technologies such as smartphones are unlikely to provide meaningful contexts in which to interpret information.
    - [B] Television programs inherently lack intelligent, meaningful discourse.
    - [C] The medium in which factual content is delivered can be an important factor in how that content is interpreted.

VERBAL REASONING PRACTICE SET 4 ANSWER KEY

1. **A**
2. **B**
3. **B, E, H**
4. **A, E**
5. **B, F**
6. **A, F, H**
7. **E**
8. **E**
9. **B**
10. **D**
11. **B, E**
12. **A, E**
13. **C, D**
14. **B, D**
15. **C**
16. **A, C**
17. **A**
18. **D**
19. *"Terse reports on serious, weighty issues such as the war in Iraq are juxtaposed with trivial information, such as celebrity gossip."*
20. **A, C**

VERBAL REASONING PRACTICE SET 4 ANSWERS AND EXPLANATIONS

1. A

The word "as" signals a continuation of ideas—the vocals were hard to hear because of the way the recordings were mastered. The answer is **(A)** *maladroitly*, which means "unskillfully" or "bunglingly." Choices **(B)** *copiously*, **(C)** *ingeniously*, and **(D)** *shrewdly* are not in line with what you're looking for—these words suggest more time and care than was spent. Choice **(E)** *maliciously* is too harsh. It's doubtful the recordings were mastered with intent to harm.

2. B

Even with the road sign *nonetheless*, a contrast is not immediately clear. Consider the tone of the phrase "even her own family," which suggests an element of surprise at the family's response. Choice **(A)** *deluded* means "misled," which doesn't fit the context. Choice **(B)** *chastised* means "scolded," which makes sense, since the robber would expect her family's support, not scolding. Choices **(C)** *absolved* and **(D)** *venerated* imply support—rule these out. The last choice, **(E)** *engulfed*, doesn't make sense in context.

3. B, E, H

The first blank is a good one to start with here. It describes something that's happened to the guitar over its long history. Since the given example is the invention of the electric guitar, you can predict that the guitar has "grown" or "changed." **(B)** *evolved* is a match and is correct. **(A)** *stagnated*, or "remained the same," doesn't fit, as an innovation is specifically mentioned in the first sentence. **(C)** *regressed*, or "moved backward," does imply a change, but there's no indication that the guitar has changed in a negative or regressive fashion.

The second blank explains the relationship between a modern guitar and a 15th-century instrument. "While" is a detour road sign; it indicates that there's a contrast between this relationship and the evolution of the guitar. Furthermore, the second sentence indicates that a skilled guitarist would be able to "competently" play the *vihuela*. A good prediction would be that even though the guitar has gone through changes over the centuries, it is still *similar* to the *vihuela*. This idea is reinforced by the next sentence, which says that a modern guitarist could probably play the old instrument. **(E)** *an affinity to* is the correct answer; an *affinity* is a "similarity" or a "likeness." **(D)** *an incongruity with* and **(F)** *a divergence from* both indicate a dissimilarity with the *vihuela*, which is not supported.

The third blank is directly connected to the *vihuela*; since all that's known about it from this text is that it's from the 15th century, predict that this blank means "old." That's **(H)** *archaic*, which means "outmoded" or "antiquated." **(G)** *inferior* ("of lesser quality") is wrong because there's no support for the idea that the *vihuela* is worse than the guitar or any other instrument. **(I)** *avant-garde* may be tempting because it's a term that's often used in the context of music and other arts; however, it relates to "new" or "experimental" concepts, so it doesn't fit here.

4. A, E

The key to this sentence is the description of the wine aficionado (or expert) as a "purist," or someone who insists on the purity of things. Since he rejects the first blank, you can assume it will be an antonym of *pure*. You can predict *mixture*, which fits in the context. However, he prefers the second blank, so this should be a synonym of *pure* and the contextual word "simple."

For the first blank, the best match for your prediction is choice **(A)** *amalgamation*. This is an exact synonym of your prediction, *mixture*. Choice **(B)** *dissonance*, which means "a disagreeable combination," seems plausible. A purist would definitely find a mixture of two wines to be dissonant. However, we need a word that states this mixture has occurred for the sentence to make sense. Similarly, choice **(C)** *enigma* means "puzzle," which may also be applicable to such a mixture but, again, lacks the necessary meaning of "mixture." For the second blank, choice **(E)** *unadulterated* matches your prediction best. Choice **(D)** *pragmatic* means "practical" and does not fit as well as *unadulterated* in context. The wine aficionado does not prefer something for its practicality but for the taste; therefore, this choice would be misleading in the sentence. Choice **(F)** *opaque*, which means "impossible to see through," may similarly be applicable to the wine; however, nowhere in the sentence is the color implied or relevant.

5. B, F

Since the student is described as "belligerent," meaning "aggressive," you can assume she will be attempting to provoke the other students. Later in the sentence, the road sign "however" appears, which indicates a turn of events when the teacher takes over. You can predict *aggravate* for the first blank and *calmed* or *lessened* for the second blank. For the first blank, the best match for your prediction is **(B)** *antagonize*, which means "provoke." Choice **(A)** *satiate* means "to satisfy," which is inconsistent with the idea of belligerence. Choice **(C)** *repudiate* means "to reject the validity of," which, although it may antagonize the students, lacks the direct connotation of *aggravate*. For the second blank, choice **(F)** *assuaged* is the best match to your prediction. Choice **(D)** *exacerbated*, which means "worsened," is the exact opposite of what you are looking for. Choice **(E)** *vacillated* means "to be indecisive," which sounds plausible but does not match the prediction as well as *assuaged*, or "calmed."

6. A, F, H

Start tackling this question by looking at the last sentence. You know that the money is going to other departments, which are not necessarily the most underfunded. Therefore, you know there aren't enough donors to the English department, or they aren't generous enough. You can predict something that means "lack of" for the first blank. Choice **(A)** *paucity of*, which means "shortage," works perfectly. Hang on to that one. For the second blank, you need something that contrasts how much the English department gets with how much the other ones get. *Discrepancy* works nicely. That eliminates choice **(E)** *paradox*—this is not contrary to what might be expected. Choice **(D)** *irritation* is very tempting but wrong. Although this situation is certainly irritating, choice **(F)** *disparity* better matches your prediction of *discrepancy*. The final blank will describe the department in a manner similar to "underfunded," with which it is paired. You can therefore reject choices **(G)** *widespread* and **(I)** *newsworthy* as being incorrect. That leaves **(H)** *needy*, which matches well with "underfunded."

7. E

This is a Logic question. The correct answer will describe why or how the author used this sentence in constructing the passage. Refer to the second sentence in the second paragraph and ask this question: "Why did the author describe Hughes's relationship with Zuckerberg?" A good prediction can be found in the sentences before and after. The first sentence of this paragraph says that Hughes's success was due to his "chance selection" of Zuckerberg as a roommate, and the third sentence says his success was partly a product "of luck." So a good prediction would be "to show why Hughes believes luck was important to his success." **(E)**, though stated in the abstract, matches this prediction and is correct. The second sentence illustrates why Hughes considered his wealth to be the result of luck, the proposition presented in the first sentence of the second paragraph. **(A)** is the *content* of the clue sentence but not its function. The author does contradict the idea that the wealthy will resist redistribution of wealth, but this is not the purpose the third sentence; eliminate **(B)**. Cross **(C)** off the list; Hughes didn't write the book because he became wealthy. Eliminate **(D)** as well. The third sentence includes only facts, not an argument.

8. E

The correct answer to this question will follow from the author's point of view expressed in the passage. The only place the author expresses an opinion is in the third paragraph, with "Hughes may be commended for his ethos of generosity and his recognition of an impending social dilemma." Specifically what Hughes has proposed is discussed at the end of the first paragraph—a plan to offset job loss due to changes in technology. However, in the last paragraph, the author views Hughes's specific proposal as impractical. Thus, what the author agrees with is the general belief that something should be done to help people who lose their jobs.

(E) is a match for this prediction. While the author never makes this statement directly, her only criticism of Hughes's plan is that it cannot be implemented. Since she commends Hughes's "recognition of an impending social dilemma," she would likely want to consider some solution to this problem. While the passage includes the opinion in the first part of **(A)**, this is the point of view of "many people," not of the author. Moreover, charitable contributions are not discussed. **(B)** is not supported by the passage, which implies that technological change is inevitable and discusses only what might be done to offset its effects. **(C)** misuses some details from the passage about Hughes's life. The author does not imply that more education is a means to reduce the role of chance in allocating wealth; indeed, Hughes had access to education, yet luck was still the dominant factor in his great good fortune. **(D)** is half-right, half-wrong. Since the author commends Hughes, she likely believes his plan to be important, but she also identifies a significant problem that must be addressed before his plan could be implemented.

9. B

This is an Explain question; you're asked to explain the seemingly paradoxical position of the bicycle safety advocates, so your first task is to understand their position. Some governments have passed mandatory helmet laws in order to reduce bicycling injuries. However, safety advocates think that sometimes, these laws may produce the opposite result; in other words, that they may actually increase the number of injuries.

It's impossible to make a specific prediction here, as there are many facts that could explain this position. What you can predict, though, is that the right answer will be a fact that explains how bicycle helmets might cause injuries. **(B)** does exactly that. If a driver is more likely to drive safely around a bicyclist without a helmet, then it's possible that mandating helmet usage would actually make bicycling more dangerous as cars would not give bicyclists as much room. This is the correct answer.

(A) explains that there may be better ways for the government to achieve its goals than mandatory helmet laws but does nothing to explain how these laws could cause injuries. **(C)** may be tempting; you might think that this would be a downside of helmet laws because bicycle safety advocates would presumably like to see more people bicycling. However, like **(A)**, it does not address the advocates' concern about safety. **(D)** only makes the position of the safety advocates more difficult to explain, as it provides a reason that at least some people—children—should wear helmets. **(E)** shows that helmets may not be effective in severe crashes, but this does not mean that they aren't effective in less severe crashes, nor does it show how they would increase the likelihood of injuries.

10. D

Be sure that you separate the two claims being made. The property manager claims that the pet restriction policy will reduce the number of dog attacks, and the tenants' association claims the policy will not remedy the problem. To undermine the tenants' claim, the correct answer will provide evidence that supports the property manager's claim. **(D)** provides just that. If 90 percent of the current tenants' leases expire soon, then the tenants will be forced to adhere to the new policy. This does not *prove* that the policy will have its intended effect but does make that outcome more likely, thus weakening the tenants' position. **(A)** does not say how similar apartment complexes reduced dog bites, so it neither supports nor undermines the plan at this complex. **(B)**, if anything, supports the tenants' position that the breed restriction plan won't work. What the owner's insurance policy covers has nothing to do with whether attacks occur; eliminate **(C)**. Likewise, the fact that a majority of attacks occurred when the tenants did not have control of their dogs does not relate to what breeds those dogs are and thus does not impact the success or failure of the new policy; eliminate **(E)**.

11. B, E

You don't need to know who Caligula was to be able to answer this question: you simply need to recognize how he is being described, and be able to follow the direction the sentence is taking. Caligula is characterized as being remembered for "bacchanalian feasts," which are basically parties involving a great deal of food and alcoholic beverages. This is reinforced by the fact that the participants indulged in "every form of excess." Therefore, you can predict that the blank, which describes Caligula, will mean something like "glutton." Choices **(D)** *puritans* ("morally strict persons") and **(F)** *ascetics* ("those who renounce worldly indulgences") can both be rejected. Choice **(A)** *gadflies* are "irritating people," so that doesn't fit in this context. Choice **(B)** *sybarites* are people devoted to luxury and pleasure, so that one certainly works. That leaves choices **(C)** *philanthropists* ("humanitarians") and **(E)** *wantons* ("those who live luxuriantly"). Humanitarians aren't necessarily people who indulge in excess, and *wantons* creates a sentence with a meaning similar to the one created by *sybarites*. They're your answers.

12. A, E

After the semicolon, the word "as," meaning "because" in this context, is a straight-ahead road sign. Determine how Arthur looked upon seeing his wife, based on the fact that seeing her filled him with "elation." "Elation" means "great joy," so a good prediction for the blank would be *happy*. Choices **(A)** *ebullient* ("high-spirited") and **(E)** *ecstatic* ("delighted") both create sentences that say Arthur was happy when he saw his wife, and these are the correct answers. **(B)** *esurient*, which means "hungry" or "greedy," and **(D)** *pensive*, which means "thoughtful," do not fit the context. Choices **(C)** *peevish* ("annoyed") and **(F)** *execrable* ("detestable") have strongly negative meanings, so they're the opposite of what you need.

13. C, D

The phrase "for all his" that begins the sentence is a detour road sign that sets up a contrast between Cedric's behavior in informal vs. serious conversation. He becomes "taciturn" ("quiet") in serious conversation. In informal chats with friends and coworkers, then, he probably talks a great deal, and probably not very seriously. You can therefore reject choices that describe meaningful, articulate, or pithy speech. Choices **(A)** *oratories* and **(B)** *declamations* are both "eloquent public speeches," so they do not match the context of chats with friends. Choice **(E)** *epigrams* are witty sayings, so you can reject that as well. Choice **(F)** *opining* means "stating an opinion." This choice might be tempting, but there is no second choice that would give the sentence the same meaning. Choices **(C)** *palaver* and **(D)** *blather* are both words that describe meaningless chatter. They're the correct answers.

14. B, D

"Despite" is a classic detour road sign indicating that the sentence will change direction. You're told that the weather is bad, which normally puts people in a "foul" mood, so the blank must have a meaning opposite of that because of the detour road sign. "Happy" works well. Based on that prediction, you can reject **(A)** *disconcerted*, as that means "upset," and **(E)** *histrionic*, as that means "melodramatic." Choice **(C)** *garrulous* means "chatty," so that does work in this context, but no other answer choice creates a similar sentence. Choice **(F)** *sententious* means "given to excessive moralizing," so that doesn't work in this context. Choice **(B)** *jocund*, meaning "jolly," works and creates a sentence similar to the one created by **(D)** *genial* ("warm and friendly"). They're your answers.

15. C

Use your summary of the author's topic, scope, and purpose to answer this Global question about why the author wrote the passage—in other words, the author's purpose in writing the passage. A good prediction would be *to explain why polar bears appear white*. Keep the author's factual tone in mind when assessing the choices. **(C)** matches the prediction and is correct. The passage explains the phenomenon of the polar bear's white appearance when its hair is actually colorless. **(A)** is incorrect because the passage describes facts, not a "pattern of reasoning." **(B)** can be eliminated because polar bear color is never described as a "traditional belief." **(D)** can be eliminated because the passage's neutral tone does not match "persuading." **(E)** is incorrect because the explanation in the passage is not described as "new information" nor compared to a "previous view."

16. A, C

The correct answer(s) to this Inference question about "the composition and characteristics of polar bear hair" will be fully supported by the passage. Keep in mind the gist of the passage—polar bears aren't actually white but look that way because the inner layer of their hairs reflects light—and research each choice as needed to confirm that it's supported. **(A)** is supported because the medulla, which is "particularly well developed in polar bears," is "only found in some mammals." **(C)** is the main idea of the passage and is supported by the final three sentences. **(B)** is a distortion of information in the passage and is not supported. While the cortex does contain bundles of keratin and pigment (in other mammals), the passage does not state that the pigment is in the keratin. Furthermore, the eighth sentence ("Since the cuticle . . .") states that polar bear hair is "devoid of pigment."

17. A

For this Detail EXCEPT question, each of the four wrong answers is stated in the text. Eliminate choices that express ideas in the passage; select the answer that contradicts the passage or is simply not mentioned. **(A)** is a distortion of information in the passage and is correct. The *cuticle*, not the cortex, is described as overlapping scales of keratin. **(B)** is found in the fourth sentence, which describes the cuticle as the outermost of the three layers. **(C)** and **(D)** are mentioned in the third sentence. **(E)** is the main idea of the passage and is found in the final two sentences.

18. D

The correct answer to this question will be the choice that breaks the connection between the number of barking-dog nuisance complaints and the more frequent deliveries to homes that make dogs bark more often, louder, and longer. **(D)** provides such a situation: there is another reason people complain about barking dogs. If the real source of such complaints is a tendency to overreact to "common disturbances," then the frequency and intensity of the dog's barking are not the determining factors; there will likely be the same number of calls to the police whether the dog woofs softly and occasionally or loudly several times a day. This answer choice doesn't prove that the increase in deliveries won't result in an increase in complaints, but it weakens this prediction, and that is enough. **(A)** and **(E)** are strengtheners. Strengtheners are common trap answers to Weaken questions because a strengthener matches the terms of the argument precisely, but has the opposite effect on the argument. Both an increase in the number of homes visited by each truck daily **(A)** and lower shipping costs **(E)** indicate that there will be more deliveries and, therefore, more occasions for loud barking. **(B)** makes an irrelevant comparison. The argument does not mention, and is not affected by, the days of the week deliveries occur. **(C)** has no effect on the argument. Even if some people appreciate dogs barking at deliveries, these presumably would not be the neighbors who would call in a nuisance-barking complaint in any case. It is the people who don't like to hear dogs barking who will be more disturbed by an increased incidence of barking at deliveries.

19. *"Terse reports on serious, weighty issues such as the war in Iraq are juxtaposed with trivial information, such as celebrity gossip."*

This sentence is the only one in the passage that offers a concrete example. The other likely candidate, "This leaves the viewer unable to emotionally respond to something traumatic, as he is bombarded with disparate pieces of information in rapid succession," describes the result. That doesn't answer the question, which calls for a sentence that illustrates *how* mass media has such an effect.

20. A, C

This question is asking you to infer Postman's position from what the brief selection tells you about his views. Choice **(A)** is correct because the author noted that Postman thought "instant access to a glut of information" reduced meaningful context for that information. Thus, he would likely apply this reasoning to newer information technology that has the same effect. Choice **(B)** is subtly wrong. Postman, you're told, thought television incapable of *fostering* intelligent discourse among its viewers; you cannot conclude that he therefore thinks that no intelligent discourse *appears in* any television program. In fact, part of Postman's problem with the medium is that serious topics are juxtaposed with frivolous items. Postman would definitely agree with the statement in choice **(C)**. Given his views on television, as a medium, and those in the final sentence of the passage, you can infer that he believes that media influence how information is interpreted.

DIAGNOSE YOUR RESULTS

Diagnostic Tool

Tally up your score and write your results in the space provided.

Total

Total Correct: ________ out of 20 correct

Percentage Correct: # you got right × 100 ÷ 20: ________

By Question Type

Text Completion ________ out of 6 correct

Sentence Equivalence ________ out of 4 correct

Reading Comprehension ________ out of 10 correct

Look back at the questions you got wrong and think about your experience answering them.

VERBAL REASONING PRACTICE SET 5

Directions: For each sentence, choose one word for each set of blanks. Select the word or words that best fit(s) the meaning of the sentence as a whole.

1. A responsible business owner may easily feel _______ between her concern for the well-being of her employees and the challenges of financial shortfalls.

   Ⓐ affinity
   Ⓑ tension
   Ⓒ uneasiness
   Ⓓ trepidation
   Ⓔ dejection

2. The controversy surrounding the election dragged on for months, and the lack of a definite victor _______ governance and left people anxious about the future of their leadership.

   Ⓐ facilitated
   Ⓑ augmented
   Ⓒ forestalled
   Ⓓ lowed
   Ⓔ abetted

3. The busboy was known for his diligence rather than his celerity. During his shifts, he worked (i) _______ when cleaning up after customers. Though the chef initially found it annoying, she came to appreciate having things done thoroughly rather than (ii) _______.

Blank (i)		Blank (ii)	
A	perfunctorily	D	haphazardly
B	sedulously	E	expediently
C	desperately	F	disingenuously

4. The middle school principal believed that even a minor (i) _______ the rules demanded his attention. Such a thing could not go (ii) _______ if he were to maintain discipline. In his eyes, obedience and order were of the utmost importance.

Blank (i)	Blank (ii)
A adherence to	D unappreciated
B respect for	E unobserved
C infraction of	F unpunished

5. Ms. Barnhart, unlike previous executives at the engineering firm, eschews the practice of managing every aspect of the day-to-day activities of her team of managers. Instead, she (i) _______ based on the annual business plan. Ms. Barnhart believes that her approach avoids (ii) _______ team morale, which would inevitably and unfortunately occur under (iii) _______ management style.

Blank (i)	Blank (ii)	Blank (iii)
A maximizes annual profits	D directly influencing	G an overly imperious
B offers detailed guidance	E fundamentally supporting	H a less stringent
C delineates comprehensive goals	F unnecessarily impairing	I a less apathetic

6. As a result of poor planning and disorganization, the young team (i) _______ attacking the root of the problem until there was little recourse left to them. They were obliged to (ii) _______ a (iii) _______, last-minute solution to the problem.

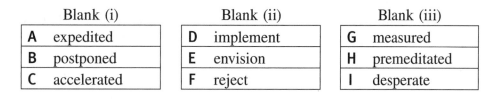

Blank (i)	Blank (ii)	Blank (iii)
A expedited	D implement	G measured
B postponed	E envision	H premeditated
C accelerated	F reject	I desperate

Questions 7–9 are based on the following passage.

The Terracotta Army, 8,000 terracotta warrior figures guarding the tomb of the first Chinese emperor, Qin Shui Huang (259–210 BCE), was discovered in Xi'an in northwest China in 1974. The finding was remarkable not only for the sheer number of figures but for the intricate details of each sculpture. While it was a well-developed art form in ancient Greece, sculpture seems to have played only a minor role in ancient Asian art until the ascension of Qin Shui Huang. The variety of ear shapes, hairstyles, and armor among the figures has archaeologists pondering the possibility that the Terracotta Army may be representations of actual individual warriors. Such a level of detail is far beyond that of any known earlier Chinese sculptures.

Experts are searching for an explanation for this seemingly sudden appearance of sophisticated sculpture in ancient China. Recent DNA analysis of human remains found in westernmost China from the period of Qin Shui Huang yielded the surprising presence of European DNA, leading anthropologists to believe that Western contact with China may significantly predate the Silk Road, usually considered the inception of the relationship between these two civilizations. What is even more remarkable, however, is one of the responses to this discovery. Professor Lukas Nickel, an art historian from the University of Vienna, speculates that the presence of the DNA indicates that a Greek sculptor may have been employed at the site of the Terracotta Army to train the locals. Nickel also cites ancient Chinese records that reveal tales of giant statues appearing in the far West, as well as narratives stating that the emperor ordered the casting of copies in bronze that were erected in front of his palace. This account supports the notion of early contact between China and the West, which Nickel says could have inspired the First Emperor not only to duplicate the giant statues but also to build the huge Terracotta Army along with other life-size sculptures. Li Xiuzhen, a Chinese archaeologist specializing in the Terracotta Army, responds that the sculptures "may be inspired by Western culture, but were uniquely made by the Chinese."

Nickel's leap from the presence of European DNA in one part of China to his conclusion strains credulity. It is, at best, an interesting hypothesis demanding further evidence and, at worst, a pernicious example of Western cultural elitism wherein artistic developments that parallel or exceed those of Western culture are considered impossible without the impetus of Western influence.

7. The primary purpose of the passage is to

   Ⓐ compare the development of sculpture as an art form in the ancient Greek and Chinese cultures
   Ⓑ challenge an interpretation of new physical evidence of the presence of Western DNA in China
   Ⓒ criticize the authenticity of recent evidence used to address the question of how the Greek and Chinese sculptural arts came to share many characteristics
   Ⓓ discuss the contribution of Greek artisans to the design and construction of the Terracotta Army
   Ⓔ present evidence that suggests an explanation for the sudden appearance of advanced sculpture techniques in China

8. The passage implies which of the following about the sculptures of the Terracotta Army?

   Ⓐ They did not include anatomical features specific to individual subjects.
   Ⓑ Their detailed features enable art historians and archaeologists to definitively identify individual warriors.
   Ⓒ They were a further development of the earlier traditions of Chinese sculpture.
   Ⓓ They were due to the training provided by Greek sculptors.
   Ⓔ They may have some similarities in style to some contemporary Greek sculptures.

9. Identify the sentence that provides an interpretation of evidence of contact between ancient Western and Chinese cultures with which the author disagrees.

Question 10 is based on the following passage.

In the field of Kafka studies and its various related subfields, perhaps the most controversial figure is Max Brod, Franz Kafka's publisher, biographer, and closest friend. Although it is thanks to Brod that we possess any of Kafka's writing—Kafka only allowed his writing to be published at Brod's insistence and had asked Brod to burn all his writing upon his death, which Brod did not do—Brod is considered by many Kafka specialists and enthusiasts to have possessed a meager understanding of his friend's writing and importance. A prolific writer, Brod's writing has in time been greatly overshadowed by Kafka's, and many find his compositions to be blunt and crude when compared to Kafka's abstruse elegance; this contrast was further emphasized by their personalities, with Brod being gregarious and a notorious womanizer, whereas Kafka was withdrawn and shy. Based on this contrast, many in the field of Kafka studies feel that Brod—being the only channel through which we know Kafka—in some ways tainted the "pure" Kafka in the editorial process, and the search for unpublished manuscripts of Kafka (free of Brod's influence) has become for many an obsession.

10. According to the passage, why is Max Brod described as a "controversial figure"?

(A) Although Brod was Kafka's closest friend, many wonder if Kafka objected to Brod's editorial alterations of his writing.
(B) Because of the divergence of their upbringings, Brod and Kafka had difficulty seeing eye to eye with one another.
(C) Although he is the only source of Kafka's writings, Brod is thought to have poorly understood Kafka's writing.
(D) Brod's lascivious behavior repulsed Kafka, who wished for someone more refined to edit his work.
(E) Upon Kafka's death, Brod burned all of Kafka's remaining writings, suggesting that he did not properly recognize his friend's incredible talent.

Directions: Select the <u>two</u> answer choices that, when inserted into the sentence, fit the meaning of the sentence as a whole <u>and</u> yield complete sentences that are similar in meaning.

11. Terrance was _______ student, always eager to participate and try his best; unfortunately, his low test scores did not reflect his efforts.

[A] a pedantic
[B] an animated
[C] an apathetic
[D] a pragmatic
[E] an assiduous
[F] a prudent

12. In addition to having sharp teeth and claws, the maned wolf emits _______ musk, which acts as a defense mechanism in the wild.

   A a malodorous
   B a pristine
   C a soporific
   D a pungent
   E an estimable
   F a charming

13. The first baseman and shortstop were both talented players with Hall of Fame credentials, but their _______ relationship exacerbated the chaos in the locker room.

   A venerable
   B prudent
   C volatile
   D stolid
   E inimical
   F stoic

14. Although the old woman had lived through the Great Depression, she _______ spent her money on her grandchildren, giving them everything she didn't have growing up.

   A liberally
   B scrupulously
   C capriciously
   D meticulously
   E lavishly
   F flintily

Questions 15 and 16 are based on the following passage.

Few babies born to HIV-infected mothers carry the disease *in utero*, even though HIV is a blood-borne virus and there is a constant flow of blood through the umbilical cord that could infect the growing fetus. As genetic testing has demonstrated, this is because the human fetal immune system may develop separately from the adult immune system, and it may provide a measure of protection. When exposed to foreign cells, immune cells "activate" to become T-cells, which defend the organism. Fetal T-cells seem to be more tolerant of HIV and do not cause the reactions typically seen in HIV infection; these cells recognize the foreign cells but do not fight them, and the virus is not stimulated to destroy the T-cells, as happens when an individual has full-blown AIDS.

15. Which sentence provides the best summary of the passage?

    (A) Foreign cells cannot enter fetuses' bloodstreams as easily as they can enter the bloodstreams of adults.
    (B) The reason few fetuses contract HIV from infected mothers is that their mothers' T-cells protect them.
    (C) The fetal immune system may not be similar to the adult immune system.
    (D) T-cells affected by HIV are not activated in the fetal immune response and therefore remain more tolerant of foreign cells.
    (E) Fetuses rarely contract HIV *in utero* because the fetal immune system operates differently than the adult system.

Consider each of the following choices separately and select all that apply.

16. Which of the following statements are suggested by the passage?

    [A] Fetuses are better protected from HIV than their mothers because of their respective immune systems.
    [B] If researchers could find a way to stop T-cells in adults from activating, adults would have the same health benefit as fetuses.
    [C] Fetal immune systems are more complicated than those of adults.

Questions 17 and 18 are based on the following passage.

While days of the chain gang are long gone, the effects of meaningful labor during imprisonment demonstrate marked benefits to both the prisoner and society. Some of these benefits take the forms of reduced recidivism, increased job skills and employability, and improved quality of life. In fact, corporations have hired jails to have their inmates perform work from manufacturing to telemarketing. However, some critics argue that prisoners who work are little more than bonded slaves, earning nothing for their labor and forced to do work that may be beyond their physical or mental capacity. Others are more concerned about the economic factors of cheap, noncompetitive labor or issues involved in giving inmates responsibility for critical components of products or providing them with lists of addresses and telephone numbers.

17. The author would most likely agree with which of the following sentences?

    (A) Working may offset deleterious psychological conditions to which prisoners are exposed.
    (B) Too many lawsuits filed against jails involve prisoners being forced to perform work they are not physically equipped to handle.
    (C) Telemarketing corporations are the main entities that stand to profit from inmates working for free or at low cost.
    (D) People in jail lack the mental skill needed to perform more challenging work.
    (E) Adjusting the current model of inmate labor to have prisoners work for money or reduced sentences would improve the penal system.

18. Choose the sentence in the passage that provides support for the main argument.

Questions 19 and 20 are based on the following passage.

The current worldwide economic recession has forced state governments to reevaluate how tax dollars should be spent. A recent statement from the Iowa State legislature indicated that they were considering cutting state-funded sabbaticals for professors working within the publicly funded Iowa University system. The justification has been that this is an inefficient use of funds, which could be better allocated elsewhere or cut out of the tax code. Critics cited the high cost of paying a professor's salary for the entire year in which they do not work. They also suggested that taxpayers should not pay for professors to take time off from teaching to write a book on a subject such as ancient mythology. There is a strong counterargument, however, which points out that not all faculty sabbaticals are, by necessity, unprofitable. Aside from the benefit of the increase of knowledge, it is not entirely clear how a sabbatical may, ultimately, return on its investment. A genetics professor who, during her sabbatical, discovers a new drug treatment methodology, for example, could potentially generate millions of dollars in grant money for the university's research department.

19. Which of the following is likely to be an opinion of the author of this passage?

(A) Public funding for sabbaticals should be cut.
(B) The value produced by a faculty sabbatical cannot be determined prior to the sabbatical.
(C) Professors should only teach, not engage in outside research.
(D) The goal of a university should be to conduct abstract research that leads to practical applications.
(E) The study of genetics is a more worthwhile pursuit than that of mythology.

Consider each of the following choices separately and select all that apply.

20. Which of the following statements is suggested by the passage?

[A] As a result of the sabbatical system, universities are doing less meaningful research than they once did.
[B] As a state, Iowa has a lower percentage of professors whose primary responsibility is teaching.
[C] Some state legislators feel that taxpayers should not have to indirectly pay for research that will not benefit them.

VERBAL REASONING PRACTICE SET 5 ANSWER KEY

1. **B**
2. **C**
3. **B, E**
4. **C, F**
5. **C, F, G**
6. **B, D, I**
7. **B**
8. **E**
9. *"Professor Lukas Nickel, an art historian from the University of Vienna, speculates that the presence of the DNA indicates the possibility that a Greek sculptor may have been employed at the site of the Terracotta Army to train the locals."*
10. **C**
11. **B, E**
12. **A, D**
13. **C, E**
14. **A, E**
15. **E**
16. **A**
17. **A**
18. *"Some of these benefits take the forms of reduced recidivism, increased job skills and employability, and improved quality of life."*
19. **B**
20. **C**

VERBAL REASONING PRACTICE SET 5 ANSWERS AND EXPLANATIONS

1. B

The sentence tells you that a relationship exists between concerns for the well-being of employees and the challenges of financial shortfalls. The two are being contrasted, so a reasonable prediction would be *stress.* Scanning the answers, you'll notice choice **(B)** *tension*, which is a synonym for stress, fits perfectly. Choice **(A)** *affinity* is the opposite of the prediction. Choice **(C)** *uneasiness* is close but does not address the conflict between the two concerns as well as *tension.* Choices **(D)** *trepidation* and **(E)** *dejection* are too negatively charged for this context; nothing in the sentence indicates that the business owner is frightened or sad, respectively.

2. C

The people are anxious because they do not know who will be leading them, which will *limit* or *hinder* leadership or governance; your answer will reflect this. Choices **(A)** *facilitated*, **(B)** *augmented*, and **(E)** *abetted* all have meanings of "strengthened" or "increased." Choice **(D)** *lowed* might be tempting because it resembles "lowered," but the verb "low" means to make the sound of a cow. Choice **(C)** *forestalled* is the only option that means "restricted" or "slowed down."

3. B, E

The detour road sign "rather than" indicates that the busboy has one of two contrasting qualities: "diligence" ("thoroughness") rather than "celerity" ("speed"). He is not quick, yet he is thorough. The chef initially disliked the busboy's work habits, but the detour road sign "though" indicates that she has come to like them, since thoroughness can be more important than rapidity. For the first blank, you need a word that means something like *thoroughly.* Choice **(B)** *sedulously*, which means "perseveringly," works well. Choice **(A)** *perfunctorily*, "superficially," is the opposite of what you need, and **(C)** *desperately* doesn't make any sense in this context. There is more information available on the second blank. The word "rather" appears again as a detour road sign. The sentence mirrors the earlier contrast in the question. The chef has come to appreciate the busboy's thoroughness even though the busboy isn't *fast.* Choice **(E)** *expediently* means "quickly," and matches the prediction perfectly. Choice **(D)** *haphazardly* means "sloppily," which is not a quality the chef would want. Choice **(F)** *disingenuously* means "insincerely," which makes no sense here.

4. C, F

You read that the principal wants to "maintain discipline" and that order is of paramount importance to him. From that context, you can determine that a *breaking of* the rules will not be tolerated. Make this your prediction for the first blank. The correct match for this is choice **(C)** *infraction of.* Both choices **(A)** *adherence to* and **(B)** *respect for* are the opposite of your prediction. For the second blank, predict that breaking rules could not go *unpunished.* This matches choice **(F)** *unpunished.* Choice **(D)** *unappreciated* doesn't make sense in context, and if the infraction was *unobserved*, choice **(E)**, the principal wouldn't know about it.

5. C, F, G

The first blank is introduced with the detour road sign "[i]nstead," so what Ms. Barnhart does contrasts with "managing every aspect" of her managers' daily activities. If you know that "eschew" means "to avoid," this is an additional clue, but even without this information, you can predict that she manages her team with a looser, more hands-off approach. *Delineates comprehensive goals*, **(C)**, matches the prediction. *Delineate* means "to outline," and *comprehensive* means "of a broad scope." Setting broad goals contrasts with managing everything her team does. While nearly every executive seeks to maximize profits, **(A)** does not fit the context of the sentence. *Offers detailed guidance*, **(B)**, is the opposite of the prediction.

For the second blank, since what Ms. Barnhart seeks to "avoid" doing to team morale would be "unfortunate," predict that she wants to avoid *harming* morale. *Unnecessarily impairing*, **(F)**, works well since *impairing* means "damaging, making worse." Neither **(D)** nor **(E)** matches the prediction.

Since Ms. Barnhart avoids hurting morale by not overmanaging her people, for the last blank, predict that the management style it describes is *too demanding* or *overbearing*. *[A]n overly imperious*, **(G)**, provides the right meaning for the sentence. *Imperious* means "controlling" or "domineering." *[A] less stringent*, **(H)**, management style would seem to describe Ms. Barnhart's approach, making **(H)** incorrect. Neither management style could accurately be described as *apathetic*, which means "not caring," so eliminate **(I)**.

6. B, D, I

The sentences provide context clues to the missing words. You learn that this disorganized team did something in the face of a problem until they had "little recourse," or few options, and had to adopt "a . . . last-minute solution." For the first blank, predict that they *delayed* dealing with the problem. **(B)** *postponed* matches this prediction and is correct. Neither **(A)** *expedited* nor **(C)** *accelerated*, which mean "acted quickly," are consistent with having to act at the last minute.

The word in the third blank will describe the "last-minute solution" that these people are "obliged" to settle on, so predict a negative word that describes their plight. **(I)** *desperate* works well. Both **(G)** *measured* ("deliberate, accurate") and **(H)** *premeditated* ("planned in advance") are the opposite of this group's approach to the situation.

The second blank has no direct road signs or context clues to help you predict, so consider the flow of the text as a whole. The team had a problem, and they finally had to solve it: predict that they were obliged to *use* a solution for it. That's **(D)** *implement*. **(E)** *envision* might have been tempting, but if all they had to do was *envision* ("imagine") a solution, time wouldn't have been an issue. And since they waited until the last minute, in effect rejecting possible actions all along, it wouldn't make sense to say they had to **(F)** *reject* a last-minute solution.

7. B

The strong language in the last paragraph, "strains credulity" and "pernicious example," are clear indicators of the author's disagreement with Nickel's assessment. A good prediction of the author's purpose would be *to rebut Nickel's interpretation of the presence of Western DNA in ancient China*. **(B)** matches the prediction and is correct. **(C)** distorts two aspects of the passage. First, the author is criticizing the interpretation of the DNA evidence, not its authenticity. Second, while the text indicates that Greek sculpture in the 3rd century BCE was more advanced than Chinese sculpture at the time, nowhere does it compare "many characteristics" of the two traditions. The remaining choices can be eliminated by a verb scan. The passage does not **(A)** *compare* cultural developments of sculpture, and the neutral verbs **(D)** *discuss* and **(E)** *present* do not accurately reflect the author's definite opinion.

8. E

The key word "implies" identifies this as an Inference question. The "sculptures of the Terracotta Army" are discussed throughout the text, so expect to compare each choice to the passage. **(A)** and **(B)** are distortions of the fourth sentence of the first paragraph. Since archaeologists are "pondering the possibility that the Terracotta Army may be representations of actual individual warriors," it is not yet known if these details do **(B)** or do not **(A)** represent individuals. **(C)** is a 180, or opposite, choice. The final sentence of the first paragraph identifies the details of these sculptures as "far beyond" those of earlier sculptures, and the first sentence of the second paragraph described their appearance as "sudden," not based on earlier traditions. **(D)** is an extreme restatement of Nickel's opinion, with which the author disagrees. That leaves **(E)**, which is not stated directly in the passage, but is supported by the point at issue. If the sculptures were in no way similar to Western sculpture, it is not likely that experts would be debating Western influence. Also, in the last sentence of the second paragraph, the Chinese expert acknowledges the possible inspiration from Western sources.

9. "Professor Lukas Nickel, an art historian from the University of Vienna, speculates that the presence of the DNA indicates the possibility that a Greek sculptor may have been employed at the site of the Terracotta Army to train the locals."

In the last paragraph, the author disagrees with Nickel's interpretation of the DNA evidence. The correct answer will be the sentence that provides Nickel's view—that's the fourth sentence of the second paragraph.

10. C

The reasons Brod is described as a controversial figure are a major focus of this passage, so researching this question should give you little trouble. The correct answer comes from the sentence in which the author tells you what "many in the field" feel about Brod: he was incapable of appreciating Kafka's work despite being its sole caretaker. Choice **(A)**, while saying nothing that directly contradicts the passage, is not supported by the passage, either. No mention is made of Kafka's feelings towards Brod's editing. That's the first choice you can eliminate. Choices **(B)** and **(D)** both possess language not contained in the passage. The passage does not discuss Kafka's and Brod's upbringings or Kafka being "repulsed" by Brod's lifestyle. Choice **(E)** sounds reminiscent of the passage, but the passage describes Kafka's wish to have his writing burned, a wish Brod denies. Choice **(E)** misstates this situation and is, thus, also incorrect. Choice **(C)**, however, paraphrases the concern of those in the field who believe that Brod did not really comprehend Kafka's writing (although he saw its importance). That is the correct answer.

11. B, E

The key to this question is the detour road sign "unfortunately." Terrance's low test scores are the exact opposite of what you would expect from such a student. You know he is an eager student who always tries his best and participates in class; any of these positive associations could fit in the blank. This allows you to immediately eliminate choice **(A)** *pedantic*, "stodgy," and **(F)** *prudent*, "restrained," which are direct opposites of our predictions. Choice **(C)** *apathetic* can be rejected for the same reason. Contrasting Terrance's ability with his idealistic actions eliminates choice **(D)** *pragmatic*, which means "realistic as opposed to idealistic." The remaining two answer choices, **(B)** *animated*, "lively," and **(E)** *assiduous*, "persistent," both create sentences that describe the type of student who would continue to participate in class when he is not experiencing success.

12. A, D

If the maned wolf's musk acts as a "defense mechanism," it probably smells pretty bad. So you can predict *foul-smelling* for the blank. For this reason, you can eliminate choice **(B)** *pristine,* "fresh," "uncorrupted," which suggests the exact opposite of a foul musk, and choice **(E)** *estimable,* "admirable," which suggests only a positive attitude toward the smell. Choice **(F)** *charming* can be rejected for similar reasons. While a **(C)** *soporific*, or "sleep-inducing," musk could conceivably serve as a defense, there is no match for it among the other choices. Choices **(A)** *malodorous,* "bad-smelling," and **(D)** *pungent,* "sharp-smelling," best fit your original prediction of *foul-smelling.*

13. C, E

Reading this sentence all the way through reveals that the missing word describes a relationship that "exacerbates," or "worsens," a chaotic situation. For this reason, you can immediately eliminate choices **(A)** *venerable* and **(B)** *prudent*, as they characterize a relationship as "respectful" and "restrained," the opposite of the relationship described here. Choice **(D)** *stolid,* "unemotional, lacking sensitivity," seems plausible at first glance, as it suggests a negative relationship. Likewise for choice **(F)** *stoic*, "indifferent to pleasure or pain." However, the context key word "chaos" suggests an emotional (albeit negative) relationship. Therefore, choice **(C)** *volatile,* "easily aroused," and **(E)** *inimical,* "hostile," are the best choices. They indicate the hostile, chaotic relationship that the sentence suggests.

14. A, E

"Although" is a detour road sign, indicating that the sentence will change direction. So, although the woman lived through the Great Depression, she can now give her grandchildren the things she couldn't afford growing up. Choice **(F)** *flintily* is wrong, as this implies she was not kindly disposed to spending money. This reasoning also eliminates choices **(B)** *scrupulously* and **(D)** *meticulously*, as these imply a restraint with money. Choice **(C)** *capriciously* is plausible, but implies a carelessness that is not evidenced in the passage. Therefore, choice **(A)** *liberally* and choice **(E)** *lavishly* are the best choices, as they indicate exuberant spending, opposite of the frugality typical of the Depression.

15. E

In this question, you are asked to select the best summary of the passage. The main idea of the passage is that fetal immune systems do not operate in the same way as adult immune systems, and that provides protection from HIV to the developing fetus. Choice **(E)** paraphrases that summary and is indeed the answer. Choice **(A)** is not true according to the passage; HIV can enter the bloodstream, but the T-cells are tolerant and don't activate, which allows the HIV to pass through without attacking the T-cells. Choice **(B)** is outside the scope; nothing is said in the passage about the mothers' T-cells. Choice **(C)** is true according to the passage, but it is not a complete summary. The critical component of HIV resistance is not included in this choice. Choice **(D)** gets the facts from the passage wrong. According to the passage, T-cells activate in the fetal immune system but do not fight HIV in the typical way.

16. A

This question asks you to evaluate the statements and select those that can be validly inferred from the passage. Choice **(A)** summarizes the passage's main point. It's one correct answer. Choice **(B)** seems reasonable, but the passage doesn't go this far. Differences between the adult and fetal immune systems beyond their respective responses to HIV may make this statement untrue. There is nothing in the passage to suggest that choice **(C)** is a valid inference. The passage does not compare the complexity of the adult and fetal immune systems.

17. A

This question asks you to evaluate possible explanations and compare them to your understanding of the information in the passage. Choice **(A)** follows from that portion of the passage in which the author tells you that prisoners see "quality of life" improvements as the result of working. Choice **(B)** falls completely outside the scope of the passage. The author says nothing about lawsuits challenging prison work programs. Choice **(C)** distorts the passage. Telemarketing is one of the jobs prisoners perform, but so is manufacturing (and maybe others). Nothing suggests that telemarketing firms have the most to gain from using prison labor. Choice **(D)** is cited as a concern of some critics, but nothing suggests that the author agrees with them. Nor can you determine whether the author would agree with choice **(E)**. The suggestion in **(E)** might address the concerns of some critics, but again, you don't know that the author shares those concerns.

18. *"Some of these benefits take the forms of reduced recidivism, increased job skills and employability, and improved quality of life."*

This sentence supports the main claim that is set up in the first sentence: "While days of the chain gang are long gone, the effects of meaningful labor during imprisonment demonstrate marked benefits to both the prisoner and society." The remainder of the passage contains counterarguments and their supporting evidence.

19. B

This question rewards you for paying attention to the author's attitude and opinions. For the most part, this author takes a neutral tone. He states facts and reports the debate over sabbaticals, but doesn't appear to take a side in that debate. Choice **(A)** is one of the sides in the debate. Nothing in the passage suggests that the author agrees with the anti-sabbatical crowd. Choice **(B)** is the correct answer. The author points out that it is not clear, prior to a sabbatical, whether the result will be profitable. He offers the biotechnology example to illustrate this point. Choice **(C)** is wrong because the author doesn't opine on this issue; he suggests a defense of research through his inclusion of the biotechnology example. Choice **(D)** is the flip side of **(C)**; while the author is positively disposed to research, nothing suggests that he considers it the sole (or even primary) mission of universities. You can reject choice **(E)** as a comparison irrelevant to the scope of this passage.

20. C

This question asks you to evaluate the statements and identify which you can infer from the passage. Choice **(A)** is incorrect because it goes beyond the scope of what the passage implies; nowhere does the author say that there is insufficient research being done within the university system or ascribe blame to the sabbatical system. Choice **(B)** may be tempting, but it is wrong. The passage employs the Iowa debate to illustrate the point, but it doesn't provide any information that compares Iowa to other states. Choice **(C)** is the only correct answer. The author mentions the example of a professor writing a book on ancient mythology during sabbatical to imply that some legislators may not consider that an adequately beneficial work product.

DIAGNOSE YOUR RESULTS

Diagnostic Tool

Tally up your score and write your results in the space provided.

Total

Total Correct: ________ out of 20 correct

Percentage Correct: # you got right × 100 ÷ 20: ________

By Question Type

Text Completion ________ out of 6 correct

Sentence Equivalence ________ out of 4 correct

Reading Comprehension ________ out of 10 correct

Look back at the questions you got wrong and think about your experience answering them.

VERBAL REASONING PRACTICE SET 6

Directions: For each sentence, choose one word for each set of blanks. Select the word or words that best fit(s) the meaning of the sentence as a whole.

1. After getting expelled from school, Patricia refused to attend any future family functions, petrified that her stern family would _______ her.

   (A) venerate
   (B) deride
   (C) raze
   (D) emulate
   (E) provoke

2. The filmmaker's highly controversial work was _______ in bringing the style of Dogme 95 to the forefront of the film industry.

   (A) a lament
   (B) an anachronism
   (C) a catalyst
   (D) an anomaly
   (E) a paradox

3. Male sperm whales, recognizable by their astonishing size, are normally (i) _______ creatures; however, when they are jealously guarding their territory, they have been known to (ii) _______ ships that they feel have encroached too far.

Blank (i)	Blank (ii)
A docile	D ignore
B aggressive	E follow
C powerful	F attack

4. Opponents of affirmative action by quota, the practice of hiring on the basis of race or sex as well as (i) _______, maintain that both the hired and the rejected suffer (ii) _______ when not judged on their abilities alone.

Blank (i)	Blank (ii)
A status	D nepotism
B creed	E parity
C competence	F injustice

5. Ancient Greek philosophers tried to (i) _______ contemporary notions of change and stability in the physical composition of the world around them. They did so by (ii) _______ the existence of the atom. For them, the atom was (iii) _______ particle from which all other varieties of matter are formed.

Blank (i)	Blank (ii)	Blank (iii)
A reconcile	D denying	G a mythical
B eliminate	E ignoring	H an indivisible
C confirm	F postulating	I a munificent

6. While many teachers extol the incorporation of Internet-based technology in the high school classroom, a vocal group of educators (i) _______ such a pedagogical approach as (ii) _______ and argues that long-standing teaching strategies would not be (iii) _______ by such technologies.

Blank (i)	Blank (ii)	Blank (iii)
A applauds	D feasible	G undermined
B repudiates	E counterproductive	H augmented
C exculpates	F beneficial	I terminated

Questions 7–8 are based on the following passage.

Ludwig Wittgenstein asserted that with the publication of his *Tractatus Logico-Philosophicus* he had solved all philosophical problems and retired to teach mathematics at the secondary level. He believed he had achieved this through his exploration of the logic of language, which he referred to as his "picture theory" of language. Wittgenstein's contention was that the world consisted of a collection of interconnected "facts" that created "pictures" of the world through propositions. These propositions are meaningful if they picture matters of empirical fact, such as "Meri is six feet tall." In order for these linguistic pictures to accurately represent facts, they must have the same logical structure as matters of empirical fact.

The problem is that philosophical propositions, such as "truth is beauty," are not matters of empirical fact. Since language itself is based on this relationship, philosophers cannot extricate themselves from the realm of language in order to actually *say* anything about whether or not the "pictures" have the same logical structure as the facts. One important consequence of this argument is that it is nonsensical to discuss philosophical problems. The propositions that philosophers commonly make are not technically wrong but nonsensical. For Wittgenstein, the ultimate goal of philosophy itself is not the actual study or pursuit of "truth." Philosophy has more to do with clarifying the relationship between language and truth than truth itself. The *Tractatus* ends up subverting its own claims by concluding that the kind of propositions of which it is composed are senseless. The most commonly quoted excerpt from the book is the proposition "What we cannot speak about we must pass over in silence."

7. The author believes Wittgenstein would likely agree with which of the following statements?

   (A) The truth is not beautiful.
   (B) Beauty is not truthful.
   (C) Something cannot be both truthful and beautiful.
   (D) The proposition "truth is beauty" is nonsensical.
   (E) Beauty is the same as truth.

8. Based on the context of the passage, the author's use of the word "empirical" most nearly means which of the following?

   (A) verifiable by experimentation
   (B) true
   (C) subjective
   (D) nonsensical
   (E) typical

Question 9 is based on the following passage.

An engineering firm specializes in installing environmentally friendly components, such as solar panels and green technology, on the rooftops of many different types of buildings in a large urban area. Each project is assigned to one of several installation teams. The owner, who is concerned with costs, is conducting an analysis of worker efficiency. Once he has completed the analysis, he plans to retrain the team that has the highest average projected completion time in order to improve that team's efficiency.

9. Which one of the following, if true, most seriously calls into question the owner's plan for selecting the team to be retrained?

   (A) The installation fees that the firm charges its customers are lower than those charged for similar projects done by other companies.
   (B) If the time that the team takes to finish a project is not lowered significantly, the firm could lose business to competitors.
   (C) The team that has the highest average completion time tends to be assigned the most complex projects.
   (D) Retraining the team will substantially increase the short-term costs of the firm and thereby impact its profitability.
   (E) Maximum efficiency can only be achieved if the team with the highest average completion rate is terminated.

Question 10 is based on the following passage.

Marcus Tullius Cicero was a Roman statesman and philosopher in the final years of the Republic and remains one of the greatest and most influential orators in Western history. Among his many famous tracts and speeches, one of the most remarkable remains the First Catilinarian Oration, a condemnation of the senator Lucius Sergius Catiline for his role in a conspiracy against the Republic. Enraged at having lost the election for consulship the previous year to Cicero, his political rival, Cataline wove a plot to assassinate Cicero and several other senators to ensure his victory in the election of 63 BCE. When the plot was uncovered and foiled, the election was postponed, and the Senate meeting moved to a more secure location the following day to discuss the conspiracy. Cataline arrived at the Senate, shocking the entire Senate, but Cicero quickly recovered and delivered the First Catilinarian Oration, a masterpiece of oratory skill, which prompted the rest of the Senate to denounce Cataline as a traitor. Cataline fled the city with his conspirators and was killed a year later in battle with Republican soldiers.

10. What is the topic of this passage?

    (A) The works of Marcus Tullius Cicero
    (B) The effects of the First Catilinarian Oration
    (C) The Catilinarian conspiracy
    (D) The First Catilinarian Oration
    (E) Famous orations

Directions: Select the two answer choices that, when inserted into the sentence, fit the meaning of the sentence as a whole and yield complete sentences that are similar in meaning.

11. Many Americans in the 1950s may have found the idea of a black president _______, but societal changes since then have made this idea a reality.

    A farcical
    B puerile
    C superannuated
    D implausible
    E perfidious
    F fastidious

12. Located in what is perhaps the most geographically remote state in the Union, Hawaii's isolated Molokai Island is known for its hidden, untouched, and _______ beaches.

    A morose
    B immaculate
    C dilapidated
    D placid
    E pristine
    F imperturbable

13. Hot yoga, a practice that takes place in a 95-degree-plus room, clears toxins out of the body through perspiration, leaving a practitioner with a sense of _______.

    A disarray
    B turbulence
    C purgation
    D quintessence
    E ablution
    F exhilaration

14. The doctor told Joe he needed to lose weight, so he began to make more _______ choices when going out to dinner.

    [A] abstemious
    [B] detrimental
    [C] gluttonous
    [D] acerbic
    [E] loquacious
    [F] austere

Question 15 is based on the following passage.

One of the most famous and influential music theorists of the latter half of the 20th century, John Cage is remembered for being to music what Marcel Duchamp was to art—someone who constantly questioned what defined music. One of his best-known interests was in removing the creator, the personal influence, from music and instead creating music based on natural patterns and chance (aleatory music). One of his famous works involved music created by laying musical bars over astrological maps and assigning notes based on the location of the stars and planets. Another famous work (perhaps his most famous), 4′33″, consisted of three movements all entirely of rests: the music, rather, was created by the ambient sounds of and around the performance hall. His stated goal was to remove personal agency and purpose from music and let music act as a reflection of the natural chaos of the world, rather than as an effort to organize and improve nature.

15. According to the passage, which of the following best paraphrases John Cage's philosophy of music?

    (A) Music must be radically changed from our current notions.
    (B) Music should be based in nature rather than on individual purpose.
    (C) Music is not really anything, but rather whatever we wish it to be.
    (D) Music is a reflection of the personal agency of the composer.
    (E) Music is inherently without meaning.

Questions 16–18 are based on the following passage.

Coffee has long been the subject of research due to its popularity as an early-morning pick-me-up and its distinct taste and aroma. Although it has often been laden with a reputation for being potentially unhealthy, many studies have shown that the opposite is true; in fact, coffee has been tied to a wide range of benefits. The acid in coffee can contribute to heartburn, and the caffeine can raise blood pressure, but when consumed in moderation (a few regular cups a day), these disadvantages are minimized.

Although coffee was once linked to cancer, that association has long been dispelled. Instead, coffee may contribute to the prevention of certain types of cancers due to its high volume of antioxidants. Minerals found in coffee, like magnesium and chromium, help the body control blood sugar by influencing insulin, and this may contribute to preventing diabetes. Similarly, although researchers aren't sure why, coffee drinkers seem to have a better chance than do non–coffee drinkers of fighting off Parkinson's disease and dementia as they age. In the short term, coffee is low in calories, stimulates alertness and concentration, and, for some people, lengthens their attention spans.

16. Which statement best summarizes the reading passage?

(A) The more coffee a person consumes, the healthier he or she will be.
(B) The benefits of drinking coffee appear to outweigh the disadvantages.
(C) Drinking coffee can prevent Parkinson's disease and dementia.
(D) Coffee consumption is unrelated to the incidence of cancer.
(E) Caffeine is the cause of high blood pressure.

Consider each of the following choices separately and select all that apply.

17. What can you infer from the passage?

[A] Decaffeinated coffee offers the same benefits as caffeinated coffee.
[B] If berries are high in antioxidants, they may help prevent cancer.
[C] Insulin has an effect on diabetes.

Consider each of the following choices separately and select all that apply.

18. The author would most likely disagree with which of the following statements?

[A] Stimulants are inherently bad for the human body.
[B] It is possible for coffee to be a part of a healthy diet.
[C] Decaffeinated coffee does not have the same benefits as caffeinated coffee.

Questions 19 and 20 are based on the following passage.

In December 2010, the Federation Internationale de Football Association (FIFA), the global governing body of soccer, announced that the 2022 World Cup would be held in Qatar. Immediately, a swirl of controversy surrounded the decision, which followed previous allegations that certain FIFA members had accepted monetary bribes in exchange for their bid votes. Soccer fans questioned how Qatar was able to win the bidding process over other bidders, such as the United States, Australia, South Korea, and Japan. In addition to the logistical problem of oppressive heat during the summer months in which the World Cup is traditionally held, Qatar is a controversial choice because of allegedly discriminatory legislation and its restrictive alcohol policy, which some claim is at odds with the activities typical of a sporting event. Additionally, Qatar would have to build venues for the event from scratch. Nonetheless, FIFA officials insist that this furthers the goal of spreading soccer to new places.

19. Which of the following is likely to be an opinion of the author of this passage?

    Ⓐ FIFA is a corrupt and unethical organization.
    Ⓑ It is improbable that Qatar will be adequately prepared for the 2022 World Cup.
    Ⓒ Japan was most deserving of winning the 2022 World Cup bid.
    Ⓓ Qatar is a controversial choice to host the 2022 World Cup.
    Ⓔ Soccer fans will be unlikely to travel to Qatar for the 2022 World Cup.

Consider each of the following choices separately and select all that apply.

20. Which of the following statements is suggested by the passage?

    [A] FIFA is likely to face criticism and come under scrutiny in the following months.
    [B] The country of Qatar is likely to change in some ways as a result of hosting the 2022 World Cup.
    [C] The choice of Qatar to host the 2022 World Cup is enough evidence to abolish FIFA and replace it.

VERBAL REASONING PRACTICE SET 6 ANSWER KEY

1. **B**
2. **C**
3. **A, F**
4. **C, F**
5. **A, F, H**
6. **B, E, H**
7. **D**
8. **A**
9. **C**
10. **D**
11. **A, D**
12. **B, E**
13. **C, E**
14. **A, F**
15. **B**
16. **B**
17. **B, C**
18. **A**
19. **D**
20. **A, B**

VERBAL REASONING PRACTICE SET 6 ANSWERS AND EXPLANATIONS

1. B

Using what you know about the "stern family" and their feelings toward failure, you can predict that the blank will be filled by a word with a negative charge. You can also deduce this negative connotation by Patricia's fear (she is "petrified") of seeing her family. **(B)** *deride,* "to speak ill of," is the correct answer; Patricia could reasonably be afraid that these unpleasant people would say mean things to her. Eliminate **(A)** *venerate* and **(D)** *emulate*, as they both indicate positive feelings. Choice **(C)** *raze* has negative connotations, but it means "physically destroy to the ground," and nothing in the text indicates her family is murderous, just that they are "stern"; the damage Patricia fears is emotional. **(E)** *provoke* can be eliminated because, while Patricia might well be *provoked*, or "angered," by her family's "stern" attitude, the sentence indicates that she is "petrified"—or terrified—of what they would do to her; you cannot deduce that she is afraid of her own reaction to them.

2. C

The key to this sentence is the relationship of the film to the film style of Dogme 95. We can predict the word *start* for the blank. For that reason, you can eliminate choice **(A)** *lament,* "expresses grief," as it directs attention to the past, not the future as is the case in this sentence. Similarly, you can eliminate choice **(E)** *paradox,* "a contradiction," which is irrelevant to the beginning of a new fad. Choices **(B)** *anachronism* and **(D)** *anomaly* are both plausible, as a controversial work is likely to be out of place. However, choice **(C)** *catalyst,* "something that brings about a change in something else," is the correct answer; it best fits your predicted word *start,* and it directly describes the relationship between the film and the change in the film industry.

3. A, F

The first word here will describe what type of creatures male sperm whales normally are. The detour road sign "however" between the clauses indicates that a contrasting point will be made. In the second clause, we learn that something happens when the whales "are jealously guarding their territory." You can predict for both blanks at once: the whales are usually *gentle* but *attack* ships when they're guarding their territory. For the first blank, choice **(A)** *docile* matches your prediction; **(B)** *aggressive* and **(C)** *powerful* are more descriptive of the whales when they're guarding their territory. For the second blank, **(D)** *ignore* is the opposite of what we expect the whales to do. Choice **(E)** *follow* is possible, but **(F)** *attack* is a match for the prediction, contrasting appropriately with *docile*: "Male sperm whales . . . are normally *docile* creatures; however, when they are jealously guarding their territory, they have been known to *attack* ships."

4. C, F

For the first blank, there are many criteria that could be used to make hiring decisions under affirmative action, so move on to the second blank. Rejected job applicants "suffer" something when not judged on their abilities. Predict some negative treatment. **(F)** *injustice* is indeed negative and fits the context; this is correct. **(D)** *nepotism* can be another kind of unfair treatment, but it is based on being related to someone, not on characteristics such as "race or sex."

(E) *parity,* "equivalence," is the opposite of what's needed. Now for the first blank, which is some quality considered in conjunction with demographic characteristics. Note that the author has set off this word from the list "race or sex," so logically it is a different sort of characteristic. Predict that the noun in this blank will align with the "abilities" that, according to the last part of the sentence, are not the sole criterion. The correct match is **(C)** *competence.* Choice **(A)** *status* and **(B)** *creed* have no connection to the idea of ability.

5. A, F, H

These philosophers were trying to do something with the notions of "change and stability." Since change and stability are opposing ideas, predict that they were trying to *harmonize* the two ideas. For the first blank, choice **(A)** *reconcile* is a match for your prediction. Neither **(B)** *eliminate* nor **(C)** *confirm* takes into account the opposing forces of change and stability.

The third blank may be easier to predict for than the second. The word in the blank will describe the kind of particle they believed the atom to be, and another description is offered in the second part of this sentence: "from which all other varieties of matter are formed." Predict something like *fundamental* or *basic* or *smallest.* **(H)** *indivisible* is correct—although you now know that atoms can be split, this was not known at the time of the Greek philosophers, and *indivisible* fits the sense of the sentence. **(G)** *mythical* doesn't work; these philosophers didn't see atoms as the stuff of myth but rather as a real particle from which all other matter was formed. **(I)** *munificent* means "generous" or "bountiful"; this wouldn't be a logical way to describe a particle.

For blank (ii), predict that they were *imagining* or *hypothesizing* the atom. **(F)** *postulating* matches this prediction. Neither **(D)** *denying* the existence of the atom nor **(E)** *ignoring* it would have helped the philosophers reconcile the concepts of change and stability.

6. B, E, H

The key to predicting for the first blank is understanding that "extol" means "to praise." The detour road sign "[w]hile" indicates that there is a "vocal group of educators" who *do not praise* technology. Instead, this group *repudiates*, **(B)**, or "rejects," such technology. *Applauds*, **(A)**, is the opposite of the prediction. *Exculpates*, **(C)**, means "to free from blame," which does not work in the context.

Since the "vocal group of educators" rejects technology, predict that they believe such "a pedagogical approach" would have negative consequences. *Counterproductive*, **(E)**, provides the right meaning for the blank. *Feasible*, **(D)**, which means "possible" or "suitable," and *beneficial*, **(F)**, do not match the prediction.

Note the detour road sign "not" before blank (iii). Given that these educators believe that a technology-based teaching approach would be *counterproductive*, the last part of the sentence should indicate that teaching strategies would not be *improved* with technology. *Augmented*, **(H)**, means either "made larger" or "improved" and matches the prediction. *Undermined*, **(G)**, provides the opposite meaning, and *terminated*, **(I)**, does not fit the context.

7. D

The passage itself is largely concerned with the philosophical relationship between logical reasoning and language. The author notes that Wittgenstein distinguishes between propositions that are "pictures" of empirical fact and those that are not. The statement "truth is beauty" falls into the latter category. Since it is not a matter of empirical fact, you cannot determine if the linguistic picture (the proposition "truth is beauty") has the same logical structure as the fact itself. Therefore, it is nonsensical. Choice **(D)** is your answer.

8. A

The word "empirical" has the meaning of "measurable." That's close to choice **(A)** *verifiable by experimentation*, which makes sense in the context of the passage. You can't measure truth or beauty, but you can measure how tall someone is, which is cited as an example of an empirical fact.

9. C

Since the question asks for a choice that seriously calls the owner's plan into question, this is a Weaken question. The owner is concerned with costs, and the owner's criterion for selecting the team to be retrained is the "highest average projected completion time." Find a choice that casts doubt on using that particular measure as a criterion for retraining. Predict that the correct answer will probably indicate that the team that takes the longest to complete projects is either not actually inefficient or is so unskilled that retraining will not help.

(C) accords with this prediction: the projects that are the most complex would reasonably take longest to complete. If a team is repeatedly assigned complex projects, the team's average completion time will inevitably be higher than that of other teams. If this is true, the owner would not be justified in concluding the workers are inefficient or in need of retraining.

(A) is an irrelevant comparison, because the installation fees that this company or other companies charge are not related to worker efficiency. While **(B)** would give the manager a reason to reduce inefficiency, this choice does not relate to his specific plan for selecting the team to retrain. **(D)** may call into question the decision to retrain any team, but the question asks you to weaken the argument for choosing the team that takes the longest to complete projects, and **(D)** does not challenge this criterion for team selection. How "maximum efficiency" could be achieved, as in **(E)**, is irrelevant to whether retraining the slowest team would improve efficiency.

10. D

Remember: the topic is the general area of the passage, while the scope is the specific purpose or focus of the passage—you should have already determined these before you began attacking the question or questions following the passage. In the case of this passage, some of the choices are *too* broad to be the topic—choice **(A)** is too broad because only one of Cicero's works is discussed, and likewise for **(E)** because only one oration is discussed. Choice **(C)** relates to the passage, but it is the setting of the passage, not the topic. Choices **(B)** and **(D)** may look similar, but you should be able to choose between them—**(B)** is too narrow to be the topic and is more akin to a possible scope. Choice **(D)** is the correct answer because it describes the general topic of the passage (the First Catilinarian Oration) rather than specific aspects of it.

11. A, D

You can use the word "but" in the sentence to deduce that the environment in the 1950s was not the same as it is now. In other words, the second half of the sentence tells us that "societal changes" have led to the reality of a black president, implying that Americans in the 1950s would not have expected such an occurrence. Choice **(E)** *perfidious,* "faithless," "disloyal," "untrustworthy," and **(F)** *fastidious,* "careful with details," can both be ruled out. These are words more likely to be used to describe people than events and ideas and would thus not make sense in this context. While **(B)** *puerile,* which means "childish, immature, or silly," could be used to describe an occurrence or event, it wouldn't make sense to describe an election of a president. Choice **(C)** *superannuated* describes something that is out-of-date or obsolete, which would be in conflict with the idea of social progress. That leaves choice **(A)** *farcical,* "absurd" or "ludicrous," and **(D)** *implausible,* "improbable" or "inconceivable." Both these words render a sentence that means about the same thing. At the beginning of the Civil Rights Movement, people would have found the idea of a black president far-fetched, rendering it both absurd and inconceivable during that era.

12. B, E

You can infer from the words "isolated," "hidden," and "untouched" that the blank must be in line with these adjectives. It wouldn't make sense for a beach to be hidden, untouched, and **(A)** *morose,* "gloomy and sullen," or **(C)** *dilapidated,* "in disrepair or run-down," so you can eliminate these choices. Choices **(D)** *placid,* "calm," and **(F)** *imperturbable,* "incapable of being disturbed," are both tempting options because it is possible that an isolated beach would be both of these things. But the sentence doesn't rule out the possibility that the beaches could be less than placid, and just because a beach hasn't been touched yet doesn't mean it is immune from being disturbed in the future. You are left with choice **(B)** *immaculate,* "without stain or flaw," and **(E)** *pristine,* "untouched" or "uncorrupted," which are both synonyms of the adjectives used elsewhere in the sentence and therefore the correct answers.

13. C, E

If your body has been cleared of toxins through sweating from exercise, there is no reason to believe that you would feel a sense of **(A)** *disarray* or **(B)** *turbulence*, which are both terms for "disorder." Additionally, choice **(D)** *quintessence* doesn't make sense in this context, since it is a word for "a most typical example" or "concentrated essence." **(F)** *exhilaration* may seem like a plausible choice if you or a friend has ever described yoga as leaving you in a state of being "energetic" or "filled with happiness." But nothing from this particular sentence implies that a person would feel especially happy after finishing a hot yoga session. Rather, this sentence highlights the fact that sweating plays a role in cleansing a person's body. Therefore, the correct choices are **(C)** *purgation,* "the process of cleansing or purification," and **(E)** *ablution,* "the act of cleansing."

14. A, F

If Joe is making an effort to lose weight, it would be in his best interest to make healthy choices when going out to dine. Therefore, making a **(C)** *gluttonous,* "tending to eat and drink excessively," or a **(B)** *detrimental,* "causing harm or injury," choice for dinner would be the opposite of what he should be doing. He may choose an **(D)** *acerbic,* "bitter" or "sharp in taste," dish for dinner, but there's no telling if that would be a healthy or unhealthy choice. Because the adjective in question applies to food, choice **(E)** *loquacious* makes no sense since it means "talkative." This leaves choices **(A)** *abstemious,* "moderate in appetite," and **(F)** *austere,* "stern" or "strict," which make sense when describing a selection that someone on a diet would make.

15. B

The key to understanding this question is to determine how the author of the passage describes John Cage's approach to music. In the passage, the author describes Cage as being concerned with "removing the creator, the personal influence, from music and instead creating music based on natural patterns." This points immediately to choice **(B)**, a paraphrase of this statement. That answer is correct, but you should take care to eliminate the other options to ensure your correct response. Choice **(A)** may seem to describe Cage's radical departure from traditional music, but the departure itself is not described as his motivation. Choices **(C)** and **(E)** are, in essence, paraphrases of one another, claiming that music has no real definition. While this relates to Cage's question of what defined music, neither choice correctly describes his philosophy of music. Choice **(D)** is clearly incorrect because it directly contradicts the paraphrase of the passage seen in **(B)**. Choice **(B)** is the correct answer.

16. B

While the general sentiment of this passage appears to be in support of coffee, it does not state that the benefits are proportionate to consumption as outlined in choice **(A)**. In fact, it recognizes that there are downsides to drinking coffee and implies that drinking it to excess could exacerbate these problems by saying that the disadvantages are minimized when coffee is consumed in moderation. Instead, choice **(B)** is the statement that most closely aligns with the message of the passage. The use of the word "appear" acknowledges the fact that there are still unknowns about coffee that researchers are studying. Although the passage states that coffee may help a person fight off Parkinson's disease and dementia, you can infer from the passage that the link is merely a correlation and not necessarily a cause-and-effect relationship, rendering **(C)** inaccurate. The passage states that coffee does not *cause* cancer, as was once believed, but that it's now known to have some properties that help fight cancer, which means choice **(D)** is false. Choice **(E)** isn't correct because, although caffeine can be a cause of high blood pressure, it is certainly possible that someone who doesn't consume caffeine can have high blood pressure as well.

17. B, C

This question asks you to evaluate the statements and identify what you can infer using material from the passage. Taking each individually, choice **(A)** may be true, but this particular passage does not address research done on both varieties of coffee. Because the antioxidants in coffee help contribute to fighting cancer, it can be inferred that choice **(B)** is correct because any other food or drink that contains antioxidants would carry the same properties. Similarly, you may deduce that if blood sugar impacts diabetes, and the magnesium and chromium in coffee interact with a person's insulin, thereby changing a person's blood sugar, choice **(C)** *insulin has an effect on diabetes* is correct.

18. A

While the passage does recognize one downside of caffeine as a stimulant (high blood pressure), it also points out a handful of benefits (higher levels of alertness and concentration as well as longer attention spans). Therefore, the author is likely to disagree with choice **(A)**. It is likely that the author would agree with choice **(B)**, since coffee has been "tied to a wide range of benefits." Although there is no evidence to say that the author would agree with choice **(C)**, because the author doesn't address research on different types of coffee, you can't infer anything about whether or not the author would disagree with that statement.

19. D

This question rewards you for correctly summarizing the author's scope and purpose in writing the passage. For the most part, this author remains objective despite reporting a controversial decision. Choice **(A)** is the attitude of some critics of the decision to have Qatar as host, but the author doesn't express agreement with the critics. The passage claims that Qatar will need to build facilities, but the author doesn't assess the likelihood that the country will or will not be ready for the World Cup by 2022; thus, choice **(B)** is incorrect. The author cites other countries that some felt were deserving, but doesn't state a preference for who should host the Cup; that knocks out choice **(C)**. Choice **(D)** is the correct answer. Without acknowledging whether the criticism is warranted, the author states that Qatar is a controversial choice. Choice **(E)** is out of scope; the likelihood that fans will attend the World Cup in Qatar simply isn't addressed in the passage.

20. A, B

This question asks you to evaluate the statements and identify any and all that you can infer, using material from the passage. Choice **(A)** follows from the passage, which reports that FIFA has already been criticized for its decision. Choice **(B)**, too, follows from the passage. Whether there are cultural or political changes as a result of hosting this global event, Qatar will at least have new stadiums and infrastructure, which the passage says must be built in anticipation of 2022. Choice **(C)** is far too extreme to qualify as a correct answer. The most rabid critics may feel this way, but nothing in the passage offers such a strong opinion.

DIAGNOSE YOUR RESULTS

Diagnostic Tool

Tally up your score and write your results in the space provided.

Total

Total Correct: ________ out of 20 correct

Percentage Correct: # you got right $\times$ 100 $\div$ 20: ________

By Question Type

Text Completion ________ out of 6 correct

Sentence Equivalence ________ out of 4 correct

Reading Comprehension ________ out of 10 correct

Look back at the questions you got wrong and think about your experience answering them.

PART THREE

Verbal Content Review

CHAPTER 6

Vocabulary

UNDERSTANDING VOCABULARY

Overview

A strong vocabulary is the greatest asset you can bring to the GRE Verbal Reasoning sections. Text Completion and Sentence Equivalence questions reward you for knowing the meanings of a large number of words. Similarly, the passages in the Reading Comprehension section contain dense, complex passages and are accompanied by questions that require you to determine the meaning of words and sentences from context.

Building a good vocabulary takes time—a lifetime for most people. However, you can increase your GRE vocabulary quickly. There are a few reasons for this:

1. The GRE tests the same words repeatedly.

Knowing the words that the GRE testmakers love to use gives you a big head start in increasing your GRE vocabulary. We have included the words that appear most often on the GRE in this chapter in the "Words in Context" section. Start learning the meanings of these words as soon as you can.

2. The GRE does not test the exact definitions of words. If you have some idea of what the word means, you can usually determine the correct answer.

You don't need to know the exact definitions of words to achieve a good verbal score on the GRE. It's better to know something about ten words than everything about one word. This is why learning words in groups is a powerful technique. We have included common word groups found on the GRE in this chapter.

Knowing the meanings of common word roots can be helpful in two ways. First, knowing the meaning of word roots can help you guess at the meanings of unfamiliar words you encounter on the GRE. Second, when you're learning new vocabulary, it's more effective to study words in groups rather than individually. Learning several words that are related by a common root will help you to learn more words faster. We have included a list of common GRE word roots in this chapter.

Once you've looked over the top GRE words and the sections on word groups, roots, and words in context, you can hone your skills using the exercises that follow each section.

Basics of Vocabulary Building

The way most people build their vocabularies is by reading words in context. Reading is ultimately the best way to increase your vocabulary, although it also takes the most time. Of course, some types of reading material contain more GRE vocabulary words than others. You should get into the habit of reading high-level publications, such as the *Wall Street Journal*, the *Economist*, and the *New York Times*. (Because you'll have to read from the computer screen on Test Day, we recommend you read these publications online, if possible. And if you read lengthy articles that require scrolling, so much the better.)

WORD GROUPS

Learning words in groups is an efficient way of increasing your GRE vocabulary, since the GRE often tests only the general sense of a word. Imagine you saw the following Sentence Equivalence question on the test:

> The prime minister _______ the actions of the cabinet member; her sanctimonious tone indicated that she wanted to put distance between herself and the lurid implications of the scandal.

- [A] denounced
- [B] rephrased
- [C] extirpated
- [D] maligned
- [E] impugned
- [F] exculpated

Let's say that you immediately recognized *denounced* as an answer choice that fits in this blank but weren't sure which other word shares this same basic meaning. If you were to look up *denounce* in a dictionary, you'd see something like this:

de•nounce (dî-nouns') *transitive verb,* de•nounced, de•nounc•ing, de•nounc•es [Middle English: *denouncen, denounsen,* fr. Latin *denoncier,* fr. *de* + *nuntiare* to report, announce, fr. *nuntius* messenger]

1. to declare (a person, an idea, behavior, a philosophy) to be censurable or evil; stigmatize or accuse, especially publicly and indignantly; inveigh against openly
2. *archaic* to announce in a public, formal, and solemn manner: to declare or publish something disastrous
3. to inform against: declare or expose a lawbreaker to the authorities

4a. *obsolete* to indicate or portend

4b. *archaic* to announce in a warning or threatening manner

5. to proclaim formally and publicly the ending of a treaty or pact
6. *Mexican Law* to offer for record legal notice of a claim for a mining concession on land held by the government

Synonym see CRITICIZE

Do you need to know all this to answer the question? No—all you need to know is that *denounce* means something like "criticize." And in the time it took you to learn the meaning of *denounce* from the dictionary, you could have memorized a whole list of other words that also mean something like "criticize": *aspersion*, *berate*, *calumny*, *castigate*, *decry*, *defame/defamation*, *deride/derisive*, *diatribe*, *impugn*, *rebuke*, and others. Note that the answer choice *impugn* is in this list: this Sentence Equivalence question is made dramatically easier! This is why learning words in groups is a better general strategy for beefing up your GRE vocabulary than working slowly through the dictionary.

Just remember, the categories in which these words are listed are *general* and not to be taken for the exact definitions of the words. The words in the list may be different parts of speech than the words in the headers.

BOLD

audacious	courageous	dauntless

CHANGING QUICKLY

capricious	mercurial	volatile

HESITATE

dither	oscillate	teeter
vacillate	waver	

ACT QUICKLY

abrupt	apace	headlong
impetuous	precipitate	

INNOCENT/INEXPERIENCED

credulous	gullible	ingenuous
naive	novitiate	tyro

DIFFICULT TO UNDERSTAND

abstruse	ambiguous	arcane
bemusing	cryptic	enigmatic
esoteric	inscrutable	obscure
opaque	paradoxical	perplexing
recondite	turbid	

EASY TO UNDERSTAND

articulate	cogent	eloquent
evident	limpid	lucid
pellucid		

SMART/LEARNED

astute	canny	erudite
perspicacious		

CRITICIZE/CRITICISM

aspersion	belittle	berate
calumny	castigate	decry
defame/defamation	denounce	deride/derisive
diatribe	disparage	excoriate
gainsay	harangue	impugn
inveigh	lambaste	objurgate
obloquy	opprobrium	pillory
rebuke	remonstrate	reprehend
reprove	revile	tirade
vituperate		

CAROUSAL

bacchanalian	debauchery	depraved
dissipated	iniquity	libertine
libidinous	licentious	reprobate
ribald	salacious	sordid
turpitude		

TRUTH

candor/candid	fealty	frankness
indisputable	indubitable	legitimate
probity	sincere	veracious
verity		

FALSEHOOD

apocryphal	canard	chicanery
dissemble	duplicity	equivocate
erroneous	ersatz	fallacious
feigned	guile	mendacious/mendacity
perfidy	prevaricate	specious
spurious		

BITING (as in wit or temperament)

acerbic	acidulous	acrimonious
asperity	caustic	mordacious
mordant	trenchant	

PRAISE

acclaim	accolade	aggrandize
encomium	eulogize	extol
fawn	laud/laudatory	venerate/veneration

HARMFUL

baleful	baneful	deleterious
inimical	injurious	insidious
minatory	perfidious	pernicious

TIMID/TIMIDITY

craven	diffident	pusillanimous
recreant	timorous	trepidation

BORING

banal	fatuous	hackneyed
insipid	mundane	pedestrian
platitude	prosaic	quotidian
trite		

WEAKEN

adulterate	enervate	exacerbate
inhibit	obviate	stultify
undermine	vitiate	

ASSIST

abet	advocate	ancillary
bolster	corroborate	countenance
espouse	mainstay	munificent
proponent	stalwart	sustenance

HOSTILE

antithetic
churlish
curmudgeon
irascible
malevolent
misanthropic
truculent
vindictive

STUBBORN

implacable
inexorable
intractable
intransigent
obdurate
obstinate
recalcitrant
refractory
renitent
untoward
vexing

BEGINNING/YOUNG

burgeoning
callow
engender
inchoate
incipient
nascent

GENEROUS/KIND

altruistic
beneficent
clement
largess
magnanimous
munificent
philanthropic
unstinting

GREEDY

avaricious
covetous
mercenary
miserly
penurious
rapacious
venal

TERSE

compendious
curt
laconic
pithy
succinct
taciturn

OVERBLOWN/WORDY

bombastic
circumlocution
garrulous
grandiloquent
loquacious
periphrastic
prolix
rhetoric
turgid
verbose

DICTATORIAL

authoritarian
despotic
dogmatic
hegemonic/hegemony
imperious
peremptory
tyrannical

HATRED

abhorrence	anathema	antagonism
antipathy	detestation	enmity
loathing	malice	odium
rancor		

BEGINNER/AMATEUR

dilettante	fledgling	neophyte
novitiate	proselyte	tyro

LAZY/SLUGGISH

indolent	inert	lackadaisical
languid	lassitude	lethargic
phlegmatic	quiescent	slothful
torpid		

PACIFY/SATISFY

ameliorate	appease	assuage
defer	mitigate	mollify
placate	propitiate	satiate
slake	soothe	

FORGIVE/MAKE AMENDS

absolve	acquit	exculpate
exonerate	expiate	palliate
redress	vindicate	

POOR

destitute	esurient	impecunious
indigent		

FAVORING/NOT IMPARTIAL

ardent/ardor	doctrinaire	fervid
partisan	tendentious	zealot

DENYING OF SELF

abnegate	abstain	ascetic
spartan	stoic	temperate

WALKING ABOUT

ambulatory	itinerant	meander
peripatetic		

INSINCERE

disingenuous	dissemble	fulsome
ostensible	unctuous	

PREVENT/OBSTRUCT

discomfit	encumber	fetter
forfend	hinder	impede
inhibit	occlude	

ECCENTRIC/DISSIMILAR

aberrant	anachronism	anomalous
discrete	eclectic	esoteric
iconoclast		

FUNNY

chortle	droll	facetious
flippant	gibe	jocular
levity	ludicrous	raillery
riposte	simper	

SORROW

disconsolate	doleful	dolor
elegiac	forlorn	lament
lugubrious	melancholy	morose
plaintive	threnody	

DISGUSTING/OFFENSIVE

defile	fetid	invidious
noisome	odious	putrid
rebarbative		

WITHDRAWAL/RETREAT

abeyance	abjure	abnegation
abortive	abrogate	decamp
demur	recant	recidivism
remission	renege	rescind
retrograde		

DEATH/MOURNING

bereave	cadaver	defunct
demise	dolorous	elegy
knell	lament	macabre
moribund	obsequies	sepulchral
wraith		

COPY

counterpart	emulate	facsimile
factitious	paradigm	precursor
simulate	vicarious	

EQUAL

equitable	equity	tantamount

UNUSUAL

aberration	anomaly	iconoclast
idiosyncrasy		

WANDERING

discursive	expatiate	forage
itinerant	peregrination	peripatetic
sojourn		

GAPS/OPENINGS

abatement	aperture	fissure
hiatus	interregnum	interstice
lull	orifice	rent
respite	rift	

HEALTHY

beneficial	salubrious	salutary

ABBREVIATED

abridge	compendium	cursory
curtail	syllabus	synopsis
terse		

WISDOM

adage, aphorism, apothegm
axiom, bromide, dictum
epigram, platitude, sententious
truism

FAMILY

conjugal, consanguine, distaff
endogamous, filial, fraternal
progenitor, scion

NOT A STRAIGHT LINE

askance, awry, careen
carom, circuitous, circumvent
gyrate, labyrinth, meander
oblique, serrated, sidle
sinuous, undulating, vortex

INVESTIGATE

appraise, ascertain, assay
descry, peruse

TIME/ORDER/DURATION

anachronism, antecede, antedate
anterior, archaic, diurnal
eon, ephemeral, epoch
fortnight, millennium, penultimate
synchronous, temporal

BAD MOOD

bilious, dudgeon, irascible
pettish, petulant, pique
querulous, umbrage, waspish

EMBARRASS

abash, chagrin, compunction
contrition, diffidence, expiate
foible, gaucherie, rue

HARD-HEARTED

asperity	baleful	dour
fell	malevolent	mordant
sardonic	scathing	truculent
vitriolic	vituperation	

NAG

admonish	belabor	cavil
enjoin	exhort	harangue
hector	martinet	remonstrate
reproof		

PREDICT

augur	auspice	fey
harbinger	portentous	precursor
presage	prescient	prognosticate

LUCK

adventitious	amulet	auspicious
fortuitous	kismet	optimum
portentous	propitiate	propitious
providential	serendipity	talisman

NASTY

fetid	noisome	noxious

HARSH-SOUNDING

cacophony	din	dissonant
raucous	strident	

PLEASANT-SOUNDING

euphonious	harmonious	melodious
sonorous		

For ease of study, these lists can also be found in Appendix A.

WORD GROUPS EXERCISE

Directions: Choose the TWO synonyms that can correctly complete the sentence.

[NOTE: While the questions in this exercise are not in GRE format, the task of choosing synonyms is good practice for the kind of thinking rewarded by Sentence Equivalence questions.]

1. The incoming freshman found the 300-level Intermediate Macroeconomic Analysis course ______; he simply did not possess the necessary background knowledge.

   Ⓐ recondite
   Ⓑ ardent
   Ⓒ enigmatic
   Ⓓ noxious
   Ⓔ salubrious

2. The man encountered a series of ______ events on his way to work, from finding $20 on the ground to winning concert tickets off the radio.

   Ⓐ lugubrious
   Ⓑ fortuitous
   Ⓒ gibe
   Ⓓ din
   Ⓔ propitious

3. The accountant became more ______ after she failed to save the company from bankruptcy.

   Ⓐ volatile
   Ⓑ torpid
   Ⓒ lackadaisical
   Ⓓ munificent
   Ⓔ acrimonious

4. Generally, parents punish bad behavior and _______ good behavior in order to teach their children.

   (A) ameliorate
   (B) exculpate
   (C) ribald
   (D) laud
   (E) extol

5. A child may find jokes about bodily functions humorous while an adult finds them _______.

   (A) caustic
   (B) noisome
   (C) pernicious
   (D) odious
   (E) credulous

6. After spending 15 years teaching in the inner city and volunteering at homeless shelters on the weekends, it was clear the teacher was _______.

   (A) beneficent
   (B) disingenuous
   (C) penurious
   (D) rapacious
   (E) altruistic

7. A _______ melody filled the band room the first time the fourth graders played their chosen instruments.

   (A) sonorous
   (B) strident
   (C) jocular
   (D) diffident
   (E) raucous

8. My sister often found her friend's conversations about celebrities and fashion _______; she was more interested in politics and science.

   (A) hackneyed
   (B) banal
   (C) limpid
   (D) trenchant
   (E) perspicacious

9. The student was able to reduce wordiness and rewrite the paper in such a _______ manner that the page count fell from 20 to 12.

   (A) garrulous
   (B) succinct
   (C) mordacious
   (D) compendious
   (E) arcane

10. After feeding the stray cat every day for a week, I watched the once _______ animal develop the audacity to walk up to my door and wait for food.

   (A) craven
   (B) churlish
   (C) iconoclastic
   (D) truculent
   (E) timorous

11. While the author swore her novel was not intended to _______ a classic work of fiction, their syntax, diction, and plot were identical.

   (A) abridge
   (B) bereave
   (C) emulate
   (D) simulate
   (E) rescind

12. The professor answered the question in such a ______ way that the student was left confused and without a straightforward explanation.

    Ⓐ respite
    Ⓑ circuitous
    Ⓒ sententious
    Ⓓ oblique
    Ⓔ presage

13. Instead of taking one piece of candy from the bowl, the ______ child took five.

    Ⓐ avaricious
    Ⓑ ingenuous
    Ⓒ salubrious
    Ⓓ dour
    Ⓔ rapacious

14. In order to ______ her crying baby, the mother gently rocked the infant and sang a lullaby.

    Ⓐ abet
    Ⓑ dither
    Ⓒ mollify
    Ⓓ obviate
    Ⓔ placate

15. The biologist was ______ when he spoke about the characteristics of the red-eyed tree frog, because he had spent nine years studying the animal in its natural habitat.

    Ⓐ perspicacious
    Ⓑ libidinous
    Ⓒ ersatz
    Ⓓ erudite
    Ⓔ acidulous

16. The executive regretted her _______ action when it later became clear that she had approved the proposal without having access to complete information.

   (A) precipitate
   (B) impecunious
   (C) discursive
   (D) impetuous
   (E) mordacious

17. The _______ side effects of chocolate ingestion can be extremely detrimental for dogs.

   (A) insipid
   (B) deleterious
   (C) injurious
   (D) irascible
   (E) vexing

18. Adam's bout of bronchitis _______ his ability to get into peak shape for the outdoor track season.

   (A) admonished
   (B) inhibited
   (C) ameliorated
   (D) stultified
   (E) exhorted

19. Being denied a partial scholarship from her dream school proved _______ for Katie because she received a full scholarship to a different school, where she met her future husband.

   (A) providential
   (B) serendipitous
   (C) raucous
   (D) scathing
   (E) temporal

20. Her constantly _______ demeanor eventually discouraged Kara's friends from inviting her to social functions.

  (A) irascible
  (B) propitious
  (C) euphonious
  (D) salutary
  (E) querulous

21. The failing economy led the company into an extended _______, resulting in substantial financial losses.

  (A) demise
  (B) precursor
  (C) hiatus
  (D) lull
  (E) recant

22. The teacher's _______ response to the girl's question deterred the student from raising her hand for the rest of the semester.

  (A) caustic
  (B) indigent
  (C) fulsome
  (D) droll
  (E) acerbic

23. Although I've been to her house several times, I've never seen her _______ little cat because he is constantly hiding.

  (A) venal
  (B) insipid
  (C) torpid
  (D) timorous
  (E) diffident

24. It wasn't a surprise that with Kristen's creativity and _______ tastes, her new restaurant was praised as "truly original."

    (A) eclectic
    (B) noxious
    (C) iconoclastic
    (D) morose
    (E) vitriolic

25. Sick of being continually _______ by her mother, Erica decided it was finally time to move out of the house and into her own apartment.

    (A) ascertained
    (B) harangued
    (C) abashed
    (D) admonished
    (E) lulled

26. One of the most simple but _______ things we can do is drink lots of water and stay hydrated.

    (A) lugubrious
    (B) beneficial
    (C) salubrious
    (D) sinuous
    (E) ludicrous

27. Once he realized the inconvenience entailed by holding up his end of the deal, Aaron tried to _______ his promise to help his friend move.

    (A) recant
    (B) lament
    (C) renege on
    (D) curtail
    (E) descry

28. Although many _______ can seem trite and jaded, there is a lot of truth to most of them.

Ⓐ aphorisms
Ⓑ scions
Ⓒ labyrinths
Ⓓ advocates
Ⓔ adages

29. Despite her dreams of exploring South America after graduating college, Caroline settled into a less-than-satisfying office job to _______ her parents.

Ⓐ abet
Ⓑ appease
Ⓒ placate
Ⓓ stultify
Ⓔ inhibit

30. Because of the capabilities resulting from scientific advancements, identical twin births are far less of an _______ than they were 50 years ago.

Ⓐ aberration
Ⓑ abatement
Ⓒ ancillary
Ⓓ anomaly
Ⓔ accolade

WORD GROUPS EXERCISE ANSWER KEY

1. **A, C**
2. **B, E**
3. **B, C**
4. **D, E**
5. **B, D**
6. **A, E**
7. **B, E**
8. **A, B**
9. **B, D**
10. **A, E**
11. **C, D**
12. **B, D**
13. **A, E**
14. **C, E**
15. **A, D**
16. **A, D**
17. **B, C**
18. **B, D**
19. **A, B**
20. **A, E**
21. **C, D**
22. **A, E**
23. **D, E**
24. **A, C**
25. **B, D**
26. **B, C**
27. **A, C**
28. **A, E**
29. **B, C**
30. **A, D**

WORD GROUPS EXERCISE ANSWERS AND EXPLANATIONS

1. A, C

Recondite and *enigmatic* are both related to "difficult to understand." *Ardent* is "favoring/not impartial." Something *noxious* is "nasty," and something *salubrious* is "healthy."

2. B, E

Fortuitous and *propitious* are both related to "luck." *Lugubrious* refers to "sorrow." A *gibe* is something "funny," and a *din* is "harsh-sounding."

3. B, C

Torpid and *lackadaisical* are both in the "lazy/sluggish" category. *Volatile* means "changing quickly." *Munificent* can be found under "assist" and *acrimonious* under "biting (as in wit or temperament)."

4. D, E

Laud and *extol* both mean "praise." *Ameliorate* is related to "pacify/satisfy." *Exculpate* means "forgive," and *ribald* is related to "carousal."

5. B, D

Noisome and *odious* both mean "disgusting/offensive." *Caustic* means "biting (as in wit or temperament)." *Pernicious* means "harmful," and *credulous* is related to "innocent/inexperienced."

6. A, E

Beneficent and *altruistic* are both related to "generous/kind." *Disingenuous* means "insincere." *Penurious* and *rapacious* are both related to "greedy."

7. B, E

Strident and *raucous* are both on the "harsh-sounding" list. *Sonorous* means "pleasant-sounding." *Jocular* is related to "funny," and *diffident* falls under "timid/timidity."

8. A, B

Hackneyed and *banal* are both related to "boring." *Limpid* is related to "easy to understand." *Trenchant* means "biting (as in wit or temperament)," and *perspicacious* is related to "smart/learned."

9. B, D

Succinct and *compendious* both fall into the "terse" category. *Garrulous* relates to "overblown/wordy." *Mordacious* means "biting (as in wit or temperament)," and *arcane* falls under "difficult to understand."

10. A, E

Craven and *timorous* are both listed under "timid/timidity." *Churlish* is related to "hostile." *Iconoclastic* is related to "eccentric/dissimilar" and "unusual," and *truculent* is related to "hard-hearted" and "hostile."

11. C, D

Emulate and *simulate* are both related to "copy." *Abridge* falls under "abbreviated communication." *Bereave* is related to "death/mourning," and *rescind* is related to "withdrawal/retreat."

12. B, D

Circuitous and *oblique* are both in the "not a straight line" category. *Respite* falls under "gap/opening." *Sententious* is related to "wisdom," and *presage* is related to "predict."

13. A, E

Avaricious and *rapacious* are both related to "greedy." *Ingenuous* can be found under "innocent/inexperienced." *Salubrious* means "healthy," and *dour* is related to "hard-hearted."

14. C, E

Mollify and *placate* both fall under "pacify/satisfy." *Abet* means "assist." *Dither* is related to "hesitate," and *obviate* is related to "weaken."

15. A, D

Perspicacious and *erudite* are both related to "smart/learned." *Libidinous* falls under "carousal." *Ersatz* is related to "falsehood," and *acidulous* is related to "biting (as in wit or temperament)."

16. A, D

Precipitate and *impetuous* are both related to "act quickly." *Impecunious* means "poor," and *discursive* is related to "wandering." *Mordacious* falls under "biting (as in wit or temperament)."

17. B, C

Deleterious and *injurious* are both related to "harmful." *Insipid* is related to "boring." *Irascible* falls under "hostile," and *vexing* falls under "stubborn."

18. B, D

Inhibited and *stultified* are both related to "weaken." *Admonished* and *exhorted* are related to "nag." *Ameliorated* is related to "pacify/satisfy."

19. A, B

Providential and *serendipitous* both refer to "luck." *Raucous* means "harsh-sounding." *Scathing* is related to "hard-hearted." *Temporal* falls under "time/order/duration."

20. A, E

Irascible and *querulous* both refer to "bad mood." *Propitious* is related to "luck." *Euphonious* means "pleasant-sounding," and *salutary* means "healthy."

21. C, D

Hiatus and *lull* are both related to "gaps/openings." *Demise* relates to "death/mourning." *Precursor* is related to "copy," and *recant* falls under "withdrawal/retreat."

22. A, E

Caustic and *acerbic* both refer to "biting (as in wit or temperament)." *Indigent* means "poor." *Fulsome* is related to "insincere," and *droll* means "funny."

23. D, E

Timorous and *diffident* both relate to "timid/timidity." *Venal* is associated with "greedy." *Insipid* is related to "boring," and *torpid* falls under "lazy/sluggish."

24. A, C

Eclectic and *iconoclastic* are both in the "eccentric/dissimilar" group. *Noxious* is related to "nasty." *Morose* relates to "sorrow," and *vitriolic* falls under "hard-hearted."

25. B, D

Harangued and *admonished* are both related to "nag." *Ascertained* is related to "investigate." *Abashed* refers to "embarrass." *Lulled* falls under "gaps/openings."

26. B, C

Beneficial and *salubrious* both refer to "healthy." *Lugubrious* relates to "sorrow." *Sinuous* falls under "not a straight line," and *ludicrous* is related to "funny."

27. A, C

Recant and *renege* are both related to "withdraw/retreat." *Lament* refers to "sorrow." *Curtail* is related to "abbreviated communication," and *descry* refers to "investigate."

28. A, E

Aphorisms and *adages* both relate to "wisdom." *Scions* are related to "family." *Labyrinths* are related to "not a straight line," and *advocates* are related to "assist."

29. B, C

Appease and *placate* are both related to "pacify/satisfy." *Abet* means "assist." *Stultify* means "weaken," and *inhibit* means "prevent/obstruct."

30. A, D

Aberration and *anomaly* are both related to "unusual." *Abatement* relates to "gaps/openings." *Ancillary* is related to "assist." *Accolade* refers to "praise."

WORD ROOTS

Introduction to the Word Root List

The following list presents some of the most common word roots—mostly Greek and Latin—that appear in English. Learning to recognize these word roots is a great help in expanding your vocabulary. Many seemingly difficult words yield their meanings easily when you recognize the word roots that make them up. *Excrescence*, for example, contains the roots *ex-*, meaning "out or out of," and *cresc-*, meaning "to grow"; once you know this, the meaning of *excrescence*, an outgrowth (whether normal, such as hair, or abnormal, such as a wart) is easily deduced.

The list concentrates on Latin and Greek roots because these are the most frequently used to form compound words in English and because they tend not to be self-explanatory to the average reader. Each entry gives the root in the most common form or forms in which it appears in English, with a brief definition. (The definition does not cover all the shades of meaning of the given root, only the most important or the most broadly applicable.) The rest of the entry is a list of some of the common English words derived from this root; this list is intended only to provide a few examples of such words, not to be exhaustive. Some words are naturally found under more than one entry. The words themselves are not defined. A longer list, including these roots and more, can be found in Appendix B. We hope these lists will encourage you to look up unfamiliar words in a dictionary.

A/AN — **NOT, WITHOUT**

agnostic, amoral, anomaly, anonymous, apathy, atheist, atrophy, atypical

AB — **OFF, AWAY FROM, APART, DOWN**

abdicate, abduct, abhor, abject, abnormal, abolish, abstinence, abstract, abstruse

ABLE/IBLE — **CAPABLE OF, WORTHY OF**

changeable, combustible, durable, indubitable, inevitable, laudable, tolerable, variable

AC/ACR — **SHARP, BITTER, SOUR**

acerbic, acid, acrid, acrimonious, acumen, acute, exacerbate

AD — **TO, TOWARD, NEAR**

(Often the *d* is dropped and the first letter after the *a* is doubled.) accede, adapt, addict, address, adequate, adhere, adjacent, adjoin, admire, advocate, accede, affiliate, aggregate, allocate, annunciation, appall, arrest, assiduous, attract

AMBI/AMPHI	**BOTH, ON BOTH SIDES, AROUND** ambidextrous, ambient, ambiguous, amphibian, amphitheater
AMBL/AMBUL	**TO GO, TO WALK** amble, ambulance, ambulatory, perambulator, preamble
ANIM	**OF THE LIFE, MIND, SOUL, BREATH** animadversion, animal, animate, animosity, equanimity, magnanimous, pusillanimous, unanimous
ANT/ANTE	**BEFORE** ancient, antebellum, antecedent, antechamber, antedate, antediluvian, anterior, anticipate, antiquity
ANTI	**AGAINST, OPPOSITE** antagonism, antibody, anticlimax, antidote, antipathy, antiphony, antipodal, antiseptic, antithesis
AQUA/AQUE	**WATER** aquamarine, aquarium, aquatic, aquatint, aqueduct, subaqueous
AUTO	**SELF** autism, autobiography, autocrat, autograph, automatic, automaton, autonomy
BELL	**WAR** antebellum, bellicose, belligerent, rebel, rebellion
BEN/BENE	**GOOD** benediction, benefactor, benefit, benevolent, benign
BI/BIN	**TWO** biennial, bifocals, bifurcate, bilateral, bilingual, binocular, binomial, bipartisan, biped, combination
BON/BOUN	**GOOD, GENEROUS** bona fide, bonus, bountiful, bounty, debonair
BREV/BRID	**SHORT, SMALL** abbreviate, abridge, brevet, breviary, breviloquent, brevity, brief
BURS	**PURSE, MONEY** bursar, bursary, disburse, reimburse

CARD/CORD/ COUR	**HEART** accord, cardiac, cardiograph, cardiology, concord, concordance, cordial, discord, encourage, record
CARN	**FLESH** carnage, carnal, carnival, carnivorous, incarnation, reincarnation
CAUS/CAUT	**TO BURN** caustic, cauterize, cautery, encaustic, holocaust
CED/CEED/ CESS	**TO GO, TO YIELD, TO STOP** abscess, accede, antecedent, cessation, concede, exceed, incessant, precede, predecessor, proceed, recede, recess, secede, succeed
CELER	**SPEED** accelerant, accelerate, celerity, decelerate
CENT	**HUNDRED, HUNDREDTH** bicentennial, cent, centennial, centigrade, centigram, centiliter, centimeter, centipede, century, percent
CHROM	**COLOR** chromatic, chrome, chromosome, monochromatic
CHRON	**TIME** anachronism, chronic, chronicle, chronology, chronometer, synchronize
CIRCU/CIRCUM	**AROUND** circuit, circuitous, circumference, circumlocution, circumnavigate, circumspect, circumstances
CO/COL/COM/ CON	**WITH, TOGETHER** coerce, collaborate, collide, commensurate, communicate, compare, compatible, conciliate, connect
COGN/CONN	**TO KNOW** cognition, cognizance, incognito, recognize, reconnaissance, reconnoiter
CONTRA/CONTRO/ COUNTER	**AGAINST** contradict, contrary, controversy, counter, counteract, counterattack, counterfeit, countermand, counterpart, counterpoint, encounter

CORP/CORS	**BODY** corporation, corps, corpse, corpulent, corpus, corpuscle, corset, incorporation
COSM	**ORDER, UNIVERSE, WORLD** cosmetic, cosmic, cosmology, cosmonaut, cosmopolitan, cosmos, microcosm
CRE/CRESC/CRET	**TO GROW** accretion, accrue, creation, excrescence, increase, increment
CRED	**TO BELIEVE, TO TRUST** accredit, credentials, credible, credit, creditable, credo, credulity, creed, incredible, incredulous
CRYPT	**HIDDEN** apocryphal, crypt, cryptic, cryptography, cryptology
CUB/CUMB	**TO LIE DOWN** concubine, cubicle, incubate, incubus, incumbent, recumbent, succubus, succumb
CULP	**FAULT, BLAME** culpable, culprit, exculpate, inculpate, mea culpa
DE	**AWAY, OFF, DOWN, COMPLETELY, REVERSAL** decipher, defame, deferential, defile, delineate, descend
DEXT	**RIGHT HAND, RIGHT SIDE, DEFT** ambidextrous, dexter, dexterity, dexterous
DI	**DAY** dial, diary, dismal, diurnal, meridian, quotidian
DI/DIA	**IN TWO, THROUGH, ACROSS** diagnose, diagonal, diagram, dialect, dialogue, diameter, diaphanous, diaphragm, diarrhea, diatribe, dichotomy
DI/DIF/DIS	**AWAY FROM, APART, REVERSAL, NOT** diffuse, dilate, dilatory, disperse, disseminate, dissipate, dissuade, distant, diverge

DIC/DICT/DIT	**TO SAY, TO TELL, TO USE WORDS** abdicate, benediction, contradict, dedicate, dictate, dictator, diction, dictionary, dictum, edict, indicate, indict, interdict, malediction, predicate, predict, valedictorian, verdict
DOL	**TO SUFFER, TO PAIN, TO GRIEVE** condole, condolence, doleful, dolorous, indolence
DORM	**SLEEP** dormant, dormitory
DORS	**BACK** dorsal, endorse
DUC/DUCT	**TO LEAD** abduct, conducive, conduct, conduit, induce, induct, produce
DULC	**SWEET** dulcet, dulcified, dulcimer
DUR	**HARD, LASTING** dour, durable, duration, duress, during, endure, obdurate, perdurable
E/EX	**OUT, OUT OF, FROM, FORMER, COMPLETELY** efface, eliminate, emanate, eradicate, evade, evict, evince, excavate, except, excerpt, exclude, execute, exhale, exile, exit, exonerate, expire, extricate
EGO	**SELF** ego, egocentric, egoism, egotist
EQU	**EQUAL, EVEN** adequate, equable, equation, equator, equidistant, equilibrium, equinox, equivocate, iniquity
ERR	**TO WANDER** aberration, arrant, err, errant, erratic, erroneous, error
EU	**GOOD, WELL** eugenics, eulogy, euphemism, euphony, euphoria, euthanasia
FAL	**TO ERR, TO DECEIVE** default, fail, fallacy, false, faux pas, infallible

FATU	**FOOLISH** fatuity, fatuous, infatuated
FERV	**TO BOIL, TO BUBBLE** effervescent, fervent, fervid, fervor
FI/FID	**FAITH, TRUST** affiance, affidavit, confide, fealty, fidelity, fiduciary, infidel
FLAGR/FLAM	**TO BURN** conflagration, flagrant, flambeau, inflame
FLECT/FLEX	**TO BEND, TO TURN** circumflex, deflect, flex, flexible, genuflect, inflect, reflect
FUG	**TO FLEE, TO FLY** centrifugal, fugitive, fugue, refuge, refugee, subterfuge
FUM	**SMOKE** fume, fumigate, perfume
GEN	**BIRTH, CREATION, RACE, KIND** carcinogenic, congenital, degenerate, engender, eugenics, gender, gene, general, generation, generous, genesis, genetics, genial, genital, genius, gentility, gentle, ingenuity, progeny, regenerate
GNI/GNO	**TO KNOW** agnostic, diagnose, ignoramus, ignore, prognosis, recognize
GRAM/GRAPH	**TO WRITE, TO DRAW** anagram, diagram, epigram, epigraph, grammar, graph, graphic, graphite, photograph, program, telegram
GREG	**FLOCK** aggregate, congregate, egregious, gregarious, segregate
HAP	**BY CHANCE** haphazard, hapless, happen, happily, happy, mishap, perhaps
HEMI	**HALF** hemicycle, hemisphere, hemistich
(H)ETERO	**DIFFERENT, OTHER** heterodox, heterodyne, heterogeneous, heterosexual

HOL	**WHOLE** catholic, holocaust, hologram, holograph, holistic
(H)OM	**SAME** anomaly, homeostasis, homogeneous, homogenize, homogenous, homologue, homonym, homophone, homosexual, homotype
HUM	**EARTH** exhume, humble, humility
ICON	**IMAGE, IDOL** icon, iconic, iconoclast, iconography, iconology
IN/IM	**NOT, WITHOUT** (Often the *n* is dropped and the first letter after the *i* is doubled.) illogical, immoral, impartial, inactive, indigent, indolence, innocuous, irrelevant
IN/IM	**IN, INTO** (Often the *n* is dropped and the first letter after the *i* is doubled.) illuminate, implicit, incarnate, indigenous, influx, intrinsic, irrigate
INTER	**BETWEEN, AMONG** interim, interloper, intermittent, intersperse, interstate, interval
INTRA	**INSIDE, WITHIN** intramural, intrastate, intravenous
IT/ITER	**WAY, JOURNEY** ambition, circuit, itinerant, itinerary, reiterate, transit
JOC	**JOKE** jocose, jocular, jocularity, jocund, joke
JOIN/JUG/JUNCT	**TO MEET, TO JOIN** adjoin, conjugal, conjunction, injunction, junction, junta, rejoin, subjugate
JOUR	**DAY** adjourn, journal, journey
JUD	**TO JUDGE** adjudicate, judiciary, judicious, prejudice

Root	Meaning and examples
JUR	**LAW, TO SWEAR** abjure, adjure, conjure, injure, juridical, jurisdiction, jurisprudence, jurist, jury, perjury
JUV	**YOUNG** juvenile, juvenilia, rejuvenate
LANG/LING	**TONGUE** bilingual, language, linguistics
LAUD	**PRAISE, HONOR** cum laude, laud, laudable, laudatory
LAV/LAU/LU	**TO WASH** ablution, antediluvian, deluge, dilute, laundry, lavatory, lave
LAX/LEAS/LES	**LOOSE** lax, laxative, laxity, lease, leash, lessee, lessor, relax, release
LEC/LEG/LEX	**TO READ, TO SPEAK** dialect, lectern, lecture, legend, legible, lesson, lexicographer, lexicon
LEV	**TO LIFT, TO RISE, LIGHT (WEIGHT)** alleviate, elevate, leaven, levee, lever, levitate, levity, levy, relevant, relieve
LI/LIG	**TO TIE, TO BIND** ally, league, liable, liaison, lien, ligament, ligature, oblige, religion, rely
LIBER	**FREE** deliver, illiberal, liberal, liberality, liberate, libertine, liberty, livery
LITH	**STONE** acrolith, lithography, lithoid, lithology, lithotomy, megalith, monolith
LOC/LOG/LOQU	**WORD, SPEECH, THOUGHT** biology, circumlocution, colloquial, dialogue, elocution, eloquent, eulogy, geology, grandiloquent, interlocutor, locution, logic, loquacious, monologue, prologue, soliloquy, ventriloquism
LUC/LUM/LUS	**LIGHT (BRIGHTNESS)** illuminate, illustrate, illustrious, lackluster, lucid, luminous, translucent

MACRO	**GREAT, LONG** macro, macrobiotics, macrocephalous, macrocosm, macroscopic
MAG/MAJ/MAX	**BIG, GREAT** magistrate, magnanimous, magnate, magnificent, magnify, magniloquent, magnitude, majesty, major, majority, master, maxim, maximum, mistress
MAL/MALE	**BAD, ILL, EVIL, WRONG** maladroit, malady, malapropism, malediction, malefactor, malfeasance, malfunction, malevolence, malicious, malign, malinger
MAN/MANU	**HAND** amanuensis, emancipate, manacle, manage, maneuver, manifest, manipulate, manner, manual, manufacture, manuscript
MAND/MEND	**TO COMMAND, TO ORDER, TO ENTRUST** command, commend, countermand, demand, mandate, mandatory, recommend, remand, reprimand
MEDI	**MIDDLE** immediate, intermediate, mean, media, median, mediate, medieval, mediocre, medium
MEGA	**LARGE, GREAT** megalith, megalomania, megalopolis, megaphone, megaton
MICRO	**VERY SMALL** microbe, microcosm, micron, microorganism, microscope
MIS	**BAD, WRONG, TO HATE** misadventure, misanthrope, misapply, miscarry, mischance, mischief, misconstrue, miscount, misfit, misinterpret
MOB/MOM/ MOT/MOV	**TO MOVE** automobile, demote, immovable, locomotion, mob, mobile, mobility, mobilize, moment, momentous, momentum, motion, motive, motor, move, mutiny, promote, remove
MOLL	**SOFT** emollient, mild, mollify, mollusk
MON/MONO	**ONE** monarchy, monism, monk, monochord, monogram, monograph, monolithic, monologue, monomania, monotonous

MOR/MORT	**DEATH** amortize, immortal, morbid, moribund, mortality, mortify, mortuary
MULT	**MANY** multiple, multiplex, multiply, multitudinous
MUT	**TO CHANGE** commute, immutable, mutation, mutual, permutation, transmute
NAT/NAS/ NAI/GNA	**BIRTH** cognate, innate, naive, nascent, natal, native, natural, nature, pregnant, renaissance
NAU/NAV	**SHIP, SAILOR** astronaut, circumnavigate, cosmonaut, nauseous, nautical, naval, nave, navy
NIHIL	**NOTHING, NONE** annihilate, nihilism
NOC/NOX	**HARM** innocent, innocuous, internecine, noxious, nuisance, obnoxious, pernicious
NOCT/NOX	**NIGHT** equinox, noctambulant, nocturnal, nocturne
NOM/NYM/ NOUN/NOWN	**NAME** acronym, anonymous, misnomer, nomenclature, nominal, nominate, noun, pronoun, pseudonym, renown, synonym
NON	**NOT** nonconformist, nonentity, nonpareil, nonpartisan
NOV/NEO/NOU	**NEW** innovate, neologism, neophyte, neoplasm, nouveau riche, novel, novice, renovate
NULL	**NOTHING** annul, null, nullify, nullity
OB	**TOWARD, TO, AGAINST, OVER** obese, obfuscate, oblique, obsequious, obstinate, obstreperous, obstruct, obtuse

OMNI	**ALL** omnibus, omnipotent, omnipresent, omniscient, omnivorous
ONER	**BURDEN** exonerate, onerous, onus
OSS/OSTE	**BONE** osseous, ossicle, ossiferous, ossify, ossuary, ostectomy, osteopathy
PALP	**TO FEEL** palpable, palpate, palpitate, palpitation
PAN/PANT	**ALL, EVERYONE** panacea, pandemic, panegyric, panoply, panorama, pantheon
PAS/PAT/PATH	**FEELING, SUFFERING, DISEASE** compassion, dispassionate, empathy, impassive, pathogenic, sociopath, sympathy
PEC	**MONEY** impecunious, peculation, pecuniary
PED	**CHILD, EDUCATION** encyclopedia, pedagogue, pedant, pediatrician
PED/POD	**FOOT** antipodes, arthropod, expedite, impede, pedal, pedestal, pedestrian, pedigree, pediment, podium, tripod
PEL	**TO DRIVE, TO PUSH** compel, dispel, expel, impel, propel
PEN/PENE	**ALMOST** antepenult, peninsula, penult, penultimate, penumbra
PERI	**AROUND** perihelion, perimeter, perineum, peripatetic, periphery, periscope
PHIL	**LOVE** bibliophile, necrophilia, philanthropy, philatelist, philharmonic, philogyny, philology, philosopher
PHOB	**FEAR** claustrophobia, hydrophobia, phobia, phobic, xenophobia

PHON	**SOUND** antiphony, euphony, megaphone, phonetics, phonograph, polyphony, saxophone, symphony, telephone
PLAC	**TO PLEASE** complacent, complaisant, implacable, placate, placebo, placid
PLE/PLEN	**TO FILL, FULL** accomplishment, complement, complete, deplete, implement, plenipotentiary, plenitude, plenty, plethora, replenish, replete, supplement
POLY	**MANY** polyandry, polygamy, polyglot, polygon, polyhedron, polynomial, polysyllable, polytechnic, polytheism
PORT	**TO CARRY** comport, deportment, disport, export, import, important, importune, portable, portage, porter, portfolio, portly, purport, rapport, reporter, supportive, transport
POST	**BEHIND, AFTER** post facto, posterior, posterity, postern, posthumous, postmeridian, postmortem, postscript, preposterous
POT	**TO DRINK** potable, potation, potion
PRE	**BEFORE, IN FRONT** preamble, precarious, precedent, precept, precocious, precursor, predict, preface, premonition, prescribe, presentiment, president
PRI/PRIM	**FIRST** primary, primal, prime, primeval, primordial, pristine
PRO	**IN FRONT, BEFORE, MUCH, FOR** problem, proceed, proclaim, procure, profuse, prolific, propound, prostrate, proselytize, protest, provident
PROP/PROX	**NEAR** approximate, propinquity, proximate, proximity
PROT/PROTO	**FIRST** protagonist, protocol, prototype, protozoan

PSEUD/PSEUDO	**FALSE** pseudepigrapha, pseudoclassic, pseudomorph, pseudonym, pseudopod, pseudoscience
PUG	**TO FIGHT** impugn, pugilist, pugnacious, repugnant
PUNC/PUNG/ POIGN	**TO POINT, TO PRICK, TO PIERCE** compunction, expunge, poignant, point, punch, punctilious, punctual, punctuate, puncture, pungent
PYR	**FIRE** pyre, pyromania, pyrometer, pyrosis, pyrotechnics
QUAD/QUAR/ QUAT	**FOUR** quadrant, quadrille, quadrinomial, quadruple, quadruplets, quart, quarter, quaternary
QUIE/QUIT	**QUIET, REST** acquiesce, acquit, coy, disquiet, quiescence, quiet, quietude, quietus, quit, requiem, requital, tranquil
QUIN/QUINT	**FIVE** quincunx, quinquennial, quintessence, quintile, quintillion, quintuple
RACI/RADI	**ROOT** deracinate, eradicate, radical, radish
RAMI	**BRANCH** ramification, ramiform, ramify
RE	**BACK, AGAIN** recline, refer, regain, remain, reorganize, repent, request
RECT	**STRAIGHT, RIGHT** correct, direct, erect, rectangle, rectify, rectilinear, rectitude, rector
REG	**KING, RULE** interregnum, realm, regal, regent, regicide, regime, regiment, region, regular, regulate
RETRO	**BACKWARD** retroactive, retrofit, retrograde, retrospective

RUB/RUD	**RED** rouge, rubella, rubicund, rubric, ruby, ruddy, russet
RUD	**CRUDE** erudite, rude, rudimentary, rudiments
SACR/SANCT	**HOLY** consecration, desecrate, execrable, sacerdotal, sacrament, sacred, sacrifice, sacrilege, sacristy, sacrosanct, saint, sanctify, sanctimonious, sanction, sanctity, sanctuary, sanctum
SAG/SAP/SAV	**TASTE, THINKING, DISCERNING** insipid, sagacious, sagacity, sage, sapient, savant, savor
SALU	**HEALTH** salubrious, salutary, salute
SALV	**TO SAVE** safe, salvage, salvation, savior
SAN	**HEALTHY** sane, sanitarium, sanitary, sanitation, sanity
SANG	**BLOOD** consanguinity, sanguinary, sanguine
SAT	**ENOUGH** assets, dissatisfied, insatiable, sate, satiate, satisfy, saturate
SCRIBE/SCRIPT	**TO WRITE** ascribe, circumscribe, conscription, describe, indescribable, inscription, postscript, prescribe, proscribe, scribble, scribe, script, scripture, scrivener, subscribe, transcript
SE	**APART, AWAY** secede, sedition, seduce, segregate, select, separate, sequester
SEC/SEQU/ SUE/SUI	**TO FOLLOW** consecutive, consequent, execute, executive, non sequitur, obsequious, obsequy, persecution, prosecute, pursue, second, sequel, sequence, sue, suitable, suite, suitor

SED/SESS/SID	**TO SIT, TO SETTLE** assiduous, dissident, insidious, preside, resident, residual, séance, sedate, sedative, sedentary, sediment, sedulous, session, siege, subside, supersede
SEM	**SEED, TO SOW** disseminate, semen, seminal, seminar, seminary
SEMI	**HALF** semicircle, semicolon, semiconscious, semifluid
SEN	**OLD** senate, senescent, senile, senior, sire
SIN/SINU	**BEND, FOLD, CURVE** cosine, insinuate, sine, sinuous, sinus
SOL	**ALONE** desolate, isolate, sole, soliloquize, solipsism, solitude, solo
SOL	**SUN** parasol, solar, solarium, solstice
SOMN	**SLEEP** insomnia, somnambulist, somniferous, somniloquist, somnolent
SOPH	**WISDOM** philosopher, sophism, sophist, sophisticated, sophistry
SOURC/SURG/ SURRECT	**TO RISE** insurgent, insurrection, resource, resurge, resurrection, source, surge
SPEC/SPIC	**TO LOOK, TO SEE** circumspect, conspicuous, despicable, inspect, perspective, perspicacious, retrospective, specious, spectrum, speculation
SPIR	**BREATH** aspire, conspire, expire, inspire, perspire, respirator, spirit, spiritual, sprightly, sprite, suspire, transpire

STRICT/STRING/ STRAN	**TO TIGHTEN, TO BIND** astringent, constrain, constrict, district, restriction, strain, strait, strangle, strict, stringent
SUA	**SWEET, PLEASING, TO URGE** assuage, dissuade, persuade, persuasive, suasion, suave, sweet
SUB/SUP	**BELOW, UNDER** subliminal, submissive, subsidiary, subterfuge, subtle, suppose
SUMM	**HIGHEST, TOTAL** consummate, sum, summary, summit
SUPER/SUR	**OVER, ABOVE** insuperable, superb, supercilious, superficial, superfluous, superior, superlative, supernatural, supersede, supervise, surmount, surpass, surrealism, surveillance, survey
SYM/SYN	**TOGETHER** symbiosis, symmetry, sympathy, symposium, synonym, synthesis
TAC/TIC	**TO BE SILENT** reticent, tacit, taciturn
TACT/TAG/ TAM/TANG	**TO TOUCH** contact, contagious, contaminate, contiguous, cotangent, intact, intangible, integral, tact, tactile, tangent, tangential
TEST	**TO BEAR WITNESS** attest, contest, detest, intestate, protest, testament, testify, testimonial
THERM	**HEAT** diathermy, thermal, thermesthesia, thermometer, thermonuclear, thermophilic, thermostat
TIM	**FEAR** intimidate, timid, timidity, timorous
TOR/TORQ/ TORT	**TO TWIST** contort, distort, extort, retort, torch, torment, torque, torsion, tort, tortuous, torture

TORP	**STIFF, NUMB** torpedo, torpid, torpor
TOX	**POISON** antitoxin, intoxication, toxemia, toxic, toxicology, toxin
TRANS	**ACROSS, BEYOND** intransigent, transaction, transcendent, transcribe, transgress, transient, transition, transmit, transparent, transport
ULT	**LAST, BEYOND** penultimate, ulterior, ultimate, ultimatum, ultramarine, ultramontane, ultraviolet
UMBR	**SHADOW** adumbrate, penumbra, somber, umber, umbrage, umbrella
UN	**NOT** unaccustomed, unruly, unseen, untold, unusual
UND	**WAVE** abound, abundance, inundate, redundant, undulant, undulate
UNI/UN	**ONE** reunion, unanimous, unicorn, uniform, union, unison, unit, unite, unity, universe
URB	**CITY** exurbanite, suburb, urban, urbane, urbanity, urbanization
VAIL/VAL	**STRENGTH, USE, WORTH** ambivalent, avail, convalescent, countervailing, equivalent, evaluate, invalid, prevalent, valediction, valiant, valid, valor, value
VER	**TRUTH** aver, veracious, verdict, verify, verily, verisimilitude, verity, very
VERB	**WORD** adverb, proverb, verb, verbal, verbalize, verbatim, verbose, verbiage
VERD	**GREEN** verdant, verdigris, verdure

VI	**LIFE** convivial, joie de vivre, revival, revive, survive, viable, vital, vitality, vivacity, vivid, viviparous, vivisection
VIL	**BASE, MEAN** revile, vile, vilify, vilification
VIRU	**POISON** virulence, virulent, viruliferous, virus
VOC/VOK	**CALL, WORD** advocate, avocation, avow, convocation, convoke, equivocate, evoke, invoke, provoke, revoke, vocabulary, vocal, vocation, vociferous
VOL	**WISH** benevolent, malevolent, volant, volatile, volition, volley, voluntary
VOLU/VOLV	**TO ROLL, TO TURN** circumvolve, convolution, devolve, evolve, involution, revolt, revolution, revolve, voluble, volume, voluminous, volute

WORD ROOTS EXERCISE

Choose the word that correctly completes the sentence. Make sure to pay attention to structural road signs and key words and use familiar roots to guide your choice.

1. The play's theme was interesting; however, the (*animated, acerbic*) monologues dampened our appreciation of the author's skills.

2. Although poets are stereotypically considered contemplative and gentle souls, composing dulcet rhymes about the vagaries of life, some of our most famous poets have been (*belligerent, breviloquent*), frequently drunk, or even criminal.

3. The intern was a delight; she completed her tasks with professionalism, (*celerity, cautery*), and good sense.

4. Flemish primitive painters such as Jan Van Eyck used a greenish substance called (*micron, verdigris*) in their portraits.

5. The math professor wrote a formula to calculate every (*neologism, permutation*) of a certain set of numbers.

6. Some behaviors are learned, while others are (*innocuous, innate*).

7. Because they had been old friends, the general shook the diplomat's hand with a (*somnolent, sanguine*) air.

8. You can easily recognize (*rubella, toxemia*) because of the raised red spots on the skin.

9. Some people consider desecration of the American flag to be treasonous or even an act of terrorism, but others refuse to treat what they consider a mere symbol as (*sacrosanct, sagacious*).

10. In frog anatomy, the major muscles of the shoulder extend from the (*dorsal, quadriceps*) area, across the shoulder joint, and into the arms.

11. At the end of the service, the general's wife gave an impromptu (*convocation, valediction*), which truly venerated his memory and profoundly moved many attendees.

12. Some families organized an effort to bring about the (*restriction, euphemism*) of the sales of illegal fireworks at the neighborhood convenience store.

13. The dog still enjoyed its vigorous morning romps through the park, but its stiff joints and patchy fur betrayed signs of (*dexterity, senescence*).

14. Around dinner time, a delicious smell (*emanated, adjourned*) from the kitchen.

15. The monorail train arrived at the station in 20-minute (*conduits, intervals*).

16. A military (*fealty, junta*) was set up to determine which party ruled, now that the old, corrupt regime had been deposed.

17. I tried to compliment my boss, but I must have overdone it; she told me to stop being so (*obsequious, salubrious*).

18. My brother was the intrepid one in the family; though I was by no means (*ambivalent, pusillanimous*), he always managed to outdo me in daredevilry.

19. The teacher was so (*peripatetic, philharmonic*) in class that when the maintenance department removed the chair at his desk, he didn't notice for weeks.

20. It was (*indubitable, laudatory*) that Inez would earn the scholarship because she clearly had the best grades and most experience.

21. I felt I had to (*succumb, intercede*) when I saw the child struggling to swim to the side of the pool and the lifeguard failed to respond.

22. The mad scientist in the movie attached a special (*diathermy, chronometer*) to the time machine so that the passengers could control the year to which they would travel.

23. We were afraid that the (*perspicuous, taciturn*) visitor did not like the presentation because she sat quietly and asked no questions.

24. Although we often remember breakthrough artists such as LL Cool J and Run-D.M.C. as the originators of rap, (*seminal, pedantic*) artists such as the Sugarhill Gang and the Fatback Band remind us that rap really started on the street and not in a studio.

25. As much as he practiced and tried to improve, Jack remained (*maladroit, pellucid*) at swimming.

26. While (*jocularity, gentility*) is appreciated in informal conversations with coworkers and colleagues, it is best not to overdo it in formal meetings such as interviews.

27. The appraiser thought she discovered an (*aberrant, indolent*) design in the antique carpet, but after further research, she determined that the pattern was actually consistent with designs in contemporaneous fashions and ornaments.

28. Since many toddlers go through a phase of independence, caregivers should be prepared to deal with frustrated, (*obdurate*, *dismal*) two-year-olds and provide patient support for this developmental process.

29. The princess arrived in plain clothes; the young ladies who had hoped to espy a beautiful woman with a flowing gown and full (*regalia, heterodoxy*) were bewildered.

30. Whenever she is nervous, my sister becomes very (*liberal, loquacious*), so when she chatted away as we were walking through the woods, I suspected she thought we might be lost.

WORD ROOTS EXERCISE ANSWER KEY

1. **acerbic**
2. **belligerent**
3. **celerity**
4. **verdigris**
5. **permutation**
6. **innate**
7. **sanguine**
8. **rubella**
9. **sacrosanct**
10. **dorsal**
11. **valediction**
12. **restriction**
13. **senescence**
14. **emanated**
15. **intervals**
16. **junta**
17. **obsequious**
18. **pusillanimous**
19. **peripatetic**
20. **indubitable**
21. **intercede**
22. **chronometer**
23. **taciturn**
24. **seminal**
25. **maladroit**
26. **jocularity**
27. **aberrant**
28. **obdurate**
29. **regalia**
30. **loquacious**

WORD ROOTS EXERCISE ANSWERS AND EXPLANATIONS

1. ACERBIC

The root ANIM in *animated* should clue you in to its meaning: "active or living." The root of *acerbic,* AC, provides a clue to its meaning: "sharp or sour."

2. BELLIGERENT

The root BELL relates to war and fighting, and *belligerent* refers to someone who is quick to get into a fight. You may recognize the roots BREV ("short") and LOQU ("speech") in *breviloquent*, which means "terse" or "brief."

3. CELERITY

The root CELER relates to speed, and *celerity* means "alacrity" or "briskness." The word *cautery* contains the root CAUT, which refers to burning. A *cautery* is an instrument used for branding (burning a mark into flesh).

4. VERDIGRIS

The root VERD is the clue to the right answer. VERD refers to green, and *verdigris* is a green pigment used by artists. The root MICRO means "very small," and a *micron* is a millionth of a meter.

5. PERMUTATION

The root MUT is the clue in this word, which refers to a change or transformation. A *permutation* is one of the possible changes or elements in a set. NEO means "new," and LOG refers to words. A *neologism* is a new word.

6. INNATE

The answer to this one is a little complicated: the prefix IN has a different meaning in each option. NAT refers to birth, and the prefix IN means "internal" or "inside." Something *innate* is born into you. The word *innocuous* contains the root NOX, meaning "harm." The prefix IN negates the meaning: an *innocuous* substance is one that will not harm you.

7. SANGUINE

In this sentence, the friendly handshake is the clue. SANG in the word *sanguine* refers to blood. In the Middle Ages, blood was considered to be the humor (or fluid) that led to a hopeful disposition, and a *sanguine* handshake is a confident one. On the other hand, SOMN refers to sleep, so a *somnolent* general would likely be yawning as he shook hands.

8. RUBELLA

Although *toxemia* contains the root TOX, which means "poison," the rash's signature red bumps suggest the answer *rubella*, which contains the root RUB, meaning "red."

9. SACROSANCT

Sacrosanct means "extremely sacred"; you may have guessed this because it contains both SACR and SANCT, both of which mean "holy." *Sagacious* means "wise" and contains the root SAG, which refers to having discernment.

10. DORSAL

If you know anatomy or you spend time at the gym, this may have been an easy one. *Dorsal* contains the root DORS, which relates to an organism's back. The *quadriceps* is a group of four (QUAD means "four") muscles in the legs.

11. VALEDICTION

A *valediction* contains the roots VAL ("strength" or "worth") and DICT ("to say"). A *valediction* is a speech given to commemorate someone or speak of his or her worth. The root CON means "together," and the root VOC means "call"; a *convocation* is a group of people who have been called together. The gathering was a *convocation*, but the speech was a *valediction*.

12. RESTRICTION

Restriction contains the root STRICT, which means "tighten." *Euphemism* contains the root EU ("good") and refers to using a pleasant term for something unpleasant. Since the families wanted to tighten the laws regarding sales of illegal fireworks, *restriction* is your answer.

13. SENESCENCE

Senescence contains the root SEN, which refers to aging or growing old. *Senescence* is the same as maturity or old age. *Dexterity* contains the root DEXT, which refers to the right side of an organism. Because most people in the world are right-handed and are therefore more agile with their right hands, *dexterity* has come to mean the same as *agility*. (If you're a lefty, remember this point of contention, and the root and word will stick with you on the test!)

14. EMANATED

Emanated contains the root E meaning "out," and indeed, it means "coming out," as does a smell. *Adjourned* contains the roots AD, which means "to," and JOUR, which means "day." *Adjourned* means "put off to another day," or finished for now.

15. INTERVALS

The root INTER means "between" or "among," and an *interval* is the time that passes between two or more repeating events. The word *conduits* contains the roots CON ("together") and DUC ("to lead"). *Conduits* are ways to get from one place to another.

16. JUNTA

The root in *junta*, JUNCT, means "join," and a *junta* is a group of people who come together for a specific purpose. The root in *fealty* is harder to see—FID or FI—and means "faith" or "loyalty."

17. OBSEQUIOUS

Obsequious comes from the roots OB, meaning "over," and SEQU, meaning "to follow." It has the sense of overdoing being a follower, or "fawning." *Salubrious* has the root SALU, meaning "health," and it means "healthy."

18. PUSILLANIMOUS

The root in *pusillanimous* is ANIM, which means "life." The other root, not given in the list, is PUSIL, which means "weak." Someone who is *pusillanimous* is "craven" or "cowardly." The word *ambivalent* contains the prefix AMBI ("both") and the root VAL ("strength") and means "pulled with equal force by two choices."

19. PERIPATETIC

The roots PERI ("around") and PED ("foot") provide the strongest clues as to the meaning of *peripatetic*, "given to walking around." *Philharmonic* contains PHIL ("love"); it means "a lover of music" and is often short for *philharmonic society* ("a group of music lovers"). Neither sense of the latter relates to this sentence.

20. INDUBITABLE

The root DUB (not given in the list, but in Appendix B) refers to doubt, and something that is *indubitable* cannot be doubted (the root IN means "not"). The root LAUD means "praise" or "honor." A *laudatory* celebration is one that is in honor of the guest.

21. INTERCEDE

The root INTER ("between") and CEDE ("go") give the meaning of *intercede* plainly: "to go between or go into a situation." The root CUMB refers to lying down or giving in, which is the meaning of *succumb*.

22. CHRONOMETER

The roots CHRON ("time") and METER ("measure") should give you the meaning of *chronometer*: "a clock." Similarly DIA ("through") and THERM ("heat"), the roots in *diathermy*, clue you into that meaning: "heating inside a body, usually through electricity."

23. TACITURN

The root TACIT means "silent," and a *taciturn* person does not speak very much. The root SPIC ("look" or "see") is a clue to the meaning of *perspicuous*: "clear or lucid."

24. SEMINAL

The root SEM refers to seeds or sowing. A *seminal* work is one that influences others (think of a seminal work as sowing creative seeds). The word *pedantic* contains the root PED (the same root as in *pediatric*), which means "child" or "education." A *pedantic* person is a teacher (and the word carries the connotation of being too much of a know-it-all!).

25. MALADROIT

The root MAL ("bad") and the word *adroit* should give you an idea of the meaning of *maladroit*: "clumsy." You may recognize the root in *pellucid*, LUC, meaning "light." Follow those instincts: *pellucid* means "translucent" or "clear."

26. JOCULARITY

You may notice the root JOC ("joke") in the word *jocularity*. *Jocularity* is "joking around" or "having a sense of humor." The word *gentility* contains the root GEN, which refers to birth or class. *Gentility*, or good manners, has been historically expected of the upper classes in society. It does not mean that only the well-off have such manners, but you can remember this connection for the exam.

27. ABERRANT

The root AB ("from") and the root ERR ("to wander") provide strong clues to the word *aberrant*, which means "different" or "off." The word *indolent* contains the root IN ("not") and DOL ("grieve"). If you think of someone who does not grieve (and possibly does not care) when something or someone is lost, you can see how the word *indolent* means "lazy" or "irresponsible."

28. OBDURATE

The roots in *obdurate*, OB ("against") and DUR ("strong") give away the meaning: "stubborn." The roots in *dismal* are actually DI ("day") and MAL ("bad"). Indeed, a *dismal* day is usually pretty lousy.

29. REGALIA

Remember that the root REG means "king" or "rule." *Regalia* thus refers to the crown, scepter, and other symbols of royalty. A *heterodoxy* is a belief or opinion (DOX, not listed here but listed in Appendix B) that is different from or at odds with (HETERO) the norm. Its antonym is "orthodoxy."

30. LOQUACIOUS

The root in *loquacious*, LOQU, refers to speech. A *loquacious* person is a talker. The root in *liberal* refers to freedom (LIBER), and those who hold *liberal* or *libertarian* ideas tend to allow more freedom to individuals to make their own choices in life.

WORDS IN CONTEXT

Some words appear on the GRE more than others. The GRE tends to test vocabulary commonly used to express ideas in academic journal articles, literature, and sophisticated journalism. Because there may be many words that could appear on the test that you are unfamiliar with, studying for the GRE Verbal section can be daunting. However, you have to start somewhere!

Here is a starting point. Learn these 10 words that might appear in a passage about someone who talks a lot. You are probably familiar with some of these words already.

DISCURSIVE	GARRULOUS	LONG-WINDED
LOQUACIOUS	PALAVEROUS	PROLIX
REDUNDANT	VERBOSE	VOLUBLE
WORDY		

Now keep going. Here are 12 words that an author might use to discuss someone who doesn't talk much:

BRUSQUE	CLOSE-MOUTHED	CURT
DUMB	LACONIC	PITHY
RETICENT	SUCCINCT	TACITURN
TERSE	UNEXPRESSIVE	UNFORTHCOMING

That's a good start! Now learn these 12 words that you might see in a text about someone who knows a lot of words, whether they use many of those words or not:

ACADEMIC	ARTICULATE	CONVERSANT
ELOQUENT	ERUDITE	FLUENT
INTELLECTUAL	LEARNED	LETTERED
LITTERATEUR	SAVANT	SCHOLAR

Trying to memorize the dictionary would be a miserable and probably futile experience, but learning a handful of related words at a time is completely feasible. Continue to expand your vocabulary by learning the words in the lists that follow.

180 Common GRE Words in Context

ABATE: to reduce in amount, degree, or severity

As the hurricane's force ABATED, the winds dropped and the sea became calm.

Words with similar meanings:

EBB	LAPSE	LET UP
MODERATE	RELENT	SLACKEN
SUBSIDE	WANE	

ABSCOND: to leave secretly
The patron ABSCONDED from the restaurant by sneaking out the back door.

Words with similar meanings:

DECAMP ESCAPE FLEE

ABSTAIN: to choose not to do something
During Lent, practicing Catholics ABSTAIN from eating meat.

Words with similar meanings:

FORBEAR REFRAIN WITHHOLD

ABYSS: an extremely deep hole
The submarine dove into the ABYSS to chart the previously unseen depths.

Related words:

ABYSSAL: pertaining to great depth
ABYSMAL: extremely bad

Words with similar meanings:

CHASM VOID

ADULTERATE: to make impure
The restaurateur made his ketchup last longer by ADULTERATING it with water.

Related words:

UNADULTERATED: pure
ADULTERY: an illicit relationship; an affair

Words with similar meanings:

DOCTOR

ADVOCATE: to speak in favor of
The vegetarian ADVOCATED a diet containing no meat.

Related words:

ADVOCACY: active support for

Words with similar meanings:

BACK CHAMPION SUPPORT

AESTHETIC: concerning the appreciation of beauty
Followers of the AESTHETIC Movement regarded the pursuit of beauty as the only true purpose of art.

Related words:

AESTHETE: someone unusually sensitive to beauty
AESTHETICISM: concern with beauty

Words with similar meanings:

ARTISTIC	TASTEFUL

AGGRANDIZE: to increase in power, influence, and reputation

The supervisor sought to AGGRANDIZE himself by claiming that the achievements of his staff were actually his own.

Words with similar meanings:

AMPLIFY	APOTHEOSIZE	AUGMENT
DIGNIFY	ELEVATE	ENLARGE
ENNOBLE	EXALT	GLORIFY
MAGNIFY	SWELL	UPLIFT
WAX		

ALLEVIATE: to make more bearable

Taking aspirin helps to ALLEVIATE a headache.

Words with similar meanings:

ALLAY	ASSUAGE	COMFORT
EASE	LESSEN	LIGHTEN
MITIGATE	PALLIATE	RELIEVE

AMALGAMATE: to combine; to mix together

Giant Industries AMALGAMATED with Mega Products to form Giant-Mega Products Incorporated.

Related words:

AMALGAM: a mixture, especially of two metals

Words with similar meanings:

ADMIX	BLEND	COMBINE
COMMINGLE	COMMIX	COMPOUND
FUSE	INTERMINGLE	INTERMIX
MERGE	MINGLE	MIX

AMBIGUOUS: doubtful or uncertain; able to be interpreted several ways

The directions he gave were so AMBIGUOUS that we disagreed on which way to turn.

Related words:

AMBIGUITY: the quality of being ambiguous

Words with similar meanings:

CLOUDY	DOUBTFUL	DUBIOUS
EQUIVOCAL	INDETERMINATE	NEBULOUS
OBSCURE	UNCLEAR	VAGUE

AMELIORATE: to make better; to improve

The doctor was able to AMELIORATE the patient's suffering using painkillers.

Words with similar meanings:

AMEND	BETTER	IMPROVE
PACIFY	UPGRADE	

ANACHRONISM: something out of place in time

The aged hippie used ANACHRONISTIC phrases, like "groovy" and "far out," that had not been popular for years.

Words with similar meanings:

ARCHAISM	INCONGRUITY

ANALOGOUS: similar or alike in some way; equivalent to

In a famous argument for the existence of God, the universe is ANALOGOUS to a mechanical timepiece, the creation of a divinely intelligent "clockmaker."

Related words:

ANALOGY: a similarity between things that are otherwise dissimilar
ANALOGUE: something that is similar in some way to something else

Words with similar meanings:

ALIKE	COMPARABLE	CORRESPONDING
EQUIVALENT	HOMOGENEOUS	PARALLEL
SIMILAR		

ANOMALY: deviation from what is normal

Albino animals may display too great an ANOMALY in their coloring to attract normally colored mates.

Related words:

ANOMALOUS: deviating from what is normal

Words with similar meanings:

ABERRANCE	ABERRATION	ABNORMALITY
DEVIANCE	DEVIATION	IRREGULARITY
PRETERNATURALNESS		

ANTAGONIZE: to annoy or provoke to anger

The child discovered that he could ANTAGONIZE the cat by pulling its tail.

Related words:

ANTAGONISTIC: tending to provoke conflict
ANTAGONIST: someone who fights another

Words with similar meanings

CLASH	CONFLICT	INCITE
IRRITATE	OPPOSE	PESTER
PROVOKE	VEX	

ANTIPATHY: extreme dislike

The ANTIPATHY between the French and the English regularly erupted into open warfare.

Words with similar meanings:

ANIMOSITY	ANIMUS	ANTAGONISM
AVERSION	ENMITY	HOSTILITY
REPELLENCE		

APATHY: lack of interest or emotion

The APATHY of voters is so great that less than half the people who are eligible to vote actually bother to do so.

Words with similar meanings:

COOLNESS	DISINTEREST	DISREGARD
IMPASSIVITY	INDIFFERENCE	INSENSIBILITY
LASSITUDE	LETHARGY	LISTLESSNESS
PHLEGM	STOLIDITY	UNCONCERN
UNRESPONSIVENESS		

ARBITRATE: to judge a dispute between two opposing parties

Since the couple could not come to an agreement, a judge was forced to ARBITRATE their divorce proceedings.

Related words:

ARBITRATION: a process by which a conflict is resolved
ARBITRATOR: a judge

Words with similar meanings:

ADJUDGE	ADJUDICATE	DECIDE
DETERMINE	JUDGE	MODERATE
REFEREE	RULE	

ARCHAIC: ancient, old-fashioned

Her ARCHAIC Commodore computer could not run the latest software.

Related words:

ARCHAISM: an outdated word or phrase

Words with similar meanings:

ANCIENT	ANTEDILUVIAN	ANTIQUE
BYGONE	DATED	DOWDY
FUSTY	OBSOLETE	OLD-FASHIONED
OUTDATED	OUTMODED	PASSÉ
PREHISTORIC	STALE	SUPERANNUATED
SUPERSEDED	VINTAGE	

ARDOR: intense and passionate feeling

Bishop's ARDOR for landscape was evident when he passionately described the beauty of the scenic Hudson Valley.

Related words:

ARDENT: expressing ardor; passionate

Words with similar meanings:

DEVOTION	ENTHUSIASM	FERVENCY
FERVIDITY	FERVIDNESS	FERVOR
FIRE	PASSION	ZEAL
ZEALOUSNESS		

ARTICULATE: able to speak clearly and expressively

She is such an ARTICULATE defender of labor that unions are among her strongest supporters.

Words with similar meanings:

ELOQUENT	EXPRESSIVE	FLUENT
LUCID	SILVER-TONGUED	SMOOTH-SPOKEN

ASSUAGE: to make something unpleasant less severe

Like many people, Philip Larkin used alcohol to ASSUAGE his sense of meaninglessness and despair.

Words with similar meanings:

ALLAY	ALLEVIATE	APPEASE
COMFORT	CONCILIATE	EASE
LIGHTEN	MITIGATE	MOLLIFY
PACIFY	PALLIATE	PLACATE
PROPITIATE	RELIEVE	SOOTHE
SWEETEN		

ATTENUATE: to reduce in force or degree; to weaken

The Bill of Rights ATTENUATED the traditional power of government to change laws at will.

Words with similar meanings:

DEBILITATE	DEVITALIZE	DILUTE
ENERVATE	ENFEEBLE	RAREFY
SAP	THIN	UNDERMINE
UNDO	UNNERVE	WATER
WEAKEN		

AUDACIOUS: fearless and daring

"And you, your majesty, may kiss my bum!" replied the AUDACIOUS peasant.

Related words:

AUDACITY: the quality of being audacious

Words with similar meanings:

ADVENTURESOME	AGGRESSIVE	ASSERTIVE
BOLD	BRAVE	COURAGEOUS
DARING	DAUNTLESS	DOUGHTY
FEARLESS	GALLANT	GAME
HEROIC	INTREPID	METTLESOME
PLUCKY	STOUT	STOUTHEARTED
UNAFRAID	UNDAUNTED	VALIANT
VALOROUS	VENTURESOME	VENTUROUS

AUSTERE: severe or stern in appearance; undecorated

The lack of decoration makes Zen temples seem AUSTERE to the untrained eye.

Related words:

AUSTERITY: severity, especially poverty

Words with similar meanings:

BLEAK	DOUR	GRIM
HARD	HARSH	SEVERE

BANAL: predictable, clichéd, boring

He used BANAL phrases like "have a nice day" and "another day, another dollar."

Related words:

BANALITY: the quality of being banal

Words with similar meanings:

BLAND	BROMIDIC	CLICHÉD
COMMONPLACE	FATUOUS	HACKNEYED
INNOCUOUS	INSIPID	JEJUNE
MUSTY	PLATITUDINOUS	PROSAIC
QUOTIDIAN	SHOPWORN	STALE
STEREOTYPIC	THREADBARE	TIMEWORN
TIRED	TRITE	VAPID
WORN-OUT		

BOLSTER: to support; to prop up

The presence of giant footprints BOLSTERED the argument that Sasquatch was in the area.

Words with similar meanings:

BRACE	BUTTRESS	PROP
SUPPORT	SUSTAIN	UNDERPIN
UPHOLD		

BOMBASTIC: pompous in speech and manner

Mussolini's speeches were mostly BOMBASTIC; his boasting and outrageous claims had no basis in fact.

Related words:

BOMBAST: pompous speech or writing

Words with similar meanings:

BLOATED	DECLAMATORY	FUSTIAN
GRANDILOQUENT	GRANDIOSE	HIGH-FLOWN
MAGNILOQUENT	OROTUND	PRETENTIOUS
RHETORICAL	SELF-IMPORTANT	

CACOPHONY: harsh, jarring noise

The junior high orchestra created an almost unbearable CACOPHONY as they tried to tune their instruments.

Words with similar meanings:

CHAOS	CLAMOR	DIN
DISCORD	DISHARMONY	NOISE

CANDID: impartial and honest in speech

The observations of a child can be charming since they are CANDID and unpretentious.

Words with similar meanings:

DIRECT	FORTHRIGHT	FRANK
HONEST	OPEN	SINCERE
STRAIGHT	STRAIGHTFORWARD	UNDISGUISED

CAPRICIOUS: changing one's mind quickly and often

Queen Elizabeth I was quite CAPRICIOUS; her courtiers could never be sure which of their number would catch her fancy.

Related words:

CAPRICE: whim, sudden fancy

Words with similar meanings:

ARBITRARY	CHANCE	CHANGEABLE
ERRATIC	FICKLE	INCONSTANT
MERCURIAL	RANDOM	WHIMSICAL
WILLFUL		

CASTIGATE: to punish or criticize harshly

Many Americans are amazed at how harshly the authorities in Singapore CASTIGATE perpetrators of what would be considered minor crimes in the United States.

Words with similar meanings:

ADMONISH	CHASTISE	CHIDE
REBUKE	REPRIMAND	REPROACH
REPROVE	SCOLD	TAX
UPBRAID		

CATALYST: something that brings about a change in something else

The imposition of harsh taxes was the CATALYST that finally brought on the revolution.

Related words:

CATALYZE: to bring about a change in something else

CAUSTIC: biting in wit

Dorothy Parker gained her reputation for CAUSTIC wit from her cutting, yet clever, insults.

Words with similar meanings:

ACERBIC	BITING	MORDANT
TRENCHANT		

CHAOS: great disorder or confusion

In most religious traditions, God created an ordered universe from CHAOS.

Related words:

CHAOTIC: jumbled, confused

Words with similar meanings:

CLUTTER	CONFUSION	DISARRANGEMENT
DISARRAY	DISORDER	DISORDERLINESS
DISORGANIZATION	JUMBLE	MESS
MUDDLE	SCRAMBLE	SNARL
TOPSY-TURVINESS	TURMOIL	

CHAUVINIST: someone prejudiced in favor of a group to which he or she belongs

The attitude that men are inherently superior to women and therefore must be obeyed is common among male CHAUVINISTS.

Words with similar meanings:

PARTISAN

CHICANERY: deception by means of craft or guile

Dishonest used car salespeople often use CHICANERY to sell their beat-up old cars.

Words with similar meanings:

ARTIFICE	CONNIVING	CRAFTINESS
DECEPTION	DEVIOUSNESS	MISREPRESENTATION
PETTIFOGGERY	SHADINESS	SNEAKINESS
SOPHISTRY	SUBTERFUGE	UNDERHANDEDNESS

COGENT: convincing and well-reasoned

Swayed by the COGENT argument of the defense, the jury had no choice but to acquit the defendant.

Related words:

COGITATE: to think deeply

Words with similar meanings:

CONVINCING	PERSUASIVE	SOLID
SOUND	TELLING	VALID

CONDONE: to overlook, pardon, or disregard

Some theorists believe that failing to prosecute minor crimes is the same as CONDONING an air of lawlessness.

Words with similar meanings:

EXCULPATE	EXCUSE	PARDON
REMIT		

CONVOLUTED: intricate and complicated

Although many people bought *A Brief History of Time*, few could follow its CONVOLUTED ideas and theories.

Words with similar meanings:

BYZANTINE	COMPLEX	ELABORATE
INTRICATE	KNOTTY	LABYRINTHINE
PERPLEXING	TANGLED	

CORROBORATE: to provide supporting evidence

Fingerprints CORROBORATED the witness's testimony that he saw the defendant in the victim's apartment.

Words with similar meanings:

AUTHENTICATE	BACK	BEAR OUT
BUTTRESS	CONFIRM	SUBSTANTIATE
VALIDATE	VERIFY	

CREDULOUS: too trusting; gullible

Although some four-year-olds believe in the Easter Bunny, only the most CREDULOUS nine-year-olds still believe in him.

Related words:

CREDULITY: the quality of being credulous

Words with similar meanings:

NAIVE	SUSCEPTIBLE	TRUSTING

CRESCENDO: steadily increasing in volume or force

The CRESCENDO of tension became unbearable as Evel Knievel prepared to jump his motorcycle over the school buses.

Words with similar meanings:

ESCALATION	INCREASE	INTENSIFICATION

DECORUM: appropriateness of behavior or conduct; propriety

The countess complained that the vulgar peasants lacked the DECORUM appropriate for a visit to the palace.

Related words:

DECOROUS: conforming to acceptable standards

Words with similar meanings:

CORRECTNESS	DECENCY	ETIQUETTE
MANNERS	MORES	PROPRIETY
SEEMLINESS		

DEFERENCE: respect, courtesy

The respectful young law clerk treated the Supreme Court justice with the utmost DEFERENCE.

Related words:

DEFER: to delay; to show someone deference
DEFERENTIAL: courteous and respectful

Words with similar meanings:

COURTESY	HOMAGE	HONOR
OBEISANCE	RESPECT	REVERENCE
VENERATION		

DERIDE: to speak of or treat with contempt; to mock

The awkward child was often DERIDED by his "cooler" peers.

Related words:

DERISION: mockery and taunts
DERISIVE: in a mocking manner

Words with similar meanings:

GIBE	JEER	MOCK
RIDICULE	SCOFF	SNEER
TAUNT		

DESICCATE: to dry out thoroughly

After a few weeks of lying on the desert's baking sands, the cow's carcass became completely DESICCATED.

Related words:

DESICCANT: something that removes water from another substance

Words with similar meanings:

DEHYDRATE	DRY	PARCH

DESULTORY: jumping from one thing to another; disconnected

Diane had a DESULTORY academic record; she had changed majors 12 times in three years.

Words with similar meanings:

AIMLESS	DISCONNECTED	ERRATIC
HAPHAZARD	INDISCRIMINATE	OBJECTLESS
PURPOSELESS	RANDOM	STRAY
UNCONSIDERED	UNPLANNED	

DIATRIBE: an abusive, condemnatory speech

The trucker bellowed a DIATRIBE at the driver who had cut him off.

Words with similar meanings:

FULMINATION	HARANGUE	INVECTIVE
JEREMIAD	MALEDICTION	OBLOQUY
TIRADE		

DIFFIDENT: lacking self-confidence

Steve's DIFFIDENT manner during the job interview stemmed from his nervous nature and lack of experience in the field.

Words with similar meanings:

BACKWARD	BASHFUL	COY
DEMURE	MODEST	RETIRING
SELF-EFFACING	SHY	TIMID

DILATE: to make larger; to expand

When you enter a darkened room, the pupils of your eyes DILATE to let in more light.

Words with similar meanings:

AMPLIFY	DEVELOP	ELABORATE
ENLARGE	EXPAND	EXPATIATE

DILATORY: intended to delay

The congressman used DILATORY measures to delay the passage of the bill.

Words with similar meanings:

DRAGGING	FLAGGING	LAGGARD
LAGGING	SLOW	SLOW-FOOTED
SLOW-GOING	SLOW-PACED	TARDY

DILETTANTE: someone with an amateurish and superficial interest in a topic
Jerry's friends were such DILETTANTES that they seemed to have new jobs and hobbies every week.

Words with similar meanings:

AMATEUR DABBLER SUPERFICIAL
TYRO

DIRGE: a funeral hymn or mournful speech
Melville wrote the poem "A DIRGE for James McPherson" for the funeral of a Union general who was killed in 1864.

Words with similar meanings:

ELEGY LAMENT

DISABUSE: to set right; to free from error
Galileo's observations DISABUSED scholars of the notion that the sun revolved around the Earth.

Words with similar meanings:

CORRECT UNDECEIVE

DISCERN: to perceive; to recognize
It is easy to DISCERN the difference between butter and butter-flavored topping.

Related words:
DISCERNMENT: taste and cultivation

Words with similar meanings:

CATCH DESCRY DETECT
DIFFERENTIATE DISCRIMINATE DISTINGUISH
ESPY GLIMPSE KNOW
SEPARATE SPOT SPY
TELL

DISPARATE: fundamentally different; entirely unlike
Although the twins appear to be identical physically, their personalities are DISPARATE.

Words with similar meanings:

DIFFERENT DISSIMILAR DIVERGENT
DIVERSE VARIANT VARIOUS

DISSEMBLE: to present a false appearance; to disguise one's real intentions or character

The villain could DISSEMBLE to the police no longer—he admitted the deed and tore up the floor to reveal the body of the old man.

Words with similar meanings:

ACT	AFFECT	ASSUME
CLOAK	COUNTERFEIT	CAMOUFLAGE
COVER UP	DISGUISE	DISSIMULATE
FAKE	FEIGN	MASK
MASQUERADE	POSE	PRETEND
PUT ON	SHAM	SIMULATE

DISSONANCE: a harsh and disagreeable combination, often of sounds

Cognitive DISSONANCE is the inner conflict produced when long-standing beliefs are contradicted by new evidence.

Words with similar meanings:

CLASH	CONTENTION	DISCORD
DISSENSION	DISSENT	DISSIDENCE
FRICTION	STRIFE	VARIANCE

DOGMA: a firmly held opinion, often a religious belief

Linus's central DOGMA was that children who believed in the Great Pumpkin would be rewarded.

Words with similar meanings:

CREED	CREDO	DOCTRINE
TEACHING	TENET	

DOGMATIC: dictatorial in one's opinions

The dictator was DOGMATIC—he, and only he, was right.

Words with similar meanings:

AUTHORITARIAN	BOSSY	DICTATORIAL
DOCTRINAIRE	DOMINEERING	IMPERIOUS
MAGISTERIAL	MASTERFUL	OVERBEARING
PEREMPTORY		

DUPE: to deceive; a person who is easily deceived

Bugs Bunny was able to DUPE Elmer Fudd by dressing up as a lady rabbit.

Words with similar meanings:

BEGUILE	BETRAY	BLUFF
COZEN	DECEIVE	DELUDE
FOOL	HOODWINK	HUMBUG
MISLEAD	TAKE IN	TRICK

ECLECTIC: selecting from or made up from a variety of sources

Budapest's architecture is an ECLECTIC mix of Eastern and Western styles.

Words with similar meanings:

BROAD	CATHOLIC	DIVERSE

EFFICACY: effectiveness

The EFFICACY of penicillin was unsurpassed when it was first introduced; the drug completely eliminated almost all bacterial infections for which it was administered.

Related words:

EFFICACIOUS: effective; productive

Words with similar meanings:

DYNAMISM	EFFECTIVENESS	EFFICIENCY
FORCE	POWER	PRODUCTIVENESS
PROFICIENCY	STRENGTH	VIGOR

ELEGY: a sorrowful poem or speech

Although Thomas Gray's "ELEGY Written in a Country Churchyard" is about death and loss, it urges its readers to endure this life and to trust in spirituality.

Related words:

ELEGIAC: like an elegy; mournful

Words with similar meanings:

DIRGE	LAMENT

ELOQUENT: persuasive and moving, especially in speech

The Gettysburg Address is moving not only because of its lofty sentiments but also because of its ELOQUENT words.

Words with similar meanings:

ARTICULATE	EXPRESSIVE	FLUENT
MEANINGFUL	SIGNIFICANT	SMOOTH-SPOKEN

EMULATE: to copy; to try to equal or excel

The graduate student sought to EMULATE his professor in every way, copying not only how she taught, but also how she conducted herself outside of class.

Words with similar meanings:

APE	IMITATE	SIMULATE

ENERVATE: to reduce in strength

The guerrillas hoped that a series of surprise attacks would ENERVATE the regular army.

Related words:

UNNERVE: to deprive of strength or courage

Words with similar meanings:

DEBILITATE	ENFEEBLE	SAP
WEAKEN		

ENGENDER: to produce, cause, or bring about

His fear and hatred of clowns was ENGENDERED when he witnessed the death of his father at the hands of a clown.

Words with similar meanings:

BEGET	GENERATE	PROCREATE
PROLIFERATE	REPRODUCE	SPAWN

ENIGMA: a puzzle; a mystery

Speaking in riddles and dressed in old robes, the artist gained a reputation as something of an ENIGMA.

Words with similar meanings:

CONUNDRUM	PERPLEXITY

ENUMERATE: to count, list, or itemize

Moses returned from the mountain with tablets on which the commandments were ENUMERATED.

Words with similar meanings:

CATALOG	INDEX	TABULATE

EPHEMERAL: lasting a short time

The lives of mayflies seem EPHEMERAL to us, since the flies' average life span is a matter of hours.

Words with similar meanings:

EVANESCENT	FLEETING	MOMENTARY
TRANSIENT		

EQUIVOCATE: to use expressions of double meaning in order to mislead

When faced with criticism of her policies, the politician EQUIVOCATED and left all parties thinking she agreed with them.

Related words:

EQUIVOCAL: undecided; trying to deceive

EQUIVOCATION: the act or state of equivocating

Words with similar meanings:

AMBIGUOUS EVASIVE WAFFLING

ERRATIC: wandering and unpredictable

The plot seemed predictable until it suddenly took a series of ERRATIC turns that surprised the audience.

Related words:

Errant: straying, mistaken, roving

Words with similar meanings:

CAPRICIOUS INCONSTANT IRRESOLUTE
WHIMSICAL

ERUDITE: learned, scholarly, bookish

The annual meeting of philosophy professors was a gathering of the most ERUDITE, well-published individuals in the field.

Related words:

ERUDITION: extensive knowledge or learning

Words with similar meanings:

SCHOLASTIC LEARNED WISE

ESOTERIC: known or understood by only a few

Only a handful of experts are knowledgeable about the ESOTERIC world of particle physics.

Words with similar meanings:

ABSTRUSE ARCANE OBSCURE

ESTIMABLE: admirable

Most people consider it ESTIMABLE that Mother Teresa spent her life helping the poor of India.

Related words:

ESTEEM: high regard

Words with similar meanings:

ADMIRABLE COMMENDABLE CREDITABLE
HONORABLE LAUDABLE MERITORIOUS
PRAISEWORTHY RESPECTABLE VENERABLE
WORTHY

EULOGY: speech in praise of someone

His best friend gave the EULOGY, outlining his many achievements and talents.

Words with similar meanings:

COMMEND EXTOL LAUD

EUPHEMISM: use of an inoffensive word or phrase in place of a more distasteful one

The funeral director preferred to use the EUPHEMISM "sleeping" instead of the word "dead."

Words with similar meanings:

CIRCUMLOCUTION WHITEWASH

EXACERBATE: to make worse

It is unwise to take aspirin to try to relieve heartburn; instead of providing relief, the drug will only EXACERBATE the problem.

Words with similar meanings:

ANNOY AGGRAVATE INTENSIFY
IRRITATE PROVOKE

EXCULPATE: to clear from blame; prove innocent

The adversarial legal system is intended to convict those who are guilty and to EXCULPATE those who are innocent.

Words with similar meanings:

ABSOLVE ACQUIT CLEAR
EXONERATE VINDICATE

EXIGENT: urgent; requiring immediate action

The patient was losing blood so rapidly that it was EXIGENT to stop the source of the bleeding.

Words with similar meanings:

CRITICAL IMPERATIVE NEEDED
URGENT

EXONERATE: to clear of blame

The fugitive was EXONERATED when another criminal confessed to committing the crime.

Words with similar meanings:

ABSOLVE ACQUIT CLEAR
EXCULPATE VINDICATE

EXPLICIT: clearly stated or shown; forthright in expression

The owners of the house left a list of EXPLICIT instructions detailing their house sitter's duties, including a schedule for watering the house plants.

Related words:

EXPLICABLE: capable of being explained
EXPLICATE: to give a detailed explanation

Words with similar meanings:

CLEAR-CUT	DEFINITIVE	PRECISE
STRAIGHTFORWARD	UNEQUIVOCAL	

FANATICAL: acting excessively enthusiastic; filled with extreme, unquestioned devotion

The stormtroopers were FANATICAL in their devotion to the Emperor, readily sacrificing their lives for him.

Words with similar meanings:

EXTREMIST	FIERY	FRENZIED
ZEALOUS		

FAWN: to grovel

The understudy FAWNED over the director in hopes of being cast in the part on a permanent basis.

Words with similar meanings:

BOOTLICK	GROVEL	PANDER
TOADY		

FERVID: intensely emotional; feverish

The fans of Maria Callas were particularly FERVID, doing anything to catch a glimpse of the great opera singer.

Related words:

FERVENT: enthusiastic
FERVOR: passion

Words with similar meanings:

BURNING	IMPASSIONED	PASSIONATE
VEHEMENT	ZEALOUS	

FLORID: excessively decorated or embellished

The palace had been decorated in a FLORID style; every surface had been carved and gilded.

Words with similar meanings:

BAROQUE	ELABORATE	FLAMBOYANT
ORNATE	OSTENTATIOUS	ROCOCO

FOMENT: to arouse or incite
The protesters tried to FOMENT feeling against the war through their speeches and demonstrations.

Words with similar meanings:

AGITATE	IMPASSION	INFLAME
INSTIGATE	KINDLE	

FRUGALITY: a tendency to be thrifty or cheap
Scrooge McDuck's FRUGALITY was so great that he accumulated enough wealth to fill a giant storehouse with money.

Words with similar meanings:

ECONOMICAL	PARSIMONY	PRUDENCE
SPARING	SCRIMPING	THRIFT

GARRULOUS: tending to talk a lot
The GARRULOUS parakeet distracted its owner with its continuous talking.

Words with similar meanings:

EFFUSIVE	LOQUACIOUS

GREGARIOUS: outgoing, sociable
She was so GREGARIOUS that when she found herself alone she felt quite sad.

Words with similar meanings:

AFFABLE	COMMUNICATIVE	CONGENIAL
SOCIABLE		

GUILE: deceit or trickery
Since he was not fast enough to catch the roadrunner on foot, the coyote resorted to GUILE in an effort to trap his enemy.

Related words:
GUILELESS: innocent, without trickery

Words with similar meanings:

ARTIFICE	CHICANERY	CONNIVERY
DUPLICITY		

GULLIBLE: easily deceived

The con man pretended to be a bank officer so as to fool GULLIBLE bank customers into giving him their account information.

Related words:

GULL: a person who is easily tricked

Words with similar meanings:

CREDULOUS EXPLOITABLE NAIVE

HOMOGENEOUS (or HOMOGENOUS): of a similar kind

The class was fairly HOMOGENEOUS, since almost all of the students were senior journalism majors.

Related words:

HOMOGENIZED: thoroughly mixed together

Words with similar meanings:

CONSISTENT STANDARDIZED UNIFORM
UNVARYING

ICONOCLAST: one who opposes established beliefs, customs, and institutions

His lack of regard for traditional beliefs soon established him as an ICONOCLAST.

Words with similar meanings:

MAVERICK NONCONFORMIST REBEL
REVOLUTIONARY

IMPERTURBABLE: not capable of being disturbed

The counselor had so much experience dealing with distraught children that she seemed IMPERTURBABLE, even when faced with the wildest tantrums.

Related words:

PERTURB: to disturb greatly

Words with similar meanings:

COMPOSED DISPASSIONATE IMPASSIVE
SERENE STOICAL

IMPERVIOUS: impossible to penetrate; incapable of being affected

A good raincoat is IMPERVIOUS to moisture.

Words with similar meanings:

RESISTANT IMPREGNABLE

IMPETUOUS: quick to act without thinking

It is not good for an investment broker to be IMPETUOUS, because much thought should be given to all the possible options.

Related words:

IMPETUS: impulse

Words with similar meanings:

IMPULSIVE, PRECIPITATE, RASH, RECKLESS, SPONTANEOUS

IMPLACABLE: unable to be calmed down or made peaceful

His rage at the betrayal was so great that he remained IMPLACABLE for weeks.

Related words:

PLACATE: to make peaceful

Words with similar meanings:

INEXORABLE, INTRANSIGENT, IRRECONCILABLE, RELENTLESS, REMORSELESS, UNFORGIVING, UNRELENTING

INCHOATE: not fully formed; disorganized

The ideas expressed in Nietzsche's mature work also appear in an INCHOATE form in his earliest writing.

Words with similar meanings:

AMORPHOUS, INCOHERENT, INCOMPLETE, UNORGANIZED

INGENUOUS: showing innocence or childlike simplicity

She was so INGENUOUS that her friends feared that her innocence and trustfulness would be exploited when she visited the big city.

Related words:

INGÉNUE: a naive girl or young woman
DISINGENUOUS: giving a false impression of innocence

Words with similar meanings:

ARTLESS, GUILELESS, INNOCENT, NAIVE, SIMPLE, UNAFFECTED

INIMICAL: hostile, unfriendly

Even though a cease-fire had been in place for months, the two sides were still INIMICAL to each other.

Words with similar meanings:

ADVERSE ANTAGONISTIC DISSIDENT
RECALCITRANT

INNOCUOUS: harmless

Some snakes are poisonous, but most species are INNOCUOUS and pose no danger to humans.

Words with similar meanings:

BENIGN HARMLESS INOFFENSIVE

INSIPID: lacking interest or flavor

The critic claimed that the painting was INSIPID, containing no interesting qualities at all.

Words with similar meanings:

BANAL BLAND DULL
STALE VAPID

INTRANSIGENT: uncompromising; refusing to be reconciled

The professor was INTRANSIGENT on the deadline, insisting that everyone turn the assignment in at the same time.

Words with similar meanings:

IMPLACABLE INEXORABLE IRRECONCILABLE
OBDURATE OBSTINATE REMORSELESS
RIGID UNBENDING UNRELENTING
UNYIELDING

INUNDATE: to overwhelm; to cover with water

The tidal wave INUNDATED Atlantis, which was lost beneath the water.

Words with similar meanings:

DELUGE DROWN ENGULF
FLOOD SUBMERGE

IRASCIBLE: easily made angry

Attila the Hun's IRASCIBLE and violent nature made all who dealt with him fear for their lives.

Related words:

IRATE: angry

Words with similar meanings:

CANTANKEROUS IRRITABLE ORNERY
TESTY

LACONIC: using few words

She was a LACONIC poet who built her reputation on using words as sparingly as possible.

Words with similar meanings:

CONCISE	CURT	PITHY
TACITURN	TERSE	

LAMENT: to express sorrow; to grieve

The children continued to LAMENT the death of the goldfish weeks after its demise.

Words with similar meanings:

BEWAIL	DEPLORE	GRIEVE
MOURN		

LAUD: to give praise; to glorify

Parades and fireworks were staged to LAUD the success of the rebels.

Related words:

LAUDABLE: worthy of praise
LAUDATORY: expressing praise

Words with similar meanings:

ACCLAIM	APPLAUD	COMMEND
COMPLIMENT	EXALT	EXTOL
HAIL	PRAISE	

LAVISH: to give unsparingly (v.); extremely generous or extravagant (adj.)

She LAVISHED the puppy with so many treats that it soon became overweight and spoiled.

Words with similar meanings:

BESTOW	CONFER	EXTRAVAGANT
EXUBERANT	LUXURIANT	OPULENT
PRODIGAL	PROFUSE	SUPERABUNDANT

LETHARGIC: acting in an indifferent or slow, sluggish manner

The clerk was so LETHARGIC that, even when the store was not busy, he always had a long line in front of him.

Words with similar meanings:

APATHETIC	LACKADAISICAL	LANGUID
LISTLESS	TORPID	

LOQUACIOUS: talkative

She was naturally LOQUACIOUS, which was a problem in situations in which listening was more important than talking.

Related words:

ELOQUENCE: powerful, convincing speaking
LOQUACITY: the quality of being loquacious

Words with similar meanings:

EFFUSIVE	GARRULOUS	VERBOSE

LUCID: clear and easily understood

The explanations were written in a simple and LUCID manner so that students were immediately able to apply what they learned.

Related words:

LUCIDITY: clarity
LUCENT: glowing with light

Words with similar meanings:

CLEAR	COHERENT	EXPLICIT
INTELLIGIBLE	LIMPID	

LUMINOUS: bright, brilliant, glowing

The park was bathed in LUMINOUS sunshine, which warmed the bodies and the souls of the visitors.

Related words:

ILLUMINATE: to shine light on
LUMINARY: an inspiring person

Words with similar meanings:

INCANDESCENT	LUCENT	LUSTROUS
RADIANT	RESPLENDENT	

MALINGER: to evade responsibility by pretending to be ill

A common way to avoid the draft was by MALINGERING—pretending to be mentally or physically ill so as to avoid being taken by the Army.

Related words:

LINGER: to be slow in leaving

Words with similar meanings:

SHIRK	SLACK

MALLEABLE: capable of being shaped

Gold is the most MALLEABLE of precious metals; it can easily be formed into almost any shape.

Words with similar meanings:

ADAPTABLE	DUCTILE	PLASTIC
PLIABLE	PLIANT	

METAPHOR: a figure of speech comparing two different things; a symbol

The METAPHOR "a sea of troubles" suggests a lot of troubles by comparing their number to the vastness of the sea.

Related words:

METAPHORICAL: standing as a symbol for something else

Words with similar meanings:

ANALOGY	COMPARISON

METICULOUS: extremely careful about details

To find all the clues at the crime scene, the investigators METICULOUSLY examined every inch of the area.

Words with similar meanings:

CONSCIENTIOUS	PRECISE	SCRUPULOUS

MISANTHROPE: a person who dislikes others

The character Scrooge in *A Christmas Carol* is such a MISANTHROPE that even the sight of children singing makes him angry.

Words with similar meanings:

CURMUDGEON	RECLUSE

MITIGATE: to soften; to lessen

A judge may MITIGATE a sentence if she decides that a person committed a crime out of need.

Words with similar meanings:

ALLAY	ALLEVIATE	ASSUAGE
EASE	LIGHTEN	MODERATE
MOLLIFY	PALLIATE	TEMPER

MOLLIFY: to calm or make less severe

Their argument was so intense that it was difficult to believe any compromise would MOLLIFY them.

Words with similar meanings:

APPEASE ASSUAGE CONCILIATE
PACIFY

MONOTONY: lack of variation

The MONOTONY of the sound of the dripping faucet almost drove the research assistant crazy.

Related words:

MONOTONE: a sound that is made at the same tone or pitch

Words with similar meanings:

DRONE TEDIUM

NAIVE: lacking sophistication or experience

Having never traveled before, the hillbillies were more NAIVE than the people they met in Beverly Hills.

Related words:

NAIVETÉ: the state of being naive

Words with similar meanings:

ARTLESS CREDULOUS GUILELESS
INGENUOUS SIMPLE UNAFFECTED

OBDURATE: hardened in feeling; resistant to persuasion

The president was completely OBDURATE on the issue, and no amount of persuasion would change his mind.

Words with similar meanings:

INFLEXIBLE INTRANSIGENT RECALCITRANT
TENACIOUS UNYIELDING

OBSEQUIOUS: overly submissive and eager to please

The OBSEQUIOUS new associate made sure to compliment her supervisor's tie and agree with him on every issue.

Related words:

OBEISANCE: a physical show of respect or submission, such as a bow

Words with similar meanings:

COMPLIANT DEFERENTIAL SERVILE
SUBSERVIENT

OBSTINATE: stubborn, unyielding

The OBSTINATE child could not be made to eat any food that he disliked.

Words with similar meanings:

INTRANSIGENT MULISH PERSISTENT
PERTINACIOUS STUBBORN TENACIOUS

OBVIATE: to prevent; to make unnecessary

The river was shallow enough to wade across at many points, which OBVIATED the need for a bridge.

Words with similar meanings:

FORESTALL PRECLUDE PROHIBIT

OCCLUDE: to stop up; to prevent the passage of

A shadow is thrown across the Earth's surface during a solar eclipse, when the light from the sun is OCCLUDED by the moon.

Words with similar meanings:

BARRICADE BLOCK CLOSE
OBSTRUCT

ONEROUS: troublesome and oppressive; burdensome

The assignment was so extensive and difficult to manage that it proved ONEROUS to the team in charge of it.

Words with similar meanings:

ARDUOUS BACKBREAKING BURDENSOME
CUMBERSOME DIFFICULT EXACTING
FORMIDABLE HARD LABORIOUS
OPPRESSIVE RIGOROUS TAXING
TRYING

OPAQUE: impossible to see through; preventing the passage of light

The heavy buildup of dirt and grime on the windows almost made them OPAQUE.

Related words:

OPACITY: the quality of being obscure and indecipherable

Words with similar meanings:

OBSCURE

OPPROBRIUM: public disgrace

After the scheme to embezzle from the elderly was made public, the treasurer resigned in utter OPPROBRIUM.

Words with similar meanings:

DISCREDIT	DISGRACE	DISHONOR
DISREPUTE	IGNOMINY	INFAMY
OBLOQUY	SHAME	

OSTENTATION: excessive showiness

The OSTENTATION of the Sun King's court is evident in the lavish decoration and luxuriousness of his palace at Versailles.

Related words:

OSTENSIBLE: apparent

Words with similar meanings:

CONSPICUOUSNESS	FLASHINESS	PRETENTIOUSNESS
SHOWINESS		

PARADOX: a contradiction or dilemma

It is a PARADOX that those most in need of medical attention are often those least able to obtain it.

Words with similar meanings:

ANOMALY	IRONY	CONTRADICTION

PARAGON: model of excellence or perfection

She is the PARAGON of what a judge should be: honest, intelligent, hardworking, and just.

Words with similar meanings:

APOTHEOSIS	IDEAL	QUINTESSENCE
STANDARD		

PEDANT: someone who shows off learning

The graduate instructor's tedious and excessive commentary on the subject soon gained her a reputation as a PEDANT.

Related words:

PEDANTIC: making an excessive display of learning

PERFIDIOUS: willing to betray one's trust

The actress's PERFIDIOUS companion revealed all of her intimate secrets to the gossip columnist.

Related words:

PERFIDY: deceit, treachery

Words with similar meanings:

DISLOYAL FAITHLESS TRAITOROUS
TREACHEROUS

PERFUNCTORY: done in a routine way; indifferent

The machinelike bank teller processed the transaction and gave the waiting customer a PERFUNCTORY smile.

Words with similar meanings:

APATHETIC AUTOMATIC MECHANICAL

PERMEATE: to penetrate

This miraculous new cleaning fluid is able to PERMEATE stains and dissolve them in minutes!

Related words:

IMPERMEABLE: unable to be permeated

Words with similar meanings:

IMBUE INFUSE SUFFUSE

PHILANTHROPY: charity; a desire or effort to promote goodness

New York's Metropolitan Museum of Art owes much of its collection to the PHILANTHROPY of private collectors who willed their estates to the museum.

Related words:

PHILANTHROPIST: someone who is generous and desires to promote goodness

Words with similar meanings:

ALTRUISM HUMANITARIANISM

PLACATE: to soothe or pacify

The burglar tried to PLACATE the snarling dog by saying, "Nice doggy," and offering it a treat.

Related words:

PLACID: tolerant; calm
IMPLACABLE: unable to be made peaceful

Words with similar meanings:

APPEASE CONCILIATE MOLLIFY

PLASTIC: able to be molded, altered, or bent

The new material was very PLASTIC and could be formed into products of vastly different shapes.

Words with similar meanings:

ADAPTABLE DUCTILE MALLEABLE
PLIANT

PLETHORA: excess

Assuming that more was better, the defendant offered the judge a PLETHORA of excuses.

Words with similar meanings:

GLUT OVERABUNDANCE SUPERFLUITY
SURFEIT

PRAGMATIC: practical as opposed to idealistic

While daydreaming gamblers think they can get rich by frequenting casinos, PRAGMATIC gamblers realize that the odds are heavily stacked against them.

Related words:

PRAGMATISM: a practical approach to problem solving

Words with similar meanings:

RATIONAL REALISTIC

PRECIPITATE: to throw violently or bring about abruptly; lacking deliberation

Upon learning that the couple married after knowing each other only two months, friends and family members expected such a PRECIPITATE marriage to end in divorce.

Related words:

PRECIPICE: a steep cliff
PRECIPITATION: weather phenomena, like rain or snow, that falls from the sky
PRECIPITOUS: very steep

Words with similar meanings:

ABRUPT HASTY HEADLONG
HURRIED ILL-CONSIDERED IMPETUOUS
IMPULSIVE PROMPT RASH
RECKLESS SUDDEN

PREVARICATE: to lie or deviate from the truth

Rather than admit that he had overslept again, the employee PREVARICATED and claimed that heavy traffic had prevented him from arriving at work on time.

Words with similar meanings:

EQUIVOCATE LIE PERJURE

PRISTINE: fresh and clean; uncorrupted

Since concerted measures had been taken to prevent looting, the archeological site was still PRISTINE when researchers arrived.

Words with similar meanings:

INNOCENT UNDAMAGED

PRODIGAL: lavish; wasteful

The PRODIGAL son quickly wasted all of his inheritance on a lavish lifestyle devoted to pleasure.

Related words:

PRODIGALITY: excessive or reckless spending

Words with similar meanings:

EXTRAVAGANT LAVISH PROFLIGATE
SPENDTHRIFT WASTEFUL

PROLIFERATE: to increase in number quickly

Although he only kept two guinea pigs initially, they PROLIFERATED to such an extent that he soon had dozens.

Related words:

PROLIFIC: very productive or highly able to reproduce rapidly

Words with similar meanings:

BREED MULTIPLY PROCREATE
PROPAGATE REPRODUCE SPAWN

PROPITIATE: to conciliate; to appease

The management PROPITIATED the irate union by agreeing to raise wages for its members.

Related words:

PROPITIOUS: advantageous, favorable

Words with similar meanings:

APPEASE	CONCILIATE	MOLLIFY
PACIFY	PLACATE	

PROPRIETY: correct behavior; obedience to rules and customs

The aristocracy maintained a high level of PROPRIETY, adhering to even the most minor social rules.

Related words:

APPROPRIATE: suitable for a particular occasion or place

Words with similar meanings:

DECENCY	DECORUM	MODESTY
SEEMLINESS		

PRUDENCE: wisdom, caution, or restraint

The college student exhibited PRUDENCE by obtaining practical experience along with her studies, which greatly strengthened her résumé.

Related words:

PRUDE: someone who is excessively concerned with propriety
PRUDISH: prissy and puritanical

Words with similar meanings:

ASTUTENESS	CIRCUMSPECTION	DISCRETION
FRUGALITY	JUDICIOUSNESS	PROVIDENCE
THRIFT		

PUNGENT: sharp and irritating to the senses

The smoke from the burning tires was extremely PUNGENT, causing neighbors to close their windows so their eyes wouldn't water.

Words with similar meanings:

ACRID	CAUSTIC	PIQUANT
POIGNANT	STINGING	

QUIESCENT: motionless

Many animals are QUIESCENT over the winter months, minimizing activity in order to conserve energy.

Related words:

QUIESCENCE: state of rest or inactivity

Words with similar meanings:

DORMANT LATENT

RAREFY: to make thinner or sparser

Since the atmosphere RAREFIES as altitudes increase, the air at the top of very tall mountains is too thin to breathe.

Related words:

RAREFACTION: the process of making something less dense

Words with similar meanings:

ATTENUATE THIN

REPUDIATE: to reject the validity of

The old woman's claim that she was Russian royalty was REPUDIATED when DNA tests showed she was of no relation to them.

Words with similar meanings:

DENY DISAVOW DISCLAIM
DISOWN RENOUNCE

RETICENT: silent, reserved

Physically small and RETICENT in her speech, Joan Didion often went unnoticed by those upon whom she was reporting.

Words with similar meanings:

COOL INTROVERTED LACONIC
STANDOFFISH TACITURN UNDEMONSTRATIVE

RHETORIC: effective writing or speaking

Lincoln's talent for RHETORIC was evident in his beautifully expressed Gettysburg Address.

Words with similar meanings:

ELOQUENCE ORATORY

SATIATE: to satisfy fully or overindulge

His desire for power was so great that nothing less than complete control of the country could SATIATE it.

Related words:

SATE: to fully satisfy or overindulge
INSATIABLE: incapable of being satisfied

Words with similar meanings:

CLOY	GLUT	GORGE
SURFEIT		

SOPORIFIC: causing sleep or lethargy

The movie proved to be so SOPORIFIC that soon loud snores were heard throughout the theater.

Related words:

SOPOR: deep sleep

Words with similar meanings:

HYPNOTIC	NARCOTIC	SLUMBEROUS
SOMNOLENT		

SPECIOUS: deceptively attractive; seemingly plausible but fallacious

The student's SPECIOUS excuse for being late sounded legitimate, but was proved otherwise when his teacher called his home.

Words with similar meanings:

ILLUSORY	OSTENSIBLE	PLAUSIBLE
SPURIOUS	SOPHISTICAL	

STIGMA: a mark of shame or discredit

In *The Scarlet Letter*, Hester Prynne was required to wear the letter "A" on her clothes as a public STIGMA for her adultery.

Related words:

STIGMATIZE: to disgrace; to label with negative terms or reputation

Words with similar meanings:

BLEMISH	BLOT	OPPROBRIUM
STAIN	TAINT	

STOLID: unemotional; lacking sensitivity

The prisoner appeared STOLID and unaffected by the judge's harsh sentence.

Words with similar meanings:

APATHETIC	IMPASSIVE	INDIFFERENT
PHLEGMATIC	STOICAL	UNCONCERNED

SUBLIME: lofty or grand

The music was so SUBLIME that it transformed the rude surroundings into a special place.

Related words:

SUBLIMATE: to elevate or convert into something of higher worth
SUBLIMINAL: existing outside conscious awareness

Words with similar meanings:

AUGUST	EXALTED	GLORIOUS
GRAND	MAGNIFICENT	MAJESTIC
NOBLE	REGAL	RESPLENDENT
SUPERB		

TACIT: done without using words

Although not a word had been said, everyone in the room knew that a TACIT agreement had been made about which course of action to take.

Related words:

TACITURN: silent, not talkative

Words with similar meanings:

IMPLICIT	IMPLIED	UNDECLARED
UNSAID	UNUTTERED	

TACITURN: silent, not talkative

The clerk's TACITURN nature earned him the nickname "Silent Bob."

Related words:

TACIT: done without using words

Words with similar meanings:

LACONIC	RETICENT

TIRADE: long, harsh speech or verbal attack

Observers were shocked at the manager's TIRADE over such a minor mistake.

Words with similar meanings:

DIATRIBE	FULMINATION	HARANGUE
OBLOQUY	REVILEMENT	VILIFICATION

TORPOR: extreme mental and physical sluggishness

After surgery, the patient experienced TORPOR until the anesthesia wore off.

Related words:

TORPID: sluggish, lacking movement

Words with similar meanings:

APATHY	LANGUOR

TRANSITORY: temporary, lasting a brief time

The reporter lived a TRANSITORY life, staying in one place only long enough to cover the current story.

Related words:

TRANSIT: to pass through; to change or make a transition
TRANSIENT: passing quickly in and out of existence; one who stays a short time

Words with similar meanings:

EPHEMERAL	EVANESCENT	FLEETING
IMPERMANENT	MOMENTARY	

VACILLATE: to sway physically; to be indecisive

The customer held up the line as he VACILLATED between ordering chocolate chip or rocky road ice cream.

Words with similar meanings:

DITHER	FALTER	FLUCTUATE
OSCILLATE	WAVER	

VENERATE: to respect deeply

In a traditional Confucian society, the young VENERATE their elders, deferring to the elders' wisdom and experience.

Related words:

VENERABLE: old, worthy of respect

Words with similar meanings:

ADORE	HONOR	IDOLIZE
REVERE		

VERACITY: truthfulness; accuracy

She had a reputation for VERACITY, so everyone trusted her description of events.

Related words:

VERITY: truth
VERACIOUS: filled with truth and accuracy

Words with similar meanings:

CANDOR	EXACTITUDE	FIDELITY
PROBITY		

VERBOSE: wordy

The professor's answer was so VERBOSE that his student forgot what the original question had been.

Related words:

VERBALIZE: to put into words
VERBATIM: using the exact words; word for word
VERBIAGE: lots of words that are usually superfluous

Words with similar meanings:

LONG-WINDED LOQUACIOUS PROLIX
SUPERFLUOUS

VEX: to annoy

The old man who loved his peace and quiet was VEXED by his neighbor's loud music.

Related words:

VEXATION: a feeling of irritation

Words with similar meanings:

ANNOY BOTHER CHAFE
EXASPERATE IRK NETTLE
PEEVE PROVOKE

VOLATILE: easily aroused or changeable; lively or explosive

His VOLATILE personality made it difficult to predict his reaction to anything.

Words with similar meanings:

CAPRICIOUS ERRATIC FICKLE
INCONSISTENT INCONSTANT MERCURIAL
TEMPERAMENTAL

WAVER: to fluctuate between choices

If you WAVER too long before making a decision about which testing site to register for, you may not get your first choice.

Words with similar meanings:

DITHER FALTER FLUCTUATE
OSCILLATE VACILLATE

WHIMSICAL: acting in a fanciful or capricious manner; unpredictable

The ballet was WHIMSICAL, delighting the children with its imaginative characters and unpredictable sets.

Related words:

WHIM: a fancy or sudden notion

Words with similar meanings:

CAPRICIOUS	ERRATIC	FLIPPANT
FRIVOLOUS		

ZEAL: passion, excitement

She brought her typical ZEAL to the project, sparking enthusiasm in the other team members.

Related words:

ZEALOT: a fanatic

Words with similar meanings:

ARDENCY	FERVOR	FIRE
PASSION		

WORDS IN CONTEXT EXERCISE

1. Which sentence uses the word **capricious** correctly, in meaning and form?

   Ⓐ When it rained during the picnic, the party shivered under a tree until John's fiancée laughed, lifting the party's *capricious* mood.

   Ⓑ Senators debated several *capricious* economic issues until the budget had been balanced.

   Ⓒ Jane's mother speculated that her daughter's failing grades were due to her carefree, *capricious* nature.

2. Which sentence uses the word **dissemble** correctly, in meaning and form?

   Ⓐ The newspaper reporter quickly *dissembled* by reporting all of the facts of the scandalous story just as they happened.

   Ⓑ Those who are camping enthusiasts benefit greatly by having a tent that they can quickly *dissemble.*

   Ⓒ To be able to *dissemble* during a press conference, a spokesperson must be able to maintain a false appearance.

3. Which sentence uses the word **paragon** correctly, in meaning and form?

   (A) Firefighters are often the biggest *paragons* of smoke detectors, fire extinguishers, and other forms of fire safety.
   (B) The decorated army commander was a *paragon* of team leadership, discipline, and professionalism.
   (C) The chief of police did not support his *paragon* views on crime reduction.

4. Which sentence uses the word **venerate** correctly, in meaning and form?

   (A) In ancient times, kings and great warriors were *venerated* by being buried with many riches.
   (B) To regain control of his soccer team, the coach *venerated* players who were not taking the sport seriously.
   (C) When the retailer *venerated* the brass bed frame, the antique piece looked like new.

5. Which sentence uses the word **cacophony** correctly, in meaning and form?

   (A) The discordant music was a dreadful *cacophony* of synthesizer, accordion, and bells.
   (B) Due to hip surgery, her *cacophony* was off-balance and clumsy.
   (C) The novel's premise was so weak that the very *cacophony* of the motivation was questionable.

6. Which sentence uses the word **chicanery** correctly, in meaning and form?

   (A) The cashmere sweater was light as *chicanery*, as if knit from the softest goose feathers.
   (B) The smells of oregano and *chicanery* wafted from the kitchen into the living room.
   (C) Though the streetwise youth was usually good at detecting *chicanery*, that swindler cheated him out of a month's pay.

7. Which sentence uses the word **impetuous(ly)** correctly, in meaning and form?

   (A) She maintained a fiercely *impetuous* hold on her job title and never let anyone else perform the office duties.
   (B) Because she'd experienced his rage before, she approached her boss *impetuously* with the updated meeting outline.
   (C) She answered the questions on the form *impetuously*, filling them in randomly and without consideration.

8. Which sentence uses the word **vacillating** correctly, in meaning and form?

   (A) The music stopped suddenly and the *vacillating* silence was deafening.
   (B) After *vacillating* for days over whether to go to the doctor, she finally made an appointment when the swelling worsened dramatically.
   (C) The *vacillating* foundation held the monument steady in the high winds.

9. Which sentence uses the word **obstinate** correctly, in meaning and form?

   (A) Old maps and charts are too imprecise to give *obstinate* locations of geographic landmarks.
   (B) The new features added to the cell phone, including Internet access and photography, make it an *obstinate* piece of equipment.
   (C) Her *obstinate* political philosophy allowed her to see her own conditioned, inherited beliefs only.

10. Which sentence uses the word **apathy** correctly, in meaning and form?

   (A) The abhorrent criminal sneered maliciously, while the uninterested detective looked on with *apathy*.
   (B) Even wearing a heavy cape and tight corset, the opera singer carried herself across the stage with great *apathy*.
   (C) When the delicate gardenia blossoms opened, a scented *apathy* filtered through the air.

11. Which sentence uses the word **banal** correctly, in meaning and form?

    Ⓐ The protesting crowd quickly formed a *banal* and crossed it to reach the locked offices of the politicians.
    Ⓑ Thoughtful as her overtures were, his sister's insistence on traditions as *banal* as birthday cards and candles on the cake irritated him.
    Ⓒ Her effervescent lightheartedness made a *banal* impression on him.

12. Which sentence uses the word **castigate** correctly, in meaning and form?

    Ⓐ They stayed a long time by the shore, to watch the boats *castigate* in the setting sun.
    Ⓑ She wrote the paper the night before it was due, so she was fully prepared for her professor to *castigate* her weak efforts.
    Ⓒ She insisted on chewing vigorously to *castigate* her food before swallowing.

13. Which sentence uses the word **cogent** correctly, in meaning and form?

    Ⓐ The doctor presented *cogent* reasons for continuing the treatment.
    Ⓑ The doctor prepared a *cogent* supply of medical resources for the patient.
    Ⓒ Not all forms of cancer have symptoms *cogent* to only one prescribed type.

14. Which sentence uses the word **lavish** correctly, in meaning and form?

    Ⓐ Her efforts to create a *lavish* party to entertain her new in-laws included a four-course dinner and live musicians.
    Ⓑ Her *lavish* stinginess eventually drew the attention of all her acquaintances.
    Ⓒ He kept his skin disorder *lavish* by concealing it discreetly beneath long sleeves.

15. Which sentence uses the word **garrulous** correctly, in meaning and form?

    Ⓐ The *garrulous* guest regaled the party with songs and stories all evening.
    Ⓑ The police set out to apprehend the *garrulous* thief who stole the vehicle.
    Ⓒ The student developed a *garrulous* model to illustrate her geography assignment.

16. Which sentence uses the word **pungent** correctly, in meaning and form?

    (A) The scent of mold assaulted her senses with its *pungent* odor.
    (B) The babysitter developed a *pungent* fondness for the children she cared for.
    (C) Nobody associated with the *pungent* student who lost his temper so easily.

17. Which sentence uses the word **onerous** correctly, in meaning and form?

    (A) Her *onerous* view of the world became apparent during the debate when she mistook libertarianism for liberalism.
    (B) In the fall, the responsibility of driving her brother to practice became more *onerous* because he played twice as many fall sports as summer sports.
    (C) Chad grew concerned that chemicals were being used for a more *onerous* purpose than to study medicine.

18. Which sentence uses the word **plethora** correctly, in meaning and form?

    (A) The new student's hilarious stories brought a lot of *plethora* to the straitlaced campus.
    (B) The newlyweds' home was filled with a *plethora* of gifts, flowers, and letters wishing them good fortune.
    (C) Elephants *plethora* before they begin a long journey.

19. Which sentence uses the word **taciturn** correctly, in meaning and form?

    (A) After his wife died, the widower grew isolated and became *taciturn* in public.
    (B) Her *taciturn* fear of public speaking caused her palms to sweat and her heart to flutter.
    (C) *Taciturn* by nature, she spoke to anyone who would listen about any subject on her mind.

20. Which sentence uses the word **efficacy** correctly, in meaning and form?

   (A) The villagers burned their overlord in *efficacy* because he taxed them heavily.
   (B) The car owner decided that a damaged fender was too negligible to warrant making an *efficacy*.
   (C) Due to the *efficacy* of his business, a store owner was able to open another branch.

21. Which sentence uses the word **repudiate** correctly, in meaning and form?

   (A) The leftover crumbs, dirty plates, and chocolate-smudged faces helped them *repudiate* what they had for dessert.
   (B) The investor *repudiated* the business plan once she demonstrated that it was nothing more than a pyramid scheme.
   (C) Gamblers work hard to conceal tics and behaviors that might *repudiate* their strategies.

22. Which sentence uses the word **deferential** correctly, in meaning and form?

   (A) The courts make it clear that *deferential* behaviors will not be tolerated during jury selection.
   (B) The miscreant kicked rocks into the yard next door with a *deferential* attitude toward the homeowners.
   (C) The young man guided his grandmother with *deferential* patience to her car.

23. Which sentence uses the word **dupe** correctly, in meaning and form?

   (A) When the boy's cousin revealed a well-known secret, the boy had to *dupe* surprise.
   (B) No one would ever *dupe* to interrupt the patriarch of the family during mealtimes.
   (C) She *duped* her boyfriend into believing she lived in a better neighborhood.

24. Which sentence uses the word **stolid** correctly, in meaning and form?

Ⓐ She painted the landscape with *stolid* and acrylic paints.
Ⓑ Mother complained about the *stolid* couple who stayed so much later than all the other guests.
Ⓒ The *stolid* professor remained unmoved by the students' story of how they had missed the exam because of the blizzard.

25. Which sentence uses the word **zealous** correctly, in meaning and form?

Ⓐ The chef made the gumbo with a secret recipe that included many *zealous* ingredients, including hot habanero peppers.
Ⓑ The candidate's *zealous* campaign impressed his supporters with his enthusiasm.
Ⓒ He had a *zealous* feeling for his boss and always made snide comments right to his face.

26. Which sentence uses the word **implacable** correctly, in meaning and form?

Ⓐ Observing a young couple, the older woman briefly felt an *implacable* grief for her lost youth.
Ⓑ She could never convince her *implacable* son to eat anything but his favorite foods.
Ⓒ The violinist in the subway station played with an *implacable* skill that no one even recognized.

27. Which sentence uses the word **insipid** correctly, in meaning and form?

Ⓐ Despite its enormous popularity, the book struck Tom as *insipid*, lacking creativity and inspiration.
Ⓑ With *insipid* legal maneuvering, the lawyer connected the witness to the crime.
Ⓒ Homeless shelters handle the *insipid* poverty of those on the streets by providing food and comfort.

28. Which sentence uses the word **transient** correctly, in meaning and form?

    (A) The thin girl pulled a shawl over her chilled, *transient* shoulders.
    (B) The sophomore regretted socializing with such *transient* abandon during his freshman year.
    (C) For a sudden, *transient* moment, the actor seemed to forget his lines completely.

29. Which sentence uses the word **naive** correctly, in meaning and form?

    (A) The film critic's *naive* comment about the classic film illustrated his lack of experience.
    (B) The shape of the yew bushes grew more *naive* when she stopped trimming them.
    (C) The pain in her side grew so intensely *naive* that she doubled over.

30. Which sentence uses the word **audacity** correctly, in meaning and form?

    (A) The *audacity* with which she voiced her complaints startled everyone in the room.
    (B) She left her parents' home in *audacity* to their wishes that she stay.
    (C) Finally leaving her parents' home, she was able to embrace her autonomy and make choices of her own *audacity*.

WORDS IN CONTEXT EXERCISE ANSWER KEY

1. **C**
2. **C**
3. **B**
4. **A**
5. **A**
6. **C**
7. **C**
8. **B**
9. **C**
10. **A**
11. **B**
12. **B**
13. **A**
14. **A**
15. **A**
16. **A**
17. **B**
18. **B**
19. **A**
20. **C**
21. **B**
22. **C**
23. **C**
24. **C**
25. **B**
26. **B**
27. **A**
28. **C**
29. **A**
30. **A**

PART FOUR

Analytical Writing

The following is a list of the types of possible Issue essay tasks you might encounter on the GRE Analytical Writing section:

- Write a response in which you examine your own position on the statement. Explore the extent to which you either agree or disagree with it, and support your reasoning with evidence and/or examples. Be sure to reflect on ways in which the statement might or might not be true, and how this informs your thinking on the subject.
- Write your own response to the recommendation in which you discuss why you either agree or disagree with it. Support your response with evidence and/or examples. Use a hypothetical set of circumstances to illustrate the consequences of accepting or rejecting the recommendation, and explain how this informs your thinking.
- Develop a response to the claim in which you discuss whether or not you agree with it. Focus specifically on the most powerful or compelling examples that could be used to refute your position.
- Write a response in which you determine which view bears the closest resemblance to your own. In justifying your reasoning and supporting your position, be sure to include your reaction to both of the views presented.
- Develop a response to the claim in which you discuss whether or not you agree with it. Focus specifically on whether or not you agree with the reason upon which the claim is based.
- Write a response discussing your reaction to the stated policy. Justify your reasoning for the position you take. Explain the potential consequences or implications for implementing such a policy and how this informs your position.

THE KAPLAN METHOD FOR ANALYTICAL WRITING

STEP 1 Take the issue/argument apart.

STEP 2 Select the points you will make.

STEP 3 Organize, using Kaplan's essay templates.

STEP 4 Type your essay.

STEP 5 Proofread your work.

How the Kaplan Method for Analytical Writing Works

Here's how the Kaplan Method for Analytical Writing works for the Issue essay:

STEP 1

Take the issue apart.

Read the assignment and consider both sides of the issue. Use your scratch paper throughout Steps 1–3. Restate the issue in your own words. Consider the other side of the issue, and put that into your own words as well.

STEP 2

Select the points you will make.

After you consider what both sides of the issue mean, think of reasons and examples for both sides and decide which side you will support or the extent to which you agree with the stated position.

STEP 3

Organize, using Kaplan's essay templates.

Organize your thoughts by outlining what you want to say so that you'll be able to approach the actual writing process confidently and focus on expressing your ideas clearly. In the introduction, restate the prompt in your own words, state whether you agree or disagree, and give a preview of the supporting points you plan to make. In the middle paragraphs, give your points of agreement (or disagreement) and provide support. Determine the evidence you'll use to support each point. Be sure to lead with your best argument. Think about how the essay as a whole will flow. Conclude by summing up your position on the issue. See the Strategy Sheet at the back of this book for concise templates describing what should go in each paragraph.

STEP 4

Type your essay.

You shouldn't proceed with this step until you've completed the three preceding ones. Graders have a limited amount of time in which to read your essay, so start out and conclude with strong statements. Be emphatic and concise with your prose, and link related ideas with transitions. This will help your writing flow and make things easier on the grader. Furthermore, you'll save time and energy by preparing your essay before you start typing it.

STEP 5

Proofread your work.

Save enough time to read quickly through the entire essay. Look for errors you can address quickly: capitalization, paragraph divisions, double-typed words, general typos, and small grammatical errors.

Apply the Kaplan Method for Analytical Writing to the Issue Essay

Now, apply the Kaplan Method for Analytical Writing to a sample Issue prompt:

Claim: High-school students should be graded on a pass/fail basis, rather than a scaled system of letter grades (A–F).

Reason: It is more important to assess whether or not students have a basic command of the subjects they take than how they fare against their peers.

Develop a response to the claim in which you discuss whether or not you agree with it. Focus specifically on whether or not you agree with the reason upon which the claim is based.

STEP 1

Take the issue apart.

Your first step is to dissect the issue. Take notes on your scratch paper. Start by restating the issue, and the claim it is based on, in your own words: "We should grade high-school students as either pass or fail because we only need to know if they understand the material, while ranking them against their peers is less important." Now, consider the other side of the issue—in your own words: "We need a scaled grading system to be able to measure students against one another, as this is important for college admissions."

STEP 2

Select the points you will make.

Your job, as stated in the directions, is to decide whether or not you agree with the statement and then to explain your decision. Some would argue that the use of scaled grades is useless, as well as demoralizing for students who test poorly. Others would say that it's imperative that we use them, as their use allows colleges and universities to distinguish between applicants. Which side do you take? Remember, this isn't about showing the essay graders your deep-seated beliefs about education—it's about demonstrating that you can formulate an argument and communicate it clearly. The position you choose for the Issue essay doesn't have to be one you actually believe in. Quickly jot down on your scratch paper the pros and cons of each side, and choose the side for which you have the most relevant support. For this topic, that process might go something like this:

Arguments *for* the use of scaled grades:

- It helps colleges differentiate between applicants.
- It will help schools determine how far behind their peers poorly performing students are.
- Grades are useful as long as they are consistently applied, and steps can be taken to make sure they aren't subjective.

Arguments *against* the use of scaled grades:

- They are subjectively determined and therefore useless as an assessment.
- They are damaging to students' self-esteem.
- Pass/fail allows schools to determine if students understand the material at a high enough level to graduate them.

Again, it doesn't matter which side you take. Strictly speaking, there is no *right* answer, as far as the testmaker is concerned. Let's say that in this case you decide to argue against the claim. Remember, the prompt asks you to argue for or against the use of a scaled grading system for high-school students and also to focus specifically on the reason upon which the claim is based.

STEP 3

Organize, using Kaplan's essay templates.

You should already have begun to think out your arguments—that's how you picked the side you support in the first place. Now is the time to write your arguments, including those that weaken the opposing side. You're writing these notes for yourself, so feel free to use abbreviations.

Paragraph 1: We should not dispense with a grading scale in favor of a pass/fail rubric.

Paragraph 2: Scaled grades are important in college admissions.

Paragraph 3: Accurate grades can help identify students who are either in need of specialized help or advanced placement.

Paragraph 4: Grades are useful as long as they are applied consistently.

Paragraph 5: The grading scale serves an important function both pedagogically and within society.

STEP 4

Type your essay.

Remember, open up with a general statement indicating that you understand the issue and then assert your position. From there, make your main points.

Sample Issue Essay 1

Proponents of a "pass/fail" grading rubric have made a case over the years that a scaled grading rubric, such as the traditional "A to F" method, should be dispensed with in favor of a system in which students would either pass or fail their classes. However, a close examination of the issue reveals that doing so would be detrimental to student welfare, as well as to society at large. The reason upon which the claim is based, that ensuring students have a basic command of the material is more important than comparing them to their peers, is misplaced as a justification for changing the grading scale that schools use.

First, we must consider the effect that such a change in assessment would have on society. Colleges and universities depend on a grading system that allows them to assess the relative academic skills of their applicant pool. One of the most expedient ways to provide that comparative scaffolding is a scaled grading system in the secondary school system. This allows institutions of higher learning to meaningfully distinguish between applicants, as a homogeneous mass of "passes" would be difficult to choose from in a nonarbitrary way. Our higher education system works because it can determine, on the basis of empirical data, what students are most academically gifted at and best suited for. Grading helps to filter the right people into the right vocations (or, at a minimum, vocations to which they are well suited).

Second, the more precise and accurate a grading system is, the more accurately the school system can determine the specific needs of individual children. Different children learn in different ways and at different rates. For example, there are children who are very proficient in mathematics but less so in language arts and reading. Scaled grades allow schools to assess how far along students are compared to their peers, and to then place them in the appropriate class with appropriate instruction, be it advanced or remedial. A student who is precociously gifted in foreign languages will not be as encouraged to pursue it if her evaluation does not go beyond the knowledge that her command of the subject is sufficient to pass the course.

A final consideration is that the reason upon which the claim is based does not necessarily lead to the claim as a conclusion. A scaled grading rubric does allow the system to determine whether or not students have reached the minimum threshold of academic ability to graduate high school. It provides for the additional benefit of being a more precise indicator of a student's grasp of the material. Some have contended that grading from A to F is detrimental to students' self-esteem. Logically, however, this is far outweighed by the disservice done to our youth by allowing them to leave high school without the best possible education.

STEP 5

Proofread your work.

Be sure to allot a few minutes after you have finished writing to review your essay. Although you don't have to write a grammatically flawless essay to score well, you should review it to correct some of the obvious mistakes. You can practice your writing skills in Chapter 9: Writing Foundations.

Assessment of Sample Issue Essay 1: "Outstanding," Score of 6

Now we'll look at how this essay would have been scored on the actual GRE Analytical Writing section:

This essay is carefully constructed throughout, enabling the reader to move effortlessly from point to point as the writer examines the multifaceted implications of the issue. The writer begins by acknowledging arguments for the opposing side, and then uses her thesis statement ("However, a close examination of the issue reveals that doing so would be detrimental to student welfare, as well as to society at large") to explain her own position on the issue. She proceeds to provide compelling reasons and examples to support the premise, and then takes the argument to an effective conclusion. The writing is clean and concise, and the grammar and usage errors minor enough not to lower the score. Sentence structure is varied, and diction and vocabulary are strong and expressive.

PACING STRATEGY

You'll have a limited amount of time to show the graders that you can think logically, analyze critically, and express yourself in clearly written English. Consequently, you'll need to know ahead of time how you're going to approach the Issue essay. The Kaplan Method for Analytical Writing will help you plan and execute a clear, organized essay in the amount of time allotted. Note that the following timing guidelines are suggestions for how you should most effectively divide the 30 minutes you'll have for the Issue essay. Different writers go through different steps at their own pace, so don't feel chained to the breakdown of time described here. As you practice, you'll get a better sense of the amount of time you need to spend on each step to produce the best essay possible.

ANALYZE AN ISSUE

Number of Questions: 1

Time per Question: 30 minutes

Keep these estimates in mind as you prepare for the test. If you use them as you work on the practice items, you will be comfortable keeping to the same amounts of time on Test Day.

- **STEP 1 TAKE THE ISSUE APART: 2 MINUTES**
- **STEP 2 SELECT THE POINTS YOU WILL MAKE: 4 MINUTES**
- **STEP 3 ORGANIZE, USING KAPLAN'S ESSAY TEMPLATES: 2 MINUTES**
- **STEP 4 TYPE YOUR ESSAY: 20 MINUTES**
- **STEP 5 PROOFREAD YOUR WORK: 2 MINUTES**

Scoring

The essay scoring for the Analytical Writing section is *holistic*, which means that the graders base your score on their overall impression of your essay, rather than deducting specific point values for errors. A holistic score emphasizes the interrelationship of content, organization, and syntax, and denotes the unified effect of these combined elements. The scoring scale is from 0–6, with 6 being the highest score. One human grader and one computer program will score each essay. If their scores differ by a certain margin, a second human grader will also score the essay, and the two human scores will be averaged.

Although the Analytical Writing section comprises two separate essays, ETS reports a single score that represents the average of your scores for the two essays, rounded to the nearest half-point. You will receive your essay score, along with your official score report, within 10–15 days of your test date.

The Scoring Rubric

The following rubric will give you a general idea of the guidelines graders have in mind when they score Issue essays.

6: "Outstanding" Essay

- Insightfully presents and convincingly supports an opinion on the issue
- Communicates ideas clearly and is generally well organized; connections are logical
- Demonstrates superior control of language: grammar, stylistic variety, and accepted conventions of writing; minor flaws may occur

5: "Strong" Essay

- Presents well-chosen examples and strongly supports an opinion on the issue
- Communicates ideas clearly and is generally well organized; connections are logical
- Demonstrates solid control of language: grammar, stylistic variety, and accepted conventions of writing; minor flaws may occur

4: "Adequate" Essay

- Presents and adequately supports an opinion on the issue
- Communicates ideas fairly clearly and is adequately organized; logical connections are satisfactory
- Demonstrates satisfactory control of language: grammar, stylistic variety, and accepted conventions of writing; some flaws may occur

3: "Limited" Essay

- Succeeds only partially in presenting and supporting an opinion on the issue
- Communicates ideas unclearly and is poorly organized
- Demonstrates less than satisfactory control of language: contains significant mistakes in grammar, usage, and sentence structure

2: "Weak" Essay

- Shows little success in presenting and supporting an opinion on the issue
- Struggles to communicate ideas; essay shows a lack of clarity and organization
- Meaning is impeded by many serious mistakes in grammar, usage, and sentence structure

1: "Fundamentally Deficient" Essay

- Fails to present a coherent opinion and/or evidence on the issue
- Fails to communicate ideas; essay is seriously unclear and disorganized
- Lacks meaning due to widespread and severe mistakes in grammar, usage, and sentence structure

0: "Unscorable" Essay

- Completely ignores topic
- Attempts to copy the task
- Written in a language other than English or contains indecipherable text

ISSUE ESSAY PRACTICE PROMPTS

The following is a list of sample Issue essay prompts similar to those you might encounter on the GRE Analytical Writing section. Those preceded by an asterisk (*) have a sample essay response in the subsequent section of this chapter.

Issue 1:

Some people believe that strong relationships can develop only after conflict and resolution have enabled the partners to speak openly and trust deeply. Others believe that each conflict creates rifts in a relationship that can never be repaired, weakening its foundation.

Write a response in which you determine which view bears the closest resemblance to your own. In justifying your reasoning and supporting your position, be sure to include your reaction to both of the views presented.

Issue 2:

Claim: Military training strategies, such as unit cohesion and drilling, are powerful techniques to use in a classroom.

Reason: These strategies allow students to focus on a task and think like a team, supporting one another to reach a goal.

Develop a response to the claim in which you discuss whether or not you agree with it. Focus specifically on whether or not you agree with the reason upon which the claim is based.

Issue 3:

A nation should ultimately be responsible for the health, welfare, and prosperity of its own citizens.

Write a response discussing your reaction to the stated policy. Justify your reasoning for the position you take. Explain the potential consequences or implications of implementing such a policy and how this informs your position.

***Issue 4:**

Because of funding limits, many schools are cutting back on what they see as "fringe" disciplines, such as music education. This is a mistake. Since music education is important even beyond the enjoyment it brings to the knowledgeable listener, its funding should be protected.

Write a response to the recommendation in which you discuss why you either agree or disagree with it, using a hypothetical set of circumstances to illustrate the consequences of accepting or rejecting the recommendation. Support your response with evidence and/or examples.

***Issue 5:**

Some people argue that confidence and optimism are critical to achieving a dream, while others believe that selfless hard work is the only way to reach a goal.

Write a response in which you determine which view bears the closest resemblance to your own. In justifying your reasoning and supporting your position, be sure to include your reaction to both of the views presented.

***Issue 6:**

Claim: The study of a nation's prominent historical leaders and figures is a poor way to study its history.

Reason: The clearest lens through which to view a nation's history is the welfare of its entire population.

Develop a response to the claim in which you discuss whether or not you agree with it. Focus specifically on whether or not you agree with the reason upon which the claim is based.

***Issue 7:**

Electronic books are preferable to books printed on paper.

Write a response in which you state your own position on the statement. In particular, explore the extent to which you either agree or disagree with it, backing up your reasoning with evidence and/or examples. Include discussion of a hypothetical situation that supports your point of view on the subject.

***Issue 8:**

Jane Jacobs: "Neither television nor illegal drugs has been the chief destroyer of American communities. Instead, the automobile has that dubious honor."

Write a response in which you explore your own position on this statement, demonstrating the degree to which you agree or disagree with it and the extent to which it might be true or false. Support your argument with evidence, examples, and/or hypotheticals.

Issue 9:

Governments in democratic societies should not restrict the public's access to information, even if it is of a sensitive or classified nature.

Write a response in which you examine your own position on the statement. Explore the extent to which you either agree or disagree with it, and support your reasoning with evidence and/or examples. Be sure to reflect on ways in which the statement might or might not be true and how this informs your thinking on the subject.

Issue 10:

Professors who work at public universities should not automatically be entitled to periodic sabbaticals, because sabbaticals are expensive and do not necessarily yield anything of value in return.

Write your own response to the recommendation in which you discuss why you either agree or disagree with it. Support your response with evidence and/or examples. Use a hypothetical set of circumstances to illustrate the consequences of accepting or rejecting the recommendation, and explain how this informs your thinking.

Issue 11:

The U.S. should dispense with regulated speed limits on interstate highways, since drivers rarely abide by them.

Write a response discussing your reaction to the stated policy. Justify your reasoning for the position you take. Explain the potential consequences or implications for implementing such a policy and how this informs your position.

Issue 12:

Claim: The educational curriculum for young children should emphasize social skills and the arts over math and reading skills.

Reason: Such a curriculum would foster important moral and social development in children and lead to them becoming well-adjusted adults.

Develop a response to the claim in which you discuss whether or not you agree with it. Focus specifically on whether or not you agree with the reason upon which the claim is based.

Issue 13:

Some economists use the measure of the total value of goods and services that a country produces annually, called the "gross domestic product," or GDP, as the measure of a nation's economic health. Others contend that the GDP is an inadequate measure, because it fails to take into account many important factors, such as unequal distribution of wealth and the health of the environment, that affect people's quality of life.

Write a response in which you determine which view bears the closest resemblance to your own. In justifying your reasoning and supporting your position, be sure to include your reaction to both of the views presented.

Issue 14:

Claim: The National Endowment for the Humanities (NEH) should be funded entirely by private foundations.

Reason: The National Endowment for the Humanities costs the U.S. government over $160 million every year. In a period of fiscal restraint and political polarization, the ends of the NEH could be better served by private funding, thereby freeing public funding for more urgent needs.

Develop a response to the claim in which you discuss whether or not you agree with it. Note the reasoning used to support the claim, identifying its strengths and weaknesses. Be sure to consider examples or evidence that could be used to counter your position.

Issue 15:

The only way to have a meaningful interaction with a foreign culture is not simply to learn the language, but to live within that culture for an extended period of time.

Write a response in which you examine your own position on the statement. Explore the extent to which you either agree or disagree with it, and support your reasoning with evidence and/or examples. Be sure to reflect on ways in which the statement might or might not be true and how this informs your thinking on the subject.

ISSUE ESSAY PRACTICE PROMPTS SAMPLE ESSAYS AND EXPLANATIONS

Here are sample top-scoring essays to five of the sample Issue prompts found in the previous section. Remember that an essay does not have to be perfect to receive a top score. Review these essays and note the qualities that earned them a score of 6.

Issue 4:

Because of funding limits, many schools are cutting back on what they see as "fringe" disciplines, such as music education. This is a mistake. Since music education is important even beyond the enjoyment it brings to the knowledgeable listener, its funding should be protected.

Write a response to the recommendation in which you discuss why you either agree or disagree with it. Support your response with evidence and/or examples.

Sample Response

Few would deny the pleasures of music. For centuries, people have enjoyed singing, performing, and listening to music in all its forms. Yet, many people argue for limiting the teaching of music education in schools solely for economic reasons. We are continually reminded by the news media, politicians, and activists that money is limited and difficult decisions must be made. For educators dealing with resource shortfalls, a "trivial" discipline like music could end up on the chopping block. This would be an unfortunate outcome, because music has value beyond the pleasure it brings.

First, working with music can help develop important skills that children need for their studies and will benefit them as adults. Brain science has shown that reasoning and coordination can both benefit from music education. The left side of the brain is concerned with logic and rote learning, and studying music can help with the development of these left-brain skills. In addition, memorizing musical passages or lyrics can help with memory retention. Performing music can help with hand-eye coordination, in the same way that participating in sports can. Moreover, music can help a child's facility with language. Studies show that children who practice music have bigger vocabularies and a better sense of grammar than do other children, and the earlier the child begins to study music, the better.

Music education can provide psychological and social benefits as well. In another similarity to sports, proficiency in music can improve a child's self-confidence and emotional development. Since practice makes perfect, children learn to create better work and so develop an interest in craft and accomplishment, boosting their self-esteem. Learning and mastering a musical instrument requires commitment, which can increase self-discipline. Even learning a simple piece of music can provide a sense of achievement. In yet another similarity to sports, performing in a musical ensemble or a choir can develop teamwork skills.

Some could argue that the use of standardized tests in schools encourages teachers to stick to the skills and knowledge that those tests focus on. As well, an increasingly diverse student body, with varying levels of English language proficiency, poses challenges to the prioritization of "fringe" disciplines. As demonstrated above, however, music education supports core skills with its benefits to logic, memory retention, and language facility. Moreover, because music requires little knowledge of any particular language, it is an ideal subject to engage all students in school, no matter their backgrounds.

Clearly, if increased developmental skills and psychological and social benefits, as well as aesthetic pleasure, are valued, then music education should be funded in schools. Music education is not a fringe element of the curriculum but a key to all-round learning.

Analysis

This is a very good essay. The author restates the prompt in his own words and recognizes that the prompt takes it as a given that people enjoy music. Then, in a well-organized discussion, he explains why the study of music is important beyond the pleasure it brings. The author supports his argument with ample evidence. In one paragraph, he discusses several skills that the study of music can enhance, referencing brain science. The next paragraph looks at psychological and social benefits. He devotes another paragraph to the counterargument, listing some reasons that music might be considered a fringe discipline and thus expendable but providing evidence to rebut this reasoning. He finishes with a satisfactory conclusion and a firmly expressed opinion.

Issue 5:

Some people argue that confidence and optimism are critical to achieving a dream, while others believe that selfless hard work is the only way to reach a goal.

Write a response in which you determine which view bears the closest resemblance to your own. In justifying your reasoning and supporting your position, be sure to include your reaction to both of the views presented.

Sample Response

Rather than relying solely on self-assurance and a positive outlook, sustained levels of effort and industry must be maintained in order to reach a goal. While some claim that a positive outlook alone can bring about good things, and others say only a nose-to-the-grindstone attitude will get you where you want to be, it seems to me that the former flows from the latter. Most truly successful people are positive and confident hard workers who derive confidence from their work ethic. Goal-seeking people put in so much time and energy because they actually believe that those goals are achievable and probable results of their efforts. This in itself is characteristic of a positive outlook and leads me to believe that these two attitudes can exist independently, but, hard work is the key ingredient to successfully achieving a goal.

Personally, while my constant optimism certainly helps me to maintain my strong work ethic, my ability to achieve a goal is grounded in hard work. When obstacles and set-backs occur, I am able to convince myself that a goal is still attainable and that a particular situation will improve if I put in the necessary work. I can offer, as anecdotal evidence, an instance in which I had three papers due on the same day for three different classes. I felt overwhelmed, as I had gotten a late start on all of them, but what motivated me was the knowledge that working hard would ultimately lead me to success. A positive attitude could not write my papers, but I was positive as a result of my drive to work hard. What pushes me to stay focused and determined is the conviction that hard work will lead directly to accomplishing a goal. While I do believe that they work best in union, there are certainly benefits to each goal-seeking approach mentioned earlier.

Hard work often results in measurable progress, a gain of experience, and skill development, to name a few. This, in and of itself, will inculcate a positive attitude that will reinforce that strong work ethic. Maintaining a positive outlook and remaining self-confident can help goal-seekers stay persistent and focused despite the inevitable setbacks that occur on the road to reaching any goal. Although these goal-seeking approaches both do have positive outcomes and can individually result in the achievement of goals, goals can only be successfully attained if the goal-seeker is driven by an indefatigable work ethic.

Analysis

This essay is a solid 6. The author adopts a personal, first-person tone, which is acceptable in this case, as that is what the prompt calls for. She tackles the issue head-on, offering her position that hard work is the key factor in achieving a dream. She goes one step further and points out that optimism can be a byproduct of such a work ethic. The personal anecdote cited in the second paragraph is perfectly suited to reinforcing the author's point. The structure of the essay is taut, and the writing is without superfluous fluff. Although the essay is in the first person, the author avoids needless self-reference. There are a few grammatical errors, as would occur under normal test conditions, and they will not detract from the score. Essays with some small errors or imperfections can still earn a score of 6. For these reasons, this essay receives a score of 6.

Issue 6:

Claim: The study of a nation's prominent historical leaders and figures is a poor way to study its history.

Reason: The clearest lens through which to view a nation's history is the welfare of its entire population.

Develop a response to the claim in which you discuss whether or not you agree with it. Focus specifically on whether or not you agree with the reason upon which the claim is based.

Sample Response

This claim is poorly supported because if a nation has had poor leaders, the people will, in turn, suffer. On a much smaller scale, how a child is raised is a reflection of how their parents raised them. If parents are attentive and loving, the children will, most likely, display similar attributes. Similarly, with regards to leaders and nations, if a leader actually cares about his country and its people, the standard of living in that country will reflect that care. People will be happier and have fewer worries. Studying historical figures, therefore, provides as much of a bellwether as studying the welfare of the people they lead.

If one were to examine the situation of a crumbling country, such as 1980s Zimbabwe, for example, one would see a prime example that backs up the above statement. The leader was corrupt and did not know how to properly run a country and, as a result, people fled the country and many who stayed starved and had very little money. In fact, the currency itself was practically worthless. With a leader who knows what he's doing, and actually cares about his citizens, Zimbabwe has the potential to thrive, and its people would have full pockets and full bellies.

Ancient Egypt can be cited as a counterexample to the claim. We know a great deal about Egypt's culture and achievements, and our knowledge comes from studying Egypt's leaders and rulers, not the welfare of its common people. The fact that Egypt's leaders were autocratic despots is beside the point; we know a great deal about Egypt's achievements and what life was like there through the study of the Pharaohs (even if the conditions for the average person were morally indefensible).

As John Donne once said, "no man is an island." This theme reflects throughout our history, for if a leader feels as though he or she is all that matters, the people under such a leader are going to suffer the consequences of his or her self-serving leadership decisions. No leader will ever be perfect, but if he or she has the right focus—that is, his people's welfare—then the decisions will be a reflection of his caring heart. A country's history will have its up and downs, but if it is able to learn from its mistakes, that can make all the difference.

A nation's history is certainly not solely about the leaders of countries and what each of them as individuals are able to accomplish, but how a leader conducts him or herself will reflect on how his or her citizens are living. If a leader becomes too power-hungry, the citizens are going to struggle as a result. Consider the situation with Hitler and Nazi Germany. He wanted ultimate control, and at whose cost? That's right, the people's. History is never one-sided, of course, and a bad leader does not necessarily mean that the country's citizens are also bad. However, a leader should be aware that how he or she behaves will affect other countries' views of his or her country. After all, if citizens are happy and content, then there will be less trouble to be recorded in the history books.

Analysis

This essay is emphatically and passionately argued. The author begins by immediately providing a justification for arguing the contrary of the claim. He insists that the qualities and actions of a nation's leader will affect the lives of the people, so studying the leader is a good way to view the nation as a whole. He supports his position with compelling evidence, drawing on notable periods of history, such as ancient Egypt, which he uses as a counterexample to refute the claim. He uses this example to support a second counterargument, which is that the study of the pharaohs and their achievements has taught us a great deal about ancient Egypt. There are a few grammatical errors, as would occur under normal test conditions, and they will not detract from the score. Essays with some small errors or imperfections can still earn a score of 6. The diction is straightforward, but effective, which is what counts when it comes to grading. For these reasons, this essay receives a score of 6.

Issue 7:

Electronic books are preferable to books printed on paper.

Write a response in which you state your own position on the statement. In particular, explore the extent to which you either agree or disagree with it, backing up your reasoning with evidence and/or examples. Include discussion of a hypothetical situation that supports your point of view on the subject.

Sample Response

Electronic books (e-books) have changed the way in which many people read and buy books, but their success should not disguise their disadvantages. E-books have limited content, do not deliver the same emotional benefits, and are less accessible when compared to their paper counterparts.

The main disadvantage of e-books has to do with their content. Although many books have been converted and made available electronically, by far most books have not. Vast numbers of titles are available only as printed books, and it would be practically impossible for most of those to be converted into digital books. Imagine if someone only read electronic books. Libraries, whether giant university libraries or local public branches, have thousands of books that are not available digitally and never will be. There are simply too many, so many titles will be out of reach. Clearly, someone who only read e-books would be missing out on a wealth of knowledge and literature.

Furthermore, there are psychological benefits to reading physical books. People gain fulfillment from browsing in bookstores, and this pleasurable activity is lost when shopping online. Scrolling through an online store simply doesn't compare, as one misses the smell and touch of books and the turning of pages as one leafs through a volume. There's also a sense of accomplishment when reading physical books that doesn't have a parallel in reading digital versions. A reader can look with pride at the finished books on the shelf. Furthermore, there is an undeniable sense of ownership in displaying much-loved books. A reader can also pass along a favorite book to a friend. Sharing a link just doesn't compare. Were physical books to disappear, an essential component of the attraction of reading for many people would also disappear, perhaps leading to a less well-read population.

Moreover, used bookstores and libraries make print books affordable for almost everyone. Libraries are trying to lend more digital books, but the selection is still limited. Digital books are always new, never used, and can cost nearly as much as physical ones, and the devices necessary to read e-books also cost money. Digital devices also break or become outmoded, and need to be replaced, at further expense. If e-books were the only option, many children and adults would have less opportunity to read.

Physical books do have negative environmental impacts (paper is sourced from trees, and books have to be shipped to stores), but electronic devices also consume resources in their manufacturing, shipping, and use. And although digital books can be convenient, that convenience pales when you consider that only a fraction of books are now available digitally. Since conversion to digital is expensive and requires special skills, there's no reason to think that an acceptable proportion of books will be converted.

Digital books have a place. For example, they may replace costly textbooks to the benefit of many students. But the hazards are considerable. Who knows what treasures will be lost forever if e-books replace the printed page? Clearly, electronic books are inferior to printed books.

Analysis

This essay takes a clear position and argues for it with ample evidence. The author considers numerous factors, from content and accessibility to environmental impact. She also cites some negative features of printed books but points out that digital books have similar drawbacks. The instructions for the essay asked for a discussion of a "hypothetical situation," and the author speculates several times on the consequences if there were no printed books but only e-books. The essay concludes with a ringing endorsement of printed books. This essay would score a 6.

Issue 8:

Jane Jacobs: "Neither television nor illegal drugs has been the chief destroyer of American communities. Instead, the automobile has that dubious honor."

Write a response in which you explore your own position on this statement, demonstrating the degree to which you agree or disagree with it and the extent to which it might be true or false. Support your argument with evidence, examples, and/or hypotheticals.

Sample Response

Jane Jacobs's statement, about the destructiveness of the automobile to communities, is far-reaching but defensible. The automobile radically altered, and even devastated, the shape of neighborhoods, communities, and cities in the United States. Widespread automobile use certainly has provided dividends, making people more mobile and far-flung destinations more accessible. The interstate road trip is a well-established vacation option and a part of American mythology as reflected in novels and films. But the very thing that is the chief strength of the automobile (the individual mobility it enables) is also the source of the damage it has caused to American communities.

Pervasive automobile use isolates individuals in a number of ways. Driving allows increases in the distances between work and home. Cars enable people to see entertainment and spend leisure time outside their communities. They can shop away from home. Automobiles split up extended, or even nuclear, families, because family members can live further away from each other than they used to. These are all detrimental outcomes from the mobility that automobiles provide, since they all serve to put distance between community members. When people are traveling considerable distances for work, play, or shopping instead of staying in their communities, they are not getting to know their neighbors, their isolation increases, their local stores and services do less business, and their communities suffer overall.

Additionally, roads themselves contribute to a neighborhood's decline. Thoroughfares, especially the complex system of freeways found in many American metropolises, create physical barriers that slice through a community's geography. These roads discourage walking, which would promote interaction among neighbors and better health. Major roads also create psychological barriers. It is not unusual for people of one race or socioeconomic status to live on one side of such a barrier and people of another race or income level to live on the other side, even when the physical features of the two neighborhoods are objectively similar.

To grasp the truth of Jacobs's statement, imagine instead a community that is connected, not atomized; where neighbors know each other and are friends; and with vibrant businesses on the street corners. Picture people biking or taking public transit, resulting in cleaner, healthier environments.

Jacobs suggests that the automobile has caused more damage than either television or illegal drugs. Again, this is a bold statement, but a little thought will demonstrate its truthfulness. Television allows entertainment and news to be available at home, increasing isolation. But television also creates communities around shows, whether big hits or cult favorites. Some shows attract millions of viewers; think of the conversations in the workplace and in social media the day after a much-watched episode. And certainly, illegal drugs create a host of social ills, such as addiction and incarceration. Remember, though, that rehabilitation and decriminalization can mitigate those detrimental outcomes.

Other countries, like Denmark and the Netherlands, and even some communities in the United States have reduced their dependency on cars, so it is possible. These communities that are not reliant on automobiles are healthier, more interconnected places that have avoided the fate that Jane Jacobs diagnosed.

Analysis

This is a well-written essay. After identifying some advantages of automobiles, the author goes on to itemize the negative consequences of their widespread use in the United States, including social isolation, health issues, and economic decline. The author goes on to mention the negative aspects of the two other phenomena that Jacobs compares to the automobile but demonstrates that although television and illicit drugs have caused harm, their negative impacts are either tempered by positives or are reversible. As invited to by the instructions, the essay includes a hypothetical example of a car-free society and refers, in the last paragraph, to some real-world societies that are less automobile dependent. This essay would score a 6.

- Write a response in which you discuss what questions would need to be answered to decide how likely the stated recommendation is to yield the predicted result. Be sure to explain how the answers to these questions would help to evaluate the recommendation.
- Write a response in which you discuss what questions would need to be answered in order to assess the reasonableness of both the prediction and the argument upon which it is based. Be sure to explain how the answers to these questions would help to evaluate the prediction.
- Write a response in which you discuss one or more viable alternatives to the proposed explanation. Justify, with support, why your explanation could rival the proposed explanation and explain how your explanation(s) can plausibly account for the facts presented in the argument.

THE KAPLAN METHOD FOR ANALYTICAL WRITING

STEP 1 Take the issue/argument apart.

STEP 2 Select the points you will make.

STEP 3 Organize, using Kaplan's essay templates.

STEP 4 Type your essay.

STEP 5 Proofread your work.

HOW THE KAPLAN METHOD FOR ANALYTICAL WRITING WORKS

Here's how the Kaplan Method for Analytical Writing works for the Argument essay:

STEP 1

Take the argument apart.

The first step in deconstructing an argument is to identify the conclusion—that is, the main point the author is trying to make. After you've nailed down the conclusion, your next step is to locate the evidence used to support the conclusion. Finally, identify the unstated assumptions (pieces of evidence that are not explicitly stated but that are necessary for the evidence to lead validly to the conclusion). Note any terms that are ambiguous and need definition.

STEP 2

Select the points you will make.

If you have identified several assumptions in Step 1, select what you feel are the two or three most important ones to use in your essay.

STEP 3

Organize, using Kaplan's essay templates.

Organize your thoughts by outlining how the essay, as a whole, will flow. In the introduction, show that you understand the argument by putting it into your own words. Point out the author's conclusion and the evidence she uses to support that conclusion. In each of the middle paragraphs, identify assumptions or overlooked alternatives, depending on the specific instructions given in the prompt, in the author's reasoning. Detail the unstated assumption(s) and explain why the argument is logically invalid if the assumptions prove unfounded, or if the prompt requires you to consider alternatives, discuss the possibilities the author of the argument has overlooked. Conclude by summarizing your main points; be sure to directly address the task given in the specific instructions. See the Strategy Sheet at the back of this book for concise templates describing what should go in each paragraph.

STEP 4

Type your essay.

You shouldn't proceed with this step until you've completed the three preceding ones. Essay graders have a limited amount of time to work with, so start out and conclude with strong statements. Be emphatic and concise with your prose, and use transitions to link related or contrasting ideas. This will help your writing flow and make your essay easier for the grader to follow.

STEP 5

Proofread your work.

Save enough time to read through your response in its entirety. As you do so, have a sense of the errors you are likely to make.

Apply the Kaplan Method for Analytical Writing to the Argument Essay

Now, apply the Kaplan Method for Analytical Writing to a sample Argument prompt:

The following memorandum is from the Edwintown City Council:

"This year, in view of our pledge to be more environmentally conscious, we will be requiring all homeowners within the city limits to recycle their glass, plastic, and paper waste. According to a recent study by Edwintown University, the volume of trash in Edwintown and its surrounding environs has increased by 20 percent over the past 15 years. The only way to combat this burden is for our citizens to actively make an effort to recycle their trash. By enforcing recycling laws for all houses within the city limits, we will improve the aesthetic and public health conditions of our area."

of this trash was and whether the items responsible for the increase are recyclable. We also do not know whether the increase in trash is unreasonable compared to the increase in population over the same time period. Further, we have no information about how and whether there has been any change over the past 15 years in the manner and cost of waste management in Edwintown. If, for instance, the city has changed from using landfills to a state-of-the-art garbage-to-energy plant, the positive environmental impact of increased recycling may be minimal.

Along with providing a more thorough examination of the university's study, the city council should also outline citizen participation. If Edwintonians have already been recycling, even without a requirement to do so, the new plan is unlikely to have much of an effect. To assess the potential efficacy of the plan, we'd need to know the current levels of recycling in the city. Other specifics of the plan are missing, too. Are there particular products, for example, that the city is or is not prepared to recycle? How can citizens decrease the amount of non-recyclable waste they produce? Would other household actions, such as developing a compost pile, also help the environment? Giving citizens this kind of information would add to the advantages of the proposal and increase their willingness to embrace new regulations.

Additionally, the city council should detail their methods for enforcing the recycling regulations. At this point, we can only speculate on the effect that various enforcement mechanisms—fines, public service, and so on—would have on citizen participation. Related to this question is the issue of how easy it will be to participate. If citizens can simply put the recycling out for pickup, participation levels should be high. If, on the other hand, they have to travel a distance and deliver recycling to a collection center, enforcement will be much more difficult. Possible disciplinary actions and incentives alike will stimulate citizen awareness and participation.

The city council's desire to improve environmental conditions is admirable. However, more information is needed before we can determine whether their proposal is likely to be effective. In any case, it is likely that informing citizens directly as to how and why these recycling regulations would be beneficial will help ensure the community's cooperation.

STEP 5

Proofread your work.

Be sure to allot some time after you have finished writing to review your essay. While a few grammatical errors here and there won't harm your score, having enough of them will, as will having a few so severe that the meaning of the essay is lost. Make sure the graders are as favorably disposed to you as possible; a well-written essay makes their job a bit less tedious.

Assessment of Sample Argument Essay 1: "Outstanding," Score of 6

Now we'll look at how this essay would have been scored on the actual GRE Analytical Writing section:

This outstanding response demonstrates the writer's insightful analytical skills. The introduction notes the prompt's specious reasoning occasioned by unsupported assumptions and a lack of definition and evidence. The writer follows this up with a one-paragraph examination of each of the root flaws in the argument. Specifically, the author exposes these points undermining the argument:

- A city-wide required program for glass, paper, and plastic recycling will help citizens become more aware of the environment.
- The recycling program will improve upon the "aesthetic and public health conditions" in the area.

Each point receives thorough and cogent development (given the time constraints) in a smooth and logically organized discourse. There are a few grammatical flaws, but minor issues of grammar and mechanics will not prevent an outstanding essay from scoring a 6. This essay is succinct, economical, and generally error-free, with sentences that vary in length and complexity, while the diction and vocabulary are precise and expressive.

PACING STRATEGY

You'll have a limited amount of time to show the graders that you can think logically, analyze critically, and express yourself in clearly written English. Consequently, you'll need to know ahead of time how you're going to approach the Argument essay. The Kaplan Method for Analytical Writing will help you plan and execute a clear, organized essay in the allotted time. Note that the following timing guidelines are suggestions for how you should most effectively divide the 30 minutes you'll have for the Argument essay. Different writers go through different steps at their own pace, so don't feel chained to the breakdown of time described here. As you practice, you'll get a better sense of the amount of time you need to spend on each step to produce the best essay possible.

Analyze an Argument

Number of Questions: 1

Time per Question: 30 minutes

Keep these estimates in mind as you prepare for the test. Use them as you work on the practice items so you'll be comfortable keeping to the same amounts of time on Test Day.

STEP 1

Take the argument apart: 2 minutes

STEP 2

Select the points you will make: 4 minutes

STEP 3

Organize, using Kaplan's essay templates: 2 minutes

STEP 4

Type your essay: 20 minutes

STEP 5

Proofread your work: 2 minutes

Scoring

The essay scoring for the Analytical Writing sections is *holistic*, which means that the graders base your score on their overall impression of your essay, rather than deducting specific point values for errors. A holistic score emphasizes the interrelationship of content, organization, and syntax, and denotes the unified effect of these combined elements. The scoring scale is from 0–6, with 6 being the highest score. One human grader and one computer program will score each essay. If their scores differ by a certain margin, a second human grader will also score the essay, and the two human scores will be averaged.

Although the Analytical Writing section is comprised of two separate essays, ETS reports a single score that represents the average of your scores for the two essays, rounded to the nearest half-point. You will receive your essay score, along with your official score report, within 10–15 days of your test date.

The Scoring Rubric

The following rubric will give you a general idea of the guidelines graders have in mind when they score Argument essays.

6: "Outstanding" Essay

- Insightfully presents and convincingly supports a critique of the argument
- Communicates ideas clearly and is generally well organized; connections are logical
- Demonstrates superior control of language: grammar, stylistic variety, and accepted conventions of writing; minor flaws may occur

5: "Strong" Essay

- Presents well-chosen examples and strongly supports a critique of the argument
- Communicates ideas clearly and is generally well organized; connections are logical
- Demonstrates solid control of language: grammar, stylistic variety, and accepted conventions of writing; minor flaws may occur

4: "Adequate" Essay

- Presents and adequately supports a critique of the argument
- Communicates ideas fairly clearly and is adequately organized; logical connections are satisfactory
- Demonstrates satisfactory control of language: grammar, stylistic variety, and accepted conventions of writing; some flaws may occur

3: "Limited" Essay

- Succeeds only partially in presenting and supporting a critique of the argument
- Communicates ideas unclearly and is poorly organized
- Demonstrates less than satisfactory control of language: contains significant mistakes in grammar, usage, and sentence structure

2: "Weak" Essay

- Shows little success in presenting and supporting a critique of the argument
- Struggles to communicate ideas; essay shows a lack of clarity and organization
- Meaning is impeded by many serious mistakes in grammar, usage, and sentence structure

1: "Fundamentally Deficient" Essay

- Fails to present a coherent critique of the argument
- Fails to communicate ideas; essay is seriously unclear and disorganized
- Lacks meaning due to widespread and severe mistakes in grammar, usage, and sentence structure

0: "Unscorable" Essay

- Completely ignores topic
- Attempts to copy the task
- Written in a language other than English or contains undecipherable text

ARGUMENT ESSAY PRACTICE PROMPTS

The following is a list of sample Argument essay prompts similar to those you might encounter on the GRE Analytical Writing section. Those preceded by an asterisk (*) have a sample essay response in the subsequent section of the chapter.

Argument 1:

Notice posted on business door:

Due to frequent customer inquires, Sunshine Restaurant will be switching to an all-vegetarian menu. Vegetarian food is better for the environment, delicious, and increasingly popular. We will be closing our establishment to renovate as we convert our kitchen to accommodate our new meatless menu. Be on the lookout for an announcement for our grand reopening!

Write a response in which you discuss what questions would need to be answered to decide how likely it is that the stated change of direction would be successful for Sunshine Restaurant, making sure to explain how the answers to these questions would help to evaluate the decision.

Argument 2:

Fifty years ago, an entomologist in Ballaland identified a new species of beetle: the scalawag. This beetle is nearly identical to the Andover mop beetle, but is slightly larger. A recent comparison of a colony of Ballaland beetles and Andover mop beetles demonstrates that the two beetles may be more similar than previously thought. The range of size between the largest beetle and the smallest beetle was identical in both colonies, and, as the beetles were physically identical in every other way, it was concluded that the two species were actually the same and that the differences in behavior and diet could be attributed to differences in habitat. Some biologists suggest that before a proposed interbreeding experiment is conducted, more research on behavior and diet of the two beetle species should be conducted.

Write a response in which you discuss what questions would need to be answered in order to assess the reasonableness of both the recommendation and the argument upon which it is based. Be sure to explain how the answers to these questions would help to evaluate the recommendation.

Argument 3:

The Streatham Portrait is a late 16th-century copy of a now-lost oil painting depicting an English woman. It was acquired by the National Portrait Gallery of London for a rumored £100,000. Although this purchase has proven controversial, there is no doubt the painting is a worthy addition to the museum's collection, as the subject is probably Lady Jane Grey, who was de facto queen of England for nine days before her execution in 1554. A faint inscription in the top-left corner reads "Lady Jayne," and experts have noticed a family resemblance between the sitter and confirmed portraits of Jane's sisters, Catherine and Mary. The sitter is richly dressed, wearing numerous pieces of jewelry, and her costume is decorated with numerous flowers that some have identified as pinks, an emblem of the Grey family.

Write a response in which you examine the assumptions of the argument. Explain how the argument depends on these assumptions and the effect on the argument if the assumptions prove unwarranted.

***Argument 4:**

The following is a memorandum from the marketing department of a computer manufacturer.

"We need a new strategy in our ads promoting our line of laptop computers. Surveys show that laptop purchasers consider reliability more important than any other quality. Thus, we should highlight that our Compulink laptop is the most technologically advanced laptop you can buy and that it uses the same hardware that NASA uses in its computers on the space station. We should also point out that our customers will save money because they won't have to bring their Compulink laptop in for costly repairs. This approach is sure to increase our market share."

Write a response in which you examine the underlying assumptions of the argument. Be sure to explain how the argument hinges on these assumptions. Comment on how any additional information could affect the argument.

***Argument 5:**

The following was written as part of an application for a permit to congregate by a religious group in the city of Gustav:

"We plan to meet at the Hunter Pavilion on the north side of the park. We expect about 200 attendees. Although we do plan to celebrate our message in words and song, we will be mindful of others who are sharing the park on that day. We have found that in the past, when our group meets in a public space, we run the risk of harassment by those who do not agree with our message. Therefore, we would like to hire five security officers to protect our congregants from religious intolerance. We would like to post one guard at the entrance to the park and others, who will dress in plain clothes, at the perimeter of our gathering. We hope you understand and will endorse this request."

Write a response in which you describe what specific examples or evidence is needed to evaluate the argument and how those examples or evidence would weaken or strengthen the argument.

***Argument 6:**

The following memo appeared in the newsletter of the Happy Sun Happy Moon daycare center:

"Since the road construction on I-72 has begun, we've noticed that parents are picking up their children after the center is officially closed. Effective immediately, parents who pick up their children more than five minutes after closing will have to pay a $10 fee. Parents who pick up their children more than one hour after closing will be subject to an additional $30 fee. We predict this will encourage parents to leave earlier from work to pick up their children on time each day."

Write a response in which you discuss what questions would need to be answered to decide how likely the stated recommendation is to yield the predicted result. Be sure to explain how these answers would help to evaluate the recommendation.

***Argument 7:**

In 2002, many farmers in Jalikistan began using a hormone designed to produce larger cows that would produce more milk. Since then, the rate of childhood obesity in Jalikistan has increased by 200 percent. The amount of milk and other dairy products consumed by children in this area has not increased or decreased. Children in the same area who are lactose intolerant, and as a result drink almond milk or soy milk, have not experienced an increase in obesity. The only clear explanation is that the introduction of the hormone is responsible for the increase in childhood obesity in Jalikistan.

Write a response in which you discuss one or more viable alternatives to the proposed explanation. Justify, with support, why the alternatives could rival the proposed explanation and explain how those explanation(s) plausibly account for the facts presented in the argument.

***Argument 8:**

The following appeared in a memo from an advertisement by Pest Protection, Inc.:

"Gardens along the coast are already being infested by the mill bug, a slimy purple pest that can decimate a vegetable garden in seconds flat. If you live within 100 miles of the coast, you need the Pest Protection cure today. Thousands of satisfied customers who have used our chemical-free treatments have never had mill bug problems. One treatment per year will ensure that you never have to lose your valuable crops to this pest."

Write a response in which you examine the underlying assumptions of the argument. Be sure to explain how the argument hinges on these assumptions and what the implications are for the argument if the assumptions prove unfounded.

Argument 9:

The following appeared in a letter to the Director of the Department of Motor Vehicles:

"The use of cell phones while driving is a source of great concern to the community, particularly to parents with young children. Teenage drivers, who are the most likely to text or talk on the phone while driving, are among the most dangerous. In our county alone there were 75 fatalities from traffic collisions. If we raise the legal driving age from 16 to 20, the problem would largely be solved because the most dangerous drivers would no longer be on the road."

Write a response in which you discuss what questions would need to be answered in order to assess the reasonableness of both the prediction and the argument upon which it is based. Be sure to explain how the answers to these questions would help to evaluate the prediction.

Argument 10:

The following memorandum is from the Media Director of the Athletic Department at Burtsdale University:

"We have decided to recommend that the school no longer offer free student access to University athletic events, regardless of level, sport, or gender of the participants. Our policy in the past has been to sell tickets only to events with significant popularity, such as men's Division I football and basketball games, and other nationally televised events. Although other sports do not typically sell out, or generate the same level of interest outside the student body, we feel it is unfair to Division II sports and the women's teams not to charge admission to their events as well. Charging admission to all events is the only way to treat all athletic teams equitably."

Write a response in which you describe what specific examples or evidence is needed to evaluate the argument and how those examples or evidence would weaken or strengthen the argument.

Argument 11:

The following is from an editorial in a legal journal:

"It is now apparent, based on data that has been collated from several independent studies, that asbestos is the cause of lung cancer, emphysema, and other respiratory illnesses in the miners of Coal Valley. The studies show a high incidence of such ailments among the miners, far higher than that of the general population. In 1920, before the mine opened, relatively few miners were known to have had such conditions. Studies published in 1960, 1980, and 2000 show that the incidence of such ailments has risen dramatically among the miners of Coal Valley."

Write a response in which you discuss one or more viable alternatives to the proposed explanation. Justify, with support, why your explanation could rival the proposed explanation and explain how your explanation(s) can plausibly account for the facts presented in the argument.

Argument 12:

The following is an excerpt from a letter to the editor of the *Billington Bugle*:

"There is no possible downside to the community in bringing the Grand Prix to Billington. Though it has not proved financially successful in other cities that have hosted the race, this will not be the case for Billington. The race's course will run through the economic center of downtown, and the organizers of the event have offered to pay to repave the downtown streets through which the race will run. Those streets are in such disrepair that having them repaired will be a tremendous boon to the city. Furthermore, though most downtown businesses (aside from restaurants and food vendors) will likely be shut down for three days, the influx of tourist dollars will be immense. Finally, the international prestige of hosting such a race will raise the city's profile significantly, generating new interest in doing business here."

Write a response in which you describe what specific examples or evidence is needed to evaluate the argument and how those examples or evidence would weaken or strengthen the argument.

Argument 13:

The following is a recommendation from the Board of Directors of the Cheshire College Preparatory Academy:

"We recommend that Cheshire College Preparatory Academy dispense with the use of standardized tests as an entrance requirement. Cheshire has been an elite school for more than 100 years, but we have recently seen a decline in enrollments. We have had particular difficulty in attracting students from non-legacy families (those who have never had a member attend Cheshire). We do not require entrance exams for legacy applicants, and those enrollments have not declined. Cutting the standardized entrance requirement will allow us to better compete with Surrey Academy, which recently dropped its exam requirements and concurrently overtook Cheshire in enrollments."

Write a response in which you discuss what questions would need to be answered to decide how likely the stated recommendation is to yield the predicted result. Be sure to explain how the answers to these questions would help to evaluate the recommendation.

Argument 14:

The Supreme Court of the United States must be composed in such a way that it accurately reflects the demographics of the country. As the highest court in the land, it functions as the final arbiter of justice. In a multicultural and multiethnic society, with a variety of races, creeds, and beliefs, it is imperative that the backgrounds of the justices on the court reflect that diversity. Since our society is not homogeneous, our judicial system must follow suit. Otherwise, it will be impossible to fairly represent the views, beliefs, and cultural norms of the entire country.

Write a response in which you describe what specific examples or evidence is needed to evaluate the argument and how those examples or evidence would weaken or strengthen the argument.

Argument 15:

The problem of poorly trained teachers that has plagued the state public school system is bound to become a good deal less serious in the future. The state has initiated comprehensive guidelines that oblige state teachers to complete a number of required credits in education and educational psychology at the graduate level before being certified.

Write a response in which you discuss how well reasoned you find the argument. In your response, describe specific examples or evidence needed to evaluate the argument and how those examples or evidence would weaken or strengthen the argument.

ARGUMENT ESSAY PRACTICE PROMPTS SAMPLE ESSAYS AND EXPLANATIONS

Here are sample top-scoring essays to five of the sample Argument prompts found in the previous section. Remember that an essay does not have to be perfect to receive a top score. Review these essays and note the qualities that earned them each a score of 6.

Argument 4:

The following is a memorandum from the marketing department of a computer manufacturer.

"We need a new strategy in our ads promoting our line of laptop computers. Surveys show that laptop purchasers consider reliability more important than any other quality. Thus, we should highlight that our Compulink laptop is the most technologically advanced laptop you can buy and that it uses the same hardware that NASA uses in its computers on the space station. We should also point out that our customers will save money because they won't have to bring their Compulink laptop in for costly repairs. This approach is sure to increase our market share."

Write a response in which you examine the underlying assumptions of the argument. Be sure to explain how the argument hinges on these assumptions. Comment on how any additional information could affect the argument.

Sample Response

The marketing department of a computer firm has proposed a new direction for advertising Compulink laptops. The evidence relates to the reliability of the Compulink, the most technologically advanced laptop on the market. This seems like a convincing argument; after all, advanced technology has introduced countless more efficient and more reliable products. But in order to determine the potential effectiveness of this new strategy, the company's executives should note several factors that the argument does not sufficiently address.

First, the key term, "reliability," is not defined. Does it mean continued service with average use or service after intense use? Or does it mean toughness of construction? (Would a Compulink laptop survive a fall from a desk—or from the roof of your car as you pull out of the driveway?) If what computer users mean by "reliability" is different from the reliability demonstrated by the Compulink, then this company's market share is unlikely to increase as a result of the proposed advertising campaign.

Another problem is that the argument treats advanced technology and reliability as same thing, but they are not. Technology can improve many features of products including, for example, energy efficiency, programming capability, and reduced weight or size. However, a technologically advanced product is not necessarily more reliable. Indeed, a computer that incorporates cutting-edge technology may be less reliable than older machines because such technology has not yet been as thoroughly tested and had the bugs worked out.

The argument also mentions that Compulink laptops use the same hardware that NASA uses in space. There's no mention, however, of what this hardware is or what it has to do with computer reliability. While one can safely assume that computers on the space station are built to be very reliable, since repairing them would be difficult, the hardware these laptops have in common with space station computers might have nothing to do with reliability. Indeed, all computers have certain elements in common, so it is possible that most laptops, not just Compulink laptops, have this hardware. If so, then the presence of NASA's hardware does not present a compelling argument to buy this brand of computer.

Finally, the recommendation states that because the Compulink laptop is so reliable, it will not need costly repairs. Even if this is true, we are not told how much a Compulink costs. If it is more expensive than a rival brand, the money saved on repairs might not offset the price difference. In this case, if laptop users want increased reliability to save money, they would not purchase a Compulink laptop.

To help this company's executives determine the potential effectiveness of the proposed shift in marketing focus, the marketing department should present certain additional facts. A survey of owners of Compulink laptops attesting to the laptop's reliability under typical use conditions would make the argument more convincing. So would statistics comparing the reliability of Compulink computers with competing brands. The marketing department should also provide details about the NASA hardware in the laptops to support the idea that the shared hardware contributes to the Compulink's reliability. Finally, a cost-benefit analysis comparing the cost of a Compulink laptop over several years with the cost of owning a rival brand over the same period would be helpful. Although an ad campaign emphasizing the Compulink's reliability might help this company increase its market share, more information is required before that conclusion can be justified.

Analysis

The essay is particularly well organized. The writer begins by noting that the argument recommends a new marketing strategy, then casts a critical eye on the elements of the argument, dedicating one paragraph to each key assumption. He points out that the author assumes "reliability" means the same thing to everyone and that technology equates to reliability. He also notes the assumption that incorporating NASA's hardware makes this laptop more reliable than other laptops or, indeed, reliable at all. Finally, he takes aim at the assumption that a laptop that does not need costly repairs is a good deal for the consumer. Then, the author lists the evidence that could make the argument stronger. This essay would score a 6.

Argument 5:

The following was written as part of an application for a permit to congregate by a religious group in the city of Gustav:

"We plan to meet at the Hunter Pavilion on the north side of the park. We expect about 200 attendees. Although we do plan to celebrate our message in words and song, we will be mindful of others who are sharing the park on that day. We have found that in the past, when our group meets in a public space, we run the risk of harassment by those who do not agree with our message. Therefore, we would like to hire five security officers to protect our congregants from religious intolerance. We would like to post one guard at the entrance to the park and others, who will dress in plain clothes, at the perimeter of our gathering. We hope you understand and will endorse this request."

Write a response in which you describe what specific examples or evidence is needed to evaluate the argument and how those examples or evidence would weaken or strengthen the argument.

Sample Response

The Bill of Rights was designed to protect the rights of the American People in the best way possible without infringing on the rights of others. Assuming that this situation takes place in the United States, this group should have the right to carry out all the requests written in this application. The main issues in question seem to be covered under freedom of religion, freedom of speech, and freedom to congregate, all of which are protected by the U.S. Constitution.

We can assume, by the request for security guards, that this group is not looked upon with favor by the community. Unfortunately for their opponents, if they go through the proper channels (such as applying for permits like this one seems to be), they are within their legal rights to gather and practice their religious ceremony nonviolently. Thus, one important question that needs to be answered in order to evaluate this argument is whether this is the proper permit and whether their request is within the laws and regulations of the city. It is one of the foundational ideals in the creation of this country that practicing an unpopular religion is entirely protected. Some of the founders of the early colonies came here to be safe from religious persecution. It would be hypocritical to cast aside a group because their views are unpopular.

The hiring of private security officers could potentially pose problems for this group. The county police force should be in charge of, and capable of, maintaining the peace in the area. It is the job of the police force to protect citizens from being harassed by intolerant fellow citizens. If the harassment gets to the point where it becomes dangerous or criminal in some way, the police should step in. The fact that this group has been harassed before, and now feel the need for additional undercover security officers, is cause for concern. To properly evaluate this argument, we would need to know what kind of harassment is going on (i.e., physical or verbal), and whether or not the police themselves are capable of handling the situation. This would obviate the need to resort to armed guards, who may or may not actually be necessary. It would help to determine whether or not the group's civil rights are being violated and whether the city would be within its legal obligations to grant such a request.

It is within the rights of private groups and citizens to hire private security officers. Celebrities, concert venues, and even high-powered business people hire security agents to maintain order when trouble is expected. Assuming there is some legal paperwork that must be filed, and this group completes it all correctly, there is no reason why they should not be allowed to hire outside help. But the outstanding factual and legal questions need to be cleared up before that conclusion is unequivocal. The group may feel it has been let down by the official police force and that they will not be safe without additional security measures.

Analysis

The author successfully identifies and analyzes this argument's contention: that the group in question should be allowed to have armed security guards at their event. In the opening paragraph, the author acknowledges that the group has the right to freedom of expression and that this should not be infringed upon. However, she draws attention to the questions that need to be answered in order to hire private security guards at a public venue.

The author also cites these points, which must be determined before assessing the argument:

- The nature of the harassment/threats being made against the group
- Whether or not the police are capable of handling the situation
- The legal considerations surrounding the hiring of private security

The author makes judicious use of well-structured paragraphs—each starts with a strong assertion followed by supporting statements. Her ideas logically flow from one sentence to the next. She uses succinct, economical diction and intersperses complex and simpler sentences. The essay concludes strongly by summarizing the conditions necessary for allowing the group to hire their guards, and, if these conditions are met, stating that they should be allowed to do so. The essay remains focused and clear throughout, earning a score of 6.

Argument 6:

The following memo appeared in the newsletter of the Happy Sun Happy Moon daycare center.

"Since the road construction on I-72 has begun, we've noticed that parents are picking up their children after the center is officially closed. Effective immediately, parents who pick up their children more than five minutes after closing will have to pay a $10 fee. Parents who pick up their children more than one hour after closing will be subject to an additional $30 fee. We predict this will encourage parents to leave earlier from work to pick up their children on time each day."

Write a response in which you discuss what questions would need to be answered to decide how likely the stated recommendation is to yield the predicted result. Be sure to explain how these answers would help to evaluate the recommendation.

Sample Response

If I were to put myself in the place of one of these parents, the first question I would have is, "How can you charge us, as parents, more if we are only a few minutes late? Traffic is always present, whether construction projects are taking place or not, so it does not seem fair to charge us extra for something that is out of our control." Six minutes late would, technically, mean a charge, and that seems a bit extreme. As such, I do not think that this recommendation would have the anticipated result. I think that some parents may leave work a bit earlier to try to get to their children earlier, but heavy traffic can begin before the standard five or six o'clock traffic, so to assume that if a parent leaves earlier they will arrive on time is false. I would imagine that some parents would arrive on time more frequently, as they would not want to be charged, but it could not be guaranteed. Without more information, the best one could say is that there's a chance that parents will always be on time. In fact, how could the daycare presume that parents could leave earlier, when some companies are quite stringent and do not allow their employees to leave before the very end of the day?

In the past, for example, I have had jobs where I could not leave early, unless I had a previously scheduled appointment. Certain tasks had to be completed by certain times, which tied me to my desk until the end of the day. Consequently, depending on traffic, sometimes I would have been late to pick up my child, and sometimes I would have been on time. I think that an hour late would warrant a fee, as the people who work at the daycare also have families to go home to, but merely a few minutes late, even up to 15 or 20 minutes late, should not be an issue.

To charge parents for being slightly late is unwarranted. Being too late is, of course, a problem, but slightly late should not be. The daycare should be more understanding and try to put themselves in the parents' shoes. Consequently, the final question that I would ask the daycare would be, "Could you only charge a fee at the end of the month to those parents who were consistently late, say, more than three times that month?" That, I think, would be a reasonable alternative. After all, if parents are dedicated to arriving on time, they will do their best to pick up their children at the appropriate hour. Naturally, they may get caught in traffic and arrive late sometimes, but if they are generally on time, I do not think that they should be penalized.

Analysis

The author begins with a provocative rhetorical question that grabs the reader's attention. He emphatically denies that the recommendation will have the predicted result. He notes that simply installing this policy will not make parents show up on time. The primary reason is that there are a number of circumstances beyond parents' control that affect their ability to arrive promptly. These include traffic and work restrictions, both of which cannot be solved simply by fining parents for being late.

Throughout the essay, the author uses well-organized paragraphs—each starts with a broad statement followed by supporting statements. He uses strong, emotional language to convey his point. The essay remains focused and clear throughout, earning a score of 6.

Argument 7:

In 2002, many farmers in Jalikistan began using a hormone designed to produce larger cows that would produce more milk. Since then, the rate of childhood obesity in Jalikistan has increased by 200 percent. The amount of milk and other dairy products consumed by children in this area has not increased or decreased. Children in the same area who are lactose intolerant, and as a result drink almond milk or soy milk, have not experienced an increase in obesity. The only clear explanation is that the introduction of the hormone is responsible for the increase in childhood obesity in Jalikistan.

Write a response in which you discuss one or more viable alternatives to the proposed explanation. Justify, with support, why the alternatives could rival the proposed explanation and explain how those explanation(s) can plausibly account for the facts presented in the argument.

Sample Response

The author claims that the only possible explanation for the increase in obesity among children in Jalikistan is that many of that country's farmers have been giving their cows a certain hormone. Evidence that this practice is the cause consists of the difference between children who drink cow's milk and children who drink milk substitutes: the cow's milk consumers have gained weight while the other children have not. While this difference may mean what the author thinks it does, there are other possibilities worth considering.

One such possibility is that the two groups of children have diets that vary in other ways, and it is these differences that cause lactose-intolerant children not to gain as much weight as their dairy-consuming peers. Perhaps parents, upon discovering that their children become sick after eating dairy, not only limit their children's access to dairy products but begin to pay a great deal of attention to their kids' diets in general. After all, if one food has made a child ill, a loving parent would be attentive to health risks posed by other foods. Such parents may limit sweets and encourage the consumption of foods known to be healthy, such as fresh fruits and vegetables and whole grains. Thus, these children may be maintaining a healthy weight because of their healthy diet. Kids who have no dietary restrictions due to lactose intolerance never evoke such concern in their parents and thus are more likely to indulge the natural sweet tooth of youth without restraint. It could be unhealthy treats, rather than milk from hormone-fed cows, that is causing these children's obesity.

Another possibility the author overlooks is that farmers seeking to increase milk yields may have made other changes to their animal husbandry practices besides administering hormones. For example, perhaps they are keeping their cows indoors instead of outside, or feeding them more grain and less hay, or breeding them more or less often. Or perhaps as they sought prescriptions from their veterinarians for hormones, they became aware of other medical interventions that could increase milk yields, such as antibiotics or other medicines. Any of these changes in how farmers cared for their animals could have changed the quality of the cows' milk. Therefore, even if the milk is responsible for the increase in childhood obesity, one cannot conclude that the hormone is responsible.

If the author could show that there are no relevant differences between the two groups of children, then the idea that the milk is causing weight gain in one group would be more plausible. In addition, if the author produced evidence that farmers have made no changes in how they treat their cows since 2002 besides starting to administer this hormone, then the hormone would be a likely culprit in the event that the milk is causing the weight gain. However, in the absence of such evidence, the author's conclusion represents an unsupported leap, underlain by assumptions rather than facts.

Analysis

The author of this essay recognizes that the argument depends on two assumptions, one about the two groups of children and another about the farmers' treatment of their cows. Beyond identifying these assumptions, the author elaborates on each, showing (as the essay prompt instructs) how alternative scenarios also fit the facts. The essay is very well organized: the first paragraph demonstrates an understanding of the argument being analyzed, the second and third paragraphs each explain a weakness in the argument, and the final paragraph discusses some evidence that could strengthen the argument before concluding that, as written, the argument is weak. Furthermore, each paragraph is coherent, beginning with a broad statement followed by supporting statements, and ideas logically flow from one sentence to the next. The essay remains focused and clear throughout, earning a score of 6.

Argument 8:

The following appeared in a memo from an advertisement by Pest Protection, Inc.:

"Gardens along the coast are already being infested by the mill bug, a slimy purple pest that can decimate a vegetable garden in seconds flat. If you live within 100 miles of the coast, you need the Pest Protection cure today. Thousands of satisfied customers who have used our chemical-free treatments have never had mill bug problems. One treatment per year will ensure that you never have to lose your valuable crops to this pest."

Write a response in which you examine the underlying assumptions of the argument. Be sure to explain how the argument hinges on these assumptions and what the implications are for the argument if the assumptions prove unfounded.

Sample Response

At first glance, the argument proffered by the advertisement seems to make sense. Those who use Pest Protection will not suffer an infestation of mill bugs. The author makes claims that seem to meet the needs of someone living in the region. However, the author relies on several unproven assumptions. First, the argument mistakenly assumes that because the mill bug "can" decimate a garden, that it will in fact do so. There's no way to assess the extent of the current infestation. Nor is there anything that states which types of vegetables or flowers the bug devours. In order to assess the validity of the advertisement, it would valuable to know the true extent of the threat that the bug poses. If it's the case that the mill bug eats only root vegetables or only flowering plants, it's unlikely that everyone within 100 miles of the coast needs Pest Protection. If "thousands of satisfied customers have never had mill bug problems," how can we even be sure that the bugs do in fact pose a serious threat?

The biggest flaw in the author's reasoning is that the author assumes, without providing proof, that there is a direct, causal relationship between using the Pest Protection cure and being free of mill bug problems. Even if both are true, that someone is using the Pest Protection cure and they do not have a mill bug problem, there is no proof that the former has caused the latter. There could be other factors at work, such as climate, migration patterns, lack of food supply, or other such extrinsic concerns.

Many who used the Pest Protection treatment may have done so unnecessarily. There is no information to suggest what the level of infestation would have been without the treatment. The advertisement's reasoning amounts to arguing that since a town began sending police officers on "Bear Patrol," no one in the town has been attacked by a bear. Depending on where the town is, there may never have been a bear attack to begin with.

Finally, the company's claim that a single, yearly treatment will ensure that customers will "never have to lose . . . valuable crops" is broad. In order to assess the argument, we need to know the price and process for this treatment. It may be price prohibitive to have annual treatments. Alternately, the treatments may have side effects. The advertisement does qualify its claim: you never have to lose crops to this pest. But, if the treatment makes it impossible to grow certain crops or depletes the soil over time, the user would lose crops in another way. Pest Protection offers no support for the claim that the treatment will last for such a long time. Many things, such as climate change and inclement weather, could mitigate or dilute the effect of such a

CHAPTER 9

Writing Foundations

OVERVIEW

The focus of the GRE writing sample is on not only how well you write, but also the thought processes you employ to formulate and articulate a position. There are two GRE Analytical Writing sections, each 30 minutes long.

You'll write essays on two different types of prompts:

- The Issue essay task provides a brief quotation on an issue of general interest and instructions on how to respond to the issue. You can discuss the issue from any perspective, making use of your own educational and personal background, examples from current or historical events, things you've read, or even relevant hypothetical situations. In this task, you will develop your own argument.
- The Argument essay task contains a short argument that may or may not be complete, and specific instructions on how to evaluate the argument's strength. You will assess the argument's cogency, analyze the author's reasoning, and evaluate her use (or lack) of evidence. In this task, you critique the argument presented in the prompt.

The Analytical Writing section allows schools to evaluate your ability to plan and compose a logical, well-reasoned essay under timed conditions. You'll write the essays on the computer, using a simple word processing program.

This section of the book will review Kaplan's 22 principles for effective writing. Numbers 1–10 relate to writing style, 11–17 to grammar, and 18–22 to mechanics. Study these principles to refine your writing skills and score well on the GRE Analytical Writing essays.

WRITING STYLE

Remember, each GRE essay is a formal writing assignment. Here are a few elements of style to keep in mind while you're writing:

Concision

- Omit words, phrases, and sentences that do not add to your argument or support your position. An experienced GRE essay grader can spot such padding a mile away. Make every word count.
- Avoid redundant phrases such as *refer back*, *serious crisis*, and *general consensus*, which weaken your writing.

Structure

- Use transition words and phrases to show the relationship between your ideas.
- Start a new paragraph for every new topic or example.

Formal and Forceful

- Don't use slang or text-message abbreviations, and don't use an ampersand (&) in place of the word *and*. This is a formal assignment—treat it as such.
- Avoid weak sentence openings, such as *There is* or *There are*.
- Avoid the passive voice: *I finished my essay* is stronger and more concise than *The essay was finished by me*.
- Avoid clichés and overused terms or phrases. Remember, the graders are reading a lot of these; try to make your essays memorable.
- Use precise wording and avoid generalizations ("many people") and abstractions. Make your meaning clear.
- Avoid referring to your own opinion with constructions like "I think," "I feel," or "I believe." Also avoid retelling personal anecdotes or sharing your own philosophy.
- Vary sentence length and style.

In all of the exercises that follow, read the sentences given and revise them to correct any errors. The headings will give you an idea of what errors to look for.

WRITING STYLE EXERCISES

1st Principle of Effective Writing: Streamlining Wordy Phrases

1. An essential element of our consideration of the problem was finding the means to identify the more dubious aspects of the plan.

   ____

2. Foremost in their thinking was the capacity of the vehicle to traverse various kinds of terrain.

   ____

3. Anthony engaged a professional interior decorator to undertake the refurbishment of his apartment.

____

2nd Principle of Effective Writing: Eliminating Redundancy

4. At this point in time, the scout experienced a serious setback.

____

5. None of her fellow classmates were at the party.

____

6. The leader had a special reputation for being calm in a crisis situation.

____

3rd Principle of Effective Writing: Avoiding Excessive Qualification

7. In a fairly rare moment of frustration, Toni pretty much lost her temper.

____

8. Lee's actions at Gettysburg seemed relatively uncharacteristic for someone whose qualities as a commander were usually sound for the most part.

____

9. I have to say that, as an employer, Helen showed a certain amount of boldness in providing what most would regard as generous benefits to her workers.

____

4th Principle of Effective Writing: Removing Unnecessary Sentences

10. This city's transportation system is a model for urban infrastructure elsewhere. Our bus and light-rail lines are second to none.

____

11. Where would this company be without the vision of someone like Carlo? Our success as a company owes everything to his belief in the future.

____

12. The builders of medieval cathedrals were not primitive laborers who had little idea of what they were doing. They were often highly skilled masons, carpenters, and workers in stained glass who were guided by a detailed plan drawn up by a master builder.

____

5th Principle of Effective Writing: Avoiding Needless Self-Reference

13. I am of the opinion that we can design cars that are much more fuel-efficient.

____

14. From my point of view, you could increase your pottery production simply by using a different glaze.

____

15. I feel it would be a mistake to take part in such a demonstration without a clear sense of purpose.

____

6th Principle of Effective Writing: Using Active Rather than Passive Voice

16. As the prisoner was brought into court by the guards, he glared at his accuser.

____

17. The question of who is to inherit the estate has never been asked.

____

18. When do you think the problem will have been solved by them?

____

7th Principle of Effective Writing: Including Strong Openings

19. There is every possibility that the police have found your lost dog.

____

20. It is to be hoped that officials can resolve this crisis before it gets out of hand.

____

21. There is a proverb that says, "Half a loaf is better than none."

____

8th Principle of Effective Writing: Avoiding Needlessly Vague Language

22. To really demonstrate our obligation to some valued customer, we will forego the standard admission fee.

____

23. All our employees are content here.

____

24. Both kind of indigent and without much accommodation, she is indeed a sad spectacle.

____

9th Principle of Effective Writing: Rewording Clichés

25. That man sleeping on the bench looks a bit over the hill.

____

26. She always seemed to me to have ice water in her veins.

____

27. With this win, the team looks like it might finally be on a roll.

____

10th Principle of Effective Writing: Avoiding Jargon

28. The consultant said that, if a company is going to downsize, it should go for the low-hanging fruit first.

    ____

29. Let's connect ear-to-ear on this one.

    ____

30. Just give me a ballpark figure so I can consider the offer.

    ____

WRITING STYLE EXERCISES ANSWERS

1. Finding the plan's weaknesses was essential to evaluating it.
2. Their main interest was the vehicle's cross-country capability.
3. Anthony hired a professional interior decorator to redecorate his apartment.
4. The scout experienced a setback.
5. None of her classmates were at the party.
6. The leader was known to be calm in a crisis.
7. In a rare moment of frustration, Toni lost her temper.
8. Lee's actions at Gettysburg were uncharacteristic of a generally sound commander.
9. Helen showed boldness by providing generous benefits to her workers.
10. The city's transportation system, with bus and light-rail lines that are second to none, is a model for other cities.
11. The success of our company owes everything to Carlo's belief in the future.
12. The builders of medieval cathedrals were not primitive laborers, but often highly skilled masons, carpenters, and workers in stained glass, guided by a detailed plan drawn up by a master builder.
13. We can design cars that are much more fuel-efficient.
14. You could increase your pottery production simply by using a different glaze.
15. It would be a mistake to take part in such a demonstration without a clear sense of purpose.
16. As the guards brought the prisoner into court, he glared at his accuser.
17. No one has ever asked who will inherit the estate.

18. When do you think they will have solved the problem?

19. The police have quite possibly found your lost dog.

20. Hopefully, officials can resolve this crisis before it gets out of hand.

21. "Half a loaf is better than none," as the proverb says.

22. We forego the standard admission fee for a valued customer.

23. All our employees have said they are satisfied with working conditions and benefits here.

24. Poor and homeless, she is sad to see.

25. That man sleeping on the bench looks old.

26. She always seemed unemotional to me.

27. With this win, the team looks like it might finally be gaining momentum.

28. The consultant said that, if a company is going to lay off workers, it should go for the easy targets first.

29. Let's discuss the details of this on the phone.

30. Just give me a cost estimate so I can consider the offer.

GRAMMAR

On the GRE, your control of language is important. Writing that is grammatical, concise, direct, and persuasive displays the "superior facility with the conventions of standard written English" (as the testmakers term it) that earns top GRE essay scores. If your writing style isn't clear, your ideas won't come across, no matter how brilliant they are. Good GRE English is not only grammatical but also clear and concise, and by using some basic principles, you'll be able to express your ideas clearly and effectively in both of your essays. To display effective writing style in your essays, your writing must follow the rules of standard written English. If you're not confident of your mastery of grammar, brush up before the test using the exercises below.

GRAMMAR EXERCISES

11TH PRINCIPLE OF EFFECTIVE WRITING: ENSURING SUBJECT-VERB AGREEMENT

31. If you or a member of your family have this problem, contact a doctor right away.

____

32. The training given to car mechanics, particularly those who work in modern dealerships on cars with the latest electronic gadgets, are more complicated than ever.

____

33. Each of the times you spoke about overcoming troubles were inspirational to me.

____

34. Our staff are discussing this proposal in our monthly meeting on Friday.

____

35. A range of options are open to businesses hoping to expand.

____

12TH PRINCIPLE OF EFFECTIVE WRITING: AVOIDING FAULTY MODIFICATION

36. Pleading innocent to all the charges, the jury was very sympathetic to the accused.

____

37. A portrait artist would probably not be successful painting sitters without a deep appreciation of personal character.

____

38. Lost when the ship sank, the rescued passengers had no possessions when they reached shore.

39. Cynthia found the credit card she had misplaced when she looked under the bed.

40. Usually never at a loss for words, the unresponsive audience left the comedian speechless.

13th Principle of Effective Writing: Avoiding Unclear Pronoun Reference

41. Marie told her mother that it was time for her to leave home.

42. Because of heavy snow on the roads, car drivers moved at a snail's pace until they were salted.

43. Bob was generous in his praise of Gil because of his pleasant nature.

44. Whenever the sergeant and the captain met, he saluted smartly.

14th Principle of Effective Writing: Including Parallelism

45. The food you buy at the Wonder King Supermarket is less expensive than the Bislet Hypermarket.

46. Helicopter pilots use one hand to control up-and-down motion, the other hand to control motion forward, backward, and sideways, while the feet control the turns.

____

47. A good teacher knows her subject, her students, and has a good sense of humor.

____

48. Students commonly preferred the teaching of Dr. Wolf to Professor Smith.

____

15th Principle of Effective Writing: Using a Consistent Narrative Voice

49. If one is genuinely serious about helping the homeless, you must become familiar with their living conditions.

____

50. From my perspective, you have to be truthful all the time. I don't see how we can claim to have integrity if we do anything less.

____

51. When we vote, we take part in an extraordinary process. One chooses not a ruler but a representative for all of us.

____

52. Each of you has a special responsibility to yourself and to others. We all have our own talents that we should develop for our own benefit and for the good of our families, our friends, and everyone we meet.

____

16TH PRINCIPLE OF EFFECTIVE WRITING: AVOIDING SLANG AND COLLOQUIALISMS

53. It was agreed that, if James wanted to get to the theater on time, he had better get on the stick.

____

54. When the city councilwoman tried to cover up her mistakes with lies, she just jumped from the frying pan into the fire.

____

55. The city high-school football team creamed their opponents, 35 to nothing.

____

56. According to fund-raising gurus, you should concentrate on people with deep pockets.

____

17TH PRINCIPLE OF EFFECTIVE WRITING: AVOIDING SENTENCE FRAGMENTS AND RUN-ONS

57. Bad drivers seem to be on the road in large numbers, many never signal what they intend to do.

____

58. High-speed trains are once again a popular topic. Especially among businesspeople.

____

59. Ever since our earliest ancestors discovered fire. We have needed to live near reasonable sources of fuel.

____

60. In England, lawyers are usually either solicitors or barristers, in the past, solicitors gave advice to clients and practiced in lower courts, while barristers practiced before the "bar" in the higher courts.

____

GRAMMAR EXERCISES ANSWERS

31. If you or a member of your family has this problem, contact a doctor right away.

32. The training given to car mechanics, particularly those who work in modern dealerships on cars with the latest electronic gadgets, is more complicated than ever.

33. Each of the times you spoke about overcoming troubles was inspirational to me.

34. Our staff is discussing this proposal in our monthly meeting on Friday.

35. A range of options is open to businesses hoping to expand.

36. The jury was very sympathetic to the accused, who pled innocent to all the charges.

37. A portrait artist without a deep appreciation of personal character would probably not be successful painting sitters.

38. Lost when the ship sank, the rescued passengers' possessions were gone when the passengers reached shore.

39. When she looked under the bed, Cynthia found the credit card she had misplaced.

40. Usually never at a loss for words, the comedian was speechless before the unresponsive audience.

41. Marie decided it was time for her to leave home, and she told her mother so.

42. Because of heavy snow, car drivers moved at a snail's pace until the roads were salted.

43. Bob was generous in his praise of Gil's pleasant nature.

44. The sergeant saluted the captain smartly whenever they met.

45. The food you buy at the Wonder King Supermarket is less expensive than the food at the Bislet Hypermarket.

46. Helicopter pilots use one hand to control up-and-down motion; the other hand to control forward, backward, and sideways motion; and the feet to control turns.

47. A good teacher knows her subject and her students, and has a good sense of humor.

48. Students commonly preferred the teaching of Dr. Wolf to that of Professor Smith.

49. If you are genuinely serious about helping the homeless, you must become familiar with their living conditions.

50. We must be truthful all the time. We cannot claim to have integrity if we do anything less.

51. When we vote, we take part in an extraordinary process. We choose not a ruler but a representative for all of us.

52. Each of you has a special responsibility to yourself and to others. You all have your own talents that you should develop for your own benefit and for the good of your families, your friends, and everyone you meet.

53. It was agreed that, if James wanted to get to the theater on time, he would have to hurry.

54. When the city councilwoman tried to cover up her mistakes with lies, she went from a bad situation to a worse one.

55. The city high-school football team overwhelmed their opponents by a score of 35 to 0.

56. According to fund-raising experts, you should concentrate on people with plenty of money.

57. Bad drivers seem to be on the road in large numbers. Many never signal what they intend to do.

58. High-speed trains are once again a popular topic, especially among businesspeople.

59. Ever since our earliest ancestors discovered fire, we have needed to live near reasonable sources of fuel.

60. In England, lawyers are usually either solicitors or barristers. In the past, solicitors gave advice to clients and practiced in lower courts, while barristers practiced before the "bar" in the higher courts.

MECHANICS

Mechanics are more technical in nature than grammatical issues. They are the established conventions of punctuation, capitalization, pronouns, and so on. Remember, minor grammatical errors will not ruin your score. Many test takers mistakenly believe that they'll lose points because of a few mechanical missteps such as misplaced commas, spelling errors, or other minor mistakes. In fact, the testmakers' description of a top-scoring essay acknowledges that there may be minor grammatical flaws. The graders understand that you are writing first-draft essays under timed conditions. However, if your errors obscure your meaning or make your essay difficult to follow, this will most likely be reflected in your scores.

To write an effective essay, you must be concise, forceful, and correct. An effective essay wastes no words, makes its point in a clear, direct way, and conforms to the generally accepted rules of grammar and form.

MECHANICS EXERCISES

18TH PRINCIPLE OF EFFECTIVE WRITING: CORRECTLY USING COMMAS

61. By federal law, interstate drivers of heavy trucks may be on duty for 14 straight hours, but must then take a 10-hour break.

____

62. Monica, who was normally a conscientious agreeable colleague shocked her coworkers with her angry outburst.

____

63. Spectators argued that the motorcycle stunt was an example of, sheer bravado, enormous courage, or arrant stupidity.

____

64. Historically mounting a horse from the left side, dates back to the time when knights wore their swords on their left hip and could swing their right leg onto the horse's back without the sword getting in the way.

____

65. Seeing the opportunity to make a quick breakthrough against her chess opponent she risked her queen by moving her remaining bishop well ahead of her pawns.

____

66. During the American Civil War, doctors regularly treated ill soldiers with "blue mass," a concoction made up of ingredients such as mercury, honey, glycerol and, licorice.

____

19th Principle of Effective Writing: Correctly Using Semicolons

67. We try to watch as little television as possible in our house, moreover we encourage reading by buying each other books as presents.

____

68. We did not know what to do, we could either run, stay, or hide.

____

69. Bringing a book to publication has often taken years, today, however, a book can appear on the Internet in a matter of weeks or even less.

____

70. The success of the operation was particularly due to the efforts of Dr. Williams, a heart specialist with an innovative approach to surgery, Dr. Mallory, the anesthesiologist, who first noted the patient's breathing problems, and Dr. Thurman, the blood specialist, who overcame dangerous clotting that could have traveled to the patient's lungs.

____

71. In recent weeks, Jake skimped on his training, therefore, his weak performance kept him from entering the tennis finals.

____

72. The 19th-century scholar Thomas Malthus wrote that limited food supplies would ultimately halt world population growth through starvation, this observation, highly influential at the time, may have prompted the historian Thomas Carlyle to describe economics as "the dismal science."

____

20th Principle of Effective Writing: Correctly Using Colons

73. A tragic hero may be: a powerful individual, a monarch, or, in modern tragedy, an ordinary person.

____

74. In recent years, Canada has produced a large number of world-class artists: including the following, the author Margaret Atwood, comedian Jim Carrey, singer Celine Dion, musician Neil Young, and actor Donald Sutherland.

____

75. The Navajo code talkers of World War II created special terms for wartime topics such as the following, submarine (iron fish), Britain (between waters), Germany (iron hat), dive bomber (chicken hawk), and August (big harvest).

____

76. I have one goal I really want to accomplish in my life, and that is: to scuba dive off the Great Barrier Reef.

____

77. The Empire State Building's special lighting system has been used: to honor only two non-Americans, Queen Elizabeth II of England and South Africa's Nelson Mandela.

____

78. Among the most sought-after qualities in a leader are the following character, enthusiasm, determination, confidence, cool-headedness, and decisiveness.

____

21st Principle of Effective Writing: Correctly Using Hyphens and Dashes

79. The company upgraded its technology system to what it called "a 21st century standard."

____

80. In a soon to be released statement, the chairman of the local soccer club reveals details of the club's new strip.

____

81. Only a few of the original members signed up for the forty seventh reunion of the class.

____

82. My objection—insignificant as it may seem, is the product of a lot of careful thought.

____

83. Almost certain ruin, the collapse of everything we have striven for, awaits us, such is the inevitable result of this change of policy.

____

84. It is to this extraordinary woman, and to her alone—that the credit for the reversal of this unjust law must go.

____

22nd Principle of Effective Writing: Correctly Using Apostrophes

85. You do know, I trust, that youre no longer just the assistant manager.

____

86. The dealership was selling tire's and rim's at less than list price.

____

87. The passengers confidence faded every time their bus broke down.

____

88. Youd be surprised how many childrens books are now collectors items.

____

89. Its easy for some people to say, "Go out and get a job," but they dont know how few jobs are open to you if you dont have a car.

____

90. The veterinarian has no idea why the cat has lost most of it's fur.

____

MECHANICS EXERCISES ANSWERS

61. By federal law, interstate drivers of heavy trucks may be on duty for 14 straight hours but must then take a 10-hour break.

62. Monica, who was normally a conscientious, agreeable colleague, shocked her coworkers with her angry outburst.

63. Spectators argued that the motorcycle stunt was an example of sheer bravado, enormous courage, or arrant stupidity.

64. Historically, mounting a horse from the left side dates back to the time when knights wore their swords on their left hip and could swing their right leg onto the horse's back without the sword getting in the way.

65. Seeing the opportunity to make a quick breakthrough against her chess opponent, she risked her queen by moving her remaining bishop well ahead of her pawns.

66. During the American Civil War, doctors regularly treated ill soldiers with "blue mass," a concoction made up of ingredients such as mercury, honey, glycerol, and licorice.

67. We try to watch as little television as possible in our house; moreover, we encourage reading by buying each other books as presents.

68. We did not know what to do; we could either run, stay, or hide.

69. Bringing a book to publication has often taken years; today, however, a book can appear on the Internet in a matter of weeks or even less.

70. The success of the operation was particularly due to the efforts of Dr. Williams, a heart specialist with an innovative approach to surgery; Dr. Mallory, the anesthesiologist, who first noted the patient's breathing problems; and Dr. Thurman, the blood specialist, who overcame dangerous clotting that could have traveled to the patient's lungs.

71. In recent weeks, Jake skimped on his training; therefore, his weak performance kept him from entering the tennis finals.

72. The 19th-century scholar Thomas Malthus wrote that limited food supplies would ultimately halt world population growth through starvation; this observation, highly influential at the time, may have prompted the historian Thomas Carlyle to describe economics as "the dismal science."

73. A tragic hero may be a powerful individual, a monarch, or—in modern tragedy—an ordinary person.

74. In recent years, Canada has produced a large number of world-class artists, including the following: author Margaret Atwood, comedian Jim Carrey, singer Celine Dion, musician Neil Young, and actor Donald Sutherland.

75. The Navajo code talkers of World War II created special terms for wartime topics such as the following: submarine (iron fish), Britain (between waters), Germany (iron hat), dive bomber (chicken hawk), and August (big harvest).

76. I have one goal I really want to accomplish in my life, and that is to scuba dive off the Great Barrier Reef.

77. The Empire State Building's special lighting system has been used to honor only two non-Americans: Queen Elizabeth II of England and Nelson Mandela of South Africa.

78. Among the most sought-after qualities in a leader are the following: character, enthusiasm, determination, confidence, cool-headedness, and decisiveness.

79. The company upgraded its technology system to what it called "a 21st-century standard."

80. In a soon-to-be-released statement, the chairman of the local soccer club will reveal details of the club's new strip.

81. Only a few of the original members signed up for the forty-seventh reunion of the class.

82. My objection—insignificant as it may seem—is the product of a lot of careful thought.

83. Almost certain ruin, the collapse of everything we have striven for, awaits us—such is the inevitable result of this change of policy.

Kaplan's Word Groups

The following lists contain a lot of common GRE words grouped together by meaning. Make flashcards from these lists and look over your cards a few times a week from now until the day of the test. Look over the word group lists once or twice a week every week until the test. If you don't have much time until the exam date, look over your lists more frequently. Then, by the day of the test, you should have a rough idea of what most of the words on your lists mean.

Note: The categories in which these words are listed are *general* and should *not* be interpreted as the exact definitions of the words.

A

Abbreviated Communication
abridge
compendium
cursory
curtail
syllabus
synopsis
terse

Act Quickly
abrupt
apace
headlong
impetuous
precipitate

Assist
abet
advocate
ancillary
bolster
corroborate
countenance
espouse
mainstay
munificent
proponent
stalwart
sustenance

B

Bad Mood
bilious
dudgeon
irascible
pettish
petulant
pique
querulous
umbrage
waspish

Beginner/Amateur
dilettante
fledgling
neophyte
novitiate
proselyte
tyro

Beginning/Young
burgeoning
callow
engender
inchoate
incipient
nascent

Biting (as in wit or temperament)
acerbic
acidulous
acrimonious
asperity
caustic
mordacious
mordant
trenchant

Bold
audacious
courageous
dauntless

Boring
banal
hackneyed
insipid
mundane
pedestrian
platitude
prosaic
quotidian
trite

C

Carousal
bacchanalian
debauchery
depraved
dissipated
iniquity
libertine
libidinous
licentious

reprobate
ribald
salacious
sordid
turpitude

Changing Quickly

capricious
mercurial
volatile

Copy

counterpart
emulate
facsimile
factitious
paradigm
precursor
simulate
vicarious

Criticize/Criticism

aspersion
belittle
berate
calumny
castigate
decry
defame/defamation
denounce
deride/derisive
diatribe
disparage
excoriate
gainsay
harangue
impugn
inveigh
lambaste
objurgate
obloquy
opprobrium
pillory
rebuke
remonstrate
reprehend
reprove
revile
tirade
vituperate

D

Death/Mourning

bereave
cadaver
defunct
demise
dolorous
elegy
knell
lament
macabre
moribund
obsequies
sepulchral
wraith

Denying of Self

abnegate
abstain
ascetic
spartan
stoic
temperate

Dictatorial

authoritarian
despotic
dogmatic
hegemonic/
hegemony
imperious
peremptory
tyrannical

Difficult to Understand

abstruse
ambiguous
arcane
bemusing
cryptic
enigmatic
esoteric
inscrutable
obscure
opaque
paradoxical
perplexing
recondite
turbid

Disgusting/Offensive

defile
fetid
invidious
noisome
odious
putrid
rebarbative

E

Easy to Understand

articulate
cogent
eloquent
evident
limpid
lucid
pellucid

Eccentric/Dissimilar

aberrant
anachronism
anomalous
discrete
eclectic
esoteric
iconoclast

Embarrass

abash
chagrin
compunction
contrition
diffidence
expiate
foible
gaucherie
rue

Equal

equitable
equity
tantamount

F

Falsehood

apocryphal
canard
chicanery
dissemble
duplicity
equivocate
erroneous
ersatz
fallacious
feigned
guile
mendacious/
mendacity
perfidy
prevaricate
specious
spurious

Family

conjugal
consanguine
distaff
endogamous
filial
fraternal
fratricide
progenitor
scion

Favoring/Not Impartial

ardent/ardor
doctrinaire
fervid
partisan
tendentious
zealot

Forgive/Make Amends

absolve
acquit
exculpate
exonerate
expiate
palliate
redress
vindicate

Funny

chortle
droll
facetious
flippant
gibe
jocular
levity
ludicrous

raillery
riposte
simper

G

Gaps/Openings
abatement
aperture
fissure
hiatus
interregnum
interstice
lull
orifice
rent
respite
rift

Generous/Kind
altruistic
beneficent
clement
largess
magnanimous
munificent
philanthropic
unstinting

Greedy
avaricious
covetous
mercenary
miserly
penurious
rapacious
venal

H

Hard-Hearted
asperity
baleful
dour
fell
malevolent
mordant
sardonic
scathing
truculent
vitriolic
vituperation

Harmful
baleful
baneful
deleterious
inimical
injurious
insidious
minatory
perfidious
pernicious

Harsh-Sounding
cacophony
din
dissonant
raucous
strident

Hatred
abhorrence
anathema
antagonism
antipathy
detestation
enmity
loathing
malice
odium
rancor

Healthy
beneficial
salubrious
salutary

Hesitate
dither
oscillate
teeter
vacillate
waver

Hostile
antithetic
churlish
curmudgeon
irascible
malevolent
misanthropic
truculent
vindictive

I

Innocent/Inexperienced
credulous
gullible
ingenuous
naive
novitiate
tyro

Insincere
disingenuous
dissemble
fulsome
ostensible
unctuous

Investigate
appraise
ascertain
assay
descry
peruse

L

Lazy/Sluggish
indolent
inert
lackadaisical
languid
lassitude
lethargic
phlegmatic
quiescent
slothful
torpid

Luck
amulet
auspicious
fortuitous
kismet
optimum
portentous
propitiate
propitious
providential
serendipity
talisman

N

Nag
admonish
belabor
cavil
enjoin
exhort
harangue
hector
martinet
remonstrate
reproof

Nasty
fetid
noisome
noxious

Not a Straight Line
askance
awry
careen
carom
circuitous
circumvent
gyrate
labyrinth
meander
oblique
serrated
sidle
sinuous
undulating
vortex

O

Overblown/Wordy
bombastic
circumlocution
garrulous
grandiloquent
loquacious
periphrastic
prolix
rhetoric
turgid
verbose

P

Pacify/Satisfy
ameliorate

appease
assuage
defer
mitigate
mollify
placate
propitiate
satiate
slake
soothe

Pleasant-Sounding
euphonious
harmonious
melodious
sonorous

Poor
destitute
esurient
impecunious
indigent

Praise
acclaim
accolade
aggrandize
encomium
eulogize
extol
fawn
laud/laudatory
venerate/veneration

Predict
augur
auspice
fey
harbinger
portentous
precursor
presage
prescient
prognosticate

Prevent/Obstruct
discomfit
encumber
fetter
forfend
hinder
impede
inhibit
occlude

S

Smart/Learned
astute
canny
erudite
perspicacious

Sorrow
disconsolate
doleful
dolor
elegiac
forlorn
lament
lugubrious
melancholy
morose
plaintive
threnody

Stubborn
implacable
inexorable
intractable
intransigent
obdurate
obstinate
recalcitrant
refractory
renitent
untoward
vexing

T

Terse
compendious
curt
laconic
pithy
succinct
taciturn

Time/Order/Duration
anachronism
antecede
antedate
anterior
archaic
diurnal
eon
ephemeral
epoch
fortnight
millennium
penultimate
synchronous
temporal

Timid/Timidity
craven
diffident
pusillanimous
recreant
timorous
trepidation

Truth
candor/candid
fealty
frankness
indisputable
indubitable
legitimate
probity
sincere
veracious
verity

U

Unusual
aberration
anomaly
iconoclast
idiosyncrasy

W

Walking About
ambulatory
itinerant
meander
peripatetic

Wandering
discursive
expatiate
forage
itinerant
peregrination
peripatetic
sojourn

Weaken
adulterate
enervate
exacerbate
inhibit
obviate
stultify
undermine
vitiate

Wisdom
adage
aphorism
apothegm
axiom
bromide
dictum
epigram
platitude
sententious
truism

Withdrawal/Retreat
abeyance
abjure
abnegation
abortive
abrogate
decamp
demur
recant
recidivism
remission
renege
rescind
retrograde

APPENDIX B

Kaplan's Root List

Kaplan's Root List can boost your knowledge of GRE-level words, and that can help you get more questions right. No one can predict exactly which words will show up on your test, but the testmakers favor certain words. The Root List gives you the component parts of many typical GRE words. Knowing these words can help you because you may run across them on your GRE. Also, becoming comfortable with the types of words that pop up will reduce your anxiety about the test.

Knowing roots can help you in two more ways. First, instead of learning one word at a time, you can learn a whole group of words that contain a certain root. They'll be related in meaning, so if you remember one, it will be easier for you to remember others. Second, roots can often help you decode an unknown GRE word. If you recognize a familiar root, you could get a good enough grasp of the word to answer the question.

This list is a starting point and a quick review, not an exhaustive guide. Roots are given in their most common forms, with their most common or broadest definitions; often, other forms and meanings exist. Similarly, the definitions for the words given as examples may be incomplete, and other senses of those words may exist. Get into the habit of looking up unfamiliar words in a good, current dictionary—whether on paper or on the Internet—and be sure to check their etymologies while you're there.

A

A/AN: not, without

agnostic: one who believes the existence of God is not provable
amoral: neither moral nor immoral; having no relation to morality
anomaly: an irregularity
anonymous: of unknown authorship or origin
apathy: lack of interest or emotion
atheist: one who does not believe in God
atrophy: the wasting away of body tissue
atypical: not typical

AB: off, away from, apart, down

abdicate: to renounce or relinquish a throne
abduct: to take away by force
abhor: to hate, detest
abject: cast down; degraded
abnormal: deviating from a standard
abolish: to do away with, make void
abstinence: forbearance from any indulgence of appetite
abstract: conceived apart from concrete realities, specific objects, or actual instances
abstruse: hard to understand; secret, hidden

ABLE/IBLE: capable of, worthy of

changeable: able to be changed
combustible: capable of being burned; easily inflamed
inevitable: impossible to be avoided; certain to happen
presentable: suitable for being presented

AC/ACR: sharp, bitter, sour

acerbic: sour or astringent in taste; harsh in temper
acid: something that is sharp, sour, or ill-natured
acrimonious: caustic, stinging, or bitter in nature
acumen: mental sharpness; quickness of wit
acute: sharp at the end; ending in a point
exacerbate: to increase bitterness or violence; aggravate

ACT/AG: to do, to drive, to force, to lead

agile: quick and well-coordinated in movement; active, lively
agitate: to move or force into violent, irregular action
pedagogue: a teacher
prodigal: wastefully or recklessly extravagant
synagogue: a gathering or congregation of Jews for the purpose of religious worship

ACOU: hearing

acoustic: pertaining to hearing; sound made through mechanical, not electronic, means

AD: to, toward, near

(Often the *d* is dropped and the first letter to which *a* is prefixed is doubled.)
accede: to yield to a demand; to enter office
adapt: adjust or modify fittingly
addict: to give oneself over, as to a habit or pursuit
address: to direct a speech or written statement to
adhere: to stick fast; cleave; cling
adjacent: near, close, or contiguous; adjoining
adjoin: to be close or in contact with
admire: to regard with wonder, pleasure, and approval
advocate: to plead in favor of
attract: to draw either by physical force or by an appeal to emotions or senses

AL/ALI/ALTER: other, another

alias: an assumed name; another name
alibi: the defense by an accused person that he was verifiably elsewhere at the time of the crime with which he is charged
alien: one born in another country; a foreigner
allegory: figurative treatment of one subject under the guise of another
alter ego: the second self; a substitute or deputy
alternative: a possible choice
altruist: a person unselfishly concerned for the welfare of others

AM: love

amateur: a person who engages in an activity for pleasure rather than financial or professional gain
amatory: of or pertaining to lovers or lovemaking
amiable: having or showing agreeable personal qualities
amicable: characterized by exhibiting good will
amity: friendship; peaceful harmony
amorous: inclined to love, esp. sexual love

enamored: inflamed with love; charmed; captivated

inamorata: a female lover

AMBI/AMPHI: both, on both sides, around

ambidextrous: able to use both hands equally well

ambient: moving around freely; circulating

ambiguous: open to various interpretations

amphibian: any cold-blooded vertebrate, the larva of which is aquatic and the adult of which is terrestrial; a person or thing having a twofold nature

AMBL/AMBUL: to go, to walk

ambulance: a vehicle equipped for carrying sick people (from a phrase meaning "walking hospital")

ambulatory: of, pertaining to, or capable of walking

perambulator: one who makes a tour of inspection on foot

preamble: an introductory statement (originally: to walk in front)

ANIM: of the life, mind, soul, breath

animal: a living being

animosity: a feeling of ill will or enmity

equanimity: mental or emotional stability, especially under tension

magnanimous: generous in forgiving an insult or injury

unanimous: of one mind; in complete accord

ANNUI/ENNI: year

annals: a record of events, esp. a yearly record

anniversary: the yearly recurrence of the date of a past event

annual: of, for, or pertaining to a year; yearly

annuity: a specified income payable at stated intervals

perennial: lasting for an indefinite amount of time

ANT/ANTE: before

antebellum: before the war (especially the American Civil War)

antecedent: existing, being, or going before

antedate: precede in time

antediluvian: belonging to the period before the biblical flood; very old or old-fashioned

anterior: placed before

ANTHRO/ANDR: man, human

androgen: any substance that promotes masculine characteristics

androgynous: being both male and female

android: a robot; a mechanical man

anthropocentric: regarding humanity as the central fact of the universe

anthropology: the science that deals with the origins of humankind

misanthrope: one who hates humans or humanity

philanderer: one who carries on flirtations

ANTI: against, opposite

antibody: a protein naturally existing in blood serum that reacts to overcome an antigen

antidote: a remedy for counteracting the effects of poison, disease, etc.

antipathy: aversion

antipodal: on the opposite side of the globe

antiseptic: free from germs; particularly clean or neat

APO: away

apocalypse: revelation; discovery; disclosure

apocryphal: of doubtful authorship or authenticity

apogee: the highest or most distant point

apology: an expression of one's regret or sorrow for having wronged another

apostasy: a total desertion of one's religion, principles, party, cause, etc.

apostle: one of the 12 disciples sent forth by Jesus to preach the Gospel

AQUA/AQUE: water

aquamarine: a bluish-green color

aquarium: a tank for keeping fish and other underwater creatures

aquatic: having to do with water

aqueduct: a channel for transporting water

subaqueous: underwater

ARCH/ARCHI/ARCHY: chief, principal, ruler

anarchy: a state or society without government or law

archenemy: chief enemy

architect: the devisor, maker, or planner of anything

monarchy: a government in which the supreme power is lodged in a sovereign

oligarchy: a state or society ruled by a select group

ARD: to burn

ardent: burning; fierce; passionate

ardor: flame; passion

arson: the crime of setting property on fire

AUTO: self

autocrat: an absolute ruler

automatic: self-moving or self-acting

autonomy: independence or freedom

B

BE: about, to make, to surround, to affect (often used to transform words into transitive verbs)

belie: to misrepresent; to contradict

belittle: to make small; to make something appear smaller

bemoan: to moan for; to lament

bewilder: to confuse completely (that is, to make one mentally wander)

BEL/BELL: beautiful

belle: a beautiful woman

embellish: to make beautiful; to ornament

BELL: war

antebellum: before the war (especially the American Civil War)

belligerent: warlike, given to waging war

rebel: a person who resists authority, control, or tradition

BEN/BENE: good

benediction: act of uttering a blessing

benefit: anything advantageous to a person or thing

benevolent: desiring to do good to others

benign: having a kindly disposition

BI/BIN: two

biennial: happening every two years

bilateral: pertaining to or affecting two or both sides

bilingual: able to speak one's native language and another with equal facility

binocular: involving two eyes

bipartisan: representing two parties

combination: the joining of two or more things into a whole

BON/BOUN: good, generous

bona fide: in good faith; without fraud

bonus: something given over and above what is due

bountiful: generous

BREV/BRID: short, small

abbreviate: to shorten

abridge: to shorten

brevet: an honorary promotion with no additional pay

breviloquent: laconic; concise in one's speech

brevity: shortness

brief: short

BURS: purse, money

bursar: treasurer

bursary: treasury

disburse: to pay

reimburse: to pay back

C

CAD/CID: to fall, to happen by chance

accident: happening by chance; unexpected

cascade: a waterfall descending over a steep surface

coincidence: a striking occurrence of two or more events at one time, apparently by chance

decadent: decaying; deteriorating

recidivist: one who repeatedly relapses, as into crime

CANT/CENT/CHANT: to sing

accent: prominence of a syllable in terms of pronunciation

chant: a song; singing

enchant: to subject to magical influence; bewitch

incantation: the chanting of words purporting to have magical power

incentive: that which incites action

recant: to withdraw or disavow a statement

CAP/CIP/CEPT: to take, to get

anticipate: to realize beforehand; foretaste or foresee

capture: to take by force or stratagem

emancipate: to free from restraint

percipient: having perception; discerning; discriminating

precept: a commandment or direction given as a rule of conduct

susceptible: capable of receiving, admitting, undergoing, or being affected by something

CAP/CAPIT/CIPIT: head, headlong

capital: the city or town that is the official seat of government

capitulate: to surrender unconditionally or on stipulated terms

caption: a heading or title

disciple: one who is a pupil of the doctrines of another

precipice: a cliff with a vertical face

precipitate: to hasten the occurrence of; to bring about prematurely

CARD/CORD/COUR: heart

cardiac: pertaining to the heart

concord: agreement; peace, amity

concordance: agreement, concord, harmony

discord: lack of harmony between persons or things

encourage: to inspire with spirit or confidence

CARN: flesh

carnage: the slaughter of a great number of people

carnival: a traveling amusement show

carnivorous: eating flesh

incarnation: a being invested with a bodily form

reincarnation: rebirth of a soul in a new body

CAST/CHAST: to cut

cast: to throw or hurl; fling

caste: a hereditary social group, limited to people of the same rank

castigate: to punish in order to correct

chaste: free from obscenity; decent

chastise: to discipline, esp. by corporal punishment

CAUS/CAUT: to burn

caustic: burning or corrosive

cauterize: to burn or deaden

cautery: an instrument used for branding; branding

holocaust: a burnt offering; complete destruction by fire or other means

CED/CEED/CESS: to go, to yield, to stop

accede: to yield to a demand; to enter office

antecedent: existing, being, or going before

cessation: a temporary or complete discontinuance

concede: to acknowledge as true, just, or proper; admit

incessant: without stop

predecessor: one who comes before another in an office, position, etc.

CELER: speed

accelerant: something used to speed up a process

accelerate: to increase in speed

celerity: speed; quickness

decelerate: to decrease in speed

CENT: hundred, hundredth

bicentennial: two-hundredth anniversary

cent: a hundredth of a dollar

centigrade: a temperature system with one hundred degrees between the freezing and boiling points of water

centimeter: one-hundredth of a meter

centipede: a creature with many legs

century: one hundred years

percent: in every hundred

CENTR: center

centrifuge: an apparatus that rotates at high speed and separates substances of different densities using centrifugal force

centrist: of or pertaining to moderate political or social ideas

concentrate: to bring to a common center; to converge, to direct toward one point

concentric: having a common center, as in circles or spheres

eccentric: off-center

CERN/CERT/CRET/CRIM/CRIT: to separate, to judge, to distinguish, to decide

ascertain: to make sure of; to determine

certitude: freedom from doubt

criterion: a standard of judgment or criticism

discreet: judicious in one's conduct of speech, esp. with regard to maintaining silence about something of a delicate nature

discrete: detached from others, separate

hypocrite: a person who pretends to have beliefs that she does not

CHROM: color
chromatic: having to do with color
chrome: a metallic element (chromium) used to make vivid colors or something plated with chromium
chromosome: genetic material that can be studied by coloring it with dyes
monochromatic: having only one color

CHRON: time
anachronism: something that is out-of-date or belonging to the wrong time
chronic: constant, habitual
chronology: the sequential order in which past events occurred
chronometer: a highly accurate clock or watch
synchronize: to occur at the same time or agree in time

CIRCU/CIRCUM: around
circuit: a line around an area; a racecourse; the path traveled by electrical current
circuitous: roundabout, indirect
circumference: the outer boundary of a circular area
circumspect: cautious; watching all sides
circumstances: the existing conditions or state of affairs surrounding and affecting an agent

CIS: to cut
exorcise: to seek to expel an evil spirit by ceremony
incision: a cut, gash, or notch
incisive: penetrating, cutting
precise: definitely stated or defined
scissors: cutting instrument for paper

CLA/CLO/CLU: to shut, to close
claustrophobia: an abnormal fear of enclosed places
cloister: a courtyard bordered with covered walks, esp. in a religious institution
conclude: to bring to an end; finish; to terminate
disclose: to make known, reveal, or uncover
exclusive: not admitting of something else; shutting out others
preclude: to prevent the presence, existence, or occurrence of

CLAIM/CLAM: to shout, to cry out
clamor: a loud uproar
disclaim: to deny interest in or connection with
exclaim: to cry out or speak suddenly and vehemently
proclaim: to announce or declare in an official way
reclaim: to claim or demand the return of a right or possession

CLI: to lean toward
climax: the most intense point in the development of something
decline: to cause to slope or incline downward
disinclination: aversion, distaste
proclivity: inclination, bias
recline: to lean back

CO/COL/COM/CON: with, together
coerce: to compel by force, intimidation, or authority
collaborate: to work with another, cooperate
collide: to strike one another with a forceful impact
commensurate: suitable in measure, proportionate
compatible: capable of existing together in harmony
conciliate: to placate, win over
connect: to bind or fasten together

COGN/CONN: to know
cognition: the process of knowing
incognito: with one's name or identity concealed
recognize: to identify as already known

CONTRA/CONTRO/COUNTER: against
contradict: to oppose; to speak against
contrary: opposed to; opposite
controversy: a disputation; a quarrel
counterfeit: fake; a false imitation
countermand: to retract an order
encounter: a meeting, often with an opponent

CORP/CORS: body
corporation: a company legally treated as an individual
corps: a body (an organized group) of troops
corpse: a dead body
corpulent: obese; having a lot of flesh
corset: a garment used to give shape and support to the body
incorporation: combining into a single body

COSM: order, universe, world

cosmetic: improving the appearance (making it look better ordered)

cosmic: relating to the universe

cosmology: a theory of the universe as a whole

cosmonaut: an astronaut; an explorer of outer space

cosmopolitan: worldly

cosmos: the universe; an orderly system; order

microcosm: a small system that reflects a larger whole

COUR/CUR: running, a course

concur: to accord in opinion; agree

courier: a messenger traveling in haste who bears news

curriculum: the regular course of study

cursive: handwriting in flowing strokes with the letters joined together

cursory: going rapidly over something; hasty; superficial

excursion: a short journey or trip

incursion: a hostile entrance into a place, esp. suddenly

recur: to happen again

CRE/CRESC/CRET: to grow

accretion: an increase by natural growth

accrue: to be added as a matter of periodic gain

creation: the act of producing or causing to exist

excrescence: an outgrowth

increase: to make greater in any respect

increment: something added or gained; an addition or increase

CRED: to believe, to trust

credentials: anything that provides the basis for belief

credit: trustworthiness

credo: any formula of belief

credulity: willingness to believe or trust too readily

incredible: unbelievable

CRYPT: hidden

apocryphal: of doubtful authorship or authenticity

crypt: a subterranean chamber or vault

cryptography: procedures of making and using secret writing

cryptology: the science of interpreting secret writings, codes, ciphers, and the like

CUB/CUMB: to lie down

cubicle: any small space or compartment that is partitioned off

incubate: to sit upon for the purpose of hatching

incumbent: holding an indicated position

recumbent: lying down; reclining; leaning

succumb: to give away to superior force; yield

CULP: fault, blame

culpable: deserving blame or censure

culprit: a person guilty of an offense

inculpate: to charge with fault

mea culpa: through my fault; my fault

D

DAC/DOC: to teach

didactic: intended for instruction

docile: easily managed or handled; tractable

doctor: someone licensed to practice medicine; a learned person

doctrine: a particular principle advocated, as of a government or religion

indoctrinate: to imbue a person with learning

DE: away, off, down, completely, reversal

decipher: to make out the meaning; to interpret

defame: to attack the good name or reputation of

deferential: respectful; to yield to judgment

defile: to make foul, dirty, or unclean

delineate: to trace the outline of; sketch or trace in outline

descend: to move from a higher to a lower place

DELE: to erase

delete: erase; blot out; remove

indelible: impossible to erase; lasting

DEM: people

democracy: government by the people

demographics: vital and social statistics of populations

endemic: peculiar to a particular people or locality

epidemic: affecting a large number of people at the same time and spreading from person to person

pandemic: general, universal

DEXT: right hand, right side, deft
ambidextrous: equally able to use both hands
dexter: on the right
dexterity: deftness; adroitness

DI: day
dial: a device for seeing the hour of the day; a clock face; rotatable discs or knobs used as a control input
diary: a record of one's days
dismal: gloomy (from "bad days")
diurnal: daily
meridian: a direct line from the North Pole to the South Pole; the highest point reached by the sun; noon
quotidian: everyday; ordinary

DI/DIA: in two, through, across
diagnose: to identify disease or fault from symptoms
dialogue: a conversation between two or more persons
diameter: a line going through a circle, dividing it in two
dichotomy: division into two parts, kinds, etc.

DI/DIF/DIS: away from, apart, reversal, not
diffuse: to pour out and spread, as in a fluid
dilate: to make wider or larger; to cause to expand
dilatory: inclined to delay or procrastinate
disperse: to drive or send off in various directions
disseminate: to scatter or spread widely; promulgate
dissipate: to scatter wastefully
dissuade: to deter by advice or persuasion

DIC/DICT/DIT: to say, to tell, to use words
dictionary: a book containing a selection of the words of a language
interdict: to forbid; prohibit
predict: to tell in advance
verdict: a judgment or decision

DIGN: worth
condign: well deserved; fitting; adequate
deign: to think fit or in accordance with one's dignity
dignitary: a person who holds a high rank or office
dignity: nobility or elevation of character; worthiness
disdain: to look upon or treat with contempt

DOG/DOX: opinion
dogma: a system of tenets, as of a church
orthodox: sound or correct in opinion or doctrine
paradox: an opinion or statement contrary to accepted opinion

DOL: to suffer, to pain, to grieve
condolence: expression of sympathy with one who is suffering
doleful: sorrowful, mournful
dolorous: full of pain or sorrow, grievous
indolence: a state of being lazy or slothful

DON/DOT/DOW: to give
anecdote: a short narrative about an interesting event
antidote: something that prevents or counteracts ill effects
donate: to present as a gift or contribution
endow: to provide with a permanent fund
pardon: kind indulgence, forgiveness

DORM: sleep
dormant: sleeping; inactive
dormitory: a place for sleeping; a residence hall

DORS: back
dorsal: having to do with the back
endorse: to sign on the back; to vouch for

DUB: doubt
dubiety: doubtfulness
dubious: doubtful
indubitable: unquestionable

DUC/DUCT: to lead
abduct: to carry off or lead away
conducive: contributive, helpful
conduct: personal behavior, way of acting
induce: to lead or move by influence
induct: to install in a position with formal ceremonies
produce: to bring into existence; give cause to

DULC: sweet
dulcet: sweet; pleasing
dulcified: sweetened; softened
dulcimer: a musical instrument

DUR: hard, lasting
dour: sullen, gloomy (originally: hard, obstinate)
durable: able to resist decay

duration: the length of time something exists
duress: compulsion by threat, coercion
endure: to hold out against; to sustain without yielding
obdurate: stubborn, resistant to persuasion

DYS: faulty, abnormal
dysfunctional: poorly functioning
dyslexia: difficulty in learning to read and interpret symbols
dyspepsia: impaired digestion
dystrophy: faulty or inadequate nutrition or development

E

E/EX: out, out of, from, former, completely
efface: to rub or wipe out; surpass, eclipse
evade: to escape from, avoid
exclude: to shut out; to leave out
exonerate: to free or declare free from blame
expire: to breathe out; to breathe one's last; to end
extricate: to disentangle, release

EGO: self
ego: oneself; the part of oneself that is self-aware
egocentric: focused on oneself
egoism/egotism: selfishness; self-absorption

EM/EN: in, into
embrace: to clasp in the arms; to include or contain
enclose: to close in on all sides

EPI: upon
epidemic: affecting a large number of people at the same time and spreading from person to person
epidermis: the outer layer of the skin
epigram: a witty or pointed saying tersely expressed
epilogue: a concluding part added to a literary work
epithet: a word or phrase, used invectively as a term of abuse

EQU: equal, even
adequate: equal to the requirement or occasion
equation: the act of making equal
equidistant: equally distant
iniquity: gross injustice; wickedness

ERR: to wander
err: to go astray in thought or belief, to be mistaken
errant: wandering or traveling, especially in search of adventure
erratic: deviating from the proper or usual course in conduct
error: a deviation from accuracy or correctness

ESCE: becoming
adolescent: between childhood and adulthood
convalescent: recovering from illness
incandescent: glowing with heat, shining
obsolescent: becoming obsolete
reminiscent: reminding or suggestive of

EU: good, well
eugenics: improvement of qualities of race by control of inherited characteristics
eulogy: speech or writing in praise or commendation
euphemism: pleasant-sounding term for something unpleasant
euphony: pleasantness of sound
euthanasia: killing a person painlessly, usually one who has an incurable, painful disease

EXTRA: outside, beyond
extract: to take out, obtain against a person's will
extradite: to hand over (person accused of crime) to state where crime was committed
extraordinary: beyond the ordinary
extrapolate: to estimate (unknown facts or values) from known data
extrasensory: derived by means other than known senses

F

FAB/FAM: to speak
affable: friendly, courteous
defame: to attack the good name of
fable: fictional tale, esp. legendary
famous: well-known, celebrated
ineffable: too great for description in words; that which must not be uttered

FAC/FIC/FIG/FAIT/FEIT/FY: to do, to make
configuration: manner of arrangement, shape
counterfeit: imitation, forgery
deficient: incomplete or insufficient

effigy: sculpture or model of person
faction: small dissenting group within larger one, esp. in politics
factory: building for manufacture of goods
prolific: producing many offspring or much output
ratify: to confirm or accept by formal consent

FAL: to err, to deceive
default: to fail
fail: to be insufficient; to be unsuccessful; to die out
fallacy: a flawed argument
false: not true; erroneous; lying
faux pas: a false step; a social gaffe
infallible: incapable of being wrong or being deceived

FATU: foolish
fatuity: foolishness; stupidity
fatuous: foolish; stupid
infatuated: swept up in a fit of passion, impairing one's reason

FER: to bring, to carry, to bear
confer: to grant, bestow
offer: to present for acceptance, refusal, or consideration
proffer: to offer
proliferate: to reproduce; produce rapidly
referendum: a vote on a political question open to the entire electorate

FERV: to boil, to bubble
effervescent: with the quality of giving off bubbles of gas
fervid: ardent, intense
fervor: passion, zeal

FI/FID: faith, trust
affidavit: a written statement on oath
confide: to entrust with a secret
fidelity: faithfulness, loyalty
fiduciary: of a trust; held or given in trust
infidel: disbeliever in the supposed true religion

FIN: end
confine: to keep or restrict within certain limits; imprison
definitive: decisive, unconditional, final
final: at the end; coming last
infinite: boundless; endless
infinitesimal: infinitely or very small

FLAGR/FLAM: to burn
conflagration: a large, destructive fire
flagrant: blatant, scandalous
flambeau: a lighted torch
inflame: to set on fire

FLECT/FLEX: to bend, to turn
deflect: to bend or turn aside from a purpose
flexible: able to bend without breaking
genuflect: to bend knee, esp. in worship
inflect: to change or vary pitch of
reflect: to throw back

FLU/FLUX: to flow
confluence: merging into one
effluence: flowing out of (light, electricity, etc.)
fluctuation: something that varies, rising and falling
fluid: a substance, esp. gas or liquid, capable of flowing freely
mellifluous: pleasing, musical

FORE: before
foreshadow: be warning or indication of (future event)
foresight: care or provision for future
forestall: to prevent by advance action
forthright: straightforward, outspoken, decisive

FORT: chance
fortuitous: happening by luck
fortunate: lucky, auspicious
fortune: chance or luck in human affairs

FORT: strength
forte: strong point; something a person does well
fortify: to provide with fortifications; strengthen
fortissimo: very loud

FRA/FRAC/FRAG/FRING: to break
fractious: irritable, peevish
fracture: breakage, esp. of a bone
fragment: a part broken off
infringe: to break or violate (a law, etc.)
refractory: stubborn, unmanageable, rebellious

FUG: to flee, to fly
centrifugal: flying off from the center
fugitive: on the run; someone who flees

fugue: a musical composition in which subsequent parts imitate or pursue the first part; a psychological state in which one flies from one's own identity
refuge: a haven for those fleeing
refugee: a fleeing person who seeks refuge
subterfuge: a deception used to avoid a confrontation

FULG: to shine
effulgent: shining forth
refulgent: radiant; shining

FUM: smoke
fume: smoke; scented vapor; to emit smoke or vapors
fumigate: to treat with smoke or vapors
perfume: scents, from burning incense or other sources of fragrance

FUS: to pour
diffuse: to spread widely or thinly
fusillade: continuous discharge of firearms or outburst of criticism
infusion: the act of permeating or steeping; liquid extract so obtained
profuse: lavish, extravagant, copious
suffuse: to spread throughout or over from within

G

GEN: birth, creation, race, kind
carcinogenic: producing cancer
congenital: existing or as such from birth
gender: classification roughly corresponding to the two sexes and sexlessness
generous: giving or given freely
genetics: the study of heredity and variation among animals and plants
progeny: offspring, descendants

GNI/GNO: to know
agnostic: one who believes that the existence of God is not provable
diagnose: to identify disease or fault from symptoms
ignoramus: a person lacking knowledge, uninformed
ignore: to refuse to take notice of
prognosis: to forecast, especially of disease

GRAD/GRESS: to step
aggressive: given to hostile acts or feelings
degrade: to humiliate, dishonor, reduce to lower rank
digress: to depart from the main subject
egress: going out; way out
progress: forward movement
regress: to move backward, revert to an earlier state

GRAM/GRAPH: to write, to draw
diagram: a figure made by drawing lines; an illustration
epigram: a short poem; a pointed statement
grammar: a system of language and its rules
graph: a diagram used to convey mathematical information
graphite: mineral used for writing, as the "lead" in pencils
photograph: a picture, originally made by exposing chemically treated film to light

GRAT: pleasing
gracious: kindly, esp. to inferiors; merciful
grateful: thankful
gratuity: money given for good service
ingratiate: to bring oneself into favor

GREG: flock
aggregate: a number of things considered as a collective whole
congregate: to come together in a group
egregious: remarkably bad; standing out from the crowd
gregarious: sociable; enjoying spending time with others
segregate: to separate from the crowd

H

HAP: by chance
haphazard: at random
hapless: without luck
happen: occur (originally: to occur by chance)
happily: through good fortune
happy: pleased, as by good fortune
mishap: an unlucky accident
perhaps: a qualifier suggesting something might (or might not) take place

HEMI: half
hemisphere: half a sphere; half of the Earth
hemistich: half a line of poetry

HER/HES: to stick

adherent: able to adhere; believer or advocate of a particular thing

adhesive: tending to remain in memory; sticky; an adhesive substance

coherent: logically consistent; having waves in phase and of one wavelength

inherent: involved in the constitution or essential character of something

(H)ETERO: different, other

heterodox: different from acknowledged standard; holding unorthodox opinions or doctrines

heterogeneous: of other origin; not originating in the body

heterosexual: of or pertaining to sexual orientation toward members of the opposite sex; relating to different sexes

HOL: whole

catholic: universal

holocaust: a burnt offering; complete destruction by fire or other means

hologram: a sort of three-dimensional image

holograph: a document written entirely by the person whose name it's in

holistic: considering something as a unified whole

(H)OM: same

anomaly: deviation from the common rule

homeostasis: a relatively stable state of equilibrium

homogeneous: of the same or a similar kind of nature; of uniform structure of composition throughout

homonym: one of two or more words spelled and pronounced alike but different in meaning

homosexual: of, relating to, or exhibiting sexual desire toward a member of one's own sex

HUM: earth

exhume: unearth

humble: down-to-earth

humility: the state of being humble

HYPER: over, excessive

hyperactive: excessively active

hyperbole: purposeful exaggeration for effect

hyperglycemia: an abnormally high concentration of sugar in the blood

HYPO: under, beneath, less than

hypochondriac: one affected by extreme depression of mind or spirits, often centered on imaginary physical ailments

hypocritical: pretending to have beliefs one does not

hypodermic: relating to the parts beneath the skin

hypothesis: assumption subject to proof

I

ICON: image, idol

icon: a symbolic picture; a statue; something seen as representative of a culture or movement

iconic: being representative of a culture or movement

iconoclast: one who attacks established beliefs; one who tears down images

iconology: symbolism

IDIO: one's own

idiom: a language, dialect, or style of speaking particular to a people

idiosyncrasy: peculiarity of temperament; eccentricity

idiot: an utterly stupid person

IN/IM: in, into

(Often the *m* is dropped and the first letter to which *i* is prefixed is doubled.)

implicit: not expressly stated; implied

incarnate: given a bodily, esp. a human, form

indigenous: native; innate, natural

influx: the act of flowing in; inflow

intrinsic: belonging to a thing by its very nature

IN/IM: not, without

(Often the *m* is dropped and the first letter to which *i* is prefixed is doubled.)

immoral: not moral; evil

impartial: not partial or biased; just

inactive: not active

indigent: poor, needy, lacking in what is needed

indolence: showing a disposition to avoid exertion; slothful

innocuous: not harmful or injurious

INTER: between, among

interim: a temporary or provisional arrangement; meantime

interloper: one who intrudes in the domain of others

intermittent: stopping or ceasing for a time

intersperse: to scatter here and there

interstate: connecting or jointly involving states

INTRA: inside, within

intramural: within a school; inside a city

intrastate: within a state

intravenous: inside the veins

IT/ITER: way, journey

ambition: strong desire to achieve (from "going around" for votes)

circuit: a line around an area; a racecourse; the path traveled by electrical current

itinerant: traveling

itinerary: travel plans

reiterate: to repeat

transit: traveling; means of transportation

J

JECT: to throw, to throw down

abject: utterly hopeless, humiliating, or wretched

conjecture: formation of opinion on incomplete information

dejected: sad, depressed

eject: to throw out, expel

inject: to place (quality, etc.) where needed in something

JOC: joke

jocose: given to joking; playful

jocular: in a joking manner; funny

jocund: merry; cheerful

joke: a witticism; a humorous anecdote; something funny

JOIN/JUG/JUNCT: to meet, to join

adjoin: to be next to and joined with

conjugal: related to marriage

conjunction: joining; occurring together; a connecting word

injunction: a command; an act of enjoining

junction: the act of joining; combining; a place where multiple paths join

junta: a group of military officers who join together to run a country; a council

rejoinder: to reply, retort

subjugate: to make subservient; to place under a yoke

JOUR: day

adjourn: to close a meeting; to put off further proceedings for another day

journal: a record of one's days

journey: a trip (originally: a day's travel)

JUD: to judge

adjudicate: to act as a judge

judiciary: a system of courts; members of a court system

judicious: having good judgment

prejudice: a previous or premature judgment; bias

JUR: law, to swear

abjure: to renounce on oath

adjure: to beg or command

jurisprudence: a system of law; knowledge of law

perjury: willful lying while on oath

JUV: young

juvenile: young; immature

juvenilia: writings or art produced in one's youth

rejuvenate: to refresh; to make young again

L

LANG/LING: tongue

bilingual: speaking two languages

language: a system of (usually spoken) communication

linguistics: the study of language

LAUD: praise, honor

cum laude: with honors

laudable: praiseworthy

laudatory: expressing praise

LAV/LAU/LU: to wash

ablution: act of cleansing

antediluvian: before the biblical flood; extremely old

deluge: a great flood of water

dilute: to make thinner or weaker by the addition of water

laundry: items to be, or that have been, washed
lavatory: a room with equipment for washing hands and face

LAX/LEAS/LES: loose

lax: loose; undisciplined
laxative: medicine or food that loosens the bowels
lease: to rent out (that is, to let something loose for others' use)
leash: a cord used to hold an animal while giving it some freedom to run loose
relax: loosen; be less strict; calm down
release: let go; set free

LEC/LEG/LEX: to read, to speak

dialect: a manner of speaking; a regional variety of a language
lectern: a reading desk
lecture: an instructional speech
legend: a story; a written explanation of a map or illustration
legible: readable
lesson: instruction (originally: part of a book or oral instruction to be studied and repeated to a teacher)
lexicographer: a writer of dictionaries
lexicon: a dictionary

LECT/LEG: to select, to choose

collect: to gather together or assemble
eclectic: selecting ideas, etc. from various sources
elect: to choose; to decide
predilection: preference, liking
select: to choose with care

LEV: to lift, to rise, light (weight)

alleviate: to make easier to endure, lessen
levee: an embankment against river flooding
levitate: to rise in the air or cause to rise
levity: humor, frivolity, gaiety
relevant: bearing on or pertinent to information at hand
relieve: to mitigate; to free from a burden

LI/LIG: to tie, to bind

ally: to unite; one in an alliance
league: an association; a group of nations, teams, etc. that have agreed to work for a common cause
liable: legally responsible; bound by law
liaison: a connection; one who serves to connect
lien: the right to hold a property due to an outstanding debt
ligament: a band holding bones together; a bond
ligature: a connection between two letters; a bond
oblige: to obligate; to make indebted or form personal bonds by doing a favor
rely: to depend upon (originally: to come together; to rally)

LIBER: free

deliver: to set free; to save; to hand over
liberal: generous; giving away freely
liberality: generosity
liberate: set free
libertine: one who follows one's own path, without regard for morals or other restrictions
liberty: freedom
livery: a uniform; an emblem indicating an owner or manufacturer (originally: an allowance of food or other provisions given to servants)

LITH: stone

acrolith: a statue with a stone head and limbs (but a wooden body)
lithography: a printing process that originally involved writing on a flat stone
lithology: the study of rocks and stones
lithotomy: an operation to remove stones from the body
megalith: a very big stone
monolith: a single block of stone, often shaped into a monument

LOC/LOG/LOQU: word, speech, thought

colloquial: of ordinary or familiar conversation
dialogue: a conversation, esp. in a literary work
elocution: art of clear and expressive speaking
eulogy: a speech or writing in praise of someone
grandiloquent: pompous or inflated in language
loquacious: talkative
prologue: introduction to a poem, play, etc.

LUC/LUM/LUS: light (brightness)

illuminate: to supply or brighten with light

illustrate: to make intelligible with examples or analogies
illustrious: highly distinguished
lackluster: lacking brilliance or radiance
lucid: easily understood, intelligible
luminous: bright, brilliant, glowing
translucent: permitting light to pass through

LUD/LUS: to play
allude: to refer casually or indirectly
delude: to mislead the mind or judgment of, deceive
elude: to avoid capture or escape defection by
illusion: something that deceives by producing a false impression of reality
ludicrous: ridiculous, laughable
prelude: a preliminary to an action, event, etc.

M

MACRO: great, long
macro: broad; large; a single computer command that executes a longer set of commands
macrobiotics: a system intended to prolong life
macrocephalous: having a large head
macrocosm: the universe; a large system that is reflected in at least one of its subsets
macroscopic: large enough to be visible to the naked eye

MAG/MAJ/MAX: big, great
magnanimous: generous in forgiving an insult or injury
magnate: a powerful or influential person
magnify: to increase the apparent size of
magnitude: greatness of size, extent, or dimensions
maxim: an expression of general truth or principle
maximum: the highest amount, value, or degree attained

MAL/MALE: bad, ill, evil, wrong
maladroit: clumsy; tactless
malady: a disorder or disease of the body
malapropism: humorous misuse of a word
malediction: a curse
malfeasance: misconduct or wrongdoing often committed by a public official
malfunction: failure to function properly
malicious: full of or showing malice
malign: to speak harmful untruths about, to slander

MAN/MANU: hand
emancipate: to free from bondage
manifest: readily perceived by the eye or the understanding
manual: operated by hand
manufacture: to make by hand or machinery

MAND/MEND: to command, to order, to entrust
command: to order; an order; control
commend: to give something over to the care of another; to praise
countermand: to retract an order
demand: to strongly ask for; to claim; to require
mandatory: commanded; required
recommend: to praise and suggest the use of; to advise
remand: to send back

MEDI: middle
immediate: nearest; having nothing in between
intermediate: in the middle
mean: average; in the middle
mediate: to serve as a go-between; to try to settle an argument
medieval: related to the Middle Ages
mediocre: neither good nor bad; so-so
medium: size between small and large; a substance or agency that things travel through (as, for example, light travels through air, and news is conveyed by television and newspapers)

MEGA: large, great
megalith: a very big stone
megalomania: a mental condition involving delusions of greatness; an obsession with doing great things
megalopolis: a very large city
megaphone: a device for magnifying the sound of one's voice
megaton: explosive power equal to 1,000 tons of TNT

MICRO: very small
microbe: a very small organism
microcosm: a small system that reflects a larger whole

micron: a millionth of a meter

microorganism: a very small organism

microscope: a device that magnifies very small things for viewing

MIN: small

diminish: to lessen

diminution: the act or process of diminishing

miniature: a copy or model that represents something in greatly reduced size

minute: a unit of time equal to one-sixtieth of an hour

minutiae: small or trivial details

MIN: to project, to hang over

eminent: towering above others; projecting

imminent: about to occur; impending

preeminent: superior to or notable above all others

prominent: projecting outward

MIS: bad, wrong, to hate

misadventure: bad luck; an unlucky accident

misanthrope: one who hates people or humanity

misapply: to use something incorrectly

mischance: bad luck; an unlucky accident

mischief: bad or annoying behavior

misconstrue: to take something in a way that wasn't intended; to understand something incorrectly

misfit: somebody or something that doesn't fit in

MIS/MIT: to send

emissary: a messenger or agent sent to represent the interests of another

intermittent: stopping and starting at intervals

remission: a lessening of intensity or degree

remit: to send money

transmit: to send from one person, thing, or place to another

MISC: mixed

miscellaneous: made up of a variety of parts or ingredients

promiscuous: consisting of diverse and unrelated parts or individuals; indiscriminate

MOB/MOM/MOT/MOV: to move

automobile: a vehicle that moves under its own power; a motorized car

demote: to move downward in an organization

immovable: incapable of being moved; unyielding

locomotion: moving from place to place; the ability to do so

mob: the rabble; a disorderly group of people (from the Latin *mobile vulgus*, meaning "the fickle crowd")

mobile: movable

mobilize: to make ready for movement; to assemble

moment: an instant; importance

momentous: of great importance (originally: having the power to move)

momentum: the force driving a moving object to keep moving; a growing force

motion: movement

motive: a reason for action; what moves a person to do something

motor: a device that makes something move

mutiny: rebellion against authority, esp. by sailors

promote: to move to a higher rank in an organization

remove: to take away; to move away

MOLL: soft

emollient: something that softens or soothes (e.g., a lotion)

mild: gentle; kind

mollify: soothe; soften; calm

mollusk: a phylum of invertebrate animals—including octopuses, squids, oysters, clams, and slugs—with soft bodies

MON/MONIT: to remind, to warn

admonish: to counsel against something; caution

monitor: one that admonishes, cautions, or reminds

monument: a structure, such as a building, tower, or sculpture, erected as a memorial

premonition: forewarning, presentiment

remonstrate: to say or plead in protest, objection, or reproof

summon: to call together; convene

MON/MONO: one

monarchy: rule by a single person

monk: a man in a religious order living apart from society (originally: a religious hermit)

monochord: a musical instrument with a single string

monogram: a design combining multiple letters into one

monograph: a scholarly study of a single subject

monologue: a speech or other dramatic composition recited by one person

monomania: an obsession with a single subject

monotonous: boring; spoken using only one tone

MOR/MORT: death

immortal: not subject to death

morbid: susceptible to preoccupation with unwholesome matters

moribund: dying, decaying

MORPH: shape

amorphous: without definite form; lacking a specific shape

anthropomorphism: attribution of human characteristics to inanimate objects, animals, or natural phenomena

metamorphosis: a transformation, as by magic or sorcery

MULT: many

multiple: many, having many parts; a number containing some quantity of a smaller number without remainder

multiplex: having many parts; a movie theater or other building with many separate units

multiply: to increase; to become many

multitudinous: very many; containing very many; having very many forms

MUT: to change

commute: to substitute; exchange; interchange

immutable: unchangeable, invariable

mutation: the process of being changed

permutation: a complete change; transformation

transmute: to change from one form into another

N

NAT/NAS/NAI/GNA: birth

cognate: related by blood; having a common ancestor

naive: lacking worldliness and sophistication; artless

nascent: starting to develop

native: belonging to one by nature; inborn; innate

natural: present due to nature, not to artificial or man-made means

renaissance: rebirth, esp. referring to culture

NAU/NAV: ship, sailor

astronaut: one who travels in outer space

circumnavigate: to sail all the way around

cosmonaut: one who travels in outer space

nauseous: causing a squeamish feeling (originally: seasickness)

nautical: related to sailing or sailors

naval: related to the navy

nave: the central portion of a church (which resembles the shape of a ship)

navy: a military force consisting of ships and sailors

NIHIL: nothing, none

annihilate: wipe out; reduce to nothing

nihilism: denial of all moral beliefs; denial that existence has any meaning

NOC/NOX: harm

innocent: uncorrupted by evil, malice, or wrongdoing

innocuous: not harmful or injurious

noxious: injurious or harmful to health or morals

obnoxious: highly disagreeable or offensive

NOCT/NOX: night

equinox: one of two times in a year when day and night are equal in length

noctambulant: walking at night; sleepwalking

nocturnal: related to the night; active at night

nocturne: a dreamlike piece of music; a painting set at night

NOM: rule, order

astronomy: the scientific study of the universe beyond the Earth

autonomy: independence, self-governance

economy: the careful or thrifty use of resources, as of income, materials, or labor

gastronomy: the art or science of good eating

taxonomy: the science, laws, or principles of classification

NOM/NYM/NOUN/NOWN: name

acronym: a word formed from the initial letters of a name

anonymous: having an unknown or unacknowledged name
nomenclature: a system of names; systematic naming
nominal: existing in name only; negligible
nominate: to propose by name as a candidate
noun: a word that names a person, place, or thing
renown: fame; reputation
synonym: a word having a meaning similar to that of another word of the same language

NON: not
nonconformist: one who does not conform to a church or other societal institution
nonentity: something that doesn't exist; something that is unimportant
nonpareil: something with no equal
nonpartisan: not affiliated with a political party

NOUNC/NUNC: to announce
announce: to proclaim
pronounce: to articulate
renounce: to give up, especially by formal announcement

NOV/NEO/NOU: new
innovate: to begin or introduce something new
neologism: a newly coined word, phrase, or expression
neophyte: a beginner; a new convert; a new worker
neoplasm: a new growth in the body; a tumor
nouveau riche: one who has lately become rich
novice: a person new to any field or activity
renovate: to restore to an earlier condition

NULL: nothing
annul: to cancel; to make into nothing
nullify: to cancel; to make into nothing
nullity: the condition of being nothing

O

OB: toward, to, against, over
obese: extremely fat, corpulent
obfuscate: to render indistinct or dim; darken
oblique: having a slanting or sloping direction
obsequious: overly submissive
obstinate: stubbornly adhering to an idea, inflexible
obstreperous: noisily defiant, unruly
obstruct: to block or fill with obstacles
obtuse: not sharp, pointed, or acute in any form

OMNI: all
omnibus: an anthology of the works of one author or of writings on related subjects
omnipotent: all powerful
omnipresent: everywhere at one time
omniscient: having infinite knowledge

ONER: burden
exonerate: to free from blame (originally: to relieve of a burden)
onerous: burdensome; difficult
onus: a burden; a responsibility

OSS/OSTE: bone
ossify: to become bone; to harden; to become callous
ossuary: a place where bones are kept; a charnel house
osteopathy: a medical system based on the belief that many illnesses can be traced to issues in the skeletal system

P

PAC/PEAC: peace
appease: to bring peace to
pacifier: something or someone that eases the anger or agitation of
pacify: to ease the anger or agitation of
pact: a formal agreement, as between nations

PALP: to feel
palpable: capable of being felt; tangible
palpate: to feel; to examine by feeling
palpitate: to beat quickly, as the heart; to throb

PAN/PANT: all, everyone
pandemic: widespread, general, universal
panegyric: formal or elaborate praise at an assembly
panoply: a wide-ranging and impressive array or display
panorama: an unobstructed and wide view of an extensive area

pantheon: a public building containing tombs or memorials of the illustrious dead of a nation

PAR: equal

apartheid: any system or caste that separates people according to race, etc.

disparage: to belittle, speak disrespectfully about

disparate: essentially different

par: an equality in value or standing

parity: equally, as in amount, status, or character

PARA: next to, beside

parable: a short, allegorical story designed to illustrate a moral lesson or religious principle

paragon: a model of excellence

parallel: extending in the same direction

paranoid: suffering from a baseless distrust of others

parasite: an organism that lives on or within a plant or animal of another species, from which it obtains nutrients

parody: to imitate for purposes of satire

PAS/PAT/PATH: feeling, suffering, disease

compassion: a feeling of deep sympathy for someone struck by misfortune, accompanied by a desire to alleviate suffering

dispassionate: devoid of personal feeling or bias

empathy: the identification with the feelings or thoughts of others

impassive: showing or feeling no emotion

pathogenic: causing disease

sociopath: a person whose behavior is antisocial and who lacks a sense of moral responsibility

sympathy: harmony or agreement in feeling

PAU/PO/POV/PU: few, little, poor

impoverish: to deplete

paucity: smallness of quantity; scarcity; scantiness

pauper: a person without any personal means of support

poverty: the condition of being poor

puerile: childish, immature

pusillanimous: lacking courage or resolution

PEC: money

impecunious: having no money; penniless

peculation: embezzlement

pecuniary: relating to money

PED: child, education

encyclopedia: book or set of books containing articles on various topics, covering all branches of knowledge or of one particular subject

pedagogue: a teacher

pedant: one who displays learning ostentatiously

pediatrician: a doctor who primarily has children as patients

PED/POD: foot

antipodes: places that are diametrically opposite each other on the globe

expedite: to speed up the progress of

impede: to retard progress by means of obstacles or hindrances

pedal: a foot-operated lever or part used to control

pedestrian: a person who travels on foot

podium: a small platform for an orchestra conductor, speaker, etc.

PEL: to drive, to push

compel: to force; to command

dispel: to drive away; to disperse

expel: to drive out; to banish; to eject

impel: to force; to drive forward

propel: to drive forward

PEN/PENE: almost

peninsula: a landmass that is mostly surrounded by water, making it almost an island

penultimate: second-to-last

penumbra: a shaded area between pure shadow and pure light

PEN/PUN: to pay, to compensate

penal: of or pertaining to punishment, as for crimes

penalty: a punishment imposed for a violation of law or rule

penance: a punishment undergone to express regret for a sin

penitent: contrite

punitive: serving for, concerned with, or inflicting punishment

PEND/PENS: to hang, to weight, to pay
appendage: a limb or other subsidiary part that diverges from the central structure
appendix: supplementary material at the end of a text
compensate: to counterbalance, offset
depend: to rely; to place trust in
indispensable: absolutely necessary, essential, or requisite
stipend: a periodic payment; fixed or regular pay

PER: completely
perforate: to make a way through or into something
perfunctory: performed merely as routine duty
perplex: to cause to be puzzled or bewildered over what is not understood
persistent: lasting or enduring tenaciously
perspicacious: shrewd, astute
pertinacious: resolute, persistent
peruse: to read with thoroughness or care

PERI: around
perimeter: the border or outer boundary of a two-dimensional figure
peripatetic: walking or traveling about; itinerant
periscope: an optical instrument for seeing objects in an obstructed field of vision

PET/PIT: to go, to seek, to strive
appetite: a desire for food or drink
centripetal: moving toward the center
compete: to strive to outdo another
impetuous: characterized by sudden or rash action or emotion
petition: a formally drawn request soliciting some benefit
petulant: showing sudden irritation, esp. over some annoyance

PHIL: love
bibliophile: one who loves or collects books
philatelist: one who loves or collects postage stamps
philology: the study of literary texts to establish their authenticity and determine their meaning
philosopher: one who investigates the truths and principles of being, knowledge, or conduct (originally: lover of wisdom)

PHOB: fear
claustrophobia: fear of enclosed places
hydrophobia: fear of water, which is a symptom of rabies; rabies
phobia: fear; an irrational fear
xenophobia: fear of foreigners; hatred of foreigners

PHON: sound
euphony: the quality of sounding good
megaphone: a device for magnifying the sound of one's voice
phonetics: the study of the sounds used in speech
polyphony: the use of simultaneous melodic lines to produce harmonies in musical compositions
telephone: a device for transmitting sound at a distance

PHOTO: light
photograph: a picture, originally made by exposing chemically treated film to light
photon: a packet of light or other electromagnetic radiation
photosynthesis: a process by which plants create carbohydrates when under light

PLAC: to please
complacent: self-satisfied, unconcerned
complaisant: inclined or disposed to please
implacable: unable to be pleased
placebo: a substance with no pharmacological effect that acts to placate a patient who believes it to be a medicine
placid: pleasantly calm or peaceful

PLE/PLEN: to fill, full
complete: having all parts or elements
deplete: to decrease seriously or exhaust the supply of
implement: an instrument, tool, or utensil for accomplishing work
plenitude: fullness
plethora: excess, overabundance
replete: abundantly supplied
supplement: something added to supply a deficiency

PLEX/PLIC/PLY: to fold, twist, tangle, or bend
complex: composed of many interconnected parts

duplicity: deceitfulness in speech or conduct, double-dealing

implicate: to show to be involved, usually in an incriminating manner

implicit: not expressly stated, implied

replica: any close copy or reproduction

supplicate: to make humble and earnest entreaty

POLY: many

polyandry: the practice of having multiple husbands

polygamy: the practice of having multiple wives

polyglot: someone who speaks many languages

polygon: a figure with many sides

polytheism: belief in many gods

PON/POS/POUND: to put, to place

component: a constituent part, elemental ingredient

expose: to lay open to danger, attack, or harm

expound: to set forth in detail

juxtapose: to place close together or side by side

repository: a receptacle or place where things are deposited

PORT: to carry

deportment: conduct, behavior

disport: to divert or amuse oneself

export: to transmit abroad

import: to bring in from a foreign country

importune: to urge or press with excessive persistence

portable: easily carried

POST: behind, after

post facto: after the fact

posterior: situated at the rear

posterity: future generations

posthumous: after death

POT: to drink

potable: drinkable; safe to drink; a drink

potation: drinking; a drink

potion: a drinkable medicine, poison, or other concoction

PRE: before, in front

precarious: dependent on circumstances beyond one's control

precedent: an act that serves as an example for subsequent situations

precept: a commandment given as a rule of action or conduct

precocious: unusually advanced or mature in mental development or talent

premonition: a feeling of anticipation over a future event

presentiment: foreboding

PREHEND/PRISE: to take, to get, to seize

apprehend: to take into custody

comprise: to include or contain

enterprise: a project undertaken

reprehensible: deserving rebuke or censure

reprisals: retaliation against an enemy

surprise: to strike with an unexpected feeling of wonder or astonishment

PRI/PRIM: first

primal: original; most important

primary: first; most important

prime: first in quality; best

primeval: ancient; going back to the first age of the world

pristine: original; like new; unspoiled; pure

PRO: in front, before, much, for

problem: a difficult question (originally: one put before another for solution)

proceed: to go forward

profuse: spending or giving freely

prolific: highly fruitful

propound: to set forth for consideration

proselytize: to convert or attempt to recruit

provident: having or showing foresight

PROB: to prove, to test

approbation: praise, consideration

opprobrium: the disgrace incurred by shameful conduct

probe: to search or examine thoroughly

probity: honesty, high-mindedness

reprobate: a depraved or wicked person

PROP/PROX: near

approximate: very near; close to being accurate

proximate: nearby; coming just before or just after

proximity: nearness; distance

PROT/PROTO: first

protagonist: the main character in a play or story

protocol: diplomatic etiquette; a system of proper conduct; the original record of a treaty or other negotiation
prototype: the first version of an invention, on which later models are based
protozoan: belonging to a group of single-celled animals, which came before more complex animals

PSEUD/PSEUDO: false
pseudonym: a false name; a pen name
pseudopod: part of a single-celled organism that can be stuck out (like a foot) and used to move around
pseudoscience: false science; something believed to be based on the scientific method but that actually is not

PUG: to fight
impugn: to challenge as false
pugilist: a fighter or boxer
pugnacious: to quarrel or fight readily
repugnant: objectionable or offensive

PUNC/PUNG/POIGN: to point, to prick, to pierce
compunction: a feeling of uneasiness for doing wrong
expunge: to erase, eliminate completely
point: a sharp or tapering end
punctilious: strict or exact in the observance of formalities
puncture: the act of piercing
pungent: caustic or sharply expressive

PYR: fire
pyre: a bonfire, usually for burning a dead body
pyromania: an urge to start fires
pyrosis: heartburn
pyrotechnics: fireworks

Q

QUAD/QUAR/QUAT: four
quadrant: a quarter of a circle; a 90-degree arc
quadrille: a square dance involving four couples
quadruple: four times as many
quadruplets: four children born in one birth
quart: one-fourth of a gallon
quaternary: the number four; the fourth in a series

QUE/QUIS: to seek
acquire: to come into possession of
conquest: the act gaining control by force
exquisite: of special beauty or charm
inquisitive: given to research, eager for knowledge
perquisite: a gratuity, tip
querulous: full of complaints
query: a question, inquiry

QUIE/QUIT: quiet, rest
acquiesce: to comply, give in
disquiet: lack of calm or peace
quiescence: the condition of being at rest, still, inactive
quiet: making little or no sound
tranquil: free from commotion or tumult

QUIN/QUINT: five
quinquennial: a five-year period; a fifth anniversary
quintessence: the essential part of something (originally: the "fifth essence," which was believed to permeate everything and be what stars and planets were made of)
quintuple: five times as many

R

RACI/RADI: root
deracinate: to uproot
eradicate: to uproot; to wipe out
radical: pertaining to roots; questioning everything, even basic beliefs; going to root causes; thorough
radish: a root vegetable

RAMI: branch
ramification: a branch; an offshoot; a collection of branches; a consequence
ramiform: branchlike

RE: back, again
recline: to lean back; to lie down
regain: to gain again; to take back
remain: to stay behind; to be left; to continue to be
reorganize: to organize again
request: to ask (originally: to seek again)

RECT: straight, right
correct: to set right

direct: to guide; to put straight
erect: upright; starting up straight
rectangle: a four-sided figure in which every angle is a right angle
rectitude: moral uprightness; moral straightness

REG: king, rule

interregnum: a period between kings
realm: a kingdom; a domain
regal: kingly; royal
regent: one who serves on behalf of a king; one who rules
regicide: killing a king; one who kills a king
regiment: a body of troops in an army; to form into such a body; to subject to strict rule
regular: having a structure following some rule; orderly; normally used; average

RETRO: backward

retroactive: extending to things that happened in the past
retrofit: to install newer parts into an older device or structure
retrograde: moving backward; appearing to move backward
retrospective: looking back at the past

RID/RIS: to laugh

derision: the act of mockery
risible: causing laughter

ROG: to ask

abrogate: to abolish by formal means
arrogant: making claims to superior importance or rights
arrogate: to claim unwarrantably or presumptuously
derogatory: belittling, disparaging
interrogate: to ask questions of, esp. formally
surrogate: a person appointed to act for another

RUB/RUD: red

rouge: a red powder used as makeup
rubella: German measles; a disease marked by red spots
rubicund: reddish; rosy-cheeked
rubric: a rule; a guide for scoring tests; a heading in a book set in red letters
russet: reddish-brown; a coarse cloth, usually reddish-brown; a type of apple or pear, typically reddish-brown

RUD: crude

erudite: scholarly; learned (that is, trained out of crudeness)
rude: uncivilized; impolite
rudimentary: undeveloped; related to rudiments
rudiments: first principles; imperfect first step of one's training

S

SACR/SANCT: holy

execrable: abominable
sacrament: something regarded as possessing sacred character
sacred: devoted or dedicated to a deity or religious purpose
sacrifice: the offering of some living or inanimate thing to a deity in homage
sacrilege: the violation of anything sacred
sanctify: to make holy
sanction: authoritative permission or approval

SAG/SAP/SAV: taste, thinking, discerning

insipid: tasteless
sagacious: perceptive; discerning; insightful
sage: wise
sapient: wise
savant: a learned person
savor: taste; to enjoy flavors

SAL: salt

salary: payment for services (originally: money for Roman soldiers to buy salt)
saline: containing salt; salty

SAL/SIL/SAULT/SULT: to leap, to jump

assault: a sudden or violent attack
desultory: at random, unmethodical
exult: to show or feel triumphant joy
insolent: boldly rude or disrespectful
insult: to treat with contemptuous rudeness
resilient: able to spring back to an original form after compression
salient: prominent or conspicuous
somersault: to roll the body end over end, making a complete revolution

SALU: health
salubrious: healthful
salutary: healthful
salute: to greet; a gesture of greeting (originally: to wish good health)

SALV: to save
salvage: to save; something saved or recovered
salvation: being saved
savior: one who saves

SAN: healthy
sane: mentally healthy
sanitarium: a place of healing
sanitary: promoting health; related to conditions that affect health, such as cleanliness

SANG: blood
consanguinity: being related by blood
sanguinary: bloody; bloodthirsty
sanguine: hopeful; confident (from the "sanguine humor," which was believed to be associated with those traits)

SAT: enough
assets: property; possessions (originally: enough property to cover one's debts)
dissatisfied: feeling that one does not have enough
sate: to fill
satisfy: to meet one's desires; to meet an obligation; to provide with enough
saturate: to fill completely; to entirely satisfy

SCI: to know
conscience: the inner sense of what is right or wrong, impelling one toward right action
conscious: aware of one's own existence
omniscient: knowing everything
prescient: having knowledge of things before they happen
unconscionable: unscrupulous

SCRIBE/SCRIPT: to write
ascribe: to credit or assign, as to a cause or course
circumscribe: to draw a line around
conscription: draft
describe: to tell or depict in words
postscript: any addition or supplement
proscribe: to condemn as harmful or odious
scribble: to write hastily or carelessly
script: handwriting
transcript: a written or typed copy

SE: apart, away
secede: to withdraw formally from an association
sedition: incitement of discontent or rebellion against a government
seduce: to lead astray
segregate: to separate or set apart from others
select: to choose in preference to another
separate: to keep apart, divide
sequester: to remove or withdraw into solitude or retirement

SEC/SEQU/SUE/SUI: to follow
non sequitur: an inference or a conclusion that does not follow from the premises
obsequious: fawning
prosecute: to seek to enforce by legal process
pursue: to chase after
second: next after the first
sequence: the following of one thing after another
suite: a series; a set (originally: a train of followers)

SED/SESS/SID: to sit, to settle
assiduous: diligent, persistent, hardworking (literally, "sitting down" to business)
dissident: disagreeing, as in opinion or attitude (literally, "sitting apart")
insidious: intended to entrap or beguile; lying in wait to entrap
preside: to exercise management or control; to sit in the leader's chair
resident: a person who lives in a place
residual: remaining, leftover
sediment: the matter that settles to the bottom of a liquid
session: a meeting at which people sit together in discussion

SEM: seed, to sow
disseminate: to spread; to scatter around
semen: seed (of male animals)
seminary: a school, esp. for religious training (originally: a place for raising plants)

SEMI: half
semicircle: half a circle
semiconscious: only partly conscious; half awake

SEN: old
senate: the highest legislative body (from "council of elders")
senescent: getting old
senile: relating to old age; experiencing memory loss or other age-related mental impairments
sire: a title for a king; a father (originally: an important person, an old man)

SENS/SENT: to feel, to be aware
dissent: to differ in opinion, esp. from the majority
insensate: without feeling or sensitivity
presentiment: a feeling that something is about to happen
resent: to feel or show displeasure
sense: any of the faculties by which humans and animals perceive stimuli originating outside the body
sensory: of or pertaining to the senses or sensation
sentiment: an attitude or feeling toward something
sentinel: a person or thing that stands watch

SIN/SINU: bend, fold, curve
insinuate: to introduce in sneaky or winding ways
sinuous: moving in a bending or wavy manner
sinus: a curved or irregularly shaped cavity in the body, such as those related to the nostrils

SOL: alone
desolate: deserted; laid waste; left alone
isolate: to set apart from others
soliloquize: talk to oneself; talk onstage as if to oneself
solipsism: the belief that the only thing that really exists, or can really be known, is oneself
solitude: the state of being alone

SOL: to loosen, to free
absolution: forgiveness for wrongdoing
dissolute: indifferent to moral restraints
dissolution: the act or process of dissolving into parts or elements
dissolve: to make a solution of, as by mixing in a liquid
resolution: a formal expression of opinion or intention made
soluble: capable of being dissolved or liquefied

SOL: sun
parasol: an umbrella that protects from the sun
solar: related to the sun
solarium: a sunroom; a room with windows for taking in the sun
solstice: one of two days when the sun reaches its highest point at noon and seems to stand still

SOMN: sleep
insomnia: inability to sleep
somnambulist: a sleepwalker
somniferous: sleep-inducing
somniloquist: one who talks while asleep
somnolent: sleep-inducing; sleepy; drowsy

SOPH: wisdom
philosopher: one who studies logic, beauty, truth, etc.; one who seeks wisdom
sophism: a superficially appealing but fallacious argument
sophisticated: complex; worldly; experienced

SOURC/SURG/SURRECT: to rise
insurgent: rising up in revolution; rushing in
insurrection: rising up in armed rebellion
resurrection: coming back to life; rising again
source: where something comes from (such as spring water rising out of the ground)
surge: to rise up forcefully, as ocean waves

SPEC/SPIC: to look, to see
circumspect: watchful and discreet, cautious
conspicuous: easily seen or noticed; readily observable
perspective: one's mental view of facts, ideas, and their interrelationships
perspicacious: having keen mental perception and understanding
retrospective: contemplative of past situations
specious: deceptively attractive

spectrum: a broad range of related things that form a continuous series

speculation: the contemplation or consideration of some subject

SPIR: breath

aspire: to desire; to pant for (originally: to breathe on)

expire: to breathe out; to breathe one's last; to come to an end

spirit: the breath of life; the soul; an incorporeal supernatural being; an outlook; a lively quality

STA/STI: to stand, to be in place

apostasy: renunciation of an object of one's previous loyalty

constitute: to make up

destitute: without means of subsistence

obstinate: stubbornly adhering to a purpose, opinion, or course of action

stasis: the state of equilibrium or inactivity caused by opposing equal forces

static: of bodies or forces at rest or in equilibrium

STRICT/STRING/STRAN: to tighten, to bind

astringent: causing to tighten

constrain: to confine; to bind within certain limits

restriction: a limitation

strangle: to kill by suffocation, usually by tightening a cord or one's hand around the throat

SUA: sweet, pleasing, to urge

assuage: to make less severe, ease, relieve

dissuade: to deter; to advise against

persuade: to encourage; to convince

suave: smoothly agreeable or polite; sweet

SUB/SUP: below, under

subliminal: existing or operating below the threshold of consciousness

submissive: inclined or ready to submit

subsidiary: serving to assist or supplement

subterfuge: an artifice or expedient used to evade a rule

subtle: thin, tenuous, or rarefied

suppose: to put down as a hypothesis; to use as the underlying basis of an argument; to assume

SUMM: highest, total

consummate: highly qualified; complete; perfect

sum: total; amount of money

summary: concise statement of the total findings on a subject; comprehensive

summit: highest point

SUPER/SUR: over, above

supercilious: arrogant, haughty, condescending

superfluous: extra, more than necessary

superlative: the highest kind or order

supersede: to replace in power, as by another person or thing

surmount: to get over or across, to prevail

surpass: to go beyond in amount, extent, or degree

surveillance: a watch kept over someone or something

SYM/SYN: together

symbiosis: living together in a mutually beneficial relationship

symmetry: balanced proportions; having opposite parts that mirror one another

sympathy: affinity; feeling affected by what happens to another

symposium: a meeting at which ideas are discussed (originally: a party at which people drink together)

synonym: a word that means the same thing as another

synthesis: combining things to create a new whole

T

TAC/TIC: to be silent

reticent: disposed to be silent or not to speak freely

tacit: unspoken understanding

taciturn: uncommunicative

TACT/TAG/TAM/TANG: to touch

contact: to touch; to get in touch

contagious: able to spread by contact, as disease

contaminate: to corrupt, taint, or otherwise damage the integrity of something by contact or mixture

contiguous: directly touching; sharing a boundary

intact: untouched; whole

intangible: unable to be touched
tactile: pertaining to touch; touchable

TAIN/TEN/TENT/TIN: to hold
abstention: the act of refraining voluntarily
detain: to keep from proceeding
pertain: to have reference or relation
pertinacious: persistent, stubborn
sustenance: nourishment, means of livelihood
tenable: capable of being held, maintained, or defended
tenacious: holding fast
tenure: the holding or possessing of anything

TEND/TENS/TENT/TENU: to stretch, to thin
attenuate: to weaken or reduce in force
contentious: quarrelsome, disagreeable, belligerent
distend: to expand by stretching
extenuating: making less serious by offering excuses
tendentious: having a predisposition toward a point of view
tension: the act of stretching or straining
tentative: of the nature of, or done as a trial, attempt

TEST: to bear witness
attest: bear witness
contest: to dispute (from bringing a lawsuit by calling witnesses)
detest: to despise; to hate (originally: to curse something by calling upon God to witness it)
protest: a dissent; a declaration, esp. of disagreement
testament: a statement of a person's wishes for the disposal of his or her property after death; a will
testify: bear witness

THEO: god
apotheosis: glorification, glorified ideal
atheist: one who does not believe in a deity or divine system
theocracy: a form of government in which a deity is recognized as the supreme ruler
theology: the study of divine things and the divine faith

THERM: heat
thermal: relating to heat; retaining heat
thermometer: a device for measuring heat
thermonuclear: relating to a nuclear reaction that takes place at high temperatures
thermostat: a device for regulating heat

TIM: fear
intimidate: to strike fear into; to make fearful
timid: fearful; shy

TOR/TORQ/TORT: to twist
contort: to twist; to distort
distort: to pull out of shape, often by twisting; to twist or misrepresent facts
extort: to wring money, property, or services out of somebody using threats or force
torch: a portable flame used for light (perhaps derived from hemp twisted around sticks, then dipped in pitch)
torque: twisting force; a force that creates rotation
tort: a wrongful act (other than breach of contract) that legally entitles one to damages
torture: to inflict pain (including by twisting instruments like the rack or wheel)

TORP: stiff, numb
torpedo: a explosive weapon used to sink ships (originally: a fish—the electric ray—that could shock victims to numbness)
torpid: numbed; sluggish
torpor: numbness; listlessness; apathy

TOX: poison
antitoxin: an antibody that counteracts a given poison
intoxication: being poisoned; drunkenness
toxic: poisonous

TRACT: to drag, to pull, to draw
abstract: to draw or pull away, remove
attract: to draw either by physical force or by an appeal to emotions or senses
contract: a legally binding document
detract: to take away from, esp. a positive thing
protract: to prolong, draw out, extend
tractable: easily managed or controlled
tractor: a powerful vehicle used to pull farm machinery

TRANS: across, beyond
intransigent: refusing to agree or compromise

transaction: the act of carrying on or conduct to a conclusion or settlement

transcendent: going beyond ordinary limits

transgress: to violate a law, command, or moral code

transition: a change from one way of being to another

transparent: easily seen through, recognized, or detected

U

ULT: last, beyond

penultimate: second-to-last

ulterior: beyond what is immediately present; future; beyond what is stated; hidden

ultimate: last; final

ultimatum: final offer; final terms

ultraviolet: beyond the violet end of the spectrum

UMBR: shadow

adumbrate: to foreshadow; to sketch; to overshadow

penumbra: a shaded area between pure shadow and pure light

somber: gloomy; darkened

umbrage: shade; shadow; displeasure; resentment

umbrella: a device providing shade from the sun or protection from rain

UN: not

unseen: not seen

unusual: not usual; exceptional; strange

UND: wave

abound: to be plentiful; to overflow (from water flowing in waves)

inundate: to flood

undulate: to move in a wavelike way

UNI/UN: one

reunion: a meeting that brings people back together

unanimous: of one mind; in complete accord

unicorn: a mythical animal with a single horn

uniform: of one kind; consistent

universe: all things considered as one whole

URB: city

suburb: a residential area just outside a city; an outlying area of a city

urban: relating to a city

urbane: polite; refined; polished (considered characteristic of those in cities)

urbanization: the process of an area becoming more like a city

US/UT: to use

abuse: to use wrongly or improperly

usage: a customary way of doing something

usurp: to seize and hold

utilitarian: efficient, functional, useful

V

VAIL/VAL: strength, use, worth

ambivalent: being caught between contradictory feelings of equal power or worth

avail: to have force; to be useful; to be of value

convalescent: recovering strength; healing

equivalent: of equal worth, strength, or use

evaluate: to determine the worth of

invalid: having no force or strength; void

valediction: a farewell (from wishing that someone be well; i.e., that someone have strength)

valid: having force; legally binding; effective; useful

value: worth

VEN/VENT: to come or to move toward

adventitious: accidental

contravene: to come into conflict with

convene: to assemble for some public purpose

intervene: to come between disputing factions, mediate

venturesome: showing a disposition to undertake risks

VER: truth

aver: to affirm, to declare to be true

veracious: habitually truthful

verdict: a judgment or decision

verisimilitude: the appearance or semblance of truth

verity: truthfulness

VERB: word

proverb: an adage; a byword; a short, commonly known saying

verbatim: exactly as stated; word-for-word

verbose: wordy
verbiage: excessive use of words; diction

VERD: green
verdant: green with vegetation; inexperienced
verdure: fresh, rich vegetation

VERS/VERT: to turn
aversion: dislike
avert: to turn away from
controversy: a public dispute involving a matter of opinion
diverse: of a different kind, form, character
extrovert: an outgoing person
inadvertent: unintentional
introvert: a person concerned primarily with inner thoughts and feelings
revert: to return to a former habit

VI: life
convivial: sociable
joie de vivre: joy of life (French expression)
viable: capable of living
vivacity: the quality of being lively, animated, spirited
vivid: strikingly bright or intense

VID/VIS: to see
adviser: one who gives counsel
evident: plain or clear to the sight or understanding
survey: to view in a general or comprehensive way
video: elements pertaining to the transmission or reception of an image
vista: a view or prospect

VIL: base, mean
revile: to criticize with harsh language
vile: loathsome, unpleasant
vilify: to slander, to defame

VIRU: poison
virulent: acrimonious; very bitter; very poisonous
viruliferous: containing a virus
virus: a submicroscopic agent that infects an organism and causes disease

VOC/VOK: call, word
advocate: to support or urge by argument
avocation: something one does in addition to a principle occupation
convoke: to call together
equivocate: to use ambiguous or unclear expressions
invoke: to call on a deity
vocabulary: the stock of words used by or known to a particular person or group
vocation: a particular occupation
vociferous: crying out noisily

VOL: wish
benevolent: characterized by or expressing goodwill
malevolent: characterized by or expressing bad will
volition: free choice, free will; act of choosing
voluntary: undertaken of one's own accord or by free choice

VOLU/VOLV: to roll, to turn
convolution: a twisting or folding
evolve: to develop naturally; literally, to unfold or unroll
revolt: to rebel; to turn against those in authority
revolve: to rotate; to turn around
voluble: easily turning; fluent; changeable
volume: a book (originally: a scroll); size or dimensions (originally: of a book)

VOR: to eat
carnivorous: meat-eating
omnivorous: eating or absorbing everything
voracious: having a great appetite

APPENDIX C

Common GRE-Level Words in Context

The GRE tests the same kinds of words over and over again. Here you will find some common GRE-level words with their definitions in context to help you to remember them. If you see a word that's unfamiliar to you, take a moment to study the definition and, most importantly, reread the sentence with the word's definition in mind.

Remember: learning vocabulary words in context is one of the best ways for your brain to retain the words' meanings. A broader vocabulary will serve you well on all four GRE Verbal question types and will also be extremely helpful in the Analytical Writing section.

A

ABATE: to reduce in amount, degree, or severity
As the hurricane's force ABATED, the winds dropped and the sea became calm.

ABSCOND: to leave secretly
The patron ABSCONDED from the restaurant without paying his bill by sneaking out the back door.

ABSTAIN: to choose not to do something
She ABSTAINED from choosing a mouthwatering dessert from the tray.

ABYSS: an extremely deep hole
The submarine dove into the ABYSS to chart the previously unseen depths.

ADULTERATE: to make impure
The chef made his ketchup last longer by ADULTERATING it with water.

ADVOCATE: to speak in favor of
The vegetarian ADVOCATED a diet containing no meat.

AESTHETIC: concerning the appreciation of beauty
Followers of the AESTHETIC Movement regarded the pursuit of beauty as the only true purpose of art.

AGGRANDIZE: to increase in power, influence, and reputation
The supervisor sought to AGGRANDIZE herself by claiming that the achievements of her staff were actually her own.

ALLEVIATE: to make more bearable
Taking aspirin helps to ALLEVIATE a headache.

AMALGAMATE: to combine; to mix together
Giant Industries AMALGAMATED with Mega Products to form Giant-Mega Products Incorporated.

AMBIGUOUS: doubtful or uncertain; able to be interpreted several ways
The directions she gave were so AMBIGUOUS that we disagreed on which way to turn.

AMELIORATE: to make better; to improve
The doctor was able to AMELIORATE the patient's suffering using painkillers.

ANACHRONISM: something out of place in time
The aged hippie used ANACHRONISTIC phrases, like "groovy" and "far out," that had not been popular for years.

ANALOGOUS: similar or alike in some way; equivalent to
In the Newtonian construct for explaining the existence of God, the universe is ANALOGOUS to a mechanical timepiece, the creation of a divinely intelligent "clockmaker."

ANOMALY: deviation from what is normal
The near-boiling river in Peru called Shanay-timpishka is a geological ANOMALY: it is the only naturally heated body of water that is not heated by its proximity to a volcano.

ANTAGONIZE: to annoy or provoke to anger
The child discovered that he could ANTAGONIZE the cat by pulling its tail.

ANTIPATHY: extreme dislike
The ANTIPATHY between the French and the English regularly erupted into open warfare.

APATHY: lack of interest or emotion
The APATHY of voters is so great that less than half the people who are eligible to vote actually bother to do so.

ARBITRATE: to judge a dispute between two opposing parties
Since the couple could not come to an agreement, a judge was forced to ARBITRATE their divorce proceedings.

ARCHAIC: ancient, old-fashioned
Her ARCHAIC Commodore computer could not run the latest software.

ARDOR: intense and passionate feeling
Bishop's ARDOR for the landscape was evident when he passionately described the beauty of the scenic Hudson Valley.

ARTICULATE: able to speak clearly and expressively
She is such an ARTICULATE defender of labor that unions are among her strongest supporters.

ASSUAGE: to make something unpleasant less severe
Serena used aspirin to ASSUAGE her pounding headache.

ATTENUATE: to reduce in force or degree; to weaken
The Bill of Rights ATTENUATED the traditional power of governments to change laws at will.

AUDACIOUS: fearless and daring
Her AUDACIOUS nature allowed her to fulfill her dream of skydiving.

AUSTERE: severe or stern in appearance; undecorated
The lack of decoration makes military barracks seem AUSTERE to the civilian eye.

B

BANAL: predictable, clichéd, boring
He used BANAL phrases like "have a nice day" and "another day, another dollar."

BOLSTER: to support; to prop up
The presence of giant footprints BOLSTERED the argument that Sasquatch was in the area.

BOMBASTIC: pompous in speech and manner
The ranting of the radio talk-show host was mostly BOMBASTIC; his boasting and outrageous claims had no basis in fact.

C

CACOPHONY: harsh, jarring noise
The junior high orchestra created an almost unbearable CACOPHONY as they tried to tune their instruments.

CANDID: impartial and honest in speech
The observations of a child can be charming since they are CANDID and unpretentious.

CAPRICIOUS: changing one's mind quickly and often
Queen Elizabeth I was quite CAPRICIOUS; her courtiers could never be sure which of their number would catch her fancy.

CASTIGATE: to punish or criticize harshly
Many Americans are amazed at how harshly the authorities in Singapore CASTIGATE perpetrators of what would be considered minor crimes in the United States.

CATALYST: something that brings about a change in something else
The imposition of harsh taxes was the CATALYST that finally brought on the revolution.

CAUSTIC: biting in wit
Dorothy Parker gained her reputation for CAUSTIC wit from her cutting, yet clever, insults.

CHAOS: great disorder or confusion
In many religious traditions, God created an ordered universe from CHAOS.

CHAUVINIST: someone prejudiced in favor of a group to which he or she belongs
The attitude that men are inherently superior to women and therefore must be obeyed is common among male CHAUVINISTS.

CHICANERY: deception by means of craft or guile
Dishonest used car salespeople often use CHICANERY to sell their beat-up old cars.

COGENT: convincing and well reasoned
Swayed by the COGENT argument of the defense, the jury had no choice but to acquit the defendant.

CONDONE: to overlook, pardon, or disregard
Some theorists believe that failing to prosecute minor crimes is the same as CONDONING an air of lawlessness.

CONVOLUTED: intricate and complicated
Although many people bought *A Brief History of Time,* few could follow its CONVOLUTED ideas and theories.

CORROBORATE: to provide supporting evidence
Fingerprints CORROBORATED the witness's testimony that he saw the defendant in the victim's apartment.

CREDULOUS: too trusting; gullible
Although some four-year-olds believe in the Easter Bunny, only the most CREDULOUS nine-year-olds still believe in him.

CRESCENDO: steadily increasing volume or force
The CRESCENDO of tension became unbearable as Evel Knievel prepared to jump his motorcycle over the school buses.

D

DECORUM: appropriateness of behavior or conduct; propriety
The countess complained that the vulgar peasants lacked the DECORUM appropriate for a visit to the palace.

DEFERENCE: respect, courtesy
The respectful young law clerk treated the Supreme Court justice with the utmost DEFERENCE.

DERIDE: to speak of or treat with contempt; to mock
The awkward child was often DERIDED by his "cooler" peers.

DESICCATE: to dry out thoroughly
After a few weeks of lying on the desert's baking sands, the cow's carcass became completely DESICCATED.

DESULTORY: jumping from one thing to another; disconnected
Diane had a DESULTORY academic record; she had changed majors 12 times in three years.

DIATRIBE: an abusive, condemnatory speech
The trucker bellowed a DIATRIBE at the driver who had cut him off.

DIFFIDENT: lacking self-confidence
Steve's DIFFIDENT manner during the job interview stemmed from his nervous nature and lack of experience in the field.

DILATE: to make larger; to expand
When you enter a darkened room, the pupils of your eyes DILATE to let in more light.

DILATORY: intended to delay
The congressman used DILATORY measures to delay the passage of the bill.

DILETTANTE: someone with an amateurish and superficial interest in a topic
Jerry's friends were such DILETTANTES that they seemed to have new jobs and hobbies every week.

DIRGE: a funeral hymn or mournful speech
Melville wrote the poem "A DIRGE for James McPherson" for the funeral of a Union general who was killed in 1864.

DISABUSE: to set right; to free from error
Galileo's observations DISABUSED scholars of the notion that the Sun revolved around the Earth.

DISCERN: to perceive; to recognize
It is easy to DISCERN the difference between butter and butter-flavored topping.

DISPARATE: fundamentally different; entirely unlike
Although the twins appear to be identical physically, their personalities are DISPARATE.

DISSEMBLE: to present a false appearance; to disguise one's real intentions or character
The villain could DISSEMBLE to the police no longer—he admitted the deed and tore up the floor to reveal the body of the old man.

DISSONANCE: a harsh and disagreeable combination, often of sounds
Cognitive DISSONANCE is the inner conflict produced when long-standing beliefs are contradicted by new evidence.

DOGMA: a firmly held opinion, often a religious belief
Linus's central DOGMA was that children who believed in the Great Pumpkin would be rewarded.

DOGMATIC: dictatorial in one's opinions
The dictator was DOGMATIC—he, and only he, was right.

DUPE: to deceive; a person who is easily deceived
Bugs Bunny was able to DUPE Elmer Fudd by dressing up as a lady rabbit.

E

ECLECTIC: selecting from or made up from a variety of sources
Budapest's architecture is an ECLECTIC mix of Eastern and Western styles.

EFFICACY: effectiveness
The EFFICACY of penicillin was unsurpassed when it was first introduced; the drug completely eliminated almost all bacterial infections for which it was administered.

ELEGY: a sorrowful poem or speech
Although Thomas Gray's "ELEGY Written in a Country Churchyard" is about death and loss, it urges its readers to endure this life and to trust in spirituality.

ELOQUENT: persuasive and moving, especially in speech
The Gettysburg Address is moving not only because of its lofty sentiments but also because of its ELOQUENT words.

EMULATE: to copy; to try to equal or excel
The graduate student sought to EMULATE his professor in every way, copying not only how she taught but also how she conducted herself outside of class.

ENERVATE: to reduce in strength
The guerrillas hoped that a series of surprise attacks would ENERVATE the regular army.

ENGENDER: to produce, cause, or bring about
His fear and hatred of clowns was ENGENDERED when he witnessed the death of his father at the hands of a clown.

ENIGMA: a puzzle; a mystery
Speaking in riddles and dressed in old robes, the artist gained a reputation as something of an ENIGMA.

ENUMERATE: to count, list, or itemize
Moses returned from the mountain with tablets on which the commandments were ENUMERATED.

EPHEMERAL: lasting a short time
The lives of mayflies seem EPHEMERAL to us, since the flies' average life span is a matter of hours.

EQUIVOCAL: open to more than one interpretation; misleading
Asked a pointed question, the politician nevertheless gave an EQUIVOCAL answer.

EQUIVOCATE: to use expressions of double meaning in order to mislead
When faced with criticism of her policies, the politician EQUIVOCATED and left all parties thinking she agreed with them.

ERRATIC: wandering and unpredictable
The plot seemed predictable until it suddenly took a series of ERRATIC turns that surprised the audience.

ERUDITE: learned, scholarly, bookish
The annual meeting of philosophy professors was a gathering of the most ERUDITE, well-published individuals in the field.

ESOTERIC: known or understood by only a few
Only a handful of experts are knowledgeable about the ESOTERIC world of particle physics.

ESTIMABLE: admirable
Most people consider it ESTIMABLE that Mother Teresa spent her life helping the poor of India.

EULOGY: speech in praise of someone
His best friend gave the EULOGY, outlining his many achievements and talents.

EUPHEMISM: use of an inoffensive word or phrase in place of a more distasteful one
The funeral director preferred to use the EUPHEMISM "sleeping" instead of the word "dead."

EXACERBATE: to make worse
It is unwise to take aspirin to try to relieve heartburn; instead of providing relief, the drug will only EXACERBATE the problem.

EXCULPATE: to clear from blame; prove innocent
The adversarial legal system is intended to convict those who are guilty and to EXCULPATE those who are innocent.

EXIGENT: urgent; requiring immediate action
The patient was losing blood so rapidly that it was EXIGENT to stop the source of the bleeding.

EXONERATE: to clear of blame
The fugitive was EXONERATED when another criminal confessed to committing the crime.

EXPLICIT: clearly stated or shown; forthright in expression
The owners of the house left a list of EXPLICIT instructions detailing their house sitter's duties, including a schedule for watering the house plants.

F

FANATICAL: acting excessively enthusiastic; filled with extreme, unquestioned devotion
The stormtroopers were FANATICAL in their devotion to the emperor, readily sacrificing their lives for him.

FAWN: to grovel
The understudy FAWNED over the director in hopes of being cast in the part on a permanent basis.

FERVID: intensely emotional; feverish
The fans of Maria Callas were unusually FERVID, doing anything to catch a glimpse of the great opera singer.

FLORID: excessively decorated or embellished
The palace had been decorated in a FLORID style; every surface had been carved and gilded.

FOMENT: to arouse or incite
The protesters tried to FOMENT feeling against the war through their speeches and demonstrations.

FRUGALITY: a tendency to be thrifty or cheap
Scrooge McDuck's FRUGALITY was so great that he accumulated enough wealth to fill a giant storehouse with money.

G

GARRULOUS: tending to talk a lot
The GARRULOUS parakeet distracted its owner with its continuous talking.

GREGARIOUS: outgoing, sociable
She was so GREGARIOUS that when she found herself alone, she felt quite sad.

GUILE: deceit or trickery
Since he was not fast enough to catch the roadrunner on foot, the coyote resorted to GUILE in an effort to trap his enemy.

GULLIBLE: easily deceived
The con man pretended to be a bank officer so as to fool GULLIBLE bank customers into giving him their account information.

H

HOMOGENEOUS (or HOMOGENOUS): of a similar kind
The class was fairly HOMOGENEOUS, since almost all of the students were senior journalism majors.

I

ICONOCLAST: one who opposes established beliefs, customs, and institutions
His lack of regard for traditional beliefs soon established him as an ICONOCLAST.

IMPERTURBABLE: not capable of being disturbed
The counselor had so much experience dealing with distraught children that she seemed IMPERTURBABLE, even when faced with the wildest tantrums.

IMPERVIOUS: impossible to penetrate; incapable of being affected
A good raincoat will be IMPERVIOUS to moisture.

IMPETUOUS: quick to act without thinking
It is not good for an investment broker to be IMPETUOUS, since much thought should be given to all the possible options.

IMPLACABLE: unable to be calmed down or made peaceful
His rage at the betrayal was so great that he remained IMPLACABLE for weeks.

INCHOATE: not fully formed; disorganized
The ideas expressed in Nietzsche's mature work also appear in an INCHOATE form in his earliest writing.

INGENUOUS: showing innocence or childlike simplicity
She was so INGENUOUS that her friends feared that her innocence and trustfulness would be exploited when she visited the big city.

INIMICAL: hostile, unfriendly
Even though the children had grown up together, they were INIMICAL to each other at school.

INNOCUOUS: harmless
Some snakes are poisonous, but most species are INNOCUOUS and pose no danger to humans.

INSIPID: lacking interest or flavor
The critic claimed that the painting was INSIPID, containing no interesting qualities at all.

INTRANSIGENT: uncompromising; refusing to be reconciled
The professor was INTRANSIGENT on the deadline, insisting that everyone turn the assignment in at the same time.

INUNDATE: to overwhelm; to cover with water
The tidal wave INUNDATED Atlantis, which was lost beneath the water.

IRASCIBLE: easily made angry
Attila the Hun's IRASCIBLE and violent nature made all who dealt with him fear for their lives.

L

LACONIC: using few words
She was a LACONIC poet who built her reputation on using words as sparingly as possible.

LAMENT: to express sorrow; to grieve
The children continued to LAMENT the death of the goldfish weeks after its demise.

LAUD: to give praise; to glorify
Parades and fireworks were staged to LAUD the success of the rebels.

LAVISH: to give unsparingly (v.); extremely generous or extravagant (adj.)
She LAVISHED the puppy with so many treats that it soon became overweight and spoiled.

LETHARGIC: acting in an indifferent or slow, sluggish manner
The clerk was so LETHARGIC that, even when the store was slow, he always had a long line in front of him.

LOQUACIOUS: talkative

She was naturally LOQUACIOUS, which was a problem in situations in which listening was more important than talking.

LUCID: clear and easily understood

The explanations were written in a simple and LUCID manner so that students were immediately able to apply what they learned.

LUMINOUS: bright, brilliant, glowing

The park was bathed in LUMINOUS sunshine, which warmed the bodies and the souls of the visitors.

M

MALINGER: to evade responsibility by pretending to be ill

A common way to avoid the draft was by MALINGERING—pretending to be mentally or physically ill so as to avoid being taken by the Army.

MALLEABLE: capable of being shaped

Gold is the most MALLEABLE of precious metals; it can easily be formed into almost any shape.

METAPHOR: a figure of speech comparing two different things; a symbol

The METAPHOR "a sea of troubles" suggests a lot of troubles by comparing their number to the vastness of the sea.

METICULOUS: extremely careful about details

To find all the clues at the crime scene, the investigators METICULOUSLY examined every inch of the area.

MISANTHROPE: a person who dislikes others

The character Scrooge in *A Christmas Carol* is such a MISANTHROPE that even the sight of children singing makes him angry.

MITIGATE: to soften; to lessen

A judge may MITIGATE a sentence if she decides that a person committed a crime out of need.

MOLLIFY: to calm or make less severe

Their argument was so intense that it was difficult to believe any compromise would MOLLIFY them.

MONOTONY: lack of variation

The MONOTONY of the sound of the dripping faucet almost drove the research assistant crazy.

N

NAIVE: lacking sophistication or experience

Having never traveled before, the elementary school students were more NAIVE than their high school counterparts on the field trip.

O

OBDURATE: hardened in feeling; resistant to persuasion

The president was completely OBDURATE on the issue, and no amount of persuasion would change his mind.

OBSEQUIOUS: overly submissive and eager to please

The OBSEQUIOUS new associate made sure to compliment her supervisor's tie and agree with him on every issue.

OBSTINATE: stubborn, unyielding

The OBSTINATE child could not be made to eat any food that he disliked.

OBVIATE: to prevent; to make unnecessary

The river was shallow enough to wade across at many points, which OBVIATED the need for a bridge.

OCCLUDE: to stop up; to prevent the passage of

A shadow is thrown across the earth's surface during a solar eclipse, when the light from the sun is OCCLUDED by the moon.

ONEROUS: troublesome and oppressive; burdensome

The assignment was so extensive and difficult to manage that it proved ONEROUS to the team in charge of it.

OPAQUE: impossible to see through; preventing the passage of light

The heavy buildup of dirt and grime on the windows almost made them OPAQUE.

OPPROBRIUM: public disgrace

After the scheme to embezzle the elderly was made public, the treasurer resigned in utter OPPROBRIUM.

OSTENTATION: excessive showiness

The OSTENTATION of the Sun King's court is evident in the lavish decoration and luxuriousness of his palace at Versailles.

P

PARADOX: a contradiction or dilemma
It is a PARADOX that those most in need of medical attention are often those least able to obtain it.

PARAGON: model of excellence or perfection
She is the PARAGON of what a judge should be: honest, intelligent, hardworking, and just.

PEDANT: someone who shows off learning
The graduate instructor's tedious and excessive commentary on the subject soon gained her a reputation as a PEDANT.

PERFIDIOUS: willing to betray one's trust
The actress's PERFIDIOUS companion revealed all of her intimate secrets to the gossip columnist.

PERFUNCTORY: done in a routine way; indifferent
The machinelike bank teller processed the transaction and gave the waiting customer a PERFUNCTORY smile.

PERMEATE: to penetrate
This miraculous new cleaning fluid is able to PERMEATE stains and dissolve them in minutes!

PHILANTHROPY: charity; a desire or effort to promote goodness
New York's Metropolitan Museum of Art owes much of its collection to the PHILANTHROPY of private collectors who willed their estates to the museum.

PLACATE: to soothe or pacify
The burglar tried to PLACATE the snarling dog by saying, "Nice doggy," and offering it a treat.

PLASTIC: able to be molded, altered, or bent
The new material was very PLASTIC and could be formed into products of vastly different shapes.

PLETHORA: excess
Assuming that more was better, the defendant offered the judge a PLETHORA of excuses.

PRAGMATIC: practical as opposed to idealistic
While daydreaming gamblers think they can get rich by frequenting casinos, PRAGMATIC gamblers realize that the odds are heavily stacked against them.

PRECIPITATE: to throw violently or bring about abruptly; lacking deliberation
Upon learning that the couple married after knowing each other only two months, friends and family members expected such a PRECIPITATE marriage to end in divorce.

PREVARICATE: to lie or deviate from the truth
Rather than admit that he had overslept again, the employee PREVARICATED and claimed that heavy traffic had prevented him from arriving at work on time.

PRISTINE: fresh and clean; uncorrupted
Since concerted measures had been taken to prevent looting, the archeological site was still PRISTINE when researchers arrived.

PRODIGAL: lavish, wasteful
The PRODIGAL son quickly wasted all of his inheritance on a lavish lifestyle devoted to pleasure.

PROLIFERATE: to increase in number quickly
Although she only kept two guinea pigs initially, they PROLIFERATED to such an extent that she soon had dozens.

PROPITIATE: to conciliate; to appease
The management PROPITIATED the irate union by agreeing to raise wages for its members.

PROPRIETY: correct behavior; obedience to rules and customs
The aristocracy maintained a high level of PROPRIETY, adhering to even the most minor social rules.

PRUDENCE: wisdom, caution, or restraint
The college student exhibited PRUDENCE by obtaining practical experience along with her studies, which greatly strengthened her résumé.

PUNGENT: sharp and irritating to the senses
The smoke from the burning tires was extremely PUNGENT.

Q

QUIESCENT: motionless
Many animals are QUIESCENT over the winter months, minimizing activity in order to conserve energy.

R

RAREFY: to make thinner or sparser
Since the atmosphere RAREFIES as altitudes increase, the air at the top of very tall mountains is too thin to breathe.

REPUDIATE: to reject the validity of
The old woman's claim that she was Russian royalty was REPUDIATED when DNA tests showed she was of no relation to them.

RETICENT: silent, reserved
Physically small and RETICENT in her speech, Joan Didion often went unnoticed by those upon whom she was reporting.

RHETORIC: effective writing or speaking
Lincoln's talent for RHETORIC was evident in his beautifully expressed Gettysburg Address.

S

SATIATE: to satisfy fully or overindulge
His desire for power was so great that nothing less than complete control of the country could SATIATE it.

SOPORIFIC: causing sleep or lethargy
The movie proved to be so SOPORIFIC that soon loud snores were heard throughout the theater.

SPECIOUS: deceptively attractive; seemingly plausible but fallacious
The student's SPECIOUS excuse for being late sounded legitimate but was proved otherwise when her teacher called her home.

STIGMA: a mark of shame or discredit
In *The Scarlet Letter*, Hester Prynne was required to wear the letter *A* on her clothes as a public STIGMA for her adultery.

STOLID: unemotional; lacking sensitivity
The prisoner appeared STOLID and unaffected by the judge's harsh sentence.

SUBLIME: lofty or grand
The music was so SUBLIME that it transformed the rude surroundings into a special place.

T

TACIT: done without using words
Although not a word had been said, everyone in the room knew that a TACIT agreement had been made about which course of action to take.

TACITURN: silent, not talkative
The clerk's TACITURN nature earned him the nickname "Silent Bob."

TIRADE: long, harsh speech or verbal attack
Observers were shocked at the manager's TIRADE over such a minor mistake.

TORPOR: extreme mental and physical sluggishness
After surgery, the patient experienced TORPOR until the anesthesia wore off.

TRANSITORY: temporary, lasting a brief time
The reporter lived a TRANSITORY life, staying in one place only long enough to cover the current story.

V

VACILLATE: to sway physically; to be indecisive
The customer held up the line as he VACILLATED between ordering chocolate chip or rocky road ice cream.

VENERATE: to respect deeply
In a traditional Confucian society, the young VENERATE their elders, deferring to the elders' wisdom and experience.

VERACITY: truthfulness; accuracy
She had a reputation for VERACITY, so everyone trusted her description of events.

VERBOSE: wordy
The professor's answer was so VERBOSE that his student forgot what the original question had been.

VEX: to annoy
The old man who loved his peace and quiet was VEXED by his neighbor's loud music.

VOLATILE: easily aroused or changeable; lively or explosive
His VOLATILE personality made it difficult to predict his reaction to anything.

W

WAVER: to fluctuate between choices
If you WAVER too long before making a decision about which testing site to register for, you may not get your first choice.

WHIMSICAL: acting in a fanciful or capricious manner; unpredictable
The ballet was WHIMSICAL, delighting the children with its imaginative characters and unpredictable sets.

Z

ZEAL: passion, excitement
She brought her typical ZEAL to the project, sparking enthusiasm in the other team members.

COMMONLY CONFUSED WORDS

ALREADY: by this or that time, previously
He already completed his work.

ALL READY: completely prepared
The students were all ready to take their exam.

ALTOGETHER: entirely, completely
I am altogether certain that I turned in my homework.

ALL TOGETHER: in the same place
She kept the figurines all together on her mantle.

CAPITAL: a city containing the seat of government; the wealth or funds owned by a business or individual; resources
Atlanta is the capital of Georgia.
The company's capital gains have diminished in recent years.

CAPITOL: the building in which a legislative body meets
Our trip included a visit to the Capitol building in Washington, D.C.

COARSE: rough, not smooth; lacking refinement
The truck's large wheels enabled it to navigate the coarse, rough terrain.
His coarse language prevented him from getting hired for the job.

COURSE: path, series of classes or studies
James's favorite course is biology.
The doctor suggested that Amy rest and let the disease run its course.

HERE: in this location
George Washington used to live here.

HEAR: to listen to or to perceive by the ear
Did you hear the question?

ITS: a personal pronoun that shows possession
Please put the book back in its place.

IT'S: the contraction of "it is" or "it has"
It's snowing outside.
It's been too long.

LEAD: to act as a leader, to go first, or to take a superior position
The guide will lead us through the forest.

LED: past tense of "lead"
The guide led us through the forest.

LEAD: a metal
It is dangerous to inhale fumes from paint containing lead.

LOOSE: free, to set free, not tight
She always wears loose clothing when she does yoga.

LOSE: to become without
Use a bookmark so you don't lose your place in your book.

PASSED: the past tense of "pass"; a euphemism for someone dying
We passed by her house on Sunday.

PAST: that which has gone by or elapsed in time
In the past, Abby never used to study.
We drove past her house.

PRINCIPAL: the head of a school; main or important
The quarterback's injury is the principal reason the team lost.
The principal of the school meets with parents regularly.

PRINCIPLE: a fundamental law or truth
The laws of motion are among the most important principles in physics.

STATIONARY: fixed, not moving
Thomas rode a stationary bicycle at the gym.

STATIONERY: paper used for letter writing
The principal's stationery has the school's logo on the top.

THEIR: possessive of "they"
Paul and Ben studied for their test together.

THERE: a place; in that matter or respect
There are several question types on the GRE.
Please hang up your jacket over there.

THEY'RE: contraction of "they are"
Be careful of the bushes, as they're filled with thorns.